MW00535093

RELIGIOUS CONFLICT IN BRAZIL

Religious Conflict in Brazil

Protestants, Catholics, and
the Rise of Religious Pluralism
in the Early Twentieth Century

ERIKA HELGEN

Yale
UNIVERSITY PRESS
NEW HAVEN AND LONDON

Published with assistance from the Kingsley Trust Association Publication Fund
established by the Scroll and Key Society of Yale College

Yale University Press books may be purchased in quantity for educational, business,
or promotional use. For information, please e-mail sales.press@yale.edu (U.S. office)
or sales@yaleup.co.uk (U.K. office).

Set in Electra type by IDS Infotech, Ltd., Chandigarh, India.
Printed in the United States of America.

Library of Congress Control Number: 2019953615
ISBN 978-0-300-24335-2 (hardcover : alk. paper)

A catalogue record for this book is available from the British Library.

This paper meets the requirements of ANSI/NISO Z39.48–1992
(Permanence of Paper).

10 9 8 7 6 5 4 3 2 1

CONTENTS

CONTENTS

ACKNOWLEDGMENTS

I would never have been able to write this book without the help of a great many people. First and foremost I would like to thank my wonderful doctoral advisors, Gil Joseph and Stuart Schwartz, for their constant support and encouragement. Gil guided and accompanied me throughout each stage of this process, always asking the right questions at the right moment, and remaining patient as I took a meandering path toward my eventual book project. Stuart's mentorship has enriched my graduate experience in countless ways—my research, teaching, and development as a scholar have been indelibly shaped by our conversations. Both he and María Jordán have served as unending sources of sage advice and positive energy. My ability to call myself a historian of religion owes a great deal to Carlos Eire. He has helped me look beyond the geographical and temporal boundaries of my project and make connections to broader currents of global religious history. It is difficult to adequately express my gratitude to Ralph Della Cava, who not only has given me invaluable feedback on my work through its many and varied stages but also has welcomed me into the Brazilianist community in New York. Through his generosity, kindness, and insightfulness he has served as a model for the kind of scholar I hope to one day become. Kenneth Serbin, Stanley Blake, Barbara Weinstein, Oliver Dinius, Ben Fallaw, Andrew Chesnut, Edward Wright-Rios, Celso Castilho, Virginia Garrard-Burnett, and Dain Borges also read my work and counseled me at critical stages of the research and writing process. I would not have gone to graduate school had it not been for Jack Womack, who was the first to tell me I could make a career out of reading and writing about Latin American history. I am especially grateful to the late Patricia Pessar, whose work on popular religiosity in Brazil fundamentally influenced the nature and direction of my project, and whose stories about her fieldwork experiences taught me how to navigate the research process with courage and humor.

So many of my fellow graduate students have given me their friendship and help throughout my time in New Haven and New York. Christine Mathias and Mike Bustamante were the best cohort-mates that an incoming (and slightly nervous and intimidated) graduate student could ever hope to have, and Jenny Lambe, Taylor Jardno, and Nazanin Sullivan are living proof that your best friends will be your best motivation to do good work. I feel forever lucky to have crossed paths with Clara Sampaio when she came to study in New Haven, and I will never be able to adequately thank her for welcoming me into her home in São Paulo. Marian Schlotterbeck, from the day she became my graduate student mentor, has been an invaluable source of counsel, encouragement, and friendship. I am grateful that my research in Brazil allowed me to meet Laura Premack and Courtney Campbell, who are wonderful colleagues and even better friends and whose work has inspired my own. I have also benefited from the friendship of Ingrid Castañeda, Fredy González, Richard Anderson, Sarah Bowman, Gerardo Con Diaz, Lisa Pinley Covert, Adrián Lerner, Santiago Muñoz, Jonathan Graham, Carmen Kordick, Cecily Raynor, Drew Konove, Ezer Vierba, Michael Rom, Andra Chastain, and Marcel García.

In Brazil I am in debt to so many scholars, archivists, priests, pastors, students, and friends that it seems impossible to be able to thank them adequately here, but I will try my best. In Rio de Janeiro, Marcelo Timotheo da Costa was the first scholar with whom I met, and he proved to be an invaluable source of encouragement and help throughout all of the years that followed. My work also benefited from conversations with Cecília Loreto Mariz, Luiz Alberto Gómez de Souza, Lúcia Ribeiro, Jessie Jane Vieira de Sousa, and Padre Luiz Fernando Klein. Dom Pascoal, Daniel Guitarelli, Aline Vianna, and Fátima Argon made my experience in the archives of Rio and Petrópolis both productive and fun. I am grateful to Néfer Muñoz not only for his friendship but also for having introduced me to Sônia and Eyleen Oliveira Marenco, who gave me so much more than just a place to stay. In São Paulo, Gedeon Freire de Alencar and Marina Correa welcomed me into their community of religious scholars, sharing their insights, ideas, resources, and archival documents with me. Their passion for Pentecostal history was contagious. I also want to thank José Claúdio Ribeiro, Leonildo Silveira Campos, Edin Sued de Abumanssur, Edênio Valle, José Oscar Beozzo, and Fernando Londoño for discussing my project with me. Jair Mongelli Júnior and Rev. Eliezer Bernardes da Silva provided crucial archival support.

In the Northeast I incurred debts in every city and town I visited. Dirceu Marroquim has been a true friend and interlocutor, and I will never forget how he welcomed me into the research community in Recife. José Roberto de Souza, Zaqueu Moreira, Manoel Geraldo da Silva Júnior, and José Bonifácio de Sousa e Silva all spoke with me about my project, pointed me toward crucial archives and libraries, and shared their extensive knowledge of northeastern religious history. Gibran Araújo proved to be an upstanding colleague, and I thank him for facilitating my access to local archives and libraries in Mossoró and Areia Branca. In Recife and João Pessoa I benefited from the help of many archivists, including Cícero Souza, Sandra Veríssimo, Acácia Coutinho, and Ricardo Grisi Veloso. Frei Jociel Gomes, who is responsible for promoting Frei Damião de Bozzano's sainthood cause, gave me access to the documents relating to Frei Damião and the Capuchin Order that are housed in the Convento Nossa Senhora da Penha. In Cuité, Crisólito Marques shared his extensive personal archive regarding Cuitense religious life in general and Padre Luiz Santiago in particular. I am so grateful for his generosity. I also thank Rev. Armando Valdevino and his family for welcoming me into their home in Catolé do Rocha as well as introducing me to invaluable contacts in the Congregational community. Additionally, Frei Severino Pinheiro, Padre Márcio Henrique Mendes Fernandes, Padre Binu George, José Antonio de Souza, Padre Luciano, and Beto Duro greatly facilitated my research. And of course I cannot even begin to express the depth of my gratitude to Graça Ataíde, who became my surrogate family in Recife and who was my constant supporter, sounding board, and model of generosity and kindness.

My travel and research were supported by the Macmillan Center for International and Area Studies at Yale University, the Andrew W. Mellon Foundation, the Fulbright/IIE Foundation, and the Robert M. Leylan Fellowship. I want to especially thank the Fulbright Commission staff members Patricia Rodrigues Grijo and Luana Smeets for providing me with support and assistance throughout my time in Brazil, as well as for organizing two wonderful conferences that allowed me to forge long-lasting relationships with fellow Fulbright scholars. I would also like to thank Bowdoin College and Vanderbilt University for hosting seminars in which I was able to present early drafts of my work.

The Collegeville Institute for Ecumenical and Cultural Research gave me funds, office space, and a lively scholarly community while I was putting the finishing touches on this book. I am grateful to my colleagues at Yale Divinity School for their advice and friendship while I was preparing the manuscript for publication and learning how to be a professor. Heather Gold at Yale University Press has been a wonderful source of knowledge, support, and patience, and I would like to thank her as well as the two anonymous readers who gave me feedback on my manuscript for making this a better book.

Finally, I would like to thank my family: my parents, Michele and Hank, and my siblings, Brigit and Thomas. They have been there for me throughout this entire endeavor, and I would not be where I am today without them. I would also like to thank my newest family members, Antonio, Marilú, and Isabel, who have become some of my greatest cheerleaders and who showed infinite amounts of patience and understanding when I spent large amounts of my time in Spain in front of my laptop, writing and editing the pages that follow.

This book could not be dedicated to anyone other than Antonio. Words cannot express what he means to me, and how much of him is in this project. *Te quiero para siempre.*

The Battle Has Already Begun

Day after day, Protestantism continues to grow among us. To see this, one simply has to take a quick look at the growth of sects (12), missionary societies (7), and cooperative societies (4) that work intelligently and persistently to proselytize. Their churches, headquarters, and prayer houses are multiplying. Their propaganda projects, new centers, house visits, and prayer invites are intensifying. . . . Do we allow them to proliferate? No, because we will fight back against [Protestants], or better said, we will continue fighting, because the battle has already begun.
—*A questão protestante no Brasil*, São Paulo seminary pamphlet, 1940[1]

In August 1940 the Central Seminary of Ipiranga, one of the most prominent and prestigious seminaries in Brazil, held a week-long conference titled the "Protestant Question in Brazil." During the conference future priests learned about "statistics that demonstrate the advances of the Protestant movement," "weapons against Protestantism and methods of combat," "how a priest should deal with Protestants in his parish," and "common accusations that Protestants make against Catholics," among other topics. Each student was responsible for completing an in-depth study of one of the course topics and presenting his findings to the seminar, along with lists of "responses to possible objections" and "practical actions that should be taken" to confront the Protestant activity or tactic under review. The conference emphasized that it was the responsibility of each and every individual priest to take action at the local level to protect his flock from Protestant "infiltration." At the end of the week seminarians were supposed to be prepared to identify, combat, and suppress any Protestant movement that should arise during their tenure as priests.

The Ipiranga seminar was just one manifestation of a broader movement in which Brazilian Catholics sought to "fight back" against the growth of Protestantism in their local communities. In Brazil the first half of the twentieth century was a period of religious conflict, as both Catholics and Protestants struggled to come to terms with the demands of a newly pluralistic society. To Catholics, the rise of religious pluralism was linked to the rise of a host of other dangerous -isms that plagued the modern world: liberalism, humanism, positivism, modernism, secularism, individualism, republicanism, and communism, to name just a few. In what has been called the Catholic Restoration, Brazilian church leaders believed that only by zealously defending Catholicism's hegemony in the public sphere could they protect both the political and spiritual integrity of the Brazilian nation. Between 1916 and 1945 Restorationist Catholics sought to remake Brazilian society in the corporatist image of the church. Protestantism, with its emphasis on free inquiry and its insistence on the separation of church and state, was seen as the most direct assault on the holy foundation of Brazil's national religious identity and the root of many of the other dangerous -isms. Restorationists predicted that once Brazilians began to deny a single religious Truth, their denial of social and political norms would not be long in coming. "The Protestant sects spread hatred against the [Catholic] Church and will end up paganizing the masses," wrote a Jesuit priest in 1942. Unless a revival of a nationalist Catholicism took place to protect Brazilians against the "hundreds of sects imported from the United States," the Jesuit priest was certain that Protestant converts would eventually "give their bodies and souls over to the fomenters of revolution."[2] Catholic Restorationists, like many other Catholic leaders around the world, believed they were their nation's last defense against an amoral, chaotic, secular, and perhaps even communist world.

This book contends that Restorationist anti-Protestantism was not solely a discursive project, as it promoted, facilitated, and shaped religious conflicts between Protestants and Catholics at the local level. In parishes and dioceses throughout Brazil, Catholic bishops, priests, and friars organized intense campaigns against Protestantism, strategically recasting religious intolerance as a necessary corollary to the nationalist and modernizing project of the Catholic Restoration. Public processions, preaching tours, rallies, and *santas missões populares* (weeklong revival missions) were meant to demonstrate Catholicism's power in the public sphere, strengthen local Catholic identity and solidarity, and intimidate Protestants. At times intimidation crossed over into violence, as Catholics threatened and attacked pastors, vandalized and burned down Protestant places of worship, and, in the most extreme, albeit rare, cases, killed members of the Protestant faithful. While the vast majority of conflicts did not involve death or serious injury, the terror felt in Protestant communities was real. The ultimate aim of local anti-Protestant campaigns was to get Protestants to leave the parish, a goal which, unfortunately, many campaigns achieved. Far from being spontaneous outbursts of riotous rage, anti-Protestant actions were fueled by a complex combination of religious and political forces, all of which were inextricably connected to broader struggles over the future of Brazilian religious identity.

Although religious conflict and campaigns against Protestantism occurred throughout Brazil, this book focuses on Catholic–Protestant relations in the Brazilian Northeast. Following the publication of Euclides da Cunha's *Os sertões* [*Rebellion in the Backlands*] in 1902 the Northeast became famous as a place of economic backwardness, political feuds, crippling droughts, popular unrest, and, most important to my analysis here, so-called religious fanaticism.[3] Da Cunha's account of the Brazilian military's confrontation with and eventual destruction of the allegedly fanatical millenarian community of Canudos, located in the far interior of the northeastern state of Bahia, would reverberate for decades to come, making regional and national elites continuously fearful of the violent potential of northeastern religiosity. As Durval Muniz de Albuquerque Júnior has shown in his groundbreaking study *The Invention of the Brazilian Northeast*, the first half of the twentieth century represented an especially critical moment in the invention of the Northeast's identity as an impoverished, violent, and fanatical region. It was during this period that writers and intellectuals like Gilberto Freyre, José Lins do Rego, Graciliano Ramos, and Rachel de Queiroz presented backlanders as nostalgic representatives of traditional Brazilian identity while at the same time highlighting their misery, unorthodox religious fervor, and potential for revolt.[4]

At first glance the Northeast would seem an unlikely place in which to study Catholic–Protestant relations during the early twentieth century. Seen as a stronghold of Brazilian popular Catholicism, the region is often thought of as being nearly devoid of Protestantism, particularly during the period before the Pentecostal boom of the 1960s and 1970s. It is certainly true that Protestant numbers have historically been lower in the Northeast than in other Brazilian regions. As Francisco Cartaxo Rolim has noted, "In terms of percentage of Protestants, [the Northeast] has been different from [other regions]," constantly lagging behind.[5] In 1940 only 0.73 percent of the northeastern population was Protestant, while the national average was three times that percentage, at 2.61 percent. The situation did not change much over time: in 1980 the percentage of Protestants in the Northeast had crept up to only 3.35 percent, half the national average of 6.62 percent, and by 2009 it had risen to 15 percent, still much less than the national average of 22 percent.[6] Perhaps for this reason scholars have largely overlooked northeastern Protestantism, especially in its historical context. However, to ignore the Northeast is to miss a fundamental part of Brazilian Protestant history. The relatively small number of Protestants had an outsized impact on northeastern religious culture during the 1920s, 1930s, and 1940s, when regional Protestantism was undergoing a dramatic transformation. During this period Protestantism in the Northeast was changing from a religion directed by foreign missionaries working in the large coastal cities to a Brazilian-led movement that created permanent church communities throughout the region, including the rural interior. In doing so, Protestants fundamentally altered the way they interacted with the Catholic community, as Catholics now regarded Protestants as embodying an urgent internal threat to the traditional heart of Brazilian Catholic culture.

Moreover, the central, tension-ridden place of the Northeast in the national Brazilian imaginary meant that the rise of Protestantism there was threatening to both national and regional leaders of the Catholic Restoration. As the traditional heart of Brazilian Catholicism, the Northeast was seen by Catholic leaders as a region that was inherently and necessarily

4

Catholic and where the mere presence of Protestantism represented an aggressive offense against Brazilian culture and identity. Catholic leaders believed that the supposed ignorance of the region's inhabitants made them vulnerable to Protestant seduction and trickery, for they could not rely on Catholic doctrinal knowledge to defend themselves against Protestant evangelization. It was up to Catholic bishops, priests, and friars to protect their flocks from the threat of conversion by leading dramatic anti-Protestant campaigns in their parishes.

And yet, as was so often the case with northeastern religious actors, civil and religious leaders believed there was a thin line between the zealous Catholic who was protecting Brazilian religious traditions and the violent religious renegade who was fanaticizing *nordestinos*. The few instances in which authorities punished Catholic perpetrators of violence involved deep-seated fears that nordestinos were going to spark a "new Canudos." Protestants were protagonists in campaigns to identify, prosecute, and punish so-called fanaticism in the Northeast, understanding that it was one of the only ways for them to obtain justice and protection. Protestant leaders believed that by connecting nordestino Catholic activism to the specter of religious fanaticism they could unmask the savagery and backwardness of Catholic campaigns against Protestantism. Yet by supporting and participating in the punishment of religious fanaticism, Protestants were ultimately promoting the Catholic Restorationist agenda, which similarly sought to police and suppress religious movements that were not sufficiently orthodox.

Protestantism in Brazil: From Immigrant Protestantism to Pentecostalism

Protestantism has a long, complex history in Brazil, full of starts and stops, growth and stagnation, political and social transformations. The earliest manifestations of Protestantism were short-lived. French and Dutch Calvinists who competed with the Catholic Portuguese for supremacy in the New World during the sixteenth and seventeenth centuries ultimately retreated in defeat, giving way to a Portuguese colonial project that effectively banned all non-Catholics from Brazil. Protestantism would not establish a permanent presence in Brazil until after 1810, when the Portuguese Crown signed treaties with Great Britain that opened Brazilian ports to British commerce and allowed foreigners, especially British Anglicans, to come to Brazil and practice their faith. The establishment of Anglican churches in Brazil marked the beginning of what scholars have called immigrant Protestantism (*protestantismo de imigração*), the first of three waves of Protestantism in Brazil.[7] Throughout the nineteenth century, encouraged by the Brazilian Empire's policies promoting European immigration, new immigrant groups like German Lutherans brought their faith with them when they arrived in Brazil. Although immigrant Protestant communities established churches throughout the country, their societal influence was limited by the fact that their main goal was not to proselytize and convert Brazilian Catholics but to maintain the faith and traditions of the religion and culture of the immigrant communities themselves. When immigration from majority-Protestant countries diminished in the twentieth century, the prominence of the denominations associated with immigrant Protestantism, such as Lutheranism, diminished as well.

Protestantism became a social force in Brazil with the rise of missionary Protestantism (*protestantismo de missão*), when U.S. and British missionaries from historical Protestant denominations—Congregationalists, Methodists, Presbyterians, and Baptists—began to actively evangelize in Brazil, explicitly seeking to convert Brazilian Catholics and establish Portuguese-speaking churches throughout the country.[8] While Methodists established a short-lived missionary project in 1835, the first permanent missionary activities did not begin until 1855, when a Scottish Congregationalist, Robert Reid Kalley, began preaching and founding churches in Rio de Janeiro. Presbyterian missionaries (PCUSA) followed in 1859, and the first Methodist congregation among Brazilians was founded in 1876. Events in the United States also hastened U.S. Protestant work in Brazil. After the U.S. Civil War, former Confederates unhappy with the outcome of the war decided to emigrate, looking for new lands that would be more hospitable to their political and social views. Brazil, where slavery was still legal and where Dom Pedro II was encouraging the immigration of white Europeans and North Americans, was an obvious choice. When the Confederates established colonies in

6

São Paulo and the Amazon in the 1860s and 1870s they appealed to their home congregations for religious assistance. Thus in the 1860s, 1870s, and 1880s Southern Presbyterians, Southern Methodists, and Southern Baptists all began to send missionaries to Brazil.[9] While they initially focused on attending to the religious needs of the Confederate colonists, the missionaries quickly expanded their evangelization activities to other cities and states, especially in the North and Northeast. By the beginning of the Brazilian Republic in 1889, all of the major Protestant denominations had a presence in Brazil. However, their numbers were still small, representing just 1 percent of the total Brazilian population.

The numbers and influence of Brazilian Protestants began to grow more rapidly in the first half of the twentieth century, partly due to the introduction of the third and final wave of Protestantism: Pentecostalism. In 1910 and 1911 the first two Pentecostal churches, the Congregação Cristã no Brasil and the Assembléia de Deus, were established in Brazil. While the Congregação Cristã remained confined largely to southern Brazil in its first decades, the Assembléia de Deus spread rapidly throughout the country.[10] The Assembléia de Deus was founded by two Swedish Baptists who had begun evangelizing Brazilians, many of whom were migrant laborers from the Northeast, in the rubber-tapping regions of the Amazon in 1911. When the rubber market collapsed in the 1910s, large numbers of new Pentecostal converts returned to their hometowns in the Northeast and founded their own Pentecostal congregations. In this way, the Assembléia de Deus spread from north to south, the Northeast being a particular area of growth.[11] By the early twentieth century Brazil was seeing all three types of Protestantism— immigrant, missionary, and Pentecostal—gaining a foothold in nearly every region of the country.

Uniting Protestantism and Restoring Catholicism: Religion and Nation in Twentieth-Century Brazil

The year 1916 marked the beginning of a new era in the respective religious histories of Catholics and historical Protestants. The Panama Congress, in which North American and Latin American Protestants came together to prepare a unified plan for the evangelization of the continent, took place that year. The congress was convoked in response to the lack of Latin American representation at the 1910 World Missionary Conference in Edinburgh, which had excluded the "Latin American question" because Catholics, conference organizers argued, were not pagans like the populations in Africa or Asia and thus were not in sufficient need of evangelization. The Panama Congress argued the opposite: that Latin America was in just as dire need of Protestant conversion as any other region because Latin American Catholics were not sufficiently Christian. Latin American Protestants believed that the Catholic Church had distorted and paganized the Christian message to such an extent that it could no longer be called Christianity. They believed that only a sustained, unified Protestant evangelization effort could bring salvation to those who had been trapped in religious superstition and ignorance.[12]

The congress had a transformative effect on Protestant culture in Brazil. As Antonio Gouvêa Mendonça has argued, 1916 was the beginning of a new era in Brazilian Protestant history, one he called the "period of cooperation and unionism."[13] Over the next three decades the disparate and oftentimes competitive Protestant denominations attempted to come together to form a cohesive religious force capable of confronting Catholic hegemony in the public sphere and exposing the threat of supposed Catholic backwardness. A great number of ecumenical organizations were founded: the Comissão Brasileira de Cooperação (Brazilian Committee on Cooperation), Federação de Igrejas Evangélicas do Brasil (Federation of Evangelical Churches in Brazil), Conselho Evangélico de Educação Religiosa do Brasil (Evangelical Council on Religious Education in Brazil), Federação de Escolas Evangélicas do Brasil (Federation of Evangelical Schools of Brazil), and the Centro Brasileiro de Publicidade (Brazilian Center of Publicity). In 1934 all of these organizations were brought together to form the Confederação Evangélica do Brasil. The confederation's stated purpose was to give Protestants a bigger and more impactful voice in Brazilian society so that churches, when confronting issues that were "of common or general interest," could "make themselves heard in the name of the greater collectivity."[14] By uniting with one another, Protestants were able to both formulate and advocate the issues, policies, and values they wanted to see flourish in Brazilian society. In essence they were able to put forth their vision for the future of the Brazilian nation: a future centered on the formation of a laicist, disestablished state in which the freedom of religion was aggressively protected and the influence of the Catholic Church diminished.

The rise of Protestantism in the national public sphere was met by an equally dramatic rise of Catholic social and political action in Brazil. For Brazilian Catholics, 1916 can be considered the year that the Catholic Restoration officially began. That year a young prelate named Sebastião Leme de Silveira Cintra was appointed to the prestigious position of archbishop of Olinda and Recife and wrote his first pastoral letter to the residents of his archdiocese. A typical pastoral greeting was often short on substance and filled with religious platitudes and abstract devotional language. Dom Leme, however, used his pastoral letter to outline an ambitious national reform project that sought to restore the Catholic Church's rightful place in Brazilian society.[15] He began the letter with a scathing condemnation of the Brazilian Catholic Church's passive acceptance of secular liberal dominance of the public sphere: "What *Catholic majority* is this, so passive in the face of laws, governments, literature, schools, press, industry, commerce, and all other functions of national life that reveal themselves to be contrary and foreign to the principles and practices of Catholicism? . . . We form *a great national force, but a force that neither acts nor influences, an inert force. We are, therefore, an inefficient majority.*[16]

Dom Leme wanted to reignite the religious energy of this Catholic majority and channel it toward the creation of a society that respected and valued Catholic doctrine and traditions. In doing so, he was attempting to restore the power and influence the Catholic Church had lost during the previous century. Throughout the period of the Brazilian Empire the Catholic Church was a weak and divided institution. Although Catholicism was the official religion of Brazil, the Catholic Church found itself subordinated to the imperial state, unable either to control its future or to strengthen its hierarchical authority. Under the regime of the religiously indifferent Emperor Dom Pedro II, religious orders fell into steep decline, and the number and vitality of Catholic dioceses stagnated.[17] During this period priests were known for their worldly ways, openly flouting the dictates of Rome as they broke their vows of celibacy and aligned themselves with Masonic lodges.[18] And while individual priests and bishops became involved in politics and government, the Catholic Church as a whole—and in particular the religious and moral influence of the church hierarchy—largely retreated from national public life. This is not to say the Catholic religion ceased to be important in the lives of everyday Brazilians. Religious festivals, pilgrimages, devotions, and religious brotherhoods (*irmandades*) continued to be central elements of Brazilian culture, constituting the main ways in which people encountered the sacred. While the institutional leadership of the Catholic Church had been severely weakened, laity-led and private religious activities flourished.[19]

As the nineteenth century progressed, however, a growing number of Catholic bishops and priests came to view the church's subordinate position vis-à-vis the state as deeply troubling and ultimately harmful to the institution's broader objectives. Known as ultramontanes or Romanizers, they advocated greater Vatican control over the national Brazilian church and greater Catholic hierarchical control over local religious life. Two of the fiercest champions of ultramontane authority were Dom Vital Maria Gonçalves de Oliveira and Dom Antônio Macedo de Costa, bishops who had received their theological and pastoral training at Romanized seminaries in France. In 1872 they decided to take a public stand against what they believed was the corruption of Brazilian Catholicism being perpetrated by a host of irreligious, anticlerical forces. In what later became known as the Questão Religiosa (Religious Question), their protest took the form of barring members of Masonic lodges from joining in the activities of irmandades, the Brazilian religious brotherhoods that dominated much of lay religious life. Brazilian ultramontanes viewed Masonry as a singularly insidious and anti-Catholic organization, and the Vatican had long prohibited Masons from taking part in Catholic organizations. Nevertheless, the laws of the Brazilian Empire contradicted the Vatican's decree, and Masons had been openly participating in Brazilian church life for much of the nineteenth century. The bishops' prohibition of Masonry led to a standoff between church and state that eventually led to the imprisonment of both

Dom Vital and Dom Antônio. For the time being, Masons were allowed to remain members of Catholic irmandades.[20]

But the state's victory over the ultramontane church proved to be short-lived. With the advent of the Republic in 1889 and the approval of a new constitution in 1891, the Catholic Church was officially disestablished and separated from the state. Initially, Catholic leaders were wary of the church–state separation, fearing the rise of an explicitly anticlerical republican government. However, disestablishment proved to be a blessing for the Romanizing church. Free to control its finances, determine its leadership structure, and reform its seminaries, the Brazilian Catholic Church was able to greatly strengthen its institutional power and hierarchical authority during the first decades of the Republic. The structural effects were seen immediately: between 1889 and 1930 the number of Brazilian dioceses grew from twelve to sixty-eight, and most boasted new and reformed seminaries.[21] Priests were increasingly taught that obedience to their hierarchical superiors was supreme among all virtues, and more and more seminaries put an emphasis on orthodox, Romanized theological and pastoral training for their priests. The bishops and archbishops whom priests were now to unquestioningly obey were also coming from increasingly rarified educational and cultural backgrounds. By the early twentieth century national and regional Catholic leaders were chosen from an ever-expanding pool of graduates from the elite Pontificio Collegio Pio Latinoamericano, a seminary in Rome dedicated to producing the next generation of Latin American bishops, archbishops, and cardinals. When the students returned to their home countries and assumed their ecclesiastical positions, they proved to be zealous Romanizers.[22]

By 1916 the Brazilian church had begun to reform and strengthen its internal ecclesiastical structures. Yet Catholicism's presence in broader Brazilian society was still weak. Catholic leaders had little political or cultural influence, and the church's stances on moral and social issues were largely ignored by the Brazilian elite. While the advent of the Republic did not bring the acrimonious church–state conflicts seen in other Latin American nations, the positivist, liberal, and largely secularist nature of the First Republic meant that early relations between the two institutions were far from harmonious. While Catholicism still dominated the religious culture of the nation, it was precisely this culture that was being sidelined from the Brazilian public sphere.

With the Restoration, militant Catholics wanted to bring the church to the center of Brazilian society, making it socially and politically relevant to modern citizens. Dom Leme believed that Catholicism's mission was ultimately a social mission: Catholics needed to unite in an effort to Christianize and purify secular society, shaping civil institutions in the image and likeness of the church. In his 1916 pastoral letter the archbishop pointed to two means by which the Catholic Church could promote a more active religious presence in society: religious education and Catholic Action.[23] Regarding the first point, Dom Leme believed that many Catholics did not defend their faith in broader society because they did not have the spiritual and doctrinal knowledge to do so. The vast majority of Brazilian Catholics were, in Dom Leme's eyes, ignorant, superstitious, and lacking respect for the sacraments and hierarchy of the institutional church. "They go to church and visit all of the altars . . . but they don't visit the Holy Sacrament," Dom Leme complained. "They will never miss their rosary prayers or novenas, but they have no problem being absent from Mass."[24] No longer content to allow Brazilians to perform their faith only in the feminized private sphere, Dom Leme demanded that Brazilians, especially Brazilian men, become religiously educated through a modernized catechism program. Once Catholics gained a sufficiently strong foundation in Catholic doctrine, they could become public ambassadors of their faith. This was the idea behind Catholic Action. It sought to promote the militancy of everyday laypeople who would infuse their homes, streets, and workplaces with the counterrevolutionary Catholic spirit, thereby "consecrat[ing] society for Christ."[25] The goal of Catholic Action was to create an official "lay apostolate" that would engender activity, excitement, and commitment from previously passive Catholics, while ensuring they remained under the close watch of the ecclesiastical hierarchy, from whom they received their "mandate and directives."[26] During the first half of the 1920s Catholic Action strove to create an intellectual vanguard that would provide the vision and leadership necessary for establishing the parish-level lay associations that would be founded toward the end of the decade.[27] In 1921 elite Catholic intellectuals led by the right-wing thinker Jackson de Figueiredo came together to found the Centro Dom Vital, whose mission was to "defend society . . . against the enemies of God, whose attack on Religion grows ever more intense."[28] The "enemies of God" were numerous: communists, Masons, liberals, atheists, and all those who advocated for a laicist state, including Protestants. Like churches around the world, the Brazilian Catholic Church had spent much of the late nineteenth and early twentieth centuries feeling besieged by the intellectual and political forces of modern society. The Restorationist intellectuals who would come to form the core of the Centro Dom Vital believed these ideologies had taken hold in Brazil. They denounced its leaders' acceptance of a "bourgeois philosophy of [political and social] life" that disdained and disestablished Catholicism without directly attacking it, thereby creating a religiously indifferent citizenry that was ill-prepared to defend itself against even more dangerous ideologies, particularly communism.[29] They compared these liberal attitudes to "termites" that "work in the shadows," gradually eating away at family, faith, and (Catholic) education, the moral foundations of Brazilian nationality.[30] Only a "spiritual counterrevolution" mounted by Catholic activists committed to exterminating the termites and restoring Brazil's Catholic culture would be able to save the nation.[31]

By the late 1920s, under the influence of the Catholic intellectual Alceu Amoroso Lima (often known by his pen name, Tristão de Athayde), the Centro Dom Vital began to devote much of its efforts to founding the on-the-ground Catholic Action associations that would be the principal conduits through which the spiritual counterrevolution would be fought. The language used to describe Catholic Action was decidedly militaristic. Pius XI liked to call it an army, and its members were commonly referred to as soldiers whose mission was to wage "a war of death and extermination" against their non-Catholic foes.[32] The *Catholic Action Catechism* defined the organization as a "holy militia" that used the "weapons of the Word, example, and zeal" to deliver the nation from its liberal and laicist foes.[33] Not all Catholic Action groups were concentrated on social activism; the majority of local groups focused primarily on the spiritual development of their members and spent much of their time organizing doctrinal study groups and promoting the sacraments. However, Catholic Action's self-conscious emphasis on its militant, nationalist mission ensured that even the most spiritually centered groups contributed to the church's new social mission.

The 1930 Revolution took place in this context of competing Protestant and Catholic efforts to expand their presence in the public sphere. In October of that year a crisis in the presidential succession resulted in a young politician from Rio Grande do Sul, Getúlio Vargas, taking the presidency by force. The early days, months, and even years of the Vargas regime were full of upheaval and uncertainty, as rival political and social groups vied for power. Vargas desperately needed help in legitimizing his government's authority. And while Protestants had made great progress in promoting interdenominational unity and fostering social and political engagement, their numbers and institutional strength were no match for those of the Catholic Church, which was in the enviable position of being able to mobilize large numbers of people through multiple networks of organized lay associations. As Ralph Della Cava has argued, "The profound political vacuum created by the Revolution of 1930 . . . transfigured the [Catholic] Church into a social force absolutely indispensable to the political process," opening up the possibility for a new alliance between church and state.[34] Dom Leme recognized that the turmoil caused by the Revolution opened an opportunity for Catholic leaders to reformulate church–state relations and ultimately to regain influence over Brazilian political affairs.

To understand the Catholic Church's reemergence on the political stage, historians have often highlighted the moment in which Dom Leme famously escorted the defeated president, Washington Luís, out of the palace and to the Copacabana Fort, thereby ensuring a relatively peaceful transfer of power.[35] However, an equally dramatic demonstration of the church's strength occurred just a few weeks after Vargas's arrival in Rio de Janeiro, when Dom Leme organized a massive public demonstration of support for the new regime, called a Mass to Give Thanks for the Pacification of Brazil. On the shores of the beach that spread out before the grand Hotel Glória, over eight thousand Cariocas gathered to see the cardinal, flanked by the then provisional President Vargas and his chief advisers, give thanks to God for restoring peace, order, and stability to Brazil. In doing so, Dom Leme effectively upended a narrative that many Brazilians, including many leaders of the Catholic Church, had been promoting since the early rumblings of revolutionary unrest: that Vargas and his supporters were dangerous upstarts who threatened to plunge the nation into violence, chaos, and anarchy. Dom Leme staged an event that publicly proclaimed the opposite, portraying Vargas and his allies as keepers of, rather than threats to, peace and order in Brazil. In Rio's newspapers, journalists breathlessly recounted the impressive scene of hundreds of members of religious associations solemnly processing in front of civil authorities, singing the national anthem and the "Hymn of João Pessoa," a revolutionary song celebrating the martyrdom of Vargas's assassinated vice president.[36]

The Mass was a declaration of the Catholic Church's openness to supporting the new regime, and it was a vivid demonstration of Catholicism's newfound organizational strength. But perhaps above all, as one newspaper correspondent remarked, it was "a public demonstration of the Catholic faith of the inhabitants of the city."[37] Over the following months there would be more mass demonstrations of Brazilian Catholicism: in May 1931 thousands would take to the streets to celebrate Brazil's newly crowned patron saint, Our Lady of Aparecida, and in October a similarly large crowd would gather to witness the inauguration of the enormous statue of Christ the Redeemer as it initiated its reign at the top of Corcovado mountain. Dom Leme wanted to show Vargas and his officials that Brazil was a *Catholic nation*—its people and culture were Catholic, and its laws and government should be so too.

The 1930s saw a rise in far-right ideologies that would influence the project of the Catholic Restoration. Chief among these was Integralism, a fascistic political group whose motto was God, Homeland, and Family and whose agenda was the installation of a corporatist, authoritarian state. As Margaret Todaro has observed, Integralism was closely aligned with Catholicism, and although the nonpartisan Restorationist church could not officially ally itself with a partisan political movement such as Integralism, in practice the Ação Integralista Brasileira (AIB), Integralism's political party, could count on the support, collaboration, and membership of Restorationist Catholic leaders, both lay and ecclesiastical.[38] From its founding in 1932 until its demise in 1937 Integralism was closely tied to the Catholic political project. Yet the relationship between Integralism and Protestantism was complicated. There was not a direct correlation between a Catholic's anti-Protestant zeal and their commitment to the Integralist cause. Padre Hélder Câmara, one of the most famous Catholic Integralists in Brazil and the Northeast, was a moderate voice when it came to Protestant issues, and even a small number of Protestants joined the Integralist movement.[39] And yet the ideological overlap between Restorationist Catholicism and Integralism meant that many Integralists subscribed to the beliefs on which Catholic anti-Protestantism was founded: anti-liberalism and anti-laicism, xenophobia and anti-U.S. sentiment, and Catholic corporatism.

Ultimately, the rise of the Catholic Restoration left no room for alternative expressions of Brazilian religiosity. To be Brazilian was to be Catholic, and to adhere to a non-Catholic religion was to betray the traditional cultural values that formed the foundation of Brazilian national strength. Anti-Protestantism during the first half of the twentieth century was not a lamentable holdover from an earlier era but a central element of the modern Restoration itself. In the Restorationist mindset Protestants were deemed to be unpatriotic and a threat to social and political stability, as they supposedly sowed discord and undermined the unity of the Brazilian populace. Catholic fears were confirmed when Protestants used their newly founded ecumenical organizations to vigorously contest the political project of the Catholic Restoration, proposing a liberal, laicist alternative to the Catholic corporatist vision of Brazil's modern future. As fascist Integralism and the Catholic Right in Brazilian politics became salient, the foreignness of Protestantism and its connections to U.S. missionary organizations made it a frequent target of Catholic nationalist critiques. While the Brazilian state did not actively persecute Protestants in the Northeast, its alliance with the Catholic Church gave state officials few incentives to protect Protestants from Catholic persecution, and the vast majority of perpetrators of anti-Protestant violence were never punished.[40] Catholics came to see Protestants as the enemies not only of the Catholic Church but also of the social body of their local and national communities. As the twentieth century progressed, the concept of what it meant to be a good Catholic and, in particular, a "good priest," increasingly came to include the commitment to battling Protestantism in the local community, using whatever methods and tools were at one's disposal.

Religious Pluralism and Religious Conflict in Brazilian History

The history of religious pluralism and Catholic–Protestant relations in Brazil has received little attention from historians. Sociologists and anthropologists have dominated the field, and thus much of the scholarship on religious pluralism has treated the period after the Pentecostal boom of the 1960s and 1970s. The rapid growth of Pentecostalism in this period caused the percentage of the Protestant population in Brazil to jump from 5 percent to 22 percent in the span of fifty years, while the percentage of the Catholic population declined from 92 percent to 65 percent.[41] The work of Cecília Mariz, Pierre Sanchis, Andrew Chesnut, and others has drawn attention to the significance and complexities of the unprecedented growth and vitality of late twentieth-century Pentecostalism, shedding light on how the dramatic intensification of religious diversity and pluralism in Brazilian society has been reshaping the social, cultural, and religious landscape of the nation. However, scholarly enthusiasm for the Pentecostal boom has often overshadowed the longer history of Protestantism in Brazil, at times giving the (unintended) impression that Pentecostalism appeared suddenly and unexpectedly in the 1960s and 1970s and that Catholics were unprepared to meet the challenge of a newly competitive religious landscape. I demonstrate that long before the Pentecostal boom both Catholics and Protestants had been grappling with the idea that Brazil—and indeed Latin America— might not remain a monolithically Catholic society, and they undertook organized and aggressive campaigns to strengthen their own power and diminish that of their competitors. The Catholic Restoration was a national, coordinated, institutional Catholic response to the rise of religious pluralism in Brazil. This response was a dramatic failure, for it was wholly unsuccessful at preventing Protestant growth or Catholic decline. Protestants were resilient in the face of Catholic persecution, as they formed alliances, created new evangelization strategies, and attacked the Catholic Church's perceived weaknesses in the political and social spheres. Both the Restorationist campaign and the failure of that campaign would have a profound effect on the future of Brazilian interreligious relations, as it shaped the structure and terms of internal debates that both Catholics and Protestants would continue to have during the second half of the twentieth century. The allure of fundamentalism, religious nationalism, and violent religious intolerance would never fully disappear from Brazilian social or political discourse, and ecumenical projects would be plagued by memories and traditions of religious conflict and competition.

To say that sociologists and anthropologists of the late twentieth-century boom have dominated the literature on religious pluralism in Brazil does not mean that historians have neglected to write about the subject. However, historians have traditionally examined Brazilian Protestantism and Catholicism in isolation from one another, preferring to write histories that analyze a single religious or denominational tradition. One is either a historian of Catholicism or a historian of Protestantism (or even a historian of Baptists or of Pentecostals, etc.), and few scholars delve deeply into the historical relationship between different religious identities. As a result, Catholicism and Protestantism are depicted as having separate historical narratives that only occasionally came into contact, and religious conflict is frequently downplayed or erased. Although early Protestant confessional historians often wrote of the persecutions suffered by their denomination's missionaries and early converts, modern scholars have traditionally overlooked, downplayed, and dismissed episodes of religious persecution, viewing Catholic anti-Protestantism as an ideological issue of nineteenth-century elites rather than an on-the-ground reality of twentieth-century Brazilians.[42] When dealing with local processes of conversion most scholars have followed the lead of the historian Antonio Gouvêa Mendonça, whose examination of Protestantism in the São Paulo region led him to conclude that "Brazilian society did not offer any serious resistance to Protestant penetration."[43] And while some historians of Catholicism have noted the prevalence of anti-Protestant discourses and biases in the Catholic Church in the early twentieth century, analyses of anti-Protestant campaigns and especially anti-Protestant violence have been almost completely absent from Catholic historiography.[44] However, silence regarding Catholic–Protestant conflict is slowly being lifted as a new generation of students has begun to undertake studies of political, educational, and intellectual conflict that accompanied Protestantism in the early years of its existence, revealing religious relations to be more contentious than previously assumed.[45] These studies are often limited to a single Protestant denomination or Catholic writer and frequently narrow in on intellectual conflicts rather than physical clashes, but they are effective counterpoints to the conflict-free narrative of Catholic–Protestant relations. I aim to contribute to this new line of inquiry by investigating specifically the issue of religious persecution. I view moments of violence, intimidation, and confrontation as flashpoints that reveal the internal contradiction of the broader Catholic Restorationist project, as religious leaders were forced to come to terms with the practical consequences of their self-proclaimed battle to protect the integrity of Brazilian Catholic identity.

This book calls for a new religious history of modern Latin America that puts religious pluralism at the center rather than at the margins of historical analysis. It seeks to understand the ways in which religious competition and conflict redefined traditional relationships between church and state, lay and clergy, popular and official religion, and local and national interests. Faced with the steady rise of religious pluralism, however modest, during the early twentieth century, Catholics and Protestants alike needed to reconfigure their understanding of the relationship between religion and Brazilian culture. For centuries religion was seen as uniting the nation of Brazil and the continent of Latin America, more so than language, politics, or even geography. Gilberto Freyre, writing in the 1930s, famously declared that "it would, in truth, be difficult to separate the Brazilian from the Catholic: Catholicism in reality was the cement of our unity."[46] Facing the prospect of a religiously pluralistic society, Brazilians began to ask new questions: Are you a true Brazilian if you are not Catholic? Is Protestantism an inherently foreign religion? What does it mean to say a religion is modern? Can traditional Brazilian culture change, and can the growth of religious pluralism change traditional culture? Scholars of contemporary religious pluralism are still asking these questions, for, as Mariz and Roberta Campos have noted, "coming up with a sense of the Brazilian nation . . . has been *the* core project of the Brazilian intelligentsia," and religion has always been central to how Brazilians have built that sense of nation.[47] I argue here that during the first half of the twentieth century these were not only intellectual questions debated by national religious leaders but also representations of conflicts and challenges that both Catholics and Protestants were confronting in their local communities. The ways in which such questions were answered by both national and local religious actors had concrete and sometimes violent consequences in towns and cities throughout Brazil.

Pentecostal History as Protestant History

In this book I use the terms "Protestantism" and "Protestants" to refer to both historical Protestants—Baptists, Methodists, Presbyterians, Lutherans, Anglicans, and Congregationalists—and Pentecostals. My decision to study historical Protestantism and Pentecostalism together stems from a belief that Pentecostal history cannot and should not be separated from Protestant history, especially in an examination of the rise of religious pluralism and Catholic–Protestant relations in Brazil. As historians have often noted, the story of Brazilian Pentecostalism is intertwined with that of historical Protestantism in that many early converts to Pentecostalism in Brazil were not Catholics but members of historical Protestant congregations.[48] Moreover, Protestant religious identities were not as narrow or fixed as one might be tempted to think. Many Brazilians in the early twentieth century moved easily and frequently between denominations, adhering to a broader identity as a *crente* or *evangélico* rather than to a specific denomination. As Karina Kosicki Bellotti has written, Latin American Protestantism "has shown itself to be relatively fluid and transgresses rigid classifications and denominational boundaries."[49] Throughout the early twentieth century Brazilians in the Northeast undertook what I call conversion journeys. Their initial conversion from Catholicism often sparked a much longer period of spiritual searching, one in which they switched denominational allegiance multiple times, especially if they undertook physical journeys to escape drought, persecution, or unemployment. A Presbyterian who moved to a town with no

Presbyterian congregation often joined a Congregational, Baptist, or even Pentecostal church, all the while keeping her or his identity as a crente. In his magisterial study of the history of Mexican and Chicano Pentecostalism, Daniel Ramírez has called this religious fluidity "proto-evangelicalismo," which refers to "a common experience of religious dissent and marginalization vis-à-vis hegemonic Catholicism" that united, and sometimes blurred the lines between, specific Protestant denominations in Latin America.[50]

I believe that Ramírez's call to better understand proto-evangelicalismo brings with it a methodological demand for historians to look beyond (but not past) denominational affiliation when studying Latin American Protestantism, broadening the subjects, archives, and narratives with which we work. As Laura Premack has shown in her article on the relationship between Brazilian Baptists and Pentecostals, the slippages and ambiguities inherent in early Brazilian Protestant identities allowed converts to move easily between denominational narratives and appear in multiple historical archives.[51] Using a proto-evangélico methodology is especially important when examining Catholic–Protestant relations, for no one promoted the idea of a common crente/evangélico identity with more vigor or with greater consequences than Catholics themselves. In early twentieth-century Brazil Catholics often elided, whether through ignorance or design, the differences between Protestant denominations, preferring to call all Protestant groups *seitas* (sects) and their members *hereges* (heretics). Catholic anti-Protestantism was truly interdenominational, and thus it would be ahistorical to speak of religious conflict between Catholics and Presbyterians or Catholics and Pentecostals. Most Catholics made no distinction between Presbyterians and Pentecostals, and they maintained that both were the fruit of the same poisoned tree. In the same way that Brazilian Protestants often called Catholics (especially members of a religious order, such as the Capuchins) Jesuits, even when they were not Jesuits, Brazilian Catholics often called Protestants Lutherans or substituted the name of one denomination for another. Catholics could therefore use the supposed sins of one—Presbyterianism's political activities, for example, or Pentecostalism's ecstatic worship style—to attack the power of the other. Whether they liked it or not, historical Protestant churches and Pentecostal churches came to learn that their fates were deeply intertwined.

Religious Conflict, Romanization, and the New Religious History

Catholic nationalism and the emergence of a northeastern Catholic identity were not the only factors driving the nature and growth of anti-Protestant sentiment in the Northeast. In the 1920s and 1930s anti-Protestantism became deeply embedded in northeastern Catholic culture, as messages and actions against Protestants were incorporated into Catholic ritual life: religious processions, festivals, chapel inaugurations, and, especially, santas missões populares, the Capuchin-led, ritual-laden religious revivals that urged nordestinos to repent their sins and receive the holy sacraments of the church. Similar to what Natalie Zemon Davis has called the "rites of violence," these activities became both symbolic and practical sites of conflict between Catholics and Protestants, and acts of church burning, stonings, and physical assaults frequently occurred as part of a popular religious event.[52]

In examining the relationship between anti-Protestantism and northeastern religious culture, I want to contribute to the rich literature on Latin American popular religiosity that has emerged over the past decade. Scholars of this new religious history have sought to break down boundaries between material and spiritual motivational forces, tradition and modernity, public and private worship, and local and universal religious projects, viewing popular religiosity as forming an integral part rather than a separate sphere of official religious life.[53] Although much of this work has focused on Mexican religious culture, scholars like Patricia Pessar have shown how Brazilian millenarian movements like that in the northeastern town of Santa Brígida "challenge dichotomous notions that pit power holders against popular classes and religion against modernity."[54] My work builds on that of Pessar and others, as conflicts between Catholics and Protestants blurred the lines between backward and modern beliefs, elite and popular religion, fanatical and orthodox priests, and illegitimate and legitimate violence. This book also seeks to complicate how scholars view the actions and identities of ordained local religious leaders, such as priests, pastors, friars, and even local bishops. Members of the clergy, especially those in rural, purportedly backward regions such as the Northeast, are often seen as being separated from both the local religious culture of their parishioners and the dynamic reform movements and planning of their urban ecclesiastical superiors. Yet the vast majority of these priests grew up steeped in the same religious culture as that of their flock (or, in the case of Capuchin friars, in the mystical religious culture of rural Italy), and this background would leave its mark on their words and actions as religious leaders. At the same time, they could and did embrace change and reform, channeling their creativity and ambition into finding local solutions for national problems.

Yet some religious leaders found these blurred clerical identities discomforting and conflictive. Since the late nineteenth century Catholic leaders had been working to Romanize both priests and their parishioners, and too much contact with popular religious culture jeopardized this effort. Romanization was, above all, a cultural project designed to reform the Catholic people themselves: to make them more orthodox, less superstitious, and unquestionably obedient to centralized hierarchies, both religious and civil—in a word, to make Latin American Catholicism more modern.[55] The religious devotions and lay sodalities that had flourished during the Brazilian Empire needed to be either suppressed or brought under hierarchical control, and local saints and heterodox religious sentiments were to be sanitized and made newly compatible with universal, that is, European, Catholic movements that had flourished in Italy and the rest of Europe in the nineteenth and early twentieth centuries.[56] Latin American religiosity was seen to be too syncretic and too impure, the result, it was thought, of insufficient evangelization and catechistic efforts. Catholic leaders, both Brazilian and European, believed that the Catholic Reformation that had swept through Europe in the sixteenth and seventeenth centuries had never been fully implemented across the Atlantic, and thus Brazil was stuck in a medieval, pre-Tridentine, and ambiguously indigenized religious culture that allowed for too much local diversity, lay control, and heterodox devotional cultures.[57] As Kenneth Serbin and Edward Wright-Rios have argued, Romanization in Latin America was essentially a conservative modernization project in which Catholic leaders attempted to mold Latin American religious practices and sentiments in the image of their more advanced European counterparts.[58]

Many priests and friars in the Northeast were committed to Romanizing their flocks, but there was always a latent fear among religious leaders that the pull of northeastern religious culture and, in particular, the presumed fanaticism that accompanied it would prove irresistible to the priests who were surrounded by it every day, causing them to lead their parishioners down a dangerous path. In this context, the violence associated with campaigns against Protestantism was transformed from a legitimate act of religious self-defense to a menacing act of religious fanaticism. I analyze how priests and friars navigated or, in some cases, failed to navigate these blurred boundaries.

A Note on Sources

At first glance the history of Catholics and Protestants in the interior of the Northeast appears to suffer from a lack of sources. Unlike religious archives in other locales, the traditional archives of northeastern Catholic and Protestant churches, that is, archdiocesan, diocesan, and regional Protestant archives, are incomplete, and, with the exception of some provincial archives of religious orders, they contain little material pertaining to parishes and congregations outside of urban centers.[59] Many Protestant congregations in the northeastern interior dissolved, re-formed, or split apart one or more times during the early twentieth century, losing much of their historical documentation in the process. However, this does not mean that materials pertaining to northeastern religious conflicts do not exist. By traveling through the northeastern interior itself, going from town to town, I found a wealth of information and sources that had gone largely overlooked by past scholars. Lying in the basements and back rooms of local Catholic and Protestant churches were diocesan decrees, minutes from congregational meetings and disciplinary hearings, devotional images and tracts, and, most important, *livros de tombo*, which were diaries in which Catholic priests detailed daily life in their parishes. In towns' public and private libraries I found the family histories and self-published memoirs of prominent members of local society, some of whom were vital actors in local religious conflicts. Moreover, in many towns I met private individuals who possessed their own archives of primary source documents and were kind enough to share them with me. Above all, conducting research in both Protestant and Catholic archives, rather than just one or the other, allowed me to double my source material on each religion because Catholics and Protestants often spent more time detailing the growth and activities of their rivals' church communities than they did of their own. This same principle applies to the study of historical Protestantism and Pentecostalism: historical Protestants oftentimes saw Pentecostalism as posing a bigger threat to their future than the Catholic Church. Just as Catholics kept an eye on the activities of Protestants, so historical Protestants, as Laura Premack has shown, kept detailed accounts of their interactions with Pentecostals.[60] Given the above-mentioned existence of proto-evangelicalismo and the blurring of Pentecostal and non-Pentecostal identities, sources related to actors who might later identify as strictly Pente-costal or historical Protestant can frequently be found in both Pentecostal and historical Protestant archives since their early religious affiliations dif-fered or were more fluid than they would become later.

Local sources can be problematic, especially those relating to religious conflict and rivalry. They can be heavily laden with bias and distortion and must be interpreted with the utmost caution. Protestants often wrote of reli-gious persecution as forming part of a providential narrative of trials, tribula-tions, and redemption, and so it is important to read beyond and between the constructions frequently found in persecution narratives in order to un-derstand what truly transpired. Catholics, too, viewed their confrontations with Protestants as part of a broader, sometimes millenarian, struggle to pro-tect the local and national community from the attacks of Protestants. They defended their actions by writing detailed accounts of supposed Protestant provocations that had set off the initial conflicts. Nevertheless, Protestant and Catholic descriptions of religious conflict were not as contradictory as one might assume. As self-proclaimed defenders of the faith, Catholics were often proud of the anti-Protestant campaigns they organized or in which they participated, and they had few qualms about discussing them openly. Livros de tombo are full of firsthand accounts by priests of the anti-Protestant initiatives they undertook in their parishes.

The richest, although scarcest, accounts of local religious conflicts are found in judicial court cases. The refusal of most local authorities to prose-cute Catholics for anti-Protestant crimes meant that few official police or court records were created. However, three important cases were brought before the Tribunal de Segurança Nacional, a special court created by President Vargas to prosecute those who threatened the "order and stability of the nation." The extensive documentation connected to these cases offers key insights into not only the religious violence itself but also its relationship to broader political debates regarding modernization, religious freedom, northeastern fanaticism, and the centralization of state authority. By comparing, triangulating, and integrating a wide variety of sources— Protestant (historical and Pentecostal), Catholic, governmental, judicial, and periodical—I incorporate multiple religious and political perspectives into my narrative and analysis.

Chapter Outlines

Chapter 1 examines how Catholics and Protestants developed competing visions for Brazil's social and political future as each came to view the other as the primary obstacle to national progress. During the 1920s and 1930s anti-Protestantism came to be a fundamental element of the national Restorationist project. Catholics began to view Protestants as enemies who threatened not only the religious project of the Catholic Church but also the political unity and stability of the Brazilian nation. Protestants saw the Catholic Church as threatening to return Brazil to its backward, superstitious, colonial past, reversing a century of liberal achievements they believed defined Brazilian imperial and republican history. Conflicts between Catholics and Protestants played out both in the pages of polemical books and in newspaper articles, both sides attacking the other for being harmful to the health of the modern nation, as well as in the political arena as each mounted an aggressive campaign to influence the writing of the 1934 constitution. With the rise of new Catholic and Protestant institutions, such as the Secretariado Nacional de Defesa da Fé (National Secretariat for the Defense of the Faith) and the Liga Pró-Estado Leigo (League for a Laicist State), political conflicts between Catholics and Protestants expanded and intensified throughout Brazil.

Chapter 2 moves the narrative permanently to the Northeast. In this chapter I analyze the changing face of Protestantism in that region as it spread to the rural interior and came to be led by a diverse group of Brazilian pastors. I examine the rise of Pentecostalism and its impact on interreligious relations in rural areas. Chapter 3 looks at how northeastern Catholics responded to these changes. The actions of local Catholic clergymen who were tasked with leading the charge against the Protestant "invasion" of their parishes are a primary subject. I show how anti-Protestantism became an essential part of what it meant to be a "good priest," as Catholic leaders throughout the Northeast promoted distinct sets of rituals and discourses that both fueled and legitimized the use of force against Protestants.

Chapter 4 puts Catholic–Protestant conflict in the context of broader societal anxieties regarding the so-called fanaticism of northeastern religious culture. Specifically, it discusses two judicial cases that represent rare examples of Catholics being punished rather than celebrated for their acts of anti-Protestant violence. Yet a close examination of the cases makes it difficult to interpret either their process or outcome as a triumph of justice, the rule of law, or religious freedom in Brazil. The prosecutions, after all, were motivated less by the desire to protect the rights of Protestant Brazilians than by the need to assert control over unauthorized and uncontrolled expressions of northeastern religiosity. Protestants understood this nuance, and in an effort to protect themselves from campaigns of persecution they ultimately contributed to the portrayal of northeastern religiosity as a backward, dangerous redoubt of violent fanaticism. The chapter highlights the complex relationships between anti-Protestant campaigns and local political and economic culture. While local authorities often protected and promoted Catholic anti-Protestantism, the social upheavals that marked the Vargas era afforded Protestants the opportunity to forge new alliances. Protestant leaders were able to take advantage of political and religious cleavages in order to advance the interests of their congregants.

Chapters 5 and 6 deal with the relationship between Protestants and santas missões populares. The missões were a key means by which anti-Protestantism became embedded within the Catholic religious culture of the Northeast. I pay special attention to Frei Damião de Bozzano, a Capuchin missionary who gained the status of a popular saint. Today, Frei Damião is one of the most well-known religious figures in Brazil, and the

Vatican has opened a case to examine his eligibility for canonization. During the 1930s Frei Damião was one of the principal agents of northeastern anti-Protestantism, as his fire and brimstone sermons urged Catholics to purify their towns of the Protestant scourge. In a period when elites' fears of religious fanaticism were on the rise, Protestants sought to portray Frei Damião as a dangerous religious fanatic who was on the verge of provoking a millenarian uprising in the supposedly backward Northeast. In this way, Protestants hoped to provoke the condemnation and repression of Frei Damião by ecclesiastical and civil authorities. However, these chapters argue that at the same time he was gaining a reputation for being a mystical, even fanatical, religious figure, Frei Damião was working hard to present himself as a modern anti-Protestant agent who was laboring on behalf of his ecclesiastical and civil superiors. Frei Damião's dual identity—part popular saint, part modernizing anti-Protestant reformer—gave him the protection and freedom necessary to become one of the most powerful religious figures of his era.

The epilogue examines the decades following the end of the Vargas regime, which saw the emergence of social, political, and theological innovations in both Catholic and Protestant churches. While these new movements opened up new opportunities for ecumenical dialogue, they also engendered deep internal divisions within the religious denominations themselves, thereby preventing the widespread adoption of the ecumenical agenda. As the Pentecostal boom accelerated the diversification of Brazilian religious culture, Catholics and Protestants alike continued to struggle to come to terms with the religious pluralism and competition that defined the latter half of the twentieth century.

ONE

Quem Não Crê, Brasileiro Não É

The Catholic Restoration and the
Rise of Protestantism in Brazil

Aos clarins do Congresso Sagrado	Upon hearing the trumpets of the Sacred Congress
Pernambuco se ergueu varonil	Pernambuco rose up, manly,
E o Recife se fez lado a lado	And Recife, from corner to corner,
Catedral onde reza o Brasil	became a Cathedral where Brazil prays
Eis, sus, ó Leão, Leão do Norte!	There it is, take courage, oh Lion, Lion of the North!
Ruge ao mar o teu grito de fé!	Roar your cry of faith to the sea!
Creio em Ti, Hostia Santa, até a morte,	I believe in You, Holy Host, until death,
Quem não crê, brasileiro não é!	Whoever does not believe is not Brazilian!

—*Hymn of the Third National Eucharistic Congress*[1]

In September 1939 tens of thousands of Brazilian Catholics gathered in the northeastern city of Recife to celebrate the Third National Eucharistic Congress. Episcopal leaders, laypeople, and government authorities came together to publicly proclaim both their Catholic faith and their national pride. For seven days they held rallies, gave speeches, and marched through the streets while singing the official hymn of the congress: "Creio em Ti, Hostia Santa, até a morte, / Quem não crê, brasileiro não é!" (I believe in you, Holy Host, until death, / Whoever does not believe is not Brazilian!) Eucharistic Congresses were perhaps one of the most emblematic elements of the Catholic Restoration. Initiated by Dom Sebastião Leme in 1922, just one year after he arrived in Rio de Janeiro, they were dramatic displays of the spiritual and political power of the Catholic Church. Marching and singing alongside the thousands of Catholic participants were representatives of the Vargas government—*interventores* (Vargas-appointed governors), federal secretaries, and local officials—who all had come to pay their respects to the church.[2]

At their core Eucharistic Congresses were expressions of a strident form of Catholic nationalism that rejected alternative expressions of Brazilian religiosity, particularly Protestantism. The congresses' emphasis on the Real Presence of the Eucharist, a doctrine which Protestants rejected, transformed the gatherings into a defense of a particularly Catholic, rather than Christian, understanding of Brazilian nationalism and identity. Nowhere was this more apparent than at the Recife congress, the first Eucharistic Congress to be held in the Northeast. During the congress Dom Sebastião Leme gave a speech calling for the strengthening of a church–state alliance capable of fighting against "foreign enemies" of Catholicism: "We are here to reaffirm that an alliance has been made between Christ, our king, and Brazil, our country, that gives us titles and rights. . . . An alliance that we will seal, if necessary, with the seal of our blood, for this alliance is everlasting and unbreakable. No impious invader, no foreign enemy of God and enemy of Brazil that comes here to try to break this alliance will have any hope of victory. . . . I believe in the Lion of the North! The enemies of the Church flee from its roar, because it was here that Pernambuco rose up to fight the enemies of the Faith."[3]

The Recife congress was not just a rejection of Protestantism and an affirmation of the national church–state alliance but also a declaration of the Northeast's privileged place in both anti-Protestant history and Catholic Restorationism. Throughout the congress frequent references were made to Pernambuco's historic seventeenth-century battle to expel the Dutch colonizers from Brazil. Speakers at the congress recast the conflict as a religious war that pitted Portuguese Catholics against Dutch Calvinists. They frequently reminded attendees that Protestants, in the form of Dutch Calvinists, had attacked northeastern Catholic churches and congregations. The congress celebrated the aggressive, courageous response of Pernambucans to the Protestant threat and called for a new Catholic commitment to driving out its enemies, including Protestants. They were not Catholic and thus not Brazilian. They were foreigners, whether by birth or by their rejection of Brazilian culture. As such, they represented a threat to the unity and security of the nation and did not deserve the freedoms protected by the constitution.

The negation of Brazilian nationality to non-Catholics was central to the Catholic Restorationist movement from its beginning. Liberalism, positivism, laicism, secularism: in the eyes of Restorationists these were decidedly un-Brazilian ideologies that had infiltrated the country from the outside, brought in by those who sought to weaken Brazil's national unity. Perhaps no group embodied this insidious mix of foreignness, liberalism, and anti-Catholicism quite like the Protestants, and for this reason Protestantism, including its churches, its leaders, and its converts, became one of the primary targets of Restorationist attacks. Northeastern Catholics were aware of the anti-Protestant campaign being waged by Restorationist leaders in the Southeast, and they actively participated in the debates, associations, and movements related to the national anti-Protestant project.

Brazilian Protestants were alarmed by the rise of Catholic Restorationism and the growing political power of its representatives. Rather than attempt to avoid conflict, Protestants went on the offensive, publishing anti-Catholic polemics, lobbying elected officials, and creating alliances with secular liberals and anticlerical activists in an effort to thwart the growing social and political power of the Restorationist Catholic Church. Protestants, too, believed that the future of Brazil was threatened by religious forces. Catholic backwardness, they held, was trying to drag Brazil back to its colonial past, undoing the progress Brazilians had achieved in the nineteenth and twentieth centuries. By reinterpreting Brazilian history as a steady march toward the triumph of liberalism, laicism, and religious freedom, Protestants sought to defend the integrity of their Brazilian identity even as they were determined to discredit Catholic claims to represent the best interests of the nation.

The result of the increase in both Catholic and Protestant political activism was an intensely polarized religious sphere in which Catholics and non-Catholics came to regard each other not only as spiritual competitors but also as political and existential threats to the future of the Brazilian nation. The rise of polarizing religious ideologies was much more dangerous for Protestants than for Catholics, as they were members of a religious minority with little political, social, or economic power. As ideas translated into actions, religious conflict and persecution became increasingly likely outcomes of the Catholic Restorationist movement.

The Future of Brazil in Danger: Protestants as Enemies of Brazilian Nationalism

Throughout the nineteenth and twentieth centuries Protestants and Catholics argued vociferously over whose religion was best suited to promoting the social, economic, and political well-being of Brazil. Protestants had long contended that their faith was the religion of progress, modernity, and economic prosperity, and they pointed to the success of the United States, the United Kingdom, and Germany to demonstrate their point.[4] The Brazilian Catholic Church had always condemned this viewpoint and disputed it, but the task became more urgent in the 1920s and 1930s, as Restorationist leaders put forth their own vision of a Brazilian state that was both Catholic and modern. In this vision the Catholic Church was compatible with economic and social progress and uniquely suited to helping Brazil confront the dangers of the modern world. Protestantism was at the root of the liberal ills that plagued modern society, and church leaders argued that only a strong Catholic nationalist project could save Brazil from the foreign Protestants who were threatening to tear apart the social and political fabric of the nation. One of the chief proponents of anti-Protestant nationalism was Padre Leonel Franca, a Jesuit priest and strong supporter of the Centro Dom Vital as well as the future father of the first Catholic university in Brazil, the Pontifícia Universidade Católica do Rio de Janeiro (PUC-RJ). In 1923 he published *A Igreja, a reforma, e a civilização* (The church, the Reformation, and civilization), which quickly became a classic of the anti-Protestant apologetic genre, going through no fewer than seven printings by 1958. As was typical of apologetic works, Franca's book was not a stand-alone attack on Protestantism but a response to *O problema religioso da América Latina* (Latin America's religious problem), a book published three years earlier by the Presbyterian pastor and prolific polemicist Eduardo Carlos Pereira.[5] In *O problema religioso* Pereira wrote, "Two great evils overshadow Latin society: ignorance and religious indifference. And from these evils come superstition and pessimism."[6] Stuck in a premodern, authoritarian mindset impervious to reason and progress, the Catholic Church was unable to effectively civilize society and was the primary reason Latin America had failed to attain the economic and social progress of its Protestant-colonized counterparts. "The political and social inferiority of our race and the moral and religious conditions of Ibero-American societies are the result of the nefarious influence of Romanism," Pereira declared.[7]

Franca's *A Igreja* sought to rehabilitate the Catholic doctrines attacked by Pereira as well as raise a counterattack. Whereas the first two sections focused mostly on theology and authority, the third section, by far the longest at nearly the length of the first two sections combined, was determined to refute Pereira's accusations of Catholic backwardness and resistance to progress. Franca began by painstakingly disproving, country by country, the idea that Catholicism was to blame for the economic, social, and moral decline of nations. He pointed to Protestant countries that were in states of economic decline similar to those of Catholic nations, including Denmark, Sweden, and Norway. Compared to Catholic Belgium, he asserted, they were in dire economic straits. He challenged the claim that the Latin American countries that had "fallen behind" were Catholic at all: had they not been governed for most of the nineteenth century by anticlerical regimes?[8] Catholics had already proven they could reign over economic and scientific progress during the sixteenth and seventeenth centuries, when they ruled some of the richest, most successful empires in Europe. If they had declined since then, it was merely because "a combination of natural causes, acting together with a blind anti-Christian political climate, determined a relatively long and profound eclipse of the splendors of their former material glory."[9] Catholic nations had prospered before, and they could prosper again, on their own terms.

But ultimately, Padre Franca was not interested in proving that Catholic states could replicate the present-day success of Protestant nations like the United States. Following the lead of Pope Leo XIII in his groundbreaking encyclical *Rerum Novarum*, Padre Franca condemned not only the materialism of communists and socialists but also the extreme individualism and unbridled capitalism that was characterized by the "oppression of the weak and the poor, and by the subordination of the collective interests to the personal interests."[10] Brazil should not strive to copy or be dominated by the United States, he wrote, but should instead form its own path and its own system of economic and political life: "Faced with individualist excesses and socialist exaggerations, the Church opposes both, and puts forth a Christian concept of society: a living organism that is animated by a unifying principle. Each member has his function, and the diverse functions do not pose obstacles to the achievement of the common goal, which is the general happiness of all. . . . The exploitation of some by others, of the weak by the strong, should be replaced with the sacrifice of one for all, with mutual concessions, all for the common good."[11]

Padre Franca was proposing a corporatist vision of society and, more obliquely, of the state, in which the interests of corporate groups would be harmonized through their submission to a centralized authority that would work for the common good. Catholic corporatism was central to the Restoration's political and social platform, and it was supported not just by Padre Franca but by nearly all of the leading Catholic intellectual leaders, particularly those associated with the Centro Dom Vital. By the 1930s it would become the political model for the Vargas regime. Protestantism, Padre Franca and others argued, was directly opposed, even anathema, to the corporatist ideal. Its emphasis on free will and individualism as well as its defiance of centralized hierarchies and authorities made its adherents unable to sacrifice some of their immediate interests in order to promote the greater common good of Brazilian society. By the end of Padre Franca's book Protestants had gone from being members of a religious minority with an erroneous and misguided theology to being dangerous threats to the political and social peace of Brazil, disrupting the corporate unity of the nation. "To conserve national unity, it is necessary to strengthen the spiritual ties of the

Brazilian family. . . . Seen in this light," Padre Franca declared, "Protestant propaganda in Brazil seems to be an eminently anti-national project. Throughout this work we've argued that C. Pereira's book is unscientific. Now I will denounce it as unpatriotic."[12] To Padre Franca, Protestants sought to divide Brazilians among themselves, to take them away from the unifying authority of the Catholic Church and set them loose in the spiritual anarchy of Protestantism, swimming among the seemingly infinite number of sects and schisms. In doing so, they weakened the nation itself, making it difficult to sustain its corporate structure.

The debate between Pereira and Franca was not the first Protestant–Catholic conflict to be played out in print in Brazil nor would it be the last. Many of the criticisms the two clerics made of each other—that the Catholic Church fomented superstition and backwardness, that Protestantism was a force of anarchy and disunity, etc.—had been made by numerous predecessors of the padre and the pastor. Yet in the environment of the Restoration, in which both Catholics and Protestants were increasing their activism in the public sphere, what began as a relatively standard polemical spat soon turned into what Antonio Gouvêia Mendonça has called "the biggest Catholic–Protestant polemic that there ever was in Brazil."[13] Pereira died in 1923 before he could respond to Franca's book, but the debate did not end. Three other Protestant intellectuals took his place, and Franca would, in turn, respond to these new authors. The back and forth continued for nearly two decades.[14] And while it might seem that religious apologetic books would not have a great impact beyond priests and pastors, the Franca polemics, as they came to be called, received nonstop coverage in the religious press. Catholic and Protestant newspapers and journals breathlessly reported on each new book and pamphlet, giving the full overviews of the works and often summaries of the opponents' work to which the current author was responding. Thus a wider public became aware of the debates as well as of the criticisms, opinions, and insults editors and guest columnists added to the mix. "[The Protestant's] disrespect for the divine word is revolting," wrote a columnist for the Catholic newspaper O Legionário. "Here, he overlooks what is not convenient for his argument, while there, he falsifies the meaning in order to maintain a dubious position that will later allow him to make an offensive interpretation of the divine Word and Holy Spirit."[15] For their part, Protestant newspapers such as O Puritano would declare that Franca's work was "a bunch of taunts and insults, full of exegetical errors and shabby criticism."[16] Moreover, these debates were not limited to the large national newspapers, for regional religious publications also closely followed the exchanges between Franca and his interlocutors. In the Northeast the Paraíban Catholic newspaper A Imprensa called Ernesto Luiz de Oliveira's Roma, a Egreja, e o Anticristo (Rome, the Church, and the antichrist) a "rude, overstuffed, rickety work with no substance: a lot of paper, but few ideas."[17] A Presbyterian church in Recife organized a new course on apologetics with the specific aim of "preparing evangelicals to refute and respond to the new attacks from the Catholic Church, which is now armed with the works of Leonel Franca and ready to do battle with Protestantism."[18] In this way, the theological arguments of the polemicists were both disseminated and intensified, as commentators from all regions of Brazil joined the debate, becoming ever more extreme in their pronouncements.

And while Padre Leonel Franca's polemical works used specialized theological language and were part of complicated intellectual debates, other, more popular anti-Protestant writers also had a wide audience and influence in the twenties and thirties. Padre Júlio Maria de Lombaerde, for example, a Belgian priest based in Minas Gerais who became known as "the hammer of Brazilian Protestantism," published eighteen anti-Protestant books and innumerable anti-Protestant articles in his newspaper, O Lutador (The fighter).[19] Padre Júlio Maria's works were read by everyday Catholics throughout Brazil. According to Daniel Soares Simões, Padre Júlio Maria "popularized Catholic arguments against Protestants, making them more accessible to the common reader."[20] Whereas Padre Franca employed erudite apologetics to question the validity of Protestant doctrines, Padre Júlio Maria used fiery language to condemn, insult, and ridicule Protestantism, as he accused the "religion of Luther" of being both a satanic sign of the Apocalypse and a haven for ignorant, perverse, corrupt, and greedy individuals who hoped to tempt and exploit unassuming Catholics into a life of sin and damnation. But while the words and imagery of Padre Franca and Padre Júlio Maria may have been different, many of their messages were the same. Like Padre Franca, Padre Júlio Maria warned his readers of the disastrous national consequences of allowing Protestantism to grow unchecked in Brazil, thereby "planting the seed of disunion in our beloved Brazil" and putting the future of Brazilian sovereignty, culture, and tradition in jeopardy.[21]

With the advent of the 1930 Revolution and the rise of political and social unrest in the country, the conflict between Catholics and Protestants became less about how the other religion's ideas or theologies were bad for the Brazilian nation than about how the other religion's *people* were actively working to undermine future Brazilian progress and peace. Catholic nationalists thus began to echo the language and imagery of far-right Brazilian nationalist projects that were gaining adherents in the 1930s, especially Integralism. Integralists, however, did not always view Protestants as a primary target of their criticism and persecution, whereas Catholic Restorationists were adamant that Protestants posed a grave threat to the Brazilian nation and had to be treated as national enemies. As the 1930s progressed, Catholics used increasingly militaristic and counterrevolutionary language to describe Protestant individuals and organizations, speaking of "Protestant infiltration," "the Protestant threat," and "the Protestant offensive." The growth of Protestant churches and associations began to take on sinister, conspiratorial overtones for Catholics, who viewed them as vehicles for secret anti-Brazilian agendas. Thus when the YMCA came to Brazil and started opening chapters, the Archdiocese of Rio de Janeiro wrote a public advisory to all Catholics warning them not be complacent when faced with "Protestant infiltration": "Remember, Brazilian Catholics, that to de-Christianize our Fatherland through neo-paganism, or de-Catholicize it through Protestantism, is to de-nationalize it; it violates the spirit of our nation's centuries-old traditions and it attacks the living forces that cement Brazil's nationality; it represents a formidable danger that threatens our very unity and political existence. It is for this reason that Catholics have a patriotic responsibility to not support in any way Protestant youth organizations."[22] The archdiocese then ordered that the advisory be disseminated widely: read at Sunday Mass in every parish in the archdiocese, hung on the door of all of the churches, read at all public religious celebrations, and circulated "by whatever means are within the reach of the activities and zeal of all Catholics in every par-ish."[23] And while it might seem odd for Catholic leaders to have such an in-tense reaction to an organization like the YMCA, it was just such innocent organizations that stoked Catholics' deepest fears. In the eyes of Restoration-ist Catholic leaders like Alceu Amoroso Lima, the president of the Centro Dom Vital and the leader of Brazilian Catholic Action, the danger repre-sented by Protestants lay precisely in their apparent innocence: "The *words* that they will pronounce will not, at least in the case of the most responsible [Protestant leaders], contain anything *explicitly* offensive to the traditional Brazilian faith. But their *intentions* are totally different, and those who know how to read between the lines can immediately see the tremendous dangers of these indirect attacks, these secret and hidden offensives that take place in the dark in order to operate more effectively."[24]

Writing in July 1932, just after residents in São Paulo had taken up arms against the Vargas government, Lima noted how Protestants were mounting "an attack against the religious soul of the nation at a moment in which its unity [was] increasingly threatened," that is, when civil war loomed and the most prosperous Brazilian state openly defied federal authorities. "Our territorial and political unity can be maintained," Lima declared, "only if we know how to maintain our intellectual and moral unity. To be a united nation we need to start by having a united soul."[25] A united soul was a Cath-olic soul, and Restorationists like Lima forcefully argued that the expansion of Protestants' activities would serve to undermine Vargas's revolutionary project and destabilize an already precarious political situation.

Moreover, to Catholic leaders such as Lima, Protestants were a threat not only to the unity of Brazil but also to its sovereignty. In line with the rising xenophobia and anti-immigrant spirit of the 1930s as well as the anti-U.S. and pro-German sentiment that characterized much of the Brazilian Right at the time, Restorationists also attacked Protestants as "foreign infiltrators" who were being funded and controlled by the United States for unknown and possibly pernicious reasons. Catholics had no doubt that the United States was directly responsible for the growth of Protestantism in Brazil. As one Catholic priest averred, "If the North Americans stopped giving money to fund Protestant propaganda in Latin America, that propaganda would disappear."[26] Lima himself waged a spirited print war against the "North American Protestant offensive" that was supposedly responsible for destroying Brazilian culture and unity.[27] He declared that the assault "represents nothing less than the attempt to divide, weaken, and humiliate a great South American Catholic nationality that could tomorrow serve as a bulwark against the neo-pagan avalanche that is coming to us from the North."[28] According to Restorationists, Protestant missionaries dazzled Brazilians with their technological advancements and intellectual modernism, only to leave them with a hollowed-out ideology of rationalism and individualism. In the eyes of Catholics this was not by accident: Protestants were actively seeking to destroy the fabric of Brazilian society.

The Protestant Counteroffensive: In Search of a Laicist State

While Protestants were accustomed to being on the receiving end of aggressive Catholic speeches and writings, by the 1930s they sensed that the growth of Catholic nationalist anti-Protestant sentiments, coupled with the rise of Getúlio Vargas to power and the subsequent realignment of Catholic and state interests, represented a serious threat not only to their faith but also to the political vision for which they had worked and fought since they began missionary work in Brazil in the mid-nineteenth century. As early as the 1860s Protestants had allied themselves with Brazil's liberal forces in promoting a secular, laicist vision of the state in which the power of the Catholic Church was greatly reduced. During the church–state conflicts of the late nineteenth century and in particular in the years leading up to the crisis of the Questão Religiosa, prominent Protestant leaders and institutions joined forces with liberals and Masons in exerting pressure on the imperial government to take a hardline stance against the ultramontane movement that was gaining ground.[29] After the fall of the empire in 1889 Protestants became vocal advocates of the separation of church and state that would be enshrined in the 1891 constitution, and they would come to see the First Republic as a burgeoning golden age of religious freedom and liberal progress. When the Revolution of 1930 came about and Vargas began to appear at public functions with Catholic leaders, Protestants watched these displays of church–state harmony with alarm. They immediately understood that the terms of the laicist state were being renegotiated and that such changes could have a profound impact on the freedom of religion in Brazil.

In December 1930, only a few weeks after Dom Leme's "thanksgiving Mass" attended by Vargas and his cabinet members, the leadership of the Brazilian Presbyterian Church sent an open letter to the president in which they expressed their dismay at the "preferences, honors, and entitlements through which the State has revealed its poorly hidden alliance with the [Catholic] Church."[30] Brazil, they declared, was at a crossroads, facing what was essentially a new Questão Religiosa, and its government would have to decide whether to support the liberal values that had sustained it for much of its history as an independent nation or allow itself to be pulled back into the dark ages of colonial church control. Favoring the former path over the latter, the document laid out three arguments that would be central to the Protestants' response to Restorationist discourses. The first two were similar to ones made in classic polemical literature: Brazil could not be a Catholic nation because most Catholics were not really Catholics at all: they were either too ignorant and illiterate to truly understand their faith or, among the more cultured classes, they "refused to accept all of [Catholic] dogma" and thus were not truly Catholics;[31] and Catholicism was the religion of ignorance and backwardness, and Protestantism was the religion of modernity and was therefore more suited to advance the modern revolutionary agenda of the Vargas regime.

But it was the third argument that formed the heart of the letter. It was by far the most lengthy and detailed section, taking up well over 70 percent of the total text. The section was essentially an alternative history of Brazilian national identity. Instead of looking for the soul of the Brazilian nation in its colonial Catholic heritage, Protestants contended that the true spirit of Brazil could be found in its nineteenth- and twentieth-century struggle for liberal principles, freedom of conscience, and separation of church and state: "The attitude of fraternal equity came about, spontaneously and intuitively, in the infancy of Brazilian nationality, having been the noble characteristic of the liberal tendencies codified in acts and resolutions, in manifestos and platforms of political parties."[32] The authors then presented a painstaking list of the events, documents, constitutions, and speeches in which key figures of Brazilian republicanism defended the freedom of religion. "It can be affirmed," the letter concluded, "that the separation between the Churches and the State, and the consequent freedom of religion, have been a sacred ideal of our great Nation for over seventy years."[33] To be Brazilian, then, was to support the laicist state, the freedom of religion, and the liberal ideas that underpinned the First Republic.

However, if Protestants were to bring their laicist vision of Brazil to fruition they would need to become involved in politics. As Leonildo Silveira Campos has argued, prior to the Catholic Restoration Protestants preferred to avoid becoming directly involved in Brazilian politics, believing that "politics are dirty and evangelicals should not get their hands dirty."[34] With the rise of Catholic political power and the renewal of the church–state alliance, Protestants knew they could no longer stand on the political sidelines. When President Vargas announced that following a nationwide election to decide delegates a constitutional convention would be held in 1933, Protestants seized the chance to defend the laicist state and enter the realm of electoral politics.

Protestants knew they needed to quickly organize themselves politically if they were going to be able to fight back against the advances of the Catholic Church. Given their proportionally small numbers, it did not make sense for them to create a confessional political party or lobbying group. They could, however, join forces with their historical allies, secular liberals and laicists who were similarly opposed to the Catholic Church's rising power in Brazil, and work together to elect laicist constitutional delegates. In May 1931 the Liga Pró-Estado Leigo (Pro-Laicist State League, LPEL) was born. The LPEL was an anticlerical and anti-Catholic pressure group whose mission was to take "vigorous action against the clericalist invasion of friars, nuns, and charity workers who . . . devour [Brazil's] material, moral, and spiritual riches, fanaticizing and exploiting its people, particularly those who are simple and well-intentioned."[35] Protestants were central to the organization of the LPEL, and pastors occupied leadership positions in national, state, and local chapters.[36] These leagues were especially strong in northeastern cities such as Recife, whose LPELs were founded by Protestant pastors, and their leaderships were made up nearly entirely of Protestants.[37] In Pernambuco the LPEL worked in concert with other liberal groups and political parties like the Liga Eleitoral do Pensamento Livre (Free-Thinking Electoral League), encouraging Protestants to register for the elections and to vote for candidates who actively opposed the Catholic Church's agenda. In Recife the rallying cry of the LPEL was soon on the pages of the major Protestant publications and on the lips of Protestant pastors: "To the ballot box, liberals! To the ballot box, Free Pernambucans!"[38]

Protestants' entry into electoral politics brought them into direct conflict with the Catholic Church's own electoral initiatives. Determined to regain the Catholic Church's rights and privileges in the new constitution, Restorationists created the Liga Eleitoral Católica (Catholic Electoral League, LEC). The league would rally support for candidates who had pledged to support the Catholic Decalogue, ten policy demands that would guide the church's political agenda for the Constitutional Convention and the subsequent congressional elections. If a Brazilian politician, regardless of party affiliation, pledged to support the four core demands of the decalogue— putting the name of God in the constitution, opposing divorce, supporting religious instruction in public schools, and providing religious chaplains for the military, hospitals, and prisons—then LEC would officially support the candidacy.[39] LEC was larger and better organized than the LPEL, having national, state, regional, and local chapters.[40] Each local LEC committee was thus affiliated with one or more lay religious associations whose members became the primary LEC activists, working to register voters, solicit signatories to the LEC cause, convince Catholics to vote for LEC-endorsed candidates, and promote all types of LEC propaganda.[41]

In the end the 1933 elections and 1934 constitution represented a smashing success for the Catholic Restoration, demonstrating Catholicism's renewed power in the political sphere and in the Vargas government. All of the major Catholic demands, including the most controversial, religious education in public schools, were incorporated into the constitution. The major Vargas-affiliated political alliance, the União Cívica Nacional, gave its full support to LEC's political agenda, and thus the 1935 elections for national and state legislatures were considered victories for the Catholic

lobby.[42] Catholics were proud of their accomplishments, and they held rallies, processions, and thanksgiving Masses in order to celebrate what they
considered to be the triumph of good over evil. In the Northeast special *Te
Deum* Masses were held in the major cathedrals across the region, and all
local priests in the interior were directed to lead their congregations in giving thanks to God for aiding the cause of LEC.[43] The mood among Catholics was so triumphant and the victory so overwhelming that Lima felt it was
necessary to warn his compatriots against becoming overconfident. The "illusion of easiness" and the "illusion of strength" that the elections had given
Catholics threatened to infect them with "inertia, disinterest, and the temptation to rest on their laurels," he warned in an article.[44] Although the article
was originally published in the Centro Dom Vital's journal, *A Ordem*, it was
reprinted throughout the nation, including in the Northeast.[45]

Protestants understood the extent to which they had been defeated in the
elections. According to Guaraci Silveira, the only Protestant member of the
Constitutional Convention, "there was never any hope of blocking the religious amendments" to the constitution since nearly all the political parties,
especially those that affiliated with Vargas, "had made a pact with Romanism."[46] Presbyterians in the Northeast lamented that politicians had "forgot-
ten that they are not legislating for Catholics, but rather for all Brazilians,
regardless of religious or philosophical creed."[47] Since the first victory of religious instruction in schools, Protestants had predicted that pro-Catholic
government policies would give moral and political support to Catholic su-
premacist tendencies and thus lead to an intensification of persecution of
Protestants, particularly in the interior. Protestants in Piauí complained that
the religious instruction decree had emboldened the Catholic clergy, making them more aggressive toward Protestants. "The priests here are freely
and unrestrainedly acting as if the Catholic Church were, as in the times of
the monarchy, the Church of the state," declared one observer. "Such are
the first fruits brought by this wretched decree."[48] And when Baptist preachers were assaulted by Catholics in Pesqueira, Pernambuco, Baptists knew
whom to blame: Francisco de Campos, the minister of education and public health and the person who had authorized the religious instruction decree. As one Baptist author wrote, "Dr. Francisco de Campos, Minister of

Education and Public Health, should look at this case [of anti-Protestant violence] and other fruits of his disastrous decree, which appears as if it was created in the womb of the Holy Inquisition."[49] Protestants were determined to do all they could to ensure that the freedom of religion, which had survived the Constitutional Convention intact, was enforced by state officials, but they understood that the political climate had definitively shifted against them and their laicist cause.

What the Protestants did accomplish in the elections of 1933 and 1934, however, was to make abundantly clear that they were opposed to all Catholic political initiatives and to signal that they were more than willing to join forces with secularists, liberals, and Masons—and even to lead those forces—in order to block Restorationist goals. To Catholics, such attitudes meant they could be more certain than ever that Protestants were dangerous enemies of the Brazilian nation. The women and men who participated in the LEC campaign truly believed they were completing an urgent and holy mission. As one northeastern archbishop said, they were "saving Brazil."[50] The militaristic language of the Restoration was salient during the 1933 campaign season, as the mission of ensuring Catholic representation at the Constitutional Convention became laden with messianic overtones. For weeks on end Catholic newspapers published large banners on their front pages telling Catholics that "being a voter and pledging allegiance to the Liga Eleitoral Católica is currently the most serious duty of Brazilian Catholics!" and asking, "Do you want your family to be protected from the assaults of the pro-divorce groups? . . . Join the Liga Eleitoral Católica."[51] These alarmist statements were staples of LEC manifestos, as LEC supporters frequently warned Catholics of the many evils that could befall Brazil if non-LEC candidates were elected. The church's opponents—liberals, laicists, Protestants, and their allies—would not only enact anti-Church and anti-family legislation but also pave the way for even greater evils: Communism and anticlericalism. Catholic writers excelled at painting doomsday scenarios, using either / or constructions that depicted a bleak future for Brazil if LEC did not succeed. "Either Catholicism wins at the polls and the country is put on the path of religious restoration," wrote Plínio Corrêa de Oliveira in São Paulo's leading Catholic newspaper, "or extreme socialism will take control of Brazil, making it a victim of the numerous Calles and Lenins that swarm behind the scenes in our political life, eager to 'Mexicanize' or 'Sovietize' the land of the Holy Cross."[52] José Pedro Galvão de Souza, another Restorationist leader, put it in the following terms: "Either we act like real Catholics instead of simple-minded prayer machines, or Brazil will go down a path of demagoguery and Revolution. It's either our white revolution, which is actually the 'opposite of a revolution,' or it will be a red, anti-Christian, Jewish, and satanic Revolution. Now is not the time for doubts, fears, criticism, or second-guessing, but rather of action—decisive, energetic, and intense action."[53]

Catholic publications regularly trumpeted this militant, nationalist, anti-Semitic message, declaring that LEC was the means by which Brazilians could reclaim their country's true Catholic spirit and heritage. In Lima's words, LEC was the hope for ensuring that "Brazil [would] continue to be Brazilian."[54] To be Brazilian was to be Catholic, and the task of protecting Brazil from foreign influences was vigorously undertaken by LEC.

As noted above, Catholics had long seen Protestants as one of the forces of evil that threatened the success of the Restoration. However, the 1933 and 1934 elections heightened Catholics' belief that Protestants were one of their most determined enemies, for they had joined hands with anti-Catholic groups and sought to put Brazil on the road to "extreme socialism." As a result, anti-Protestant rhetoric in Catholic circles became even more heightened after the elections, above all in the Northeast, where the LPEL was highly active and received public support and leadership from Protestant pastors. In João Pessoa, where Protestants and the LPEL had staged a large public protest and procession in order to express their displeasure with the "politics of the sacristy that only satisfy personal and selfish ambitions, in detriment to the good of the people," Catholics continuously warned their brethren of the dangers posed by Protestant members of the LPEL, painting them as being at once ridiculous fringe elements and sneaky conduits of both civil and religious disorder.[55] In Pernambuco Catholics had no doubt that Protestants were their main political enemy. It was the Protestants, argued Marian Congregations in Recife, who had gathered together "Spiritists, positivists, and all species of materialists" and caused them to "coalesce into a type of 'cartel' of the Devil that, through a great amount of publicity and noise, warned the city about the dangers of what they called 'a new religious battle.'"[56] After the elections Catholics remained on the lookout for new Protestant plots designed to destroy the Catholic agenda. Pernambucan Catholics were worried about the Cruzada Nacional da Educação (National Education Crusade, CNE), a literacy campaign they believed to be a Protestant front for anti–Catholic education attacks.[57] In this new Restorationist atmosphere in which political power was featured as one of the keys, if not *the* key, to Catholic survival, Protestants had shown themselves to be one of the most powerful organized groups to explicitly fight against their political success. More than ever Catholics were convinced that if the Restoration was to survive, Protestantism had to be defeated.

Marian Congregations and the Secretariado Nacional da Defesa da Fé

Given Restorationists' conviction that they had won the battle but not the war as well as their certainty that Protestants were continuing to work to destroy Catholicism and, by extension, the Brazilian nation itself, it is not surprising that the latter part of the 1930s saw an intensification in both the presence and organizational capacity of Catholic anti-Protestantism. In 1939 Dom Leme, with the support of Pope Pius XII, convoked the Concílio Plenário Brasileiro (Brazilian Plenary Council). A historic event, it marked the first time bishops of the Brazilian Catholic Church came together and established official, nationwide norms and policies for dioceses and parishes to follow. From the beginning Protestantism was a central consideration of the agenda. In his letter approving the council and naming Dom Leme its official legate, Pope Pius XII outlined the topics the bishops should address: the promotion of priestly vocations, the organization of Catholic Action, the administration of ecclesiastical funds, and, last but not least, "the suppression and extinguishing of the evils that come from the errors of Protestantism and the practices of Spiritism."[58] The bishops of the council took the pope's directive seriously, resulting in a conciliar vote that created a permanent nationwide organization whose sole mission would be to "efficiently combat

Protestantism and Spiritism."[59] The key word here was "efficiently." The Secretariado Nacional de Defesa da Fé (National Secretariat for the Defense of the Faith, SNDF), as it was to be called, was meant to be a modern solution to the age-old problem of religious competition. It would have its own publishing house and its own executive committee, and it would create a network of supporting organizations throughout Brazil that would implement its directives, forming the vanguard of anti-Protestant propaganda and activism.

To speed up the process, Padre Cesar Dainese, S.J., the founding president of the SNDF, used the existing network of Marian Congregations as a conduit for channeling the anti-Protestant campaign. Marian Congregations were a natural choice for Padre Dainese. By explicitly promoting devotion to the Virgin Mary and the (Real Presence of the) Eucharist, they reinforced those doctrines over which Protestants and Catholics most passionately disagreed. Moreover, in addition to serving as the Marian Congregation's national director, Padre Dainese was helping them to enhance their engagement with the political and social issues of the day. He believed that greater involvement in such matters would allow Marian Congregations to compete more adeptly with their socially and politically active Catholic Action counterparts, who were receiving the majority of the resources, attention, and support from Restorationist bishops and lay leaders.[60] Padre Dainese argued that Marian Congregations needed to adopt an "offensive apostolate" when it came to confronting Protestants and Spiritists, that is, an apostolate that learned from the tactics of the enemy and used those tactics against them.[61] While Catholic Action groups had been the vanguard forces in LEC, religious education campaigns, and family values initiatives, Padre Dainese hoped Marian Congregations would lead the way in anti-Protestant activism, thereby demonstrating their ability to protect and promote the Brazilian Catholic state. The national journal of the congregations, *Estrela do Mar*, as well as various local congregation-affiliated publications, became unofficial mouthpieces for the SNDF, reprinting nearly all of the articles found in the SNDF's official bulletin, *Pro Ecclesia*, as well as promoting the SNDF's activities and campaigns.[62]

On the ground local Marian Congregations were often viewed as the first lines of defense against the arrival or growth of Protestantism in parishes or dioceses. In São Paulo the local Marian Congregation held an annual book-burning ceremony on the Day of the Pope. Hundreds of books deemed to be heretical were burned in a public ceremony. When accused of being intolerant, José de Azeredo Santos, one of the leaders of the Santa Cecília Congregation, replied by embracing the congregation's intolerance. "Those that speak of tolerance," he argued, "always refer to something bad." In the eyes of Santos, to be intolerant was to stand up for one's principles and to refuse to condone evil ideologies and behaviors.[63] "We will continue, then, to defend our faith without fear of this intolerance, because it does not exclude charity for one's neighbor," Santos declared. "We will continue to make a flaming pyre of bad books, and in the fire of our zeal we will also destroy any uncertainty regarding the wisdom and holiness of the Church."[64] Marian Congregations were often the first to both reject as well as to insist that their Catholic brethren reject any and all collaboration with Protestant organizations like Christian Youth Associations that sought Catholic collaboration on charity and social improvement projects.[65]

In the Northeast Marian Congregations had long been at the forefront of campaigns against Protestantism, publicly clashing with Protestants since before the Constitutional Convention in 1934.[66] In Paraíba Marian Congregations were explicitly represented as anti-Protestant organizations, uniquely prepared for "the fight against heresy."[67] In an article published in the Paraíban Catholic newspaper, A Imprensa, the Catholic intellectual Armando Más Leite described the Congregations as both highlighting and correcting the errors of heretical sects: "Against Protestants, who scorned the maternal intervention of Our Lady, [Marian Congregations] make the cult of the Virgin Mary their principal foundation; against the disdain for the Eucharist promoted by these same people, Marian regulations insist on the frequent taking of Communion; against the negligence of good works that results from Protestant fideism, [Marian Congregations] reiterate the calls for Christians to be Apostles."[68]

Marian Congregations took pride in their anti-Protestant identity and frequently wrote to Estrela do Mar to update the wider Marian world on their activities against Protestantism. They wrote of their campaigns against the Cruzada Nacional da Educação (National Education Crusade), which they believed to be nothing more than an "organ of Protestant propaganda." They reported as well on their fights, sometimes physical encounters, against "blasphemies against Our Lady," in which they would organize large marches and rallies to take place in front of buildings or plazas where Protestant pastors were preaching or giving public lectures.[69] Such activism was common throughout the Northeast. In Bahia the Marian Congregation of Jaguarari excitedly informed their brethren that they had "killed the Protestant temple" in their town through their rallies, meetings, and prayers.[70]

In some parishes in the northeastern interior Marian Congregations were explicitly connected with some of the most extreme campaigns against Protestants. When Padre João Verberck was in the middle of a violent and controversial campaign against Protestants in the town of Paparí, in Rio Grande do Norte, he founded a new Marian Congregation in his parish that sought to create an army of anti-Protestant crusaders. In his speech at the founding ceremony João Carvalho, the congregation's first president, told his fellow congregants that "it would be a weakness of character, and even disrespectful to God, if in these times in which the soldiers of Satan invade our lands, masquerading as Protestants, we didn't respond with courage to the appeal that we have heard countless times from the true pastors of our souls."[71] Declaring that he and his fellow members of the Marian Congregations were ready to "enter into battle as true soldiers of the Catholic religion," Carvalho reiterated that they "would not allow the land of the Holy Cross, Christian Brazil, in whose sky is reflected the image of our sacrifice, to be invaded by the Protestantism that wants to subjugate the Brazilian Fatherland that was baptized by God at the dawn of our nationality."[72]

In addition to Marian Congregations, the SNDF had an informal association with another nationwide organization, Integralism. As noted above, Integralists were not always committed to anti-Protestant campaigns, but certain Integralists viewed Protestants as enemies of the nation, and they were the ones most likely to collaborate with Catholic Restorationist campaigns against Protestantism. And although the Integralist Party was disbanded in 1937 after the Estado Novo banned all political parties, many of its leaders remained important and respected members of the Catholic activist community. Eurípides Cardoso de Menezes, the editor of the Integralist magazine *Anauê!* until its closure in 1937, was one of these former Integralist leaders. Far from being shunned in Catholic circles, Menezes became the founding secretary of the SNDF, serving as the lay counterpart and self-described apostle of Padre Cesar Dainese.[73] Menezes was a convert to Catholicism, having previously been a Protestant pastor.[74] Like many converts, he had a zeal for proselytizing and a determination to warn his new coreligionists of the evils and dangers of his former faith. Menezes saw the SNDF as an opportunity to institutionalize his message and reengage the audience he lost when his magazine and his movement were suppressed in 1937. In 1939, when the SNDF was founded, Menezes became its resident propagandist, directing *Pro Ecclesia* and writing most of its early articles and pamphlets.[75] Taking advantage of his status as a former Protestant pastor, Menezes portrayed himself as an insider who could both uncover the hidden fallacies and evils of Protestantism and show Catholics how to reach out to his former Protestant colleagues in an attempt to convert them to the True Faith. His articles often took the form of letters to Protestant pastors that attacked their doctrines and defended the purity of the Catholic faith or of exposés about the disingenuous nature of Protestant congregations, particularly the "new sects," such as Pentecostalism, Seventh-day Adventists, and Christian Scientists.[76] Menezes's racism was frequently evident in his attacks on Protestants, and he considered comparisons of Protestantism to Afro-Brazilian religions to be the most damning evidence of the danger of religious pluralism. Combining his anti-Protestant convictions with his Integralist passion for promoting an authoritarian and corporatist Catholic state, Menezes proved to be an ideal ideologue for the SNDF.

A Modern Approach to Anti-Protestantism?: Agnelo Rossi and the Formation of an Anti-Protestant Clergy

The creation of the SNDF was part of a broader effort to modernize the Catholic Church's response to Protestant growth in the 1930s and 1940s. Ultimately, the Restorationist Church wanted anti-Protestantism to be less of an ad hoc effort led by individual Catholics and more of a churchwide campaign directed by bishops and priests. Much of the credit for this "officialization" of

Restorationist campaigns against Protestantism goes to a young priest named Agnelo Rossi, who was fresh from his seminary studies in Rome. Many Restorationist Catholic activists in the 1920s–40s attacked Protestantism with their pens, but few did so with the single-mindedness and organizational fervor of Padre Rossi, a towering figure in Brazilian Catholic history. Ordained a priest at the age of twenty-three in Campinas (SP), he rose to be the archbishop of São Paulo, was elevated to cardinal, and served in various high posts in the Vatican. Central to his early identity as a rising star in the Brazilian church was his role in incorporating anti-Protestantism into the modernizing project of Restorationist Catholicism and Catholic Action. As a young seminarian in the early 1930s he traveled to Rome to become a member of the first class of students at the Pontifício Colégio Pio Brasileiro, the elite Romanizing institute originally part of the Pontifício Colégio Pio Latino-Americano. He would remain in Rome to pursue graduate studies at the Pontifical Gregorian University, where he studied under Father Camillo Crivelli, a professor of Protestant history at the university who was known as "the Columbus of Protestant propaganda in Latin America."[77] Crivelli gained this title for having revealed to the Catholic world, through his book *Directorio Protestante de la America Latina*, the inroads Protestant missionaries were making in a region previously thought to be impervious to such influences.[78] Under the direction of Crivelli, Padre Rossi studied the history and contemporary state of Protestantism in Brazil, writing his thesis on the subject.[79] As the story goes, in 1936 or 1937 the Brazilian ambassador to the Vatican, Luiz Guimarães Filho, had an audience with Pope Pius XI in which the pontiff told him about Crivelli's work on Protestantism and recommended he meet with the professor in order to learn more about the subject. Crivelli, in turn, arranged a meeting with the young seminarian Rossi, whose knowledge about "the Protestant diffusion in Brazil" so impressed the ambassador that he insisted that the Brazilian state arrange for the publication of Padre Rossi's thesis.[80]

The result, *O Diretório Protestante no Brasil*, was published in 1939, two years after the newly ordained Padre Rossi had returned to Brazil. As its title suggests, the book was less of a polemical attack on Protestantism than a practical guide to understanding the history, organization, evangelization methods, similarities, and differences of the many Protestant denominations operating in Brazil. The tone of the book was mostly sober and scholarly, and it was full of statistics, dates, and historical overviews. Yet Padre Rossi's book was far from a neutral treatise on the Protestant presence in Brazil. By way of introduction, Dom Francisco de Campos Barreto, then bishop of Campinas, described Padre Rossi's book as "giving a patriotic cry of alarm" with respect to "the serious and dangerous Protestant infiltration" of Brazil.[81] He went on to write, "Since the Protestant spirit, no matter where it goes, always brings with it the virus of a foreign influence looking to upset the racial and religious harmony of our country, the work of Padre Agnelo Rossi arises as a true wake-up call for certain elements—even clerical elements—who don't want to see the corruption that the DOLLAR and the impertinence of the Protestant sectarians does amongst simple Catholics who know little of their own Religion."[82]

The purpose of the book was to arm Catholics with the practical knowledge necessary to combat and defeat their Protestant enemies. Brazil did not need more polemical tracts and defenses of Catholic doctrine, Padre Rossi thought. "In terms of polemical, doctrinal work, we already have an abundance of publications," he declared. "We [now] want to provide the necessary knowledge to facilitate the tactics of combat. Because you can't deal with an Anglican in the same way in which you would deal with a Seventh-day Adventist."[83] Padre Rossi sought to let Catholics know how dire the Protestant situation was in Brazil—so many different sects! so much growth!—while also affording them practical advice on how to understand the various Protestant denominations and neutralize them. An entire chapter of the book titled "Rules for Preventing or Resisting Protestant Propaganda" was dedicated to giving advice on how to combat Protestants via different strategies for the three categories of Protestants: "Protestants of good faith," that is, those who refrained from attacking the Catholic Church directly, represented by a small minority of Brazilian Protestants, such as Lutherans; "Protestants of bad faith," those who attacked Catholicism in their journals, speeches, and sermons, represented by most Brazilian Protestants, especially Presbyterians and Baptists; and "apostates and converted priests," the most dangerous of all Protestants since they had influence over their fellow Catholics.[84] Depending on the type of Protestant and the type of evangelization method, whether Bible selling, pamphleteering, church building, and so forth, Catholics could deploy a specialized refutation strategy that would be more effective than a generalized campaign. Padre Rossi was developing an approach to anti-Protestantism that combined scientific knowledge of Protestant institutions, rather than just their theology, with practical plans to confront Protestants in cities and towns across Brazil.

After being ordained a priest in Rome in 1937 Padre Rossi returned to Campinas and soon began to work to spread the word about his anti-Protestant agenda. When he first arrived in Campinas he served as the personal secretary to the diocese's bishop, Dom Francisco de Campos Barreto. The bishop turned out to be a strong supporter of Padre Rossi's efforts to alert Brazil to the dangers of Protestantism. Having himself published an anti-Protestant polemic, *Catolicismo e Protestantismo perante a Bíblia*, Dom Francisco was a bishop who "was always supportive and eager to teach the clergy and other bishops about the ambushes undertaken by the enemy against [the] holy [Catholic] religion," and he encouraged and nourished Padre Rossi's interest in developing anti-Protestant projects.[85] Before long Padre Rossi was undertaking a print campaign to raise awareness of Protestantism's alarming rise. He became the editor of Biblioteca Apologética, an Editora Vozes book series devoted to apologetic and anti-Protestant tracts.[86] He was also a regular contributor to São Paulo's primary Catholic newspaper, *O Legionário*, directed by the increasingly powerful Plínio Corrêa de Oliveira, the future founder of the conservative Tradition, Family, and Property movement, as well as to a new journal for the Brazilian clergy, *Revista Eclesiástica Brasileira*. In these publications Padre Rossi chronicled Protestant activity in almost startling detail: the associations they formed, the conferences they organized, the conflicts they experienced both between and within their congregations, and, most frequently, the many purported insolent attacks on Catholics they made in their newspapers, books, speeches, and sermons. He was especially interested in alerting Catholics to the new or exotic forms of Protestantism that were emerging in Brazil, such as Pentecostalism and Seventh-day Adventism. He declared the former to be "nothing more than a mixture of Protestantism and the lowest form of Spiritism" and the latter to be an effort to "dig a deep trench of disunion in the

Brazilian family" by undermining the sanctity of Sunday worship and thereby "establishing a most pernicious division in [Brazilian] society."[87] Padre Rossi delighted in reporting the criticisms other Protestant churches made of these new sects but made sure to let readers know that even the extreme churches were born of the same "rotten seed" of Protestantism. Padre Rossi's articles were reprinted in Catholic newspapers across Brazil, including the Northeast, where periodicals like *A Ordem,* based in Natal, frequently featured them on their front pages.

Padre Rossi did not limit his anti-Protestant activities to publishing books and articles. He also traveled throughout São Paulo state to give lectures on Protestantism, and he mounted public exhibitions meant to show Catholics how extensive and pernicious the Protestant threat in Brazil had become. One such exhibition, on Protestant media activity in Brazil, featured examples of Protestant books, pamphlets, newspapers, flyers, and other materials that demonstrated "the mark that the enemy is making in diverse areas throughout our territory."[88] Padre Rossi worked hard to incorporate anti-Protestantism into the program of Catholic Action, which he believed was one of the best and most modern vehicles through which to combat religious pluralism. As noted above, the SNDF was mainly concentrated in Marian Congregations, but Padre Rossi was determined to make Catholic Action an equally powerful center of anti-Protestant activity, arguing that Protestants themselves recognized the dangerous potential of an organized Catholic lay apostolate. If the church wanted to stay one step ahead of Protestant organizing efforts, he often wrote, then it needed to invest heavily in Catholic Action.[89] Padre Rossi was so successful at promoting anti-Protestantism in Catholic Action that the SNDF was eventually taken out of the purview of Marian Congregations and became a department within Catholic Action. It was given a new name, the Departamento Nacional de Defesa da Fé e da Moral, a new acronym, DNDFM, and a new director, Padre Rossi himself.[90]

Perhaps the most significant element of Padre Rossi's campaign was his effort to influence the training of future priests. In 1940 he became a professor at the prestigious Ipiranga Central Seminary in São Paulo, where he taught soon-to-be priests from all over Brazil about the dangers of the Protestant threat. Almost immediately after taking up his post Padre Rossi sponsored a study week, or student conference, in which many of the ideas found in his book were expanded on and adapted in order to aid the formation of Brazil's future priests. During the weeklong seminar students learned about the dangers and threats posed by the alarming growth of Protestantism in their country, and they were given specific tactics and instructions regarding how to combat and suppress Protestant infiltration in their future parishes.[91] Most important, the seminar was meant to make abundantly clear that priests were expected to take active roles in promoting anti-Protestant campaigns in their parishes and that no priest in good conscience could passively allow Protestantism to exist and grow in their local communities.

The influence of Padre Rossi's seminary training program extended far beyond São Paulo. The Ipiranga seminary was the most prestigious seminary in Brazil, and young men from all over Brazil went there to study. Américo Sérgio Maia, a member of one of the most influential families in Catolé do Rocha, a small town in the interior of Paraíba that would be the scene of some of the most intense anti-Protestant violence in the region, attended the Ipiranga seminary. Maia participated in Padre Rossi's anti-Protestant seminar, giving a presentation titled "Some accusations that Protestants make against the Brazilian Church (historically)."[92] Rossi worked hard to see that anti-Protestant awareness and training were incorporated into seminary curricula throughout the country. For this reason the proceedings and speeches from his anti-Protestant seminar were gathered and published in the form of a pamphlet called *The Protestant Question in Brazil*. The pamphlet was meant to be distributed widely so that other seminaries could organize their own "Protestant study weeks" based on Rossi's data, theories, and methods.

Overall, Padre Rossi sought to give the Restorationist stamp of approval to a policy that many bishops had already been implementing in their dioceses, particularly those in the Northeast: that the "Protestant question" and its solution were ultimately the responsibility of the parish priest. According to this mind-set, Protestantism's presence and growth in Brazil did not happen naturally but were *allowed* to happen by priests who lacked the training and motivation to actively fight them. Part of being a good Restorationist priest, then, was to be an anti-Protestant priest. Priests who were truly committed to restoring the church's influence in modern Brazil would thus be expected to mount campaigns against Protestants in their parishes, taking both defensive and offensive measures in order to at once block and roll back Protestant growth. "Where there exist clerics and priests who are pious, thoughtful, prudent, and zealous in their ministry," Rossi argued, "it becomes difficult for Protestant propaganda to be fomented or spread, and many times it even disappears from where it once existed."[93] If Protestantism was fomented or spread in a priest's parish, it stood to reason that that priest was not as "pious, thoughtful, prudent, and zealous" as he should have been. Priests were now the first line of defense against Protestant infiltration, and Catholic leaders were demanding that they take their positions seriously.

One element that stands out in Padre Rossi's treatises and seminary programs is an insistence on the modernity of his anti-Protestant program. Rossi saw himself as a scholar or expert on Protestant issues, and he continuously emphasized the scientific nature of his methodology. In the same way Restorationist leaders attempted to marshal fact-based studies to guide Catholic Action's efforts to address the social question, Padre Rossi wanted to use a data-driven approach to the Protestant question that would allow Catholics to both defend themselves against and counterattack their sectarian enemies. By doing so, Padre Rossi was subtly criticizing the sporadic anti-Protestant efforts of the nineteenth and early twentieth centuries led by Catholics who were, in Padre Rossi's eyes, ignorant of the differences between Protestant groups and prone to employing theatrics and hyperbole in the service of their anti-Protestant agenda. Rossi argued that the use of insults and "zingers" merely compelled Catholics to stoop to the same level as their supposedly brutish Protestant counterparts.[94]

Padre Rossi's calls for sobriety and moderation, however, were seemingly at odds with both his alarmist rhetoric regarding the Protestant threat and his permissive attitude toward religious confrontations and violence. He did not eschew his Restorationist colleagues' nationalist anti-Protestant rhetoric. To the contrary, he used numbers, charts, and historical data to back up the idea that Brazil was indeed being invaded by Protestant agents whose mission was to foment anti-Catholic hatred and destroy Brazil's traditional values. He rarely allowed his readers to forget that his Protestant manuals and courses had one goal and one goal only: to fight back against "these corrupted brothers, who have forged an alliance with one another with the sole goal of opposing the Catholic Church and its visible Leader."[95] And while Padre Rossi never explicitly advocated violence against or persecution of Protestants, he frequently indicated that he found such acts understandable and justifiable. When confronted with violent conduct, particularly in the Northeast, he did not deny its existence. "I recognize that there have been many acts of popular defense against evangelicals who were preaching right in the middle of the public square," he admitted.[96] However, as his description of the violence as "acts of popular defense" suggests, Padre Rossi did not believe Catholics were doing anything wrong. They were merely defending themselves and their parishes against unacceptable provocations and attacks from Protestants, who dared to evangelize in public squares in Catholic-majority towns. "Why do they come to insult us (our History, our ancestors, our beliefs) in our own house?" he wrote. "These so-called preachers should be more cautious—if they don't fan the flames, they won't have to complain about a fire."[97] And yet it often seemed as if Padre Rossi, through his suggestions and advice for seminarians and priests, was the one fanning the flames of conflict. For example, in his course for seminary students Padre Rossi advised future priests to "organize caravans of young catechists and other adventurers to travel throughout regions (villages, neighborhoods, *fazendas*) that are infested with Protestants."[98] While these caravans were not explicitly told to harass Protestants or commit acts of violence against them, their mere presence would have created a large amount of religious tension in the regions they visited. It is not difficult to imagine conflict resulting from such situations.

Ultimately, the anti-Protestant nationalism espoused by Padre Rossi and other Restorationist leaders resulted in the construction of a discursive, practical framework within which to justify local acts of persecution against Protestants in the Northeast. If Protestants were a threat to the security, stability, and strength of both the Catholic Church and the Brazilian nation, then individuals and communities could claim they had the right and even the responsibility to use any means necessary to combat their presence. And in the Northeast people did precisely that, as bishops, priests, and lay Catholics created a language of self-defense that transformed illegal and unconstitutional acts against Protestants into patriotic and holy sacrifices to protect the political integrity of the nation and the spiritual integrity of the local community.

Toward a Sertanejan Church

The New Face of Protestantism in the Interior of the Northeast

On June 25, 1939, the Integralist priest João Passos Cabral published an article that appeared on the front page of the Rio-based Catholic newspaper *A Cruz*. Titled "The Protestant Invasion," the article issued a strident warning to Catholics in the southeastern region of Brazil who might have overlooked the "disturbing news" coming from the faraway land of the Northeast—or, as Padre Cabral described it, "that land that has been calcified by the equatorial sun and tortured by the scourge of drought." "A true invasion of Protestant pastors, all being paid by the United States," was afflicting the Northeast, Padre Cabral lamented, and he warned his readers that the situation had already reached "epidemic proportions." The only solution was to support northeastern Catholics in their ongoing struggle against these "invaders and conquerors" who were trying to destroy the religious and political powers in the region. Cabral compared the northeasterners' fight against the Protestants to the uprising against the Calvinist Dutch occupation in the seventeenth century: both were expelling an unwanted foreign presence from their midst, both were protecting the integrity of church and state, and both were well within their rights to use whatever means possible to defend themselves against Protestant invaders. Praising the "legitimate and energetic reaction" of northeastern Catholics to contemporary Protestant attempts to found churches in their communities, the article ended with an ominous warning: if northeasterners did not continue or even intensify their anti-Protestant campaign, the very fabric of the Brazilian nation would be at risk.[1]

Padre Cabral's article reflected the growing awareness among national Catholic leaders of an issue that northeastern Catholics had been highlighting for nearly two decades: the Northeast was especially and, some argued, uniquely afflicted by the Protestant invasion of its territory. Throughout the 1930s and 1940s there was a distinct feeling among Catholics that the Northeast—and in particular the interior of the Northeast—was in danger of being overtaken by a flood of Protestant missionaries and converts and that extreme measures needed to be taken in order to prevent the triumph of the enemy's nefarious antinational agenda.

And yet the Protestant population in the Northeast was growing no faster than that in the rest of the nation—in fact, it was growing more slowly than anywhere else in Brazil. As Francisco Cartaxo Rolim has shown, the growth of Protestantism in the Northeast consistently lagged behind that in other regions. While the Northeast was home to 35 percent of the Brazilian population in 1940, it was home to only 9.8 percent of the nation's Protestants. That same year Protestants accounted for a mere 0.73 percent of the northeastern population, the lowest percentage of all of Brazilian regions, even the northern Amazon, and less than half the national average of 2.61 percent.[2] Northeastern Catholics were far from being besieged by a rapid rise in Protestant numbers in their states. In fact, they had been exceptionally successful at preventing Protestants from gaining a notable foothold in the Northeast, a feat no other region could claim.

However, northeastern Catholics were not entirely mistaken in feeling that something was different in Protestants' evangelization efforts in the twenties and thirties, something that threatened the traditional Catholic religion of the populace. For while the absolute number of Protestant conversions had not radically grown in comparison to past decades, where and how those conversions were taking place had indeed changed. Contributing to the transformation of the religious culture in the Northeast were a shift in control from foreign to Brazilian evangelical leaders; an intensification of evangelization efforts in the rural interior; the rise of Pentecostalism; and the demographic and social upheavals caused by drought and migration. Ultimately, Protestantism in the Northeast was changing from a religion directed by foreign missionaries working in the large coastal cities to a Brazilian-led movement that created permanent church communities throughout the region, including the drought-ridden interior region known as the *sertão*. As a result, Protestants fundamentally altered the way they interacted with the Catholic community, which reacted to the changes with fear, hostility, and an intensification of anti-Protestant campaigns.

From Foreign to Brazilian Leaders

In 1932 Rev. Langdon Henderlite, a U.S. missionary for the Presbyterian Church in the United States (PCUS), wrote a report on his work in the far interior of the Pernambucan sertão.[3] He was exceptionally upbeat, predicting great success for the future of evangelization efforts in an area that had previously appeared to be impervious to Protestant penetration.[4] "Never was there a greater opportunity for our work," he wrote. "Everywhere doors hitherto closed are wide open."[5] Reverend Henderlite attributed the high scale of success to "our method of using native evangelists under our guidance," arguing that "these men are doing better work than missionaries could possibly do, for they are natives of the interior and well acquainted and fitted [with the region]."[6]

By the 1930s the situation Reverend Henderlite described had become the order of the day in the Northeast. In place of the U.S. missionaries who had heretofore traveled throughout the interior visiting far-flung Protestant congregations and opening up new mission fields, Brazilian Protestants, some ordained and some lay, would now be the chief agents of evangelization. Therefore, while the number of U.S. Baptist missionaries working in the Northeast had decreased between 1920 and 1930, the number of Brazilian Baptist pastors had more than tripled.[7] In the small Presbytery of Pernambuco the number of Brazilian Presbyterian pastors rose from four to twelve in just two years, from 1931 to 1933.[8] The Pentecostals of the Assembléia de Deus went through an even more dramatic transition when, in 1930, they held a Convention in Natal and decreed that all local pastors must be Brazilian.[9] Brazilian Protestants were spread throughout the region and most, especially those in historical Protestant denominations, were responsible not only for attending to the established churches that employed them but also for evangelizing the surrounding mission field. They were tasked with founding new congregations and supporting fledgling groups of new converts, which would in turn be led by new local Brazilian leaders. These years saw the appearance of pastors like Rev. Joel Rocha, who became the chief Presbyterian evangelist for the interior of Paraíba, and the Baptists José Alves Feitosa and José Jacintho, who "opened up" the Arcoverde[10] region in the far interior of Pernambuco.[11] "Some of these ministers have from ten to thirty preaching points each," the PCUS missionary in Garanhuns, Pernambuco, Rev. George W. Taylor, explained, adding, in what amounted to an extreme understatement, that "the Native Church is doing her part."[12] Even when the U.S. missionaries undertook work in the interior they made sure they were accompanied by a Brazilian evangelist who did most of the preaching. This was not because of a language barrier—U.S. missionaries had been preaching in Portuguese since they arrived in Brazil in the nineteenth century, and they normally delighted in demonstrating their language abilities—but because they had come to believe that "the native has access to his own people that no missionary has. . . . [T]he people are his own blood, and he knows, and understands, their customs, habits, and racial idiosyncrasies."[13] By the 1930s this opinion was widespread among the missionaries. As Rev. Harold Cook reported, "The weekly market in Brazil offers a fine opportunity for open air preaching, but the writer is of the strong opinion that it should be done by Brazilians."[14]

Although U.S. missionaries like Reverend Henderlite and Reverend Cook frequently depicted this "new strategy" as an idea conceived and supported by the missionaries themselves, in reality it was the activism of Brazilian Protestants combined with the financial difficulties related to the Great Depression that forced U.S. missionary leaders to cede more administrative and evangelistic control to the so-called natives. The paternalism of the foreign missionary project meant that most missionaries supported the idea of Brazilian helpers but not of Brazilian leaders, as Brazilians were deemed to be too immature and "swollen in their conceit" to become successful administrators of their own work.[15] The worldwide financial crisis that began in 1929 severely undercut missionaries' ability to block the growth of Brazilian leadership. As Laura Premack has noted, in the case of the Baptist Church the Great Depression curtailed the U.S. Foreign Mission Board's ability to train, send, and support U.S. missionaries in Brazil.[16] The PCUS missionaries similarly saw their work become more difficult when, in 1930, they witnessed "the worst cut ever known in our Foreign Mission history."[17] The cuts in missionary funding were acutely felt in the Northeast, where missionary numbers had already been falling due to new recruits' lack of interest in the region.[18] Among the Southern Baptists in the Brazilian Northeast the number of U.S. missionaries had fallen from thirty-nine to twenty-eight between 1923 and 1933, and no new missionaries had been appointed in over ten years. The Depression-era funding crisis meant that even more missionaries would be recalled, or sent back, to the United States and cut off from the foreign board's funding, thereby exacerbating an already difficult situation.[19] Reverend Taylor lamented that "our Mission, with only thirteen members, has a field the size of our Southland east of the Mississippi, with only one full-time evangelist. Are we going to fall down on our part?"[20] Baptist missionaries declared that the economic downturn was "making it almost impossible for us to carry on for lack of means," and they angrily wondered why Catholics seemed to be able to weather the financial storm. "The priests go to the rich man and assess him, others they dominate through fear," declared the Baptist missionary Erik Nelson. "In fact they use lotteries or any kind of means to get money from both men and governments."[21] As they attempted to adjust to their new financial circumstances, U.S. missionaries wondered how the Protestant cause in Brazil would be able to survive.

But the fact that these missionaries believed the Protestant cause in the Northeast was doomed to failure due to the weakening of U.S. missionary strength demonstrated how much they underestimated and underappreciated the work of their Brazilian counterparts. By the late 1920s there had been a sharp increase in the numbers of Brazilians who became ordained Protestant pastors, thanks in part to the official foundation of the first Protestant seminaries in the Northeast in the late 1910s and early 1920s.[22] With the rise in the number of Brazilian Protestant leaders came the rise in demands for self-determination. Brazilian Congregationalists had a long history of self-governance because they had invited foreign missionaries to be helpers in their churches, not founders or directors.[23] But Brazilian Presbyterians and Baptists had more difficult routes to independence. An early twentieth-century attempt of Brazilian Presbyterians to gain autonomy had been roundly rejected by the U.S. Presbyterians and had been partly to blame for a schism that resulted in the founding of the Independent Presbyterian Church (IPI).[24] The Northeast remained mostly under the jurisdiction of the original Presbyterian church, the Brazilian Presbyterian Church (IPB), giving PCUS missionaries control over much of the region's affairs. But by 1916, the year of the Panama Congress, calls for the nationalization of the IPB had grown stronger, and U.S. missionaries were themselves eager to be rid of some of the financial and personnel responsibilities tied to local Presbyterian churches. The result was the Brazil Plan of 1917, by which Brazilian Presbyteries would be granted full autonomy and U.S. missionaries would control only their own projects and personnel. No pastor could belong to both the Presbytery and the mission at the same time, and all self-sustaining local churches would come under the jurisdiction of the regional Presbytery.[25] The agreement gave Brazilians more control over their church structure and evangelization plan. By the 1920s and 1930s PCUS missionaries in the Northeast would participate in Presbyterian evangelization projects only if they were formally invited to do so by Brazilian leaders.[26]

However, it was the Baptists' campaign for autonomy that truly transformed the face of Protestantism in the Northeast. The Radical incident, as the campaign would be called, was acrimonious, emotional, and protracted, and it would have lasting effects on the region. Unlike other autonomy movements founded and led by Protestants from the urban centers of the Southeast, the Baptist campaign was centered in and led from the Northeast. It began in the late 1910s and early 1920s when more and more Brazilian Baptists came to reject the notion of missionary supremacy that had reigned until that time, taking offense at the ways in which missionaries demeaned Brazilians' capabilities in order to justify U.S. leadership. Northeastern Brazilians especially resented "the misrepresenting and infamous campaign made in the States about [northeastern Brazilians'] civilization and character and spirituality," a campaign in which "[Brazilians] are presented in front of the American public as a tribe of the African Congo" in an effort "to show in the states [Brazilians'] incapacity for the [evangeliza-tion] work so to make necessary the perpetuity of the missionary leadership in absolute."[27]

The issue came to a head in 1922 when a group of northeastern Brazilian Baptists staged nothing less than a separatist revolt against U.S. missionar-ies.[28] At the heart of the conflict were two related issues: control over Church finances and control over evangelization work. Brazilian Baptist leaders be-lieved that U.S. missionaries' insistence on centrally administering all funds was not only disrespectful to Brazilian Baptists, as it indicated a lack of trust in their leadership abilities, but also harmful to the evangelization cause, particularly in the rural interior of the sertão. They argued that U.S. mis-sionaries were seriously neglecting evangelization work in the interior because they were putting all of their resources into the more lucrative urban-based educational institutions. In their letter to the Foreign Mission Board northeastern Brazilian leaders lamented that "all the local Missionar-ies are engaged in educational work without a single exception, with serious disadvantage to the evangelization interprise [sic]," but "in spite of this fact they insist in keeping the direction of a work that they cannot do."[29] Brazil-ian pastors, they argued, "have the men but not the means, and tremendous opportunities are being lost, forever grieving up our hearts and souls."[30] To rectify the situation, they proposed splitting funds between the U.S. mis-sionaries and Brazilian Baptists, giving the former control of the budget for educational institutions and the latter control over funds for the evangeliza-tion project.

U.S. missionaries rejected the new funding proposal in its entirety, and they went on to accuse northeastern Brazilian leaders of being greedy and un-grateful.[31] But they ultimately underestimated the degree of support the Radi-cals held among their fellow Brazilian Baptists, who quickly rallied around the nationalist cause. The missionaries' refusal to consider the Brazilian lead-ership's demands resulted in an effective schism that was made official in 1923, when the two groups created separate conventions, churches, and seminar-ies.[32] While the schism may have seemed like only a partial victory for those promoting Brazilian church leadership, its end result was the ascendance of Brazilian Baptists in *both* the antimissionary and promissionary conventions.

As had been the case in the Presbyterian schism of the early twentieth century, the Baptist separation created a climate of competition in which for over a decade, from 1923 to 1936, U.S. missionaries needed to compete with their Radical Brazilian counterparts for the allegiance of local Baptist churches in the Northeast.[33] But in order to be successful they needed to rid themselves of the reputation of being a "missionary dictatorship" and prove their respect for Brazilian Baptist leaders. They did so by making key concessions to Brazilian demands, not only promoting more Brazilian pastors but also providing more financial support for the Brazilian Baptists who were undertaking the bulk of the evangelization work.[34] Missionaries were aware of the fragile nature of the relationship with their Brazilian supporters and sought to avoid confrontation. When the Reverend Arnold E. Hayes, a missionary in Pernambuco, heard that the Foreign Mission Board's Depression-era financial crisis had caused it to call for a 10 percent cut in the budget for "native workers," he recommended that the money come from the missionary budget because it would "amount for the same thing in the end."[35] Hayes wrote that the "socalled [sic] 'Radical' movement of 1922 and 23" had taught him to tread carefully in financial matters.[36]

By the late 1920s and early 1930s, with fewer U.S. missionaries coming to Brazil and more Brazilians undertaking evangelizing and pastoral roles, the face of Protestant evangelization in the Northeast was increasingly Brazilian. This transition presented new challenges to Protestants faced with Catholic opposition to their presence. The decrease in foreign missionaries complicated but did not deter the Catholic nationalist narrative that viewed Protestantism as a U.S.-led imperialist project meant to undermine Brazilian unity and strength. Catholics continued to denounce Protestantism for being a U.S. campaign against Brazilian independence, but the chief perpetrators of this evil were no longer the foreign missionaries but the Brazilian Protestants themselves. In Catholic denunciations Brazilian Protestants went from being pitiful, duped victims to greedy, treacherous "wolves in sheep's clothing" who "with bad faith and perverse intentions take advantage of [Catholics'] charity and spread throughout the diocese."[37] Catholic leaders portrayed Protestant evangelists as mercenaries who were willing to trade their national loyalty for U.S. dollars. The bishop of Pesqueira called them "pseudo-pastors who make a living from the ill-fated task of throwing the Catholic conscience into doubt," all at the behest of the United States, "which, as everyone knows, has a great interest in this cursed campaign."[38] As Catholics began to see their Brazilian neighbors, rather than U.S. missionaries, as the chief source of the Protestant plague, the conflict became at once more widespread, more localized, and, therefore, more worrisome.

Yet it was not just the nationality of the new pastoral workers that had changed. The class background of Brazilian evangelists had also shifted. As Gledson Ribeiro de Oliveira has shown, Brazilian Protestant ministers in Ceará had initially come from the "middle sectors of society," and their parents were commonly "midscale landowners who raised cattle and goats, liberal professionals, or public servants."[39] They were not from the most prominent families in the Northeast, but neither were they from poor or working-class backgrounds. Oliveira's assessment, however, is based on the era that predates the changes discussed here. In the 1930s, as the number of Brazilian evangelical workers multiplied, their backgrounds diversified. While many of the leading pastors in the Northeast continued to come from relatively prosperous families, more and more Protestant leaders were of working-class backgrounds. Rev. José Martins Ferreira, a Presbyterian minister who worked as an evangelist in Paraíba in the 1930s, was said to have been illiterate when he converted to the Presbyterian faith, famously learning how to read only after his wife showed him a copy of the New Testament.[40] The Baptist evangelist in Sousa was an auto mechanic who was described by a U.S. missionary as having been "a terrible drunkard and rouffian [sic], being half Indian."[41] His dissolute days predated his conversion to Protestantism, after which time he became "a devoted student of the scriptures and an ardent preacher of the gospels."[42] In Cajazeiras the Baptist congregation was led by a shoemaker who was described by a different U.S. missionary as being "an uncouth man of little culture."[43] Another recently ordained pastor, Rev. Marcionilo Carvalho, was said to be "poorly educated as to schooling, [but] a veritable graduate in personal work and soul-winning."[44] And while being a pastor certainly conferred on these humble men a higher social status within their communities, it did not necessarily solve their financial problems. Unlike their middle-class counterparts, who often had day jobs or, in many cases, side jobs that allowed them to live comfortably when their churches were not able to pay them high salaries, pastors of lesser means could easily fall into destitution, even while holding their pastoral post. In the 1930s it was not unusual to hear stories like that of the pastor of Sapé, who was not even able to afford the costs of a funeral following the death of his young son.[45]

Information on the racial identity of these pastoral workers is scarce, but some evidence suggests that the new generation of Brazilian Protestant leaders was more racially diverse than their predecessors. There had never been official policies that barred racially mixed Brazilians from pursuing leadership positions, but racism, combined with the desire for middle-class pastors, had ensured that most Brazilian leaders looked like the Gueiros family, who boasted of three generations of Presbyterian pastors and were famous among U.S. missionaries for being beautiful, which at the time meant white. But as the demand for Brazilian pastors expanded, so too did opportunities for racially mixed Brazilians. Missionaries frequently noted that new pastors were of indigenous or African descent.[46] The leading Brazilian pastors of the 1930s, such as Revs. Manoel Ferreira, Joel Rocha, and José Jacinto da Silva, represented a distinct departure from the elite, white cadre of Brazilian Protestant leaders that had dominated in previous decades, as the face of northeastern Protestantism began to closely resemble the faces of northeasterners themselves.

The diversification of Protestant leaders had many advantages: it increased the geographic reach of Protestantism in the Northeast by allowing more northeastern Brazilians to become evangelists, pastors, and lay workers; it brought new perspectives and ideas to the evangelization effort; and it made it easier for evangelists to connect to the marginalized, racially mixed populations that formed the majority of the members of their congregations. Yet the rise in working-class and mixed-race Protestant leaders also increased the amount and intensity of persecution that these men as well as their congregations would face. Protestants' political connections and economic power were often the only factors that could prevent or punish religious persecution. With less social and economic capital came less local political influence, making Protestant congregations more vulnerable to Catholic attacks.

Returning to an Abandoned Field: The Intensification of Evangelization in the Rural Interior of the Northeast

Perhaps the most notable outcome of the rise of Brazilian Protestant leadership in the Northeast was its impact on the geographical expansion of evangelization efforts. Previously concentrated on converting the inhabitants of the large coastal cities and the interior urban hubs of the Northeast, Protestants now began to give their attention to the smaller towns of the rural interior. Protestantism was not completely unknown in these places. The famous missionaries of the nineteenth century, including Solomon Ginsburg, George Butler, and Robert Reid Kalley, had traveled throughout the interior of the Northeast, distributing Bibles, preaching, and, in the case of Butler, a physician, healing the sick. As missionary efforts in the Northeast became more institutionalized, evangelization work in these rural areas decreased dramatically. U.S. missionaries poured nearly all of their resources into urban educational institutions that served middle- and upper-class Brazilians of the coastal cities. As the Presbyterian missionary James Bear recalled, the early twentieth century witnessed "the withdrawal of the missionaries from the work of direct evangelism in a wide field and their concentration in the state of Pernambuco, where they were largely engaged in institutional work."[47] In 1903 there had been thirteen U.S. Presbyterian missionaries scattered among nearly all of the northeastern states, from Alagoas to Amazonas, all of whom were doing evangelization work. By 1913 there were eleven missionaries, all stationed in Pernambuco and none doing evangelization work.[48] The Baptist Church had undergone a similar contraction: when pioneers like Reverend Ginsburg and Rev. Zachary Taylor left the field or retired to do educational work in the early twentieth century, no one replaced them. By 1923 none of the U.S. Baptist missionaries were conducting full-time evangelization work.[49]

The shift in power from U.S. missionaries to Brazilian pastors during the 1920s and 1930s resulted in a change of focus from urban schools to rural congregations. As was evident in the case of the Baptist Radical revolt of the 1920s, Brazilians believed the U.S. missionaries' singular absorption with educational institutions unjustly ignored the needs and opportunities presented by rural communities, and they explicitly connected their desire for leadership with their desire to concentrate on the evangelization of the sertão.[50] Once Brazilians attained church leadership they almost immediately turned their attention to the rural interior. In the late 1920s churches in the interior began to expand rapidly, far more quickly than those in the cities. Between 1927 and 1930 Presbyterian churches in the northeastern interior grew at twice the rate of churches in urban areas.[51] Northeastern Protestants firmly believed that their religion would not thrive unless they evangelized the unconquered territory of the rural interior.

Catholics noted the shift immediately and expressed growing alarm at the idea that "spiritual anarchy" was "winning over new territory."[52] The growth of Protestantism in the rural interior particularly offended Catholics' sensibilities because they viewed the sertão as the stronghold of traditional Catholicism. "Protestants are no longer content to remain only in the cities," lamented a Catholic observer in Paraíba. "Now they want to rob the sweet peace of the Catholic families among the rural populations. They don't know how to respect the religious happiness of those who are born, live, and die with the name of Jesus on their lips and His love in their hearts."[53] Catholic Restorationists in Rio, such as the Integralist priest Padre Olympio de Mello, similarly decried the arrival of Protestants in the northeastern sertão. Padre Olympio considered the mere act of Protestant evangelization in this region to be a heinous attack on Brazilian Catholicism's heartland and thus a threat to Catholic nationalism. Defending anti-Protestant violence in the small Pernambucan town of Floresta, Padre Olympio wrote that "Floresta is a sertanejan city in the state of Pernambuco made up of profoundly Catholic families. In this land there has never existed any religion other than Catholicism." To promote Protestantism here, Padre Olympio said, was to "provoke a division of spirits" in the nation itself.[54] Ultimately, Restorationists believed that spreading Protestantism in the sertão contaminated the wholesome core of Brazilian Catholicism. While residents of large urban cities were already under attack from secularists, communists, and other dangerous forces, rural northeastern families were thought to be pure and untouched, the last bastion of ardent, if at times unorthodox, Catholicism. In the opinion of Catholic Restorationists, Protestants' decision to target these naive communities in their attempt to "invade the various cities in the interior" needed to be rebuffed with special ferocity.[55]

Despite Catholic protests Brazilian Protestant leaders continued to promote sertanejan evangelization. After all, many of the newly minted Brazilian pastors were natives of the small towns that dotted the far northeastern interior. They therefore took a special interest in ensuring that their hometowns and those places that resembled their hometowns received the same access to the salvific message of Protestantism as urban nordestinos. Perhaps the most famous sertanejan evangelist was Rev. José Alves Feitosa, who was from the interior town of Congo, on the border between Paraíba and Pernambuco. In 1926 he set off into the far interior of Pernambuco and Paraíba, the area where he was born and raised, in order to evangelize the communities and found new congregations.[56] Reverend Feitosa was not an isolated case. As more rural sons of the interior became pastors, more returned to the interior to guide new or expanded Protestant congregations. Rev. Abel Siqueira became an evangelist in Rio Grande do Norte, his native state, because "he felt the greater need of this field."[57] Rev. Aureliano Gonçalves, born in a small town on the border between Paraíba and Pernambuco, would return to evangelize both states in the late 1920s and 1930s.[58] And while not all pastors returned to their places of birth when evangelizing, nearly all showed an intense commitment to church work in the interior. Rev. Joel Rocha, from São Bento, PE, Rev. Manuel Ferreira dos Santos, from Pesqueira, PE, Rev. Helon Dinoá Araújo, from Baturité, CE, and Rev. João Clímaco Ximenes, from Escada, PE, did not return to their home regions of Pernambuco and Ceará. Instead, they went to one of the neediest fields in the Northeast: the Paraíban sertão, where persecution of Protestants was high and churches were struggling.[59] As natives of the interior, they understood both the challenges and opportunities that such a field represented. Rather than viewing the sertão as an exotic, impenetrable place, they saw it as a familiar region full of untapped potential.

Brazilians were not the only Protestants increasing their evangelization efforts in the sertão. Perhaps ironically, given their earlier neglect of the field, U.S. missionaries began to pay serious attention to the interior region in the late twenties and early thirties. That their renewed interest in the interior began roughly around the time as that of their Brazilian counterparts was not a coincidence. The Baptist schism of 1924 created a climate of rivalry in which the two conventions, one affiliated with the Radicals, the other with the missionaries, competed to capture the greatest number of congregations possible. This meant that when the Brazilian Baptists went into the interior, U.S. missionaries followed. Sometimes the two conventions established rival churches in the same town, each declaring the other a pernicious interloper. The competition could be fierce. In Macambira the U.S. missionary-affiliated church claimed that the Radicals were gaining adherents by spreading the rumor that the U.S. missionaries would "accept gamblers and smokers [into their congregation], organize dances and all sorts of frivolities, etc."[60] To accuse a Baptist church of moral laxity was a serious charge, and it could torpedo the accused congregation's chances of progress. But while each group was convinced the other was destroying the future of the Baptist cause in the Northeast, the reality was quite the opposite. Competition compelled action, and the northeastern interior brimmed with an unprecedented evangelizing fervor. The conflict ultimately produced what Baptists would later call the "sweet result of a bitter problem," as the decade saw a sharp increase in both the number of churches and the geographical area in which those churches operated.[61] Between 1923 and 1938 the number of Baptist churches in Pernambuco alone increased by fifty-three, from thirty-two to eighty-five.[62] Some of these were new churches, and some were offshoots of already established congregations. In both cases they contributed to the feeling that the interior was experiencing explosive Protestant growth: the more churches that appeared in small towns, the more visible the Protestant presence in the interior.

Moreover, U.S. Presbyterian missionaries were also returning to the field they had abandoned decades earlier. In 1931 Reverend Henderlite began evangelization work in the far interior of the sertão, thereby initiating what U.S. Presbyterian missionaries would later call a "new start in evangelism."[63] The context of their return was quite different from that of the Baptists: rather than compete with the Brazilian Presbytery, the PCUS missionaries were invited by their Brazilian counterparts to evangelize the border region that stretched across the interior limits of Pernambuco, Paraíba, and Rio Grande do Norte. Lacking the resources to pay a full-time evangelist to take charge of the isolated area and conscious of the "urgent necessity of a worker in the Paraíban sertão," the Pernambucan Presbytery requested that Reverend Henderlite take over the field.[64] Later, in 1936, the PCUS missionaries would expand their presence in the Northeast with the arrival of Rev. Raynard Arehart in Ceará. Like Reverend Henderlite, Reverend Arehart received an invitation from the Brazilian Presbyterians to evangelize a field that had long proved difficult to penetrate.[65] And while two new missionaries might not seem to represent a large growth in missionary activity, the outsized resources they brought to their fields ensured that their impact went beyond their individual presence. They were able to pay the salaries of groups of young, up-and-coming Brazilian pastors who would otherwise not have been able to preach in areas devoid of self-sustaining churches. Pastors who would become important evangelists of the interior, such as Rev. José Martins Ferreira, got their start on the payroll of Reverends Henderlite and Arehart.[66]

Another factor contributing to the expanding presence of Protestantism in the northeastern interior was the rise of foreign evangelists associated with interdenominational or independent missionary societies. During the 1920s and 1930s relatively young missionary associations such as the Evangelical Union of South America (EUSA), the Gospel Furtherance Band (GFB), and the Mid-Missions alliance began working in the Brazilian Northeast. While each society sent only a small number of missionaries to Brazil, these evangelists worked almost exclusively in rural interior regions and had an outsized impact on the area. For example, Rev. Harry George Briault, a British EUSA missionary, was perhaps the most influential foreign missionary in the Paraíban sertão, founding and leading numerous Congregationalist churches in the far interior during the late twenties and thirties, many of which suffered attacks by Catholics.[67] Rev. Charles F. Mathews, a U.S. missionary affiliated with the Gospel Furtherance Band, was notorious among Catholics for his confrontations with their local leaders in Paraíba and Rio Grande do Norte during the thirties and forties.[68] He played a central role in the organization of a public debate between Protestants and Catholics in Campina Grande, Paraíba, in 1935, and his commitment to founding churches in rural towns in Rio Grande do Norte caused the Catholic newspaper of the state, A Ordem, to publish banner headlines warning the faithful that "the Protestant Mateus is going about distributing heretical bulletins throughout the interior."[69] The Riograndense Catholic press became quite fixated on the missionary, to the point of publishing imaginary conversations with Reverend Mathews in which the pastor lamented the fact that priests and parishioners of certain towns would not allow him to preach.[70] These so-called brave towns were meant to serve as examples for other areas threatened by the GFB missionary. "We must expel, just like [these towns have done], all of the Protestants until the last one is gone," the author of the imaginary conversation wrote. "We are a Catholic people, and we cannot be deceived by the cheap words of these foreign preachers."[71]

As their more traditional missionary counterparts frequently pointed out, not all independent missionaries were successful in founding long-lasting Protestant communities. Baptists frequently complained about the "Unionist 'faith missions' from several lands [that] are scattering over the interior in a sort of unstable missionary wanderlust . . . such men baptize (?) with eager haste, for that clinches their spoil; but the results often show they 'baptized' raw sinners . . . [who don't know that] there is more to baptism than the mere immersion of a stranger at a crossroads."[72] Needless to say, the opinions of traditional missionaries were biased. The interdenominational "faith missions" represented a threat to denominational hegemony in the region, largely in the areas of the interior that the historical Protestant Churches had neglected. Their critique of the faith missions' "wanderlust" did contain a grain of truth: these missionaries were dedicated to a near-constant schedule of travel and preaching, and they were often the first to open up an interior region previously untouched by Protestant expansion. Padre Rossi was astounded by the sheer volume of work done by these missionary societies. Referring to the EUSA, Rossi warned Catholics that "they have a frighteningly high level of activity."[73] Quoting a Protestant source, he went on to declare, "If you consider the miles covered by [EUSA missionaries] and others in 1928, they covered 15,000 miles by car or by horse. They visited Pernambuco, Alagoas, Rio Grande do Norte, Paraíba, Rio Grande do Sul, Santa Catarina, Ceará, Piauí, Maranhão, and Bahia, selling 1,274 Bibles, 21,173 partial Bibles, 2,738 New Testaments, 778 Traveler's Guide, and they distributed 25,000 pamphlets."[74]

Many churches, such as those founded by Reverend Briault, stood the test of time. Many others did not. And while their high rate of movement may not have been conducive to the founding of stable, long-lasting churches, these new missionaries and their constant travels heightened the sense among Catholics that Protestants were suddenly everywhere. When one takes into account the fact that the northeastern interior saw new activities of Brazilian pastors, U.S. missionaries, *and* interdenominational missionaries in the 1920s and 1930s, Catholics' worries about Protestant growth in the northeastern interior are understandable.

The Rise of the Assembly of God in the Northeast and the Pentecostalization of Catholic Anti-Protestantism

Paul Freston and others have called the Baptist, Presbyterian, and Congregationalist congregations that arrived in Brazil during the latter half of the nineteenth century the "traditional historical" Protestant congregations.[75] But another branch of Protestantism experienced intense growth in the Northeast during the 1920s, 1930s, and 1940s: the Assembléia de Deus (Assembly of God, AD), the Pentecostal church that arrived in Brazil a decade earlier, in 1911. Unlike historical denominations, the AD did not begin its evangelization campaign in the Brazilian Southeast. Rather, it began in the Amazonian state of Pará when two Swedish evangelists, Daniel Berg and Gunnar Vingren, broke away from their Baptist congregation and founded the Apostolic Faith Mission, a Pentecostal church later renamed the Assembléia de Deus.[76] The AD was not a religion of the rich and powerful but of the poor and marginalized. Berg and Vingren were themselves marginalized immigrants who had experienced prejudice and hardship in both Sweden and the United States.[77] Many of the AD's first converts in the Amazon were poor northeastern migrants who had traveled to Pará to work in the rubber industry. But by the 1910s the rubber boom had become a bust, and the northeastern migrants who were converting to Pentecostalism were beginning to return to their homes in the Northeast, in a reverse migratory trend that would continue throughout the next two decades. As they made the trip back to their homes they brought their faith with them. As R. Andrew

Chesnut has noted, "Many of the seringueiros (rubber tappers), returning to their native lands in the impoverished Northeast, planted the hearty seeds of Pentecostalism in one of Brazilian Catholicism's most fertile soils."[78] The loose leadership structure of the AD and its belief that the power of the Holy Spirit allowed anyone, no matter their education or training, to preach the Gospel and form congregations meant that the returning migrants could take the initiative to start their own Pentecostal communities. Such wide discretion gave them a great advantage over historical Protestant congregations, whose members needed specific educational credentials or apprenticeships or both before they could evangelize and lead their own churches.[79] In the early years of the AD all were called to preach, all were called to convert, and all were called to found new Pentecostal communities.

Thus the trajectory of AD expansion went south, from the North to the Northeast. After Pará, the first states to host AD members were Paraíba (1911), Rio Grande do Norte (1911), Ceará (1914), and Alagoas (1915).[80] The AD had no formalized evangelization plan, and so congregations grew and spread alongside the migratory movements of the northeasterners themselves. And since many of the migrants came from small towns in the rural interior, it was in the rural interior that some of the first congregations emerged. The story of Maria Nazaré, the first person to evangelize Ceará, came to represent the quintessential story of migrant evangelists. As Emílio Conde, an official historian of the AD, wrote, "It was not a missionary or a credentialed worker who brought the Pentecostal message to the State of Ceará; it was not a man who was the first person to introduce the flame of the Holy Spirit in the lands of José de Alencar. A woman who was humble, but burning with zeal, received the message when she was in Belém, Pará, and wanted her parents, who lived in Ceará, to be able to know the Good News and the full Gospel."[81]

Nazaré returned to her hometown of Serra de Uruburetama, a small town in the Cearense interior, and there she founded the first Pentecostal congregation in the state. Nazaré's story was not unique: in Paraíba the first documented congregation was formed in the interior town of Alagoa Grande, when Galdino Cândido do Nascimento, a native of the town, returned from Pará and began to preach his new faith to family and friends.[82]

In Alagoas another "humble worker" brought his faith to the state when he converted his family members in 1915.[83] The flow of migrant-evangelizers to the Northeast continued throughout the twenties and thirties. In 1934 one could still read about a resident of the interior of Piauí who converted to the AD when his brother returned from Maranhão "with a Bible in his hand."[84] Migrant-evangelists were soon joined by more official evangelizing agents, such as the Swedish missionary Joel Carlson, who arrived in Recife in 1918, and the Brazilian worker Cícero Canuto de Lima. Reverend Lima was a native of Mossoró, Rio Grande do Norte, but he had converted while working for the rubber industry in the Amazon. After being consecrated as a pastor in Belém by Vingren himself, he went to Paraíba and in 1924 became the state's first official missionary. Yet while these new official pastors would expand the AD's work in larger coastal cities such as João Pessoa, Natal, and Recife, the heart of the AD remained in the interior.[85]

The growth of the AD had a profound effect on Protestant–Catholic relations in the northeastern interior. At its most basic level Pentecostalism's arrival increased the number of Protestant congregations in the Northeast and intensified the abovementioned trends in Protestant evangelization, that is, the rise in Brazilian-led churches, the emergence of working-class Protestant leaders, and the concentration of Protestant growth in the interior of the sertão. But, perhaps more important, the arrival of Pentecostalism transformed the way Catholics viewed Protestantism in the Northeast. Pentecostalism distinguishes itself from historical Protestant denominations by its belief that the Holy Spirit remains radically present in the world today, serving as a means by which human beings can directly experience God and His revelation. In Pentecostal congregations any believer can and should receive a "Spirit baptism," the moment in which the Holy Spirit enters a person. Pentecostals believe that the age of miracles has not ended, and they thus have access to the divine gifts of the Holy Spirit, including divine healing, speaking in tongues, and prophesying. Pentecostal worship abounds in physical manifestations of the Spirit: worshippers frequently convulse, fall to the floor, speak in a strange voice, and say words that are unintelligible to others. Such actions are proof of the real transformative effects of the Holy Spirit on individual persons in the here and now.

These qualities made Pentecostalism a target of Brazilian Restorationist Catholics, who viewed it as suspiciously similar to the backward religious culture they were trying to eradicate in the Northeast. Catholics viewed Pentecostalism as a wild, superstitious, fanatical religion. The physicality of AD religious services alarmed Catholics like Padre Rossi, who was horrified that Pentecostals "flail about, shake, contort themselves, and fall to their knees, while they utter incomprehensible and disconnected words."[86] In Pentecostalism Padre Rossi saw a dangerous combination of both the "mental illness" associated with Spiritism and the fanatical superstition associated with millenarian Christianity. After declaring that Pentecostalism was "an excellent ally of Spiritism" because it "predisposes [children and adolescents] to neurological and even physical problems later in life," Padre Rossi went on to describe a "fanatical" Pentecostal church whose leader, he said, referring to the leader of the millenarian movement of Canudos, was "a new Antonio Conselheiro." "This is to cite just one example of the fanaticism that Pentecostalism can lead to," wrote Padre Rossi. Pentecostalism was dangerous precisely because it encouraged so-called fanaticism, according to Padre Rossi, and the priest warned Brazilians of the destabilizing effects Pentecostalism could have on Brazilian communities. "This might be the first sign of a new case of Canudos," he declared.[87] In the Northeast, a region whose inhabitants were thought to already harbor latent millenarian tendencies, the threat of Pentecostalism was doubly worrisome to Catholic leaders. First, the ignorant, exploitable masses were more likely to leave their Catholic faith and join the new Pentecostal churches, whose fanatical insistence on a direct relationship with the divine would be likely to attract superstitious Catholics. And, second, now those very churches were thought to be in danger of becoming, like Canudos, hotbeds of antigovernment millenarian radicalism.

The racist nature of attacks on Pentecostalism was clear: like the millenarianism of Canudos, Pentecostalism was depicted as a religion of *caboclos* that was made inferior by its closeness to Afro-Brazilian and indigenous religions. "The Pentecostal sect is nothing more than 'Protestant macumba' and extremely dangerous 'low spiritism' [also known as Afro-Brazilian spiritism]," wrote Eurípedes de Menezes, the Integralist Catholic lay leader who led the SNDF.[88] To Menezes, these characteristics made Pentecostals "the most ignorant, the most fanatical, and the most pernicious of all Protestants." Ultimately, he believed that the solution to the Pentecostal problem lay not in "lofty historical, philosophical, or theological debates, but in enlightened patriotism, professional awareness, and energetic action by the Chief of Police!"[89]

Catholics were not the only ones worried about the rise of Pentecostalism. In many ways historical Protestants were most affected by Pentecostal growth in that a large number of early Pentecostal converts were not Catholics but rather Protestants who left their congregations to join or even found a Pentecostal church.[90] Some of the most aggressive attacks on Pentecostalism came from fellow Protestants. Baptists like Rev. Pedro Tarsier railed against the "fake cures" of the Pentecostals, expressing his anger at a religion that promoted "LANGUAGES THAT ARE NOT LANGUAGES, VISIONS THAT ARE NOTHING MORE THAN MENTAL (psychological) IMAGES, FALLIBLE AND HUMAN PROPHECIES THAT PURPORT TO FORGIVE SINS, etc."[91] The Presbytery of Pernambuco was so worried about the Pentecostal threat that it commissioned one of its prominent young pastors, Rev. Jerônimo Gueiros, to write a pamphlet warning his fellow Presbyterians about the dangers of the new religion and advising them how to combat its spread.[92] Titled *The Pentecostal Heresy*, the pamphlet accused Pentecostalism of being "a dangerous combination of falsified biblical principles and harmful religious psychism portrayed as a new Pentecost."[93] Reverend Gueiros believed that Pentecostals were hypocrites at heart, claiming to be pious and to receive special favors from the Holy Spirit all while leading lives of "chronic moral dissolution." The pastor even hinted at sinister secret meetings in which Pentecostals searched for "freedom in front of the Lord" as they lost control of their bodies and minds, screaming uncontrollably and leaving all modesty behind.[94] Reverend Gueiros's pamphlet was distributed throughout the northeastern interior, going through at least two printings as well as numerous reprintings in regional evangelical newspapers.

And yet for all of their insistence that Pentecostal practices were anathema to true Protestant doctrine, members of historical Protestant denominations found that when it came to Protestant–Catholic relations they were inextricably linked to their Pentecostal brethren. Leaders of Restorationist anti-Protestant campaigns deliberately conflated Pentecostalism and historical Protestantism, holding that Pentecostalism was a reflection of the "religious anarchy" and "mania for reform" that all Protestant churches, including historical Protestant churches, embodied. "Whether [historical Protestant churches] like it or not, Pentecostalism is the natural and inevitable result of the articles of faith created by Protestants," Padre Rossi wrote.[95] Moreover, the vast majority of Catholics in the Northeast, including members of the Catholic hierarchy, simply did not distinguish between denominations of Protestants. When speaking or writing about Protestants, priests and laymen alike rarely specified an individual or church's denominational affiliation. Protestants were simply *crentes* or *evangélicos*, and their churches were *seitas*. Specific names of denominations were often used interchangeably. When a Pentecostal member of the AD was assassinated in the small Paraíban town of Cuité, the officials investigating the case frequently referred to the victim and his coreligionists as Lutherans, even though there were no Lutherans living in or near Cuité.[96] As a result of this denominational confusion, the so-called sins of one denomination often became the sins of all. The specific dangers of Pentecostalism—its supposedly anarchic religious celebrations, superstitious beliefs, exploitative practices, and psychological manipulations—became general dangers associated with all Protestant congregations.

Domestic Migration and the Journey of Conversion

The final factor that shaped Protestantism in the northeastern interior was the social and religious upheaval caused by the climate of the region itself, specifically, the frequent droughts that plagued the sertão and triggered cyclical waves of migration. When two great droughts hit the Northeast in less than a decade, peaking in 1932 and 1941, the resulting devastation of the region's agricultural and livestock industries led to a mass exodus of people from the hardest-hit areas of the states. A priest in Flores, a small town in the interior of Pernambuco, remarked that the drought of 1932 "seem[ed] like a sign of the End Times."[97] At first glance it would seem these drought crises would have hindered the advancement of Protestantism in the region. Whereas Catholic parishes, owing to their higher membership numbers and more stable funding structures, were able to weather the crises and continue to serve their drought-reduced communities, Protestant churches found themselves in more dire predicaments. In small sertanejan towns Protestant congregations were often composed of only a few extended families. This made them highly unstable and susceptible to external shocks. When one or more families left town the survival of the entire church was put into jeopardy. Baptists in Pernambuco spoke of various churches that had become extinct due to the exodus of members from the sertão.[98] The Congregationalist church in Coremas was completely dissolved because of the "incessant dispersion of believers, motivated by the three-year devastating drought."[99] A Pentecostal leader of the AD in Rio Grande do Norte wrote, "The drought is so bad that everyone is emigrating."[100] In Campina Grande Protestants wrote that "many families and brothers who had professed interest in converting have left our community in search of means of subsistence. . . . The vast majority of our brothers are unemployed and sick."[101] Some congregations disappeared forever, and for those that fought to stay or re-form, the process of rebuilding could take years, even decades, as resource-depleted churches struggled to finance new evangelization efforts.

Drought and migration also had the potential to allow Protestant denominations to gain new followers and spread to new towns in the rural interior. As Daniel Ramírez has shown in the case of Mexico, migration networks could facilitate the growth of new religious movements as converts moved across borders and brought their religion with them.[102] The decline of the rubber industry, as noted, resulted in the reverse migration of Pentecostal northeasterners, resulting in the introduction of Pentecostalism to small interior towns that no other Protestant congregation had previously visited. The sertanejan droughts of the 1930s and 1940s sparked a similar diffusion of Protestantism within the Northeast itself. While the general migratory flow went from interior towns to coastal cities such as Recife and Natal, the migratory experience was neither permanent nor uniform. Many migrants returned to their hometowns after conditions in the sertão improved, and others never went to the coastal cities at all, instead heading to midsized cities in the interior or to smaller towns where they sought the support of better-off family members. The resulting social and demographic upheaval created new opportunities for conversion and evangelization. In the cities and along the roads on which drought-stricken migrants were traveling, Protestants quickly set up aid stations. They dispensed food and water and sometimes provided housing, while introducing migrants, most of whom were Catholic, to their religious beliefs and practices. The Presbyterian missionary Raynard Arehart wrote that the "continued drought, with its economic consequences, brought added responsibilities and opportunities" as local churches worked overtime to administer to the needs of the destitute population while taking advantage of the new captive audience by teaching them about Protestant doctrine and beliefs. Reverend Henderlite wrote about how his church's superior aid efforts were allowing him to convince migrants to leave the Catholic Church: "The drought and the consequent suffering has opened the eyes of the people to the real character of the priests and the Roman church. In all the people's suffering the church has not lifted a hand to help. Their charges for baptisms, marriages, extreme unction, etc., are still the same, and the people are turning to us and giving us a sympathetic ear. That is all that the Gospel needs. If a man will listen, the Holy Spirit convicts and converts."[103]

In general Protestants felt that the drought upset social hierarchies and allowed people to reimagine their spiritual futures. In some instances desperation fueled the search for a new religious identity. The Baptist missionary Charles Stapp marveled at how the great drought of 1932 had anticipated a Protestant revival in the interior Pernambucan city of Garanhuns: "We are feeling a new spirit in our field. The extreme drought, the horrible depression, the extreme physical necesity [sic] of the people seem at last turning their thoughts to things of another world." Reverend Stapp did not want to waste the chance to convert so many lost souls. "Now is the time to press the battle to the gates," he declared. "Certainly the people are saying in their hearts: 'To whom shall we go.'"[104] Reverend Stapp and others worked hard to ensure that the people would go to the Protestant congregations.

Later, converted migrants often returned to their hometowns, bringing their new faith with them. This is what happened to a man known as Senhor Carlos, who had left his small town in the interior various times as "drought after drought had taken his crops and killed his cattle."[105] During one stay in the city (most likely Recife) Carlos converted to the Presbyterian faith. When he decided to return he did so "with an earnest endeavor to bring into the lives of some the wonderful light he had found." He started inviting his friends and neighbors to Sunday services in his home, and soon a small community of believers had formed in his town. Not all returning migrants actively evangelized their communities. But even if they did not found new congregations they played a vital role in the spread of Protestantism in the interior by becoming what could be called dormant Protestants. Dormant Protestants remained relatively inactive when they arrived in a town with no organized Protestant church, but they could be quickly awakened when a traveling minister or a new Protestant family came to their town. Such readiness allowed them to serve as a link between Protestant newcomers and the local community. Manoel Francisco de Almeida, a Pentecostal man who in 1933 moved to a town in Piauí that had no AD church, "strayed from the correct path" for five years until a Pentecostal pastor come to town. Almeida immediately offered his home as a site for AD services and converted his friends, and soon the small group attending these "house meetings" was transformed into an official church. Four years later the congregation, now thriving, was even able to send out men to evangelize surrounding towns.[106]

Drought and migration contributed as well to the multiplication of Protestant congregations in the northeastern interior, as Protestants of one denomination converted to another. While such transitions did not immediately increase the total number of Protestants in the region, they did encourage the founding of new churches, which had the potential to attract new members and disrupt the religious status quo of small towns. A case in point is Ana Alves, a former Presbyterian from Iguatú, Ceará, who escaped the 1932 drought by emigrating to Pará and working in the rubber industry. At the time there was no official Presbyterian presence in the Paraense town to which Alves migrated, but there was another Protestant church, the Pentecostal AD. Alves wrote, "[While I was in Pará] I heard that there were Protestants who were speaking in tongues. I went to a service, and it was not long before I believed in Pentecostal truths."[107] She converted and became a zealous promoter of her new faith. Two years later, in 1934, she returned to Iguatú and founded the town's first AD congregation, thereby doubling the number of Protestant churches in the small town. Two Protestant churches meant two evangelization initiatives, two distributors of two different types of Protestant publications, and eventually two physical church structures, all in the same Cearense town. The appearance of a new local Protestant denomination would have greatly intensified Catholics' sense that their town was being invaded by Protestants, even if the total number of new converts from Catholicism was not rising greatly.

The denominational conversion experienced by Protestants like Ana Alves formed part of what could be called their conversion journey, which accompanied the more literal journey of migration and displacement. In this way, Protestants experienced conversion in the way it has been defined by Edward Cleary and Timothy Steigenga, namely, as a "process, rather than an isolated event."[108] Rejecting the Pauline notion that views conversion as a single transformative moment in an individual's life, Cleary and Steigenga instead argue that "conversion takes place over time, interacts with institutional religious, network, and cultural contexts, and does not necessarily proceed in a linear or chronological fashion."[109] In the 1920s and 1930s an individual's initial conversion to a non-Catholic faith was a radical act, separating them from their community, family, and friends, but it was oftentimes only the first step on a long path of conversion and spiritual discovery. The case of José Francisco, a Pentecostal from João Pessoa, is revealing. In 1940 he published his testimony, or conversion narrative, in the Pentecostal journal *Mensageiro da Paz*. He wrote that he had been born Catholic, the grand-nephew of a Catholic priest, no less, and had been steeped in the Catholic faith until one day his "faith was thrown asunder" and he became a "lost atheist" who became dedicated to materialist and philosophical writings. But in 1936 he underwent another crisis of faith when he "recognized [his] condition as a rebel and [his] disobedience to the Word of God." He subsequently converted to the Baptist church, declaring that the "Sun of Justice (Jesus) shone in my life." Four years later he became sick with "an illness that was said to be incurable by medicine," and he turned to the Pentecostal practice of faith healing to combat the disease. The success of the healing practice convinced him of the righteousness of the Pentecostal faith, and he experienced his final (at the time of his writing) conversion, this time to the church of the Assembléia de Deus.[110] While some would say that José Francisco had converted three times, José himself saw each of his three religious transformations as part of the same soul-saving journey that led him to his ultimate spiritual destiny, Pentecostalism. "Twice I was saved from atheism," he declared, "but only at the end was I saved from sin."

While denominational conversion often arose out of practical circumstances, such as Ana Alves's migration to a town with no Presbyterian church, it could also stem from a deeper sense of spiritual malaise and a desire for a more authentic spiritual fulfillment. Pentecostals like Luiz Gomes, from Ceará, frequently described a pervasive feeling of dissatisfaction with their lives or a belief that something was missing that caused them to undergo multiple conversions in order to achieve a sense of spiritual peace. Gomes converted three times, first to the Baptist religion, then to Presbyterianism, and finally to Pentecostalism. Describing his conversion journey, Gomes wrote,

> I heard the Gospel for the first time in the Baptist church, where I accepted Jesus as my only Savior; however, my soul was not satisfied there. I began, then, to attend the Presbyterian church, in search of the truth and of real peace; but I still did not find all that for which my heart longed. Examining the Sacred Scriptures, I found the signs foretold by the Lord, which belong to those who believe. It was then that I began to attend the "Assembly of God," where I met with brothers and I saw and heard everything that my thirsty soul had lacked. I felt that there all of the signs were fulfilled; I began to search for baptism in the Holy Spirit, and I received it, speaking in new tongues and praising His holy name.[111]

For many Pentecostals the sense of one's "soul not being satisfied," as Gomes described it, came from the belief that they were not living a sufficiently rigorous spiritual life. The search for such rigor could thus involve numerous denominational changes throughout the conversion journey. Liomio Cunha, from Bahia, converted to Presbyterianism, but he soon came to believe that he "still lived with the pleasures of life" and didn't "feel the transformation of [his] life."[112] This unsettledness caused him to seek out the Assembléia de Deus, which he believed to be more stringent in its moral precepts than the Presbyterian church and more radical in its promises of self-transformation. Antônio Pedro Crespim, referring to his conversion to Presbyterianism, wrote, "I felt saved, . . . but I [still] felt carnal."[113] Others were content with their initial conversion until they discovered new religious practices that suited their spiritual needs better. José Marques Sobrinho's entire family had converted to the Baptist faith, but when his brother-in-law told the family about Spirit baptism they realized they were missing "the power of God within [their] heart."[114] A future Pentecostal from Pernambuco, Milton Gomes, spoke of how when he was a Catholic he was a "sinner, tired and oppressed." He then started to attend Spiritist meetings in an attempt to "rid [him]self of an *encosto* [suffering spirit that attaches itself to a person] or a bad spirit." But soon he began to believe that Spiritism was not making him feel better—to the contrary, he thought it "increased [his] suffering." He left Spiritism and converted to Pentecostalism, a religion he felt could attend to his feeling of spiritual malaise more effectively.[115]

Pentecostals placed great importance on conversion testimonies, which made them more likely than their historical Protestant counterparts to record, publish, and save their stories recounting their spiritual journeys. Yet Pentecostals were certainly not the only Protestants to undergo multiple conversions. In Rio Grande do Norte a photographer had become a Spiritist because "he was seeking God and reality." But once he began reading the Bible he became convinced that Spiritists did not respect the deity of Jesus sufficiently, and he sought out a Congregationalist pastor and asked to convert. However, after having a vision in which he saw a group of people being fully immersed in the waters of a river, he became unsatisfied with the Congregationalist practice of sprinkling their converts with water, and he switched to the Baptist faith.[116] There were even reports of entire congregations undergoing multiple denominational changes. A Presbyterian congregation in Paraíba was said to have "become dissatisfied with their doctrines" and asked that a Congregationalist missionary take over the leadership of their church. According to later reports by Baptist missionaries, the same congregation was still unhappy with their doctrine, "particularly in regard to baptism," and the Congregationalist pastor himself said to them, "You folks are Baptists."[117] From that point forward they were Baptists. Similar transformations occurred in other churches. Multiple historical Protestant churches decided to become Pentecostal and joined the AD.[118] A Presbyterian congregation was said to have asked Baptist missionaries to take charge of their church.[119]

In the eyes of Catholics the multiple conversions of Protestants were yet another example of the religious anarchy that they believed was inherent in Protestantism and that would infect Brazilian citizens with a disrespect for both religious and civil authorities. As the Paraíban Catholic newspaper *A Imprensa* wrote, the "monstrous variety" of Protestant denominations was the "horrible consequence of this damned Sect," and stemmed directly from the ability to "read the Bible and interpret it based on the judgment of each individual."[120] Once nordestinos began to view religion as a search for spiritual satisfaction rather than a reception of authoritative truths, Catholics wondered where it all would end. Indeed, denominational variety itself was seen as being dangerous and harmful to both individuals and society: "Divided into hundreds of doctrines, branches, and sub-branches, Protestantism, with its dozens of forms of baptism, with its different forms of communion, with its eternal biblical screeds, and, above all, with its free inquiry [*livre exame*], is truly a factory of denials and madness."[121] In the eyes of Catholic Restorationists the conversion journeys of Protestants served merely to confirm their suspicions and fears: that Protestantism would engender "anarchy, disorder, and chaos with its divergent factions, and its diabolical pastors and missionaries will work against national unity."[122] Catholic leaders had a feeling that a dam had been breached and that the forces of individualism and free inquiry had been unleashed into society. Once individuals left the authoritative embrace of the Catholic Church, they seemed to reject all authorities, even those of their new churches.

As Protestantism spread to the rural interior, so too did the belief that no corner of the Northeast was safe from the threat of conversion. This was the real threat of the new face of Protestantism that had emerged in the Northeast in the twenties and thirties: the Protestantism that was increasingly Brazilian-led, increasingly intent on evangelizing the interior, increasingly dominated by Pentecostals, and increasingly mobile. The total number of Protestants in the Northeast was not growing at an explosive pace, but the identity of Protestantism itself was transforming from a foreign-led, urban religion to a Brazilian-led faith that had followers throughout all regions of the country. New churches could be fleeting and unstable, their small numbers and geographical isolation making them vulnerable to the external shocks of drought, migration, and leadership conflicts. Yet to northeastern Catholics in the 1930s the long-term instability of certain individual churches was not yet evident, and the short-term flourishing in their numbers and geographical reach seemed to represent an existential threat to the Catholic Church. The march of Protestantism into the Brazilian sertão was deeply unsettling to Restorationist Catholics because it upended their assumptions regarding the nature of Protestantism's relationship with Brazilian society. Protestantism was supposed to remain in urban centers, where it could be considered just another incarnation of the secular/liberal/communist spirit that unfortunately pervaded all large cities. But as Protestant churches multiplied in far-flung corners of the sertão that were previously thought to be impervious to Protestant advances, thereby upsetting the "peaceful, good, simple, and profoundly orderly spirit" of the rural communities, Catholics decided they needed to take decisive action.[123]

THREE

To Be a "Good Priest"

Catholic Leadership and Local Campaigns against Protestantism in the Northeast

In May 1939 a group of policemen arrived in the small town of Nísia Floresta, Rio Grande do Norte, with orders to "guarantee the safety" of local Protestants and ensure that the religious persecution that had wracked the town the previous month would not continue.[1] With the police stationed outside their church, the local Baptist congregation was able to resume its weekly services without fear of coming under attack, as Catholics were not allowed to approach the building. At the time, the arrival of the police seemed to represent a defeat for Padre João Verberck, the local parish priest. Facing the threat of prosecution for his role in promoting the recent violence, he had fled to the nearby village of São José de Mipibú in order to "seek shelter." However, Padre Verberck's ecclesiastical career was ultimately helped rather than hindered by his clash with police forces, as he quickly became a regional hero for having stood up to the Protestants. During his short exile the priest was visited by diocesan leaders, the head priest of Natal, and various Marian Congregations, all of whom expressed their strong support of Padre Verberck and his cause.[2] When the police left Nísia Floresta a week later, having made no arrests or provisions for the future protection of the Protestant community, Padre Verberck staged a triumphant return. Flanked by representatives from Natal and surrounding towns, he was greeted by a jubilant Catholic rally complete with a public procession, speeches, a thanksgiving Mass, and fireworks. "The Protestant heresy could not have received a more devastating response," declared a reporter from the Natal-based

Catholic daily, *A Ordem*.[3] Padre Verberck, the newest leader of the anti-Protestant crusade, would continue to fight the Protestants of Nísia Floresta, going so far even as to found a Marian Congregation with the explicit intent of creating a group of laypersons "ready to enter into battle as true soldiers of the Catholic Religion." Padre Verberck was determined to "not allow the land of the Holy Cross, Christian Brazil, to be invaded by the Protestant religion that seeks to subjugate the Brazilian Fatherland baptized by God at the dawn of our nationality."[4] If anything, he had returned from his exile even more emboldened to drive any and all Protestants from his parish.

Cases like that of Padre Verberck were common throughout the Northeast in the 1920s, 1930s, and 1940s. As Catholic leaders became increasingly convinced that a Protestant invasion was under way in the interior, local priests assumed their position on the front lines of the battlefield. Their ecclesiastical superiors demanded that they take harsh, immediate action against any Protestants who were in their parishes, and priests who proved zealous in their anti-Protestant campaigns were celebrated by Catholic leaders and their parishioners. Rituals and discourses fueled and legitimized the use of force against Protestants, and the stonings, church burnings, mass expulsions, and physical assaults against Protestants were rarely spontaneous expressions of riotous rage. Instead, they were organized events that utilized common symbols, ceremonies, and actions in order to send specific messages to Protestant and Catholic communities alike. Bishops and priests were intimately involved in both the promotion and implementation of persecutory campaigns. In order to justify religious aggression, they created a discourse of self-defense that combined the language of Catholic nationalism, which depicted Protestantism as a threat to the civic unity of Brazil, with the spiritual language of purification, which saw Protestantism as a threat to the salvific and millenarian future of local communities. Catholic leaders thus engaged in a complex form of double-talk in which they condemned the idea of religious aggression but supported its practice, claiming that nordestinos had the right and, indeed, the responsibility to defend their towns from destructive Protestant forces. Although this confrontational attitude sometimes brought clerics into conflict with local authorities, most priests ultimately benefited from undertaking ambitious anti-Protestant campaigns, as they rarely received civil punishments, instead often obtaining ecclesiastical rewards in the form of appointments to more prestigious parishes or promotions to higher ecclesiastical offices. The more committed a priest was in protecting his parish from the Protestant onslaught, the more he could claim the title of the good priest: a zealous, obedient cleric who was fulfilling the aspirations of the Catholic Restoration and protecting the traditional religious culture of the northeastern interior.

I Have Come to Bring Fire: Bishops and Anti-Protestantism

Bishops set the tone for interreligious relations in their dioceses. Through circular letters sent out to all diocesan priests, pastoral visits in which they passed judgment on priestly works, pastoral letters outlining their vision and agenda for the diocese, and the distribution of ecclesiastical punishments and rewards, bishops were able to exert great influence over local parishes. With the rise of Catholic anxieties regarding Protestant growth in the interior of the Northeast during the first half of the twentieth century, many regional bishops were determined to ensure that the seeds of heresy were not planted in their dioceses. Some, like Dom José Antônio de Oliveira Lopes, the bishop of Pesqueira, became anti-Protestant crusaders in their own right, taking a leading role in expelling Protestants from their dioceses. Dom José was a native son of Pernambuco, born in Recife in 1868. When he was appointed to the bishopric of Pesqueira in 1915 he immediately proved to be a zealous reformer.[5] At the time, Pesqueira was experiencing economic and demographic growth, as the Great Western railroad was extended to reach the town and the region's main industrial employer, the canning factory Fábrica Peixe, was beginning to export its goods to both national and international markets. Dom José wanted to encourage Pesqueira's residents, new and old alike, to take an active role in promoting Catholic values in the public sphere. To that end he founded new religious associations such as Ação Social Católica (Catholic Social Action, an early precursor to Catholic Action), which not only undertook charitable projects but also encouraged public discussions on how to reconcile religion with the modern world. On one memorable evening in 1919 the group rented out the local cinema and invited the "best families and most distinguished gentlemen" of the region to listen to a priest give a lecture on the harmonious relationship between faith and science. The bishop declared the lecture a great success, saying that the scholar-priest had "left the auditorium completely satisfied."[6] Hoping to cultivate an active community of Catholic elites and intellectuals, the bishop founded a local Catholic newspaper, *Era Nova* [*New Era*], that became one of the principal means by which Romanizing and Restorationist ideas spread through the Pernambucan interior.[7] Dom José placed great emphasis on Romanizing devotions, creating a religious association solely concerned with promoting the devotion to the Sacred Heart of Jesus, and he instituted weekly sessions of Eucharistic adoration.[8] Worried about the ignorance of the rural populations of the interior, who were supposedly more vulnerable to the seductions of millenarianism, superstitions, communism, and Protestantism, Dom José created a Central Committee for Christian Doctrine to coordinate stricter catechism standards throughout the diocese. Dom José believed that enhanced catechism instruction would inculcate Pesqueirenses with the doctrinal and moral knowledge necessary to protect themselves from those who would seek to take advantage of their weak Catholic foundations.

Thus when Protestants began to arrive in Pesqueira in the 1920s, Dom José was prepared to fight back against what he believed to be a pernicious attack on the unity and peace of his community. He first fixed his attention on the traveling evangelists, most likely Baptists, who frequently visited the Pesqueira diocese. Dom José proudly wrote in his diocesan *livro de tombo* (a diary of all the activities that take place in a diocese, passed down from bishop to bishop) of how he would repel the Protestant assault, forcing Protestant workers to leave before they made serious inroads in the religious culture of the area.[9] He did not specify the methods he used to bring about the Protestant retreat, but they were aggressive enough that in 1925 Protestants asked for the local police to protect them whenever they preached in Pesqueira.[10] Catholics were furious when the local *coronel* (rural strongman) and then mayor, Cândido Britto, granted the Protestants' request. In the eyes of Padre José de Anchieta Callou, the priest of Pesqueira's parish church, Coronel Britto was doing nothing less than "protecting those perverse men" and facilitating their infiltration of the Pesqueirense community.[11] In response, Dom José and Padre

José organized a mission to preach against Protestants in the Prado neighborhood of Pesqueira, which at the time was on the outskirts of the town. For
multiple days Catholic leaders preached against the so-called Protestant
plague, urging their parishioners to drive out any Protestants in their midst.

However, the preaching tour in Pesqueira's Prado neighborhood did not
permanently rid the area of Protestants. Just two years later, in 1927, Dom José
felt that he needed to issue an open letter to all of the priests in his diocese in
which he reminded them of the urgent need to combat any representatives of
Protestantism who might try to establish themselves in a priest's parish. "It is my
responsibility, inherent to my pastoral duty," he wrote, "to call attention to the
furious propaganda of the new sects or evangelists, who are satanically committed to using their erroneous doctrines to disturb public order throughout the
entirety of this poor country."[12] The bishop was disturbed by the fact that Protestants no longer limited themselves to evangelizing urban centers such as Recife and had instead embarked into the interior, spreading disorder and chaos
in their wake. Dom José held special rancor for Brazilian evangelists, depicting
them as treacherous agents of the United States, a country that "we all know
has a great interest in this damned enterprise."[13] To Dom José, the evangelistic
work of Brazilians made them traitors to their communities and nations, exploiters of the "simple populations" in exchange for "the bread they win from
this evil job."[14] Priests were instructed to "not permit Protestants to enter [their
parish]" and to commit to helping the bishop "protect the sacred deposit of
faith that we must swear to defend, even with the sacrifice of our lives."[15] Dom
José did not explicitly advocate that priests use violence to expel Protestants
from their parishes, but it was clear he anticipated a confrontational resolution
to the situation, one that might even involve the "sacrifice" of clerics' lives.

Religious conflict in Pesqueira reached crisis levels in 1931, when a series
of attacks against Protestants took place. In separate occurrences in March,
April, and June Catholics aggressively confronted Protestants who had come
to preach in their midst. In each case Dom José was directly implicated in
promoting and supporting the conflicts. He openly boasted that in anticipation of the arrival of Protestant evangelists in April he had "convoked his
armed flock and warned them of the assault that the malicious wolf [Protes-
tantism] wanted to make on them."[16] In an unsurprising development the

Protestants were subsequently assaulted while conducting their religious service.[17] In June Dom José was said to have directed or, at the very least, allowed the parish priest of Pesqueira to ring the cathedral bells to alert Catholics to the arrival of Protestants in the city. A massive group of Catholic Pesqueirenses converged on the public square where the evangelists were preaching and attacked those gathered with rocks. Later, religious leaders were reported to have "encouraged the people to stone the Protestants in the hotel where they were staying."[18] Again, Catholic leaders did not deny they had rung the cathedral bells and instructed the people who gathered to defend the town against the supposed Protestant attack. The parish priest, Padre Alfredo de Arruda Câmara, an ardent Restorationist who had attended the Colégio Pio Latino-Americano in Rome and become an avid political supporter of the Vargas regime, wrote that he had rung the bells to gather Catholics in protest against the arrival of the Protestants. Dom José told the press the bells had been rung "after the people clamored for it," although he denied having had prior knowledge of the act.[19]

As a bishop in the Northeast, Dom José was by no means alone in spearheading campaigns against Protestants. Even when bishops did not become directly involved with specific incidents in the way Dom José did, they still played a prominent role in promoting a diocesan environment that encouraged and rewarded anti-Protestant actions. Dom Jaime de Barros Câmara, the future cardinal-archbishop of Rio de Janeiro, got his start in the newly created diocese of Mossoró, in Rio Grande do Norte. He was appointed the diocese's first bishop in 1935, although he did not arrive in Mossoró until 1936. The motto he chose for his coat of arms was, "I have come to bring fire," a biblical statement (Luke 12:49) that embodied his Restorationist, anti-Protestant mission. He wanted to rid Mossoró of its complacency, indifferentism, and lack of religious zeal in order to ensure that Mossorense Catholics would no longer turn a blind eye to the elements in their midst that weakened Catholic unity. Like Dom José, Dom Jaime was indefatigable in his promotion of diocesan progress and reform: he directed all of the priests in his diocese to found Catholic Action associations, promoted Catholic Workers' Circles, founded a diocesan seminary to address the local priest shortage and encourage the vocations of local youths, overhauled the local catechism curriculum, and initiated a campaign to combat the growth of Protestantism.[20]

When Dom Jaime arrived in Mossoró disparate campaigns against Protestants were already taking place throughout the diocese. Padre Luiz Motta, a native son of Mossoró, had traveled to the Pio Colégio Latino-Americano to complete his religious studies, returning to Mossoró in 1926, just as the first Protestants, members of the Pentecostal Assembléia de Deus church, were beginning to found congregations in the region. The young priest immediately undertook an effort to roll back Pentecostal growth in his new parish, and, in the words of his fellow Catholics, he "courageously sounded the alarm and generated a great amount of activity in order to scare back the invading wave [of Pentecostals]."[21] His colleague in Areia Branca, a small town on the northern Riograndense coast that was also the site of a new Pentecostal congregation, embarked on an even more aggressive campaign that included both anti-Protestant sermons and larger, more theatrical spectacles like Bible burnings.[22] Protestants in Areia Branca accused the priest of inciting violence against them, saying that with his consent and perhaps even instruction their church was vandalized and their congregants assaulted.[23]

When Dom Jaime arrived in Mossoró in 1936 he praised the anti-Protestant campaigns that were already under way and immediately began to use them as models for other parishes to follow. The second circular he issued as bishop of Mossoró was a manifesto against Protestantism titled "For the Union of Catholics and the Conservation of the Faith." He began the letter by congratulating past campaigns against Protestantism that had been carried out in the diocese: "It has come to my attention, with special pleasure, that in your valor as Catholics you have more than once rejected with dignity, and impeded with intrepid steadfastness, the introduction of Protestant communities in your midst. Bravo!"[24] The new bishop went on to tell priests about his previous experience dealing with Protestantism, in which he had innocently tried a more peaceful, conciliatory approach. "I treated [Protestants] like long-lost brothers, and I used a voice of generosity and serenity when explaining Catholic doctrine to them," he recalled. "But soon I realized that these so-called *crentes* were dishonest and perverse, and they saw my generosity as weakness, and took advantage of it to spread [Protestantism] throughout the interior of our beloved diocese." The only option now, he argued, was to abandon all attempts at persuasion and conciliation and instead take an aggressive stance. "Back then I wanted to save [Protestants]," he wrote, "but now, dear diocese, it is necessary to arm ourselves for battle against them." He ordered priests to do their "sacred duty" and repel Protestants from their parishes by any means possible. The letter ended with a hearty "Long live the religion of Christ! Long live the only true Religion! Long live the Catholic Religion!"[25]

Dom Jaime quickly became known for his intolerance of religious pluralism. The Catholic newspaper in Natal, A Ordem, commended him for his "burning zeal" to rid his diocese of Protestants. The paper celebrated his promotion of anti-Protestant activities, such as when he organized a pilgrimage to a Protestant-"infested" town near Mossoró in an attempt to "give courage" to its residents so they could rise up against the so-called heretics. Attendees were encouraged to bring Protestant Bibles and literature with them so that they could destroy them in a public ceremony. To Dom Jaime, the fight against Protestantism was a diocese-wide endeavor. If local Catholics in one town allowed a Protestant enclave to develop, then neighboring Catholics would need to remind them of their duties to the corporate whole. This, in essence, was the aim of the pilgrimages. "With the grace of God and the aid of Our Lady of Aparecida [the national patron saint of Brazil], we are certain that soon the disciples of Luther will fall over themselves fleeing from the Mossorense plagues," the author proclaimed. "Protestant sirs, turn back! The flock that you are trying to decimate already has a shepherd who, in the words of our Lord, 'will be willing to give his life for his sheep!' "[26]

To Be a Good Priest: Anti-Protestantism and the Rise of the Restorationist Priest

Bishops created environments that allowed religious intolerance to flourish, but priests were the clerics most directly involved in organizing anti-Protestant campaigns. Priests regarded the presence of Protestants in their parishes as signifying a failure of their personal pastoral leadership. Perhaps they had not sufficiently educated their parishioners in the doctrine of the true faith, perhaps their preaching skills were lacking, or perhaps they had not been zealous enough in their rejection of Protestant evangelization efforts. Ultimately, priests were held responsible for allowing Protestantism to thrive in their communities. Although such a mind-set may have been unfair to the clergy, as it exaggerated the control they exercised over the inhabitants of their towns, priests themselves were often the strongest proponents of such a belief. When Padre Manuel Octaviano de Moura Lima, the priest of the interior parish of Catolé do Rocha, was essentially demoted from his parish and assigned to a lesser posting, he wrote a note to his successor apologizing for his inability to eradicate the presence of the Congregationalist church that had established itself in Catolé do Rocha. "I must now leave for another parish that God has placed in my hands, and perhaps there my fight against the Protestants will be more effective," Padre Manuel wrote. "Leaving these parishioners, I pray for the triumph of my successor in directing his flock toward the true fold of our Holy Church."[27]

Just as some priests felt shame when they failed to act decisively against Protestants, others took great pride when they were able to successfully drive Protestants out of their parishes or to convince parishioners to shun them from the broader community. Priests did not downplay their role in anti-Protestant actions, even when they resulted in violence. The most striking evidence of this fact can be found in the livros de tombo which, as noted above, were akin to diaries of parish life: priests were required to write down in them all of the activities and events that took place in their parishes, as they happened. Then, when bishops would arrive to perform a pastoral visit, partly a performance evaluation of the priest and his parish, they would inspect the livro to get an idea of how the priest had been performing his duties. Priests often touted their accomplishments in the journals, writing about the activities and initiatives of which they were most proud. Campaigns against Protestantism were central components of an accomplished priest's record, and they were almost always included in a well-documented livro de tombo.[28] In the livros priests meticulously documented their anti-Protestant preaching missions, their book-burning sessions, their public rallies, and even, albeit obliquely, their violence and threats of violence. When Padre Manoel Marques, the priest of Flores, Pernambuco, was accused of physically threatening the local hotelkeeper in order to make him stop allowing Protestant preachers to stay at his establishment, the priest himself wrote in the livro de tombo that he had indeed "personally and nicely warned [the proprietor] to not continue to rent rooms to these individuals who only came to Flores to sow discord and disturb the peace."[29] And when Catholics in Cajazeiras were accused of attacking Protestants after a religious rally, prompting a police investigation of religious leaders, the local priest, Padre Fernando Gomes, did not omit or gloss over the event in the livro de tombo (as sometimes happened with other parish scandals). Instead, he described the incident in great detail, accusing the Protestants of insulting the Catholic Church and thus provoking a reaction and protest from the Catholic crowd. To Padre Fernando, the demonstration was not scandalous at all but "a time of exceptional blessings for Cajazeiras, marking yet another victory of the Church against Protestantism."[30] Priests like Padre Fernando and Padre Manoel depicted all anti-Protestant acts, even those that resulted in police inquiries and violence, as worthy endeavors capable of winning victories against Protestantism.

Livros de tombo did not contain expressions of explicit support for anti-Protestant violence. While many admitted that aggressive actions took place, most Catholic leaders contended that violence against Protestants, when it occurred, was largely the result of uncontrolled outbursts and so-called excesses of lay groups or individuals. When asked in a newspaper interview about recent accusations of violence against Protestants in Pesqueira, Bishop Lopes declared that in the face of the Protestant threat to local peace and unity, "[the people] became full of zeal and gave themselves over to hostile displays."[31] In Rio Grande do Norte Padre José Adelino Dantas attributed the aggressive persecution of Protestants to "a state of unrest that has been growing among the [Catholic] people" that made them unable to contain themselves when confronted with the insult of heresy.[32] And although priests often sought to distance themselves from the violent acts themselves, they almost never condemned them. Instead, they portrayed these excesses as virtuous expressions of religious fervor in which Catholics were displaying their decisive rejection of the Protestant faith. In Cajazeiras the conflict with Protestants was said to stem from "the piety and ardent faith of the parishioners, who cannot stand Protestant foolishness."[33]

The outbursts thus became proof of the success of the clerics' campaigns and reforms. Technically they may have been spontaneous, but priests were quick to point out that the supposedly unpremeditated actions were the result of the values that the priests themselves had instilled in the populace. Catholics who acted aggressively against Protestants were Catholics who were pious, zealous, and sufficiently knowledgeable of Catholic doctrine to not be won over by Protestant theological arguments. In short, they were good Restorationists, the faithful who rejected indifferentism and wanted to make sure Catholicism triumphed in both the private and public sphere.

Not surprisingly, then, nearly all of the priests who led the most ambitious campaigns against Protestantism, even those that resulted in violence and police inquiries, were later promoted to more prestigious ecclesiastical posts. Priests from small rural parishes were promoted to larger, more urban parishes or gained prominent ecclesiastical positions in diocesan governments. Padre José Borges do Carvalho, whom Protestants accused of spearheading "an insane battle against the [Protestant] servants of the Lord," moved from the tiny parish of Santa Luzia in the interior diocese of Cajazeiras to the more central parish of Alagoa Nova, located closer to the coast and belonging to the larger Archdiocese of Paraíba. Padre Manoel Marques, who had led an anti-Protestant campaign so aggressive that the police had opened an investigation into his activities, eventually became the head priest of the diocesan seat of Pesqueira, while Padre Joaquim de Assis Ferreira, whose parishioners had burned down a Congregational church, was later appointed to a post in the diocesan government of Cajazeiras. Some priests, like Padre Fernando Gomes, who had led the campaign against Protestants in Cajazeiras, even became bishops. After first being promoted to various highly regarded positions in the Cajazeiras diocesan government, he was named the bishop of Penedo in 1943, and later became the bishop of Aracajú and then the archbishop of Goiânia. As noted above, the famous Dom Jaime de Barros Câmara would become the archbishop and later cardinal-archbishop of Rio de Janeiro just five years after he had sent his first anti-Protestant circular in Mossoró. In fact, all of the prelates mentioned in this chapter were promoted to more prestigious posts in the years following their conflicts with Protestants.[34] The promotions were not necessarily the direct result of priests' actions against Protestants, for anti-Protestantism alone did not define a cleric as a good priest. Rather, a priest's campaign against Protestantism formed part of a broader Restorationist agenda in which the priest sought to revitalize parish culture and strengthen Catholicism's power and prestige in the local community. Anti-Protestantism was thus one aspect among many—the founding of lay religious associations, the promotion of Catholic Action, catechism reform, and so on—that designated a priest as being committed to the Restorationist cause and hence a good candidate for ecclesiastical advancement.

To Protect the Nation: Catholic Nationalism, Integralism, and Local Anti-Protestantism

When promoting local campaigns against Protestants, Catholic leaders in the Northeast developed a language of self-defense that was at once political and spiritual, combining the Restorationist rhetoric of national unity with the mystical language of purification. Priests and bishops took seriously the Restorationist vision of a united Catholic nation, and they viewed the very act of evangelization as an act of aggression. They said that inherent to Protestantism lay an attempt to sow disunity and weaken the traditional Catholic culture that formed the backbone of national and local society. "Brazil was born Catholic," declared a columnist in O Nordeste, a Catholic newspaper in Fortaleza. "The Estado Novo, through the voice of President Vargas, has shown us the merits of the nation's Catholic origins. We must defend the patrimony that is intrinsic to our civilization!"[35] Bishop Barros Câmara put the matter succinctly: "At a time when nothing should separate us, how can we allow the bonds of the Catholic faith to break—those powerful ties that bind our hearts together? . . . At a time when our nation needs the loyalty of all its children, how can we allow people to be disloyal to God and to the Religion of the Brazilian people?"[36] To bishops and priests in the Northeast, the mere presence of Protestants was an affront to local Catholics, who now were exposed to ideas that not only contradicted their Catholic faith but also criticized and belittled Catholic institutions and leaders. When Protestants came to Cajazeiras, Padre Fernando accused them of undertaking "a disrespectful and unjust propaganda campaign against the Church, the Clergy, the Christian people and the Cajazeirense family."[37] Padre Fernando did not specify the Protestant words or actions that were disrespectful to Catholicism, but he did not have to: the very fact that Protestants preached a doctrine other than that of Catholicism was enough to label their campaign as offensive and insulting, thereby legitimizing any aggressive actions taken against them.

And just as Dom Sebastião Leme and Alceu Amoroso Lima had used militaristic language to describe the necessity and mission of Catholic Action, so did northeastern Catholic leaders frame their confrontations with Protestants as battles and wars. According to Catholics, Protestants did not enter a town, they invaded, infiltrated, or penetrated it. Many Catholics argued even more forcefully that all Protestant evangelists, Brazilian and foreign alike, were antinational agents of U.S. imperialism who were willing to trade Brazilian unity and sovereignty for U.S. dollars. "Behind much of the [Protestant] propaganda there is another interest that is hidden behind the scenes," Padre Avila, a priest from Natal, declared in 1941. "It is that of the United States, which is a well-armed and imperialist state."[38] By this logic, local anti-Protestant disturbances became justified acts of self-defense against anti-Brazilian imperialist forces seeking to destroy the nation's social unity and religious heritage.

In the 1930s local northeasterners' condemnation of U.S. imperialism also informed a strident critique of liberalism that at times involved a critique of the Vargas state. For such priests as Padre Manoel Marques, the leader of the interior Pernambucan parish of Flores, the rise of "denationalizing" Protestantism was proof that the Vargas government had not sufficiently reined in the excesses of the Old Republic and was thus allowing liberalism, commercialism, and U.S. influence to invade Brazil and destroy its traditional culture. In 1933, at the height of the Constitutional Convention, Padre Manoel wrote a long anti-Protestant manifesto after having confronted Baptist evangelists who had recently founded the first Protestant congregation in his parish. He declared, "We will not accept the *Protestants*, emissaries of the Father of Lies—the Devil—and earners of dollars from the United States of North America that sent its *cashiers* with a purely commercial interest, dressed as the evangelists for a nefarious sect, which is the vehicle for discord and misery. And protected by the *Agnostic Constitution*, in which one finds the article on the *Freedom of Religion*, they insult that which our blessed Roman Catholic Apostolic Religion holds most holy and sacred, . . . and they invade our sertões, taking advantage of the sweet nature of the people in order to plant the seed that will ruin the Family, the basic cell of society."[39]

Rejection of U.S. influence and nationalistic support of the Brazilian family as the "basic cell of society" were common among local priests in the interior of the Northeast. Thus Integralism, unsurprisingly, also gained many Catholic supporters in the region. There was no direct correlation between Integralism and anti-Protestantism. The priests who were more directly involved in Integralism were not necessarily more devoted to the anti-Protestant cause, and there were certainly anti-Protestant priests who did not become involved with Integralism. However, many anti-Protestant campaigns in the northeastern interior were indeed shaped by the local Integralist presence in their parishes. Arcoverde, a Pernambucan town, had both an active Integralist movement and an intense anti-Protestant campaign.[40] Arcoverde was growing and changing rapidly in the 1920s and 1930s. Ever since the Great Western railroad had been extended to the town in 1912, making it the last stop on the line and thus a hub of commercial activity, Arcoverde had become known as a diverse, unruly frontier town. Protestants found it to be a natural center for their evangelization work in the Pernambucan interior, and by the 1930s there were Baptists, Presbyterians, and Pentecostals working in the town. The rapid social and religious changes in Arcoverde provoked a backlash among certain local elites as well as by the Catholic Church. Dismayed by the tolerance local politicians were showing the various upstarts and so-called ruffians who had flocked to the town, many of the town's conservative elites became attracted to Integralism and its firm approach to Catholic family values. From the beginning, the Catholic Church played an outsized role in the rise of Integralism in Arcoverde. The leader of the Integralist movement there, Antonio Napoleão Arcoverde, was the former mayor and a member of one of the town's most prominent families. Describing his town's Integralist "nucleus," Napoleão Arcoverde happily told his superiors that "we can count on the sympathy of the parish priest and of the Catholics of the city," and there would be a great deal of overlap between local Catholic and Integralist activists.[41] Arcoverde Integralists were extremely hostile to Protestants, whom they re-garded as one of their primary enemies in town. Integralists believed, rightly so, that the town's evangelists were opposed to their political goals and were actively working against their movement.[42] Napoleão Arcoverde called the local Protestant pastor, José Ferreira Neves, "our dangerous veiled enemy" who worked in the shadows to bring about the destruction of Integralism's ideals: Faith, Family, and Nation.[43] The local priest in Arcoverde, Padre An-tonio Faustino, felt the same way. In 1937 Padre Antonio traveled to Pesque-ira to "search for a priest who would preach in [Arcoverde] against the Protestant pastor."[44] Two priests, Antonio Vieira and Severino Jabotá, ac-companied Padre Antonio back to his town, where they "preached all night in that city, congratulated by the Catholics who filled the parish church, thereby giving a testimony of their faith. At dawn, the pastor fled [from Ar-coverde], leaving an extremely bad impression."[45] There is no evidence to suggest that Integralism played a direct role in the effort to make Protestants flee from Arcoverde. Integralism did, however, contribute to a more general climate of anti-Protestantism in small towns throughout the interior, rein-forcing the Catholic nationalist idea that these towns must be defended against the Protestant onslaught thought to be imminent. After the disband-ment of Integralism in 1937 and the entry of Brazil into World War II on the side of the Allies in 1942, much of the anti-U.S. and pro-Integralist rhetoric of Catholic priests disappeared. Yet the connections between former Inte-gralists and Catholic leaders remained, as did their conviction that Protes-tantism was a dangerous foreign attempt to undermine the unity of Brazil.

Purifying the Community: The Rites of Anti-Protestantism

Throughout the 1930s Catholic leaders advanced a narrative in which Prot-estants not only undermined the political and social unity of the nation but also jeopardized the spiritual health and salvific future of local communities. Spiritual purification was central to campaigns against Protestants in the Northeast, as Catholics were ordered to expel, purge, and reject Protestants in their midst. As Natalie Zemon Davis has pointed out in her analysis of the religious violence of Reformation-era Europe, religious conflict was often about "ridding the community of dreaded pollution."[46] Catholics in the Northeast believed that Protestants were tainted by their supposed loyalty to foreign political powers as well as by their allegiances to malicious spiritual forces that corrupted the broader social body. Northeastern Catholic leaders often referred to Protestants by means of biblical allusions with millenarian overtones. For example, Catholics frequently disparaged Protestants by calling them goats. The insult, ubiquitous in the Northeast, was used by bishops, priests, Capuchin friars, and everyday Catholics. At large Catholic gatherings and anti-Protestant demonstrations it was not unusual to hear loud chants of "Death to the goats!" emanating from the crowds.[47] Observers have given various explanations for the origin of the insult: early U.S. Protestant missionaries suggested it may have referred to the goatee of one of the first missionaries in Brazil or that it was perhaps an allusion to the beard of Uncle Sam. A closer look reveals that at least some Catholic leaders used the epithet as a biblical allusion.[48] The Parable of the Sheep and the Goats (Matthew 25:31–46, also known as the Judgment of Nations) describes the advent of the end of the world, when Jesus will return to the earth and "will sit on the throne of his glory." Then the work of Judgment will begin: "All nations will be gathered before him, and he will separate people from one another as a shepherd separates the sheep from the goats, and he will put the sheep at his right hand and the goats at the left" (Mt 25:32–33). While the sheep will be blessed by Jesus and welcomed into heaven and eternal life, the goats will suffer the opposite fate: "Then he will say to those on the left hand, 'You that are accursed, depart from me into the eternal fire prepared for the devil and his angels.'" It is easy to see why Catholics would identify Protestants with the biblical goats of Matthew: they were thought to have infiltrated and mixed in with the Catholic good sheep, and although political authorities might have refused to take severe action against them, Catholics looked forward to a millenarian future in which such spiritual imposters would be separated from the members of the True Faith. Bishop Oliveira Lopes alluded to the biblical story when he confronted the so-called Protestant assault on the Pesqueira diocese in 1931. He wrote that when he heard of the Protestants' plan to preach in his town he "convoked his armed flock and warned them of the assault being planned by the harmful wolf in sheep's clothing. There were two GOATS, who were under the direct protection of local authorities, and who wanted to plant the weeds [cizânia] of evil, immorality, and disbelief in the heart of Pesqueira."[49]

Here, in addition to the reference to goats, are two other biblical references: "wolves in sheep's clothing" and "weeds." The former refers to Matthew 7:15: "Beware of false prophets, who come to you in sheep's clothing but inwardly are ravenous wolves." And when speaking of "weeds," the bishop used a very specific word, cizânia, which translates literally into a type of ryegrass that some versions of the Bible translate as "tares." Thus the bishop was making a specific reference to the Parable of the Tares, also known as the Parable of the Weeds, in which "a man sowed good seed in his field, but while the man slept, his enemy came and sowed tares among the wheat" (Mt 13:24–25). At harvest time the man would burn the tares and put the wheat in his barn. Like the parable of the sheep and the goats, the parable of the tares was a reference to the apocalyptic judgment day: "Just as the tares are collected and burned up with fire, so will it be at the end of the age. The Son of Man will send his angels, and they will collect out of his kingdom all causes of sins and evildoers, and they will throw them into the furnace of fire, where there will be weeping and gnashing of teeth. Then the righteous will shine like the sun in the kingdom of their Father. Let anyone with ears listen!" (Mt 13:40–43).

Catholics throughout the Northeast frequently cited all three of these biblical references when referring to Protestants.[50] Taken together, they depict Protestants as evil, invasive beings who would attempt to assimilate to Catholic culture while simultaneously seeking to destroy it. To a certain extent, northeastern Catholics were precipitating the millenarian future promised in the Bible, as they took it upon themselves to purify their communities by isolating and expelling the Protestant threat. Through the actions of local Catholics the weeds would be pulled up, goats separated from the sheep, and wolves run out of town. To return to the example of the Pesqueira diocese, when the town "received an unwanted visit of eight sons of Luther," the bishop proudly declared that the local populace had "proved they did not want any creed that was not Catholic, because at night an enormous group of popular people, chanting 'Long live the Catholic Religion' and 'Death to the goats,' were able to chase the evil wolf of Protestantism far away from the sheepfold."[51] Unlike the farmer in the Parable of the Tares, Catholics would not go to sleep and allow pernicious weeds to invade their community—they would remain awake and chase the "evil wolves" away during the night. To expel Protestants was to expel all that threatened to sully and endanger the town: the "accursed" goats, the weeds that were sown by the enemy of the community, and the wolves whose "ravenous" destruction of Catholic culture was facilitated by liberal tolerance and Protestants' trickery.

In their efforts to purify their communities, northeastern Catholics frequently employed a set of common anti-Protestant actions that were used time and again in various parishes throughout the region. These "rites of purification," to use Zemon Davis's term, had both practical and symbolic significance.[52] For example, in many Catholic communities a ban on interreligious commercial activity strictly prohibited Catholics from selling to, buying from, or employing Protestants. On the one hand, the ban was a practical means by which Catholics drove Protestants from their towns and intimidated fellow Catholics who might feel compelled to come to Protestants' aid. Protestant accounts were full of stories of believers who, having been denied the ability to sustain themselves and their family, were forced to leave town in order to seek work elsewhere. In Ipojuca, Pernambuco, Baptist Silvestre Ferreira had to leave his family after he lost his job and experienced "tremendous persecution because of [his belief in] the Gospel." Unable to find work in his hometown he "ultimately had to leave his home in search of material and moral sustenance, leaving his wife and two small children in the care of fellow Baptists."[53] Catholic business owners who employed, tolerated, or promoted Protestants and their work similarly saw their finances suffer. The town of Guarabira organized a boycott of a local barbershop in which Protestants had been allowed to hold a public meeting. The local Catholic paper warned the barber what would happen if he continued to host Protestants: "Open your eyes, Mr. Owner. Guarabira will not tolerate these spectacles. You will lose your clientele if you continue with such abuses. You must be careful with these wise guys, these emissaries of Satan, slaves of the dollar, these nonentities with their forbidden fruit of knowledge."[54]

Yet the ban on commerce with Protestants was also heavily laden with religious meaning, as it promoted the idea that any contact with Protestants, however perfunctory, would contaminate both the individual and the community. From Flores came the story of a Baptist who "was a brick-maker, but the priest prohibited him from working in the brickyard, saying that the ground belonged to Our Lady and therefore a Protestant could not work there as he would contaminate the place."[55] Catholics were not even allowed to sell basic goods and necessities to their Protestant neighbors for fear the money they gained from such transactions would be tainted. Such prohibitions created situations of desperation for many Protestant families, who could not obtain food or water. Local Catholics "kicked Protestants out of the houses they were renting, merchants refused to sell foodstuffs, evangelical merchants could not sell anything, and Protestants couldn't even get water out of fountains," a Baptist newspaper reported.[56] In Cajazeiras a family became desperate when no one would sell them milk to feed their child, eventually having to resort to asking the local chief of police to help them secure it.[57] The priest in Cuité, Padre Luiz Santiago, reportedly told his parishioners to "deny bread and water" to Protestants. One Pentecostal man even spoke about the priest berating a parishioner who gave him a mere "cup of water" when he was thirsty.[58]

To Catholics in the Northeast, the denial of sustenance to Protestants took on a mystical meaning as it was incorporated into religious rituals of penance and purification. The santas missões of the Capuchin friar Damião de Bozzano often included moments in which local Catholics publicly swore to abstain from having commercial contact with Protestants.[59] In Esperança a Catholic described the scene as follows:

> On the last night [of the santa missão], at the end of the sermon, there was a blessing of the candles, rosaries, medals, etc., very similar to a papal blessing. Frei Damião, animated in front of a crowd of fifteen thousand members of the faithful, explained to them the practical method by which to combat Protestants, inciting them, through a solemn oath to the Most Holy Virgin, who is Protestants' most bitter enemy, to cease any and all commercial

transactions with these people. The crowd, satisfied and firm in their decision, promised the eminent Virgin that they would flee from all commercial contact with the followers of the Devil. A thousand thanks to God.[60]

As in all santas missões the crowd then took part in the sacrament of confession, repenting for their past sins, including that of tolerating Protestantism. The oath against commercial contact with Protestants, which, since Catholics were already barred from socializing with Protestants, effectively warded against any type of interreligious contact, was thus an oath to remove Protestants from all aspects of community life and thereby remove them from the community itself. The santa missão would purify the local spiritual community through the sacrament of confession, but in order to stay in this state of grace the community would need to eliminate all contaminating contact with the "followers of the Devil." By thus expelling Protestants from communal life, local Catholics believed they were protecting their community from damnation.

This damnation was not exclusively spiritual. Religious leaders often insinuated that the evil presence of Protestantism could have negative worldly consequences for nordestinos. This danger was particularly true in the 1930s, when drought and disease plagued the region. In Pesqueira the bishop held a penitential procession in which thousands of Catholics took to the streets to "implore God to have mercy and to relieve the suffering caused by the drought that is wracking the sertão and the invasion of the Protestant heresy among us."[61] Protestantism itself was frequently called a plague or a virus, and so when a real virus, malaria, tore through the sertão in the late thirties and early forties, Catholics associated Protestants with it. In Rio Grande do Norte a Catholic bitterly wrote about the "Protestant heresy" that, "like a plague, preceded the malaria" that had sickened and killed so many members of the community.[62] During penitential processions in which Catholics sought divine intercession against the scourge of the virus, participants sang songs featuring Protestants. In Alagoas Catholics reportedly sang a song asking for the help of Saint Sebastian, the patron saint of plagues.[63] They implored him to deliver them from malaria and Protestantism, which they saw as being equally harmful and inextricably intertwined:

Meu glorioso Sebastião	My glorious Sebastian
Meu Santo que podés	My Saint, you who have the power
Livrai-me da peste	Deliver me from the plague
E dos malditos bódes	And from the damned goats [Protestants]
Si o meu sangue tivesse	If my blood had
O novo batismo	The new baptism
Livrai-me da peste	Deliver me from the plague
E do protestantismo	And from Protestantism
(Côro)	(Chorus)
Oh! Mártir de Cristo	Oh! Martyr of Christ
Tem de mim compaixão	Take pity on me
Livrai-me dos "bodes"	Deliver me from the "goats"
São Sebastião.[64]	Saint Sebastian.

In the Northeast Protestantism became wholly pathologized, transformed into a potent virus or plague that contaminated those who came in contact with it and brought about actual physical disease and natural disaster. To purify, then, was also to sanitize, for the spiritual health of the community would determine the physical health of its members.

In their effort to purify their communities Catholics also targeted Protestant churches. Throughout the twenties, thirties, and forties Catholics vandalized, burned down, and even tore down, brick by brick, numerous Protestant churches in the northeastern interior.[65] Like the commercial boycotts, the destruction of churches had both practical and symbolic meaning for Catholics and Protestants alike. On a practical level churches allowed Protestants to have security, safety, and longevity. They would no longer have to crowd into a believer's home for services each week or rely on the goodwill of local business owners in order to rent space for an event. As noted above, Catholic leaders often waged aggressive campaigns to discourage residents from renting space to Protestants, even hotel rooms.[66] Moreover, churches allowed Protestants to consolidate disparate communities that may have been meeting in different homes throughout a region and therefore mount a more effective evangelization campaign. As Protestants in Salgado de São Felix (PB) argued, owning their own space allowed them to "centralize and definitively establish evangelical work in Salgado, bringing together all the believers from the surrounding area and creating a strategic point from which to conquer souls in the region."[67] With the construction of their own temple Protestants could realize their practical aspirations: a more aggressive evangelization campaign, greater administrative capacity, more social service initiatives, and larger, more elaborate religious services.

But beyond the practical advantages it conferred, the presence of a new Protestant church was also deeply symbolic in that it represented a Protestant denomination's permanent establishment in a town. It was public proof that Protestants had become successful members of the community. To Protestants, it often quite literally marked their transformation from dependent congregation to a self-supporting church, which entailed a new administrative status. When a congregation became economically self-sufficient, highly organized, able to support outside evangelization efforts, and able to host its own pastor, then it could gain the status of a self-supporting church, and a physical church building was an indispensable step in this process. In the 1920s and 1930s Brazilian Protestants placed great importance on church building, working hard to ensure that each congregation constructed its own church as quickly as possible. The Pernambucan Presbytery even created a special loan program, the Presbyterian Building Fund, specifically for the purpose of promoting the construction of Presbyterian temples throughout the northeastern interior.[68] As the number of churches in the Northeast grew, so too did the public presence of Protestantism.

To northeastern Catholics, a Protestant temple was a concrete manifestation of evangelical growth in the region. And while Catholic leaders did not necessarily understand the administrative nuances that accompanied the rise of self-supporting churches, they did know that the appearance of physical church structures represented the official establishment of Protestantism in their parish and, consequently, their own failure to protect their parishioners from Protestant infiltration. For this reason priests did all in their power to prohibit Protestants from building temples. In Caruaru, Pernambuco, the local priest reportedly convinced a business owner to reject Protestants' offer to buy a building for their church and instead sell it to a Catholic resident for less money.[69] A priest in Agua Preta went to court to try to block the construction of a Presbyterian church in his town, claiming the parish owned the land on which the Protestants wanted to build.[70] In Recife members of the Marian Congregation petitioned the government to suppress the establishment of a Protestant church because its position across the street from the neighborhood Catholic church was deemed an affront to local Catholic residents.[71]

Catholics eventually took a page from the Protestant playbook and embarked on their own chapel-building campaigns, which were explicitly aimed at combating the Protestant presence in outlying parish neighborhoods. The construction of Catholic chapels, like that of their Protestant counterparts, was full of symbolic meaning. In Cajazeiras, after Catholics had succeeded in expelling two Protestant pastors from the community, Padre Fernando Gomes, the local parish priest, constructed a "victory chapel" in the very place where the anti-Protestant campaign had taken place. To Padre Fernando, the construction of the chapel was meant to definitively mark the end of the successful anti-Protestant initiative and to demonstrate to the critics of the Catholic Church, including the civil authorities who had attempted, unsuccessfully, to punish Catholic leaders for their role in violence against Protestants, that the Catholic Church was the true spiritual and political authority in the region. In the parish livro de tombo Padre Fernando wrote:

> As a sign of the victory we won over Protestantism, which had tried to establish its lair in our parish, we decided to build a Chapel in honor of Saint Anthony, in the neighborhood of the same name. The reason for choosing Saint Anthony is that this neighborhood had been the place most persecuted by the [Protestant] heresy: it was there that, in spite of the firmness of the faith of its courageous inhabitants, the first Protestants established themselves, and it was from there that the last Protestants left. And so it was that on the second of August, the ninth Sunday after Pentecost, we performed a solemn ceremony to bless the laying of the first stone of the future chapel.[72]

Yet while their triumphant symbolism was reminiscent of past Catholic victories over indigenous religions in the Americas, chapel-building projects in the Northeast more aptly illustrated a core weakness of northeastern Catholicism: its neglect of the outlying and marginalized sections of rural parishes. Parishes in the northeastern interior normally covered vast expanses of geography, making it impossible for all parishioners to travel regularly to the *matriz*, or central church, to attend weekly or daily Mass. Ideally these communities would have their own chapels where priests would conduct religious services. In reality many priests largely ignored these hard-to-reach communities, preferring to remain in the town center and interact with the more elite members of local society. Unsurprisingly, Protestantism thrived in these outlying districts. In this way, the construction of victory chapels was not so much a sign of the Catholic Church's defeat of Protestantism as a defensive strategy aimed at protecting communities made vulnerable to Protestant advances by the church's previous neglect.

The defensive nature of chapel building was evident in Campina Grande, Paraíba, which spearheaded one of the most sustained and ambitious chapel-building projects of the 1930s. Protestantism had come to Campina Grande in the form of the Congregational Church, which was established there in 1920. Over the next decade Protestantism in Campina Grande grew rapidly. By 1930 the Congregationalists had built two churches, and they were no longer the only denomination in town — Presbyterians, Pentecostals, and two Baptist, one Radical, the other missionary, congregations had joined their ranks. The 1930s would see a small Protestant building boom, as these three new groups all built their respective churches. To Campina Grande's incoming parish priest, Padre José de Medeiros Delgado, the growth of Protestantism was deeply disturbing. Padre José was one of the most important priests in Campina Grande's history, leading the parish for a decade, from 1931 to 1941. During that time he became intensely devoted to the construction of rural chapels, and at the end of his tenure this would be the project of which he was most proud. Recalling his arrival in the parish in 1931, he wrote, "One of the most distressing elements about the Campina Grande parish was its abandonment of its rural population. All of the essential religious services were concentrated in the central church," which led to a great "religious ignorance" among the "abandoned" parishioners. Constructing more chapels and extending services to previously ignored regions would not only give more souls access to religious knowledge and salvation-giving sacraments but also contribute to "the defense of the Catholic population against the Protestant infiltration of the evangelical sect in those areas."[73]

One of Padre José's first acts as priest of Campina Grande was to finish the construction of a chapel that had languished, half-finished, for more than thirty-one years in a rural *sítio* called Marinho, which had become a Protestant stronghold during the 1920s. "That poor land has been besieged by Protestant heresy," Padre José wrote, "and it is [my] intention to finish the above-mentioned chapel in order to more easily return the people to the true fold of the Lord."[74] Finishing the Marinho chapel was a way to provide the religious services necessary to draw Catholics back to the church as well as to send a message that residents would no longer be ignored by their religious leaders. Soon after the Marinho chapel was finished Padre José built a chapel in Jacú, another rural area where Protestantism had grown.[75] In his first seven years as priest of Campina Grande Padre José would oversee the building of at least nine new chapels, an almost shockingly high number for a parish in the interior of Paraíba.[76]

Chapels alone did not ensure that Catholics would be inoculated against the so-called Protestant virus. Priests themselves needed to make an effort to visit the outlying communities and remind them of their duty to expel Protestants from their midst. For this reason priests adopted a powerful anti-Protestant rite: the preaching tour, sometimes called a preaching mission. When Protestants threatened to gain a foothold in an outlying region of a parish, Catholic leaders would employ a shock and awe strategy in which they would flood the area, creating a sustained presence for a few days, weeks, or even months. They would preach anti-Protestant sermons, hold public burnings of Protestant books and leaflets, and warn wayward individuals of the spiritual and secular dangers of remaining indifferent to the Protestant threat. During the 1920s, 1930s, and 1940s the anti-Protestant preaching tour became a popular tool of bishops and priests throughout the Northeast. In Cajazeiras Padre Fernando went on a preaching tour of no fewer than four peripheral neighborhoods in an effort to "curb the destructive Protestant propaganda be- ing spread in the parish."[77] In Cuité Padre Luiz Santiago would often make special trips to small chapels in far-flung areas of his Paraíban parish, famously telling worshippers that "it is not a crime to kill a Protestant."[78] And, as one would expect, Padre José de Medeiros Delgado considered preaching tours part of his mandatory pastoral responsibilities in Campina Grande because he felt the need to "defend the simple and good people" from predatory evange- lists.[79] Ultimately, these tours were more about creating a spectacle than instill- ing parishioners with long-lasting lessons on Catholic doctrine and catechism. Above all, they were a show of Catholic numbers and strength, reinforcing common rituals and discourses of anti-Protestant activism.

Throughout the early twentieth century it was common for local Catholic rituals to be transformed into anti-Protestant demonstrations. Longtime tra- ditions and annual processions that did not originally have an anti-Protestant intent became opportunities to convey a community's rejection of Protes- tantism and rally its residents to fight back against the "evil sect." As noted earlier, penitential processions asking for the intercession of God against the drought could be transformed into demonstrations of the need to purify the community of the Protestant plague that was deemed responsible for the crisis. Processions honoring key Catholic doctrines could also become mo- ments in which to aggressively defend these beliefs against Protestant criticisms. In Mossoró a Eucharistic procession became an opportunity for the doctrine of the Real Presence to be defended, as the population took its "revenge against the insults that Our Lord has received from the Protestant heretics."[80] Processions in honor of the Virgin Mary were loaded with anti- Protestant meaning in that they reminded parishioners of Protestants' pur- ported lack of respect and veneration for the Holy Mother. When the local priest in Areia Branca wanted to combat Protestantism he held a public pro- cession to transport the image of Our Lady of the Conception, the parish's patron saint, from the rectory to the public square, where he blessed it and then "gave a speech about the cult of the saints and especially about the Vir- gin Mary."[81] Since Protestants did not believe in the Immaculate Concep- tion the procession served as an ideal moment in which to combine veneration for the patron saint of the town with rejection of its Protestant population. A similar event occurred when two Baptist pastors came to preach in Jaguaquara. In their report they wrote of the ritual of rejection that greeted them on their arrival:

> Our reception was startling. The priest of the city had staged a big procession to come along just as we arrived. A highly adorned image of the Virgin and Child was borne along the shoulders of devotees, preceded by a brass band and followed by marching Catholic religious associations and then the men, and then preceded by long lines of children, girls, and women, all silently winding their way along the other side of the rectangular square, down one side of which our train crept in, parallel to the procession. It was a well-timed demonstration of the Catholic force and devotion of the population.[82]

At the height of conflicts between Catholics and Protestants in Pesqueira, a procession in honor of the local patron saint, Our Lady of the Mountains, was described with great detail:

> Today, here in the diocesan seat, a great Catholic rally took place in front of the Cathedral. Brought to preside over this rally, among cries of happiness and enthusiasm, was the venerated image of Our Lady of the Mountains, the patron saint of Cimbres [a neighborhood of Pesqueira]. Some 5,000 people were present at and took part in this event, whose objective was to avow, in a public and extraordinary manner, our faith, and also to demonstrate how great is our faith in the Mother of God and all of us, Most Holy Mary. We hope that once and for all She crushes the head of the infernal dragon, communism, and also, as the "terror of all heresies," she does not permit the evil weed of Protestantism to take root in Pesqueira.[83]

Such processions were neither inherently nor explicitly violent, but their emphasis on the militant rejection of Protestantism meant they were frequently the sites of aggressive, sometimes physical, religious confrontations.

When Protestants came to Alagoinha the local priest raised a "cry of alarm to warn his sheep of the imminent danger [Protestantism] posed to local religious life." He then organized a procession in which large crowds marched through the streets "praying the Rosary of the Virgin and preaching the sacred truths of Religion in the public square, against the errors of the Protestant heresy."[84] To Catholics, the procession represented a triumphant display of their strength. Protestants, however, portrayed the procession in a more violent light, reporting that the event ended with groups of Catholics stoning Protestants and invading the homes in which they were celebrating their religious services. And while Catholics denounced the allegations as "defamations and lies . . . by those who were terrorized by the splendor and victory of the Catholic Cause," the incidents were sufficiently disconcerting that Protestants asked for police protection during the next public Catholic event in Alagoinha.[85] Similar occurrences took place throughout the Northeast. In Cajazeiras Protestants reported multiple assaults during the "imposing processions of the faithful that the local priest has organized for the city," and in Areia Branca the local Pentecostal leader told a harrowing story of hearing a procession passing outside his small home and emerging to find "a group of men, women, and children, around 200 people, who attacked the humble hovel, like voracious wolves."[86] According to the account, they threw stones at the pastor, pushed into his home and ransacked it, tearing apart furniture and destroying religious texts. After hiding in the home of a friend, the evangelist was escorted out of town by a rather unhelpful police sergeant who did little to prevent Catholics from hitting him, throwing stones at him, and threatening his life during his journey out of town. Eventually the Pentecostal leader made it to a boat and sailed for Natal, leaving Areia Branca for good.[87]

Similar acts of aggression occurred during a wide array of anti-Protestant rites, as physical conflicts were frequently preceded by church burnings, anticommercial oaths, preaching tours, and *romarias* (religious pilgrimages). The very nature of these rites made them privileged sites of conflict, as their emphasis on purifying the community implied an urgent need to rid one's surroundings of the Protestant contaminant. In this way, participants in the rites transformed their acts of aggression into acts of self-defense, thereby becoming noble protectors of the sanctity of their families, their communities, the Virgin Mary, the communion of saints, and the Real Presence of Jesus Christ himself. As Padre José Adelino, a priest in Natal, wrote,

> It would be incredible, so incredible, to deny people being assaulted the right to defend themselves. [Protestants] want to extort, rob, tear up, and annihilate forever the treasure of the centuries-old faith, the Catholic faith, planted in the soul of our people through sacrifice, catechism, and martyrdom, during four and a half centuries of History. And when people think that this precious treasure is being violated with impunity by opportunistic outsiders from other lands, paid (and well-paid at that) with the gold from distant coffers, is it not understandable that they would be unable to contain themselves?[88]

Padre José thought the defense of the "precious treasure" of Catholicism justified the so-called excesses committed against Protestants, who by their own admission were committing the spiritual crime of "robbing and annihilating" the salvific religious traditions of Brazilians. Padre José, like almost all of his fellow Catholic prelates, did not openly advocate that his parishioners utilize violence or physical aggression to achieve the goal of protecting their communities from Protestant invasion. Yet, taken to its logical conclusion, Catholic leaders' discourse of spiritual purification, supported by their promotion of anti-Protestant rituals and rites, would seem to necessitate the use of force. How would Catholics purify their communities if not via the violent expulsion of their Protestant inhabitants? Leaders' support of the perpetrators of persecution after the fact seemed to confirm the notion that violent acts were, indeed, the intended outcome of the processions, oath ceremonies, preaching tours, and other rites.

Crime without Punishment

To Protestants, one of the greatest indignities of Catholic campaigns against them was the impunity their perpetrators enjoyed. Few people were ever punished for attacks on Protestants, and priests and bishops were often rewarded for their zeal, which formed an integral part of the Restorationist definition of a good priest. Civil authorities occasionally made tentative, halfhearted attempts to rein in aggressive anti-Protestant campaigns, but more often than not police action ended up aiding rather than hindering the anti-Protestant cause. Priests and bishops used police investigations as opportunities to express their disgust with local authorities deemed overly tolerant of Protestants, and they were able to publicize and rally even more support for their anti-Protestant cause. The persecutors became the perse-cuted, as priests cast themselves as victims of Protestant machinations that were, yet again, conspiring to destroy the foundation of Catholic culture in Brazil. In Flores Padre Manoel interpreted a police request to interview him as a terrible offense to his status as a priest. "In a Catholic country, where 96 percent of its population is born under the shadow of the Cross . . . [and] in a city that is almost completely Catholic," he wrote, referring to himself in the third person, "the Priest of Flores, Padre Manoel Marques, was *rudely* ordered, by a simple soldier of the Police, to appear at the municipal police station." He went on to compare his plight to that of Jesus Christ, writing, "I must remind myself that Our Lord also appeared before tribunals," and he vowed to continue his fight against Protestantism.[89] When Bishop Oliveira Lopes was investigated for his anti-Protestant campaign, all of the priests in his diocese signed an open letter in which they offered their "applause to [the bishop's] exemplary conduct in the heroic defense of the sacred Patri-mony of the Catholic Faith."[90] When the chief of police in Cajazeiras had the temerity to open an investigation into the anti-Protestant violence sur-rounding the mission of Frei Damião, Catholics were ultimately able to get the chief fired from his job, and Padre Fernando wrote of being overjoyed that "in this fight we have had the support of the Catholic population."[91] And, as discussed above, the case opened against Padre Verberck in Nísia Floresta prompted shows of support for his anti-Protestant cause by fellow priests, bishops, and Catholic intellectuals. None of these priests or bishops were ever brought to trial or punished in any way for the part they played in anti-Protestant violence.

Police inquiries often led priests and bishops to make strategic retreats from their parishes or dioceses—Padre Verberck went to the neighboring town of São José de Mipibú to seek the support of his fellow priests, Padre Manoel went on a vacation in order to "calm his nerves," and Dom Oliveira Lopes received a propitiously timed invitation to travel to Rio de Janeiro — but in absenting themselves they encouraged even greater celebrations of anti-Protestant zeal when they returned, victorious, to their parish or diocese, having suffered no legal consequences. These victory celebrations themselves became a sort of anti-Protestant rite in which Catholics processed through the streets waving images of the Virgin Mary, shouting, "Long live the Catholic Faith!" and "Death to the goats!," making impassioned anti-Protestant speeches, and setting off fireworks. Ultimately, civil interventions in religious affairs merely displayed religion's triumph over the law. Yet there were exceptions to this rule. In certain rare cases Catholics and even Catholic priests were punished by both civil and ecclesiastical authorities for crimes they committed against Protestants. Protestants were able to get their persecutors punished in these cases, but they were unable to do so in so many others.

FOUR

Punishing the Fanatics

Protestants, the Tribunal de Segurança Nacional, and the Prosecution of Nordestino Catholics

In the middle of the night of May 31, 1939, in the town of Brejo dos Cavalos José Alves da Silva's wife roused him from bed with an urgent message: Catholics had gathered outside the Congregational church and were shooting guns in the air and attempting to tear down the building. Brejo dos Cavalos was in the Paraíban municipality of Catolé do Rocha, which had been wracked by religious conflict for over a year. Churches had been toppled, Protestants had been assaulted, and the Congregational pastor had been forced to flee the area. José, a sixty-six-year-old farmer and member of the Congregational church, knew that attacks on Protestant churches frequently morphed into attacks on Protestant persons, and his first thought was of his adult children, who lived next to the Brejo dos Cavalos temple. Fearing they might become targets of Catholic violence, José immediately ran out of his house and headed in the direction of the commotion. When he arrived he found a chaotic, dangerous scene: fifty to sixty men armed with pickaxes, hoes, hatchets, crowbars, and shotguns were attacking the temple both inside and outside, apparently intent on tearing the entire structure down. While most of the group members were occupied with the tasks of breaking down the walls and ripping off roof tiles, others seemed more interested in firing their guns in the air and shouting anti-Protestant slogans, creating an atmosphere of raucous intimidation. Before José knew what was happening, one of the men recognized him as a Protestant and grabbed him, throwing him down to the ground. More men came and began to beat José with a blunt instrument (perhaps one of the crowbars or hoes), bruising his face and arms. At some point he was able to escape and ran into the brush, where he spent a long, fearful night together with other Protestants who had fled their homes when they heard what was taking place. Later, when questioned by the police, José was unable to identify his attackers, as it was too dark, he said, and everything had happened too quickly. His son, Amadeu, however, was certain the attack was led by a number of prominent Catolense Catholics who had "spen[t] their lives threatening [Protestants] and planning all sorts of intrigues."[1]

One year later, a little over two hundred kilometers to the east of Catolé do Rocha, thirteen men walked along a lonely dirt road. They had just attended a Pentecostal prayer service and were returning to their homes in the small town of Cuité. Suddenly the sound of gunshots rang out through the growing darkness. Shouts of panic and desperation filled the air as the men scattered and ran, not knowing where the bullets came from or who was being targeted. Most were able to dart out of harm's way, but thirty-year-old Severino Amaro, who had been walking a few paces behind his coreligionists, could not escape. Shot in the back, he fell to the ground. His friend Apolinario Gomes da Silva knelt at his side, attempting in vain to staunch the flow of blood. As the bullets continued to fly, Apolinario ran for cover. Severino died soon thereafter, alone on the deserted road. His body remained there until the next day, when the surviving witnesses brought the police and medical examiners to the scene. When investigators asked Amaro's friends and family who they believed committed the crime, they did not hesitate to answer: Catholics and, specifically, the Cuitense parish priest, Padre Luiz Santiago.[2]

The attacks on Protestants in Catolé do Rocha and Cuité were not all that noteworthy or unique, given the high number of aggressive campaigns against Protestantism occurring in the Northeast at that time. But there was one factor that both connected the two episodes and made them different from nearly every other instance of anti-Protestant violence that took place during first half of the twentieth century: in these cases Protestants were able to ensure that the alleged perpetrators were arrested, prosecuted, and ultimately convicted of their crimes. Moreover, the assailants were convicted not by local or state courts but by the Tribunal de Segurança Nacional (TSN), a special judicial body created by Getúlio Vargas's Estado

Novo to prosecute crimes that threatened the national security of Brazil. How, then, did these two episodes of local religious persecution in the rural interior of Paraíba gain the attention of federal authorities, and why did those authorities deem the anti-Protestant actions to be national security threats? A combination of two elements made the TSN prosecution of violence against Protestants possible: Protestant leaders' ability to make strategic alliances with local authorities during times of political upheaval in Paraíba; and the Vargas government's crackdown on the perceived religious fanaticism of northeastern religious movements that were thought to challenge the state's monopoly on violence. Although anti-Protestantism was not the primary target of Vargas's antifanaticism campaign, when Protestant leaders and their political allies were able to bring cases like those in Catolé do Rocha and Cuité to the attention of federal authorities, highlighting the cases' fanatical nature, the TSN took action.

While it is tempting to celebrate the TSN cases as rare instances in which Protestants were able to hold perpetrators of religious violence accountable for their actions, a close examination makes it difficult to interpret either the process or outcome of the cases as representing a triumph of justice, the rule of law, or religious freedom in Brazil. In prosecuting the supposed excesses of northeastern Catholics, the Vargas government was motivated not by the desire to protect the rights of Protestant Brazilians but by the need to assert control over unauthorized and uncontrolled expressions of northeastern religiosity. In the eyes of state and national elites the religious violence in Catolé do Rocha and Cuité revealed the potentially explosive nature of the insidious, ever-present religious fanaticism that supposedly pervaded the northeastern sertão, which both the Vargas regime and the Restorationist Catholic Church believed fomented political and social unrest. At a time when popular millenarian movements were on the rise in the Northeast, Brazilian authorities were extremely wary of any religious actors who seemed to promote unruly and unorthodox expressions of the Catholic faith. The TSN prosecutions demonstrate how both church and state attempted to draw a line between illegitimate and legitimate anti-Protestant violence that was based less on the nature and severity of the violence than on the perceived worthiness of the persons perpetrating it.

Nowhere was the line between illegitimate and legitimate anti-Protestant violence more evident than in the cases of the parish priests of Catolé do Rocha and Cuité, Padre Joaquim Assis de Ferreira and Padre Luiz Santiago, respectively. At first glance the priests seemed to be cut from the same cloth: both were zealous Restorationist reformers, both were Paraíban native sons who became priests in parishes near their hometowns, and both planned and executed intense campaigns against Protestants that resulted in violence and were condemned by TSN judges. Yet whereas Protestants argued that both were examples of Catholic fanaticism, government and Catholic Church leaders believed the two priests represented very distinct manifestations of priestly power. At the same time Padre Joaquim came to be viewed as an obedient, hardworking defender of the True Faith, Padre Luiz was regarded as a backward, hotheaded religious rogue. And although both of their anti-Protestant campaigns were prosecuted by the TSN, only Padre Luiz was named as a defendant and accused of directly causing violence. Padre Joaquim was not only spared prosecution but also received praise and promotions in the wake of the judicial indictments in Catolé do Rocha. Padre Luiz, on the other hand, was expelled from the priesthood, labeled a dangerous religious fanatic, and compelled to retreat to his rural fazenda and live the rest of his life as an outcast of the institutional Catholic Church.

The TSN cases also highlight the contradictions and dangers inherent in Protestant efforts to protect themselves from Catholic persecution. Protestants were able to bring perpetrators of violence to justice not by appealing to the constitutionally protected freedom of religion but by capitalizing on tensions and weaknesses in the Catholic nationalist project itself. In addition to forming alliances with local political enemies of Catholic clerics, Protestants exploited elites' prejudices toward the religious culture of the Northeast, which was considered to be inherently fanatical, millenarian, and prone to violence. At a time when the Catholic Church was attempting to modernize its practices and personnel, priests like Padre Luiz, who blurred the line between modern and backward, posed a threat to Restorationist orthodoxy. Although state and ecclesiastical authorities alike had a continued interest in promoting Catholic hegemony, their definition of Catholicism was a narrow one that excluded expressions of Catholic religiosity considered unorthodox and, in the case of the Brazilian Northeast, fanatical. Protestants understood this nuance and used it to their advantage. In their efforts to gain the rights and protections that they, as Brazilian citizens, demanded and deserved, Protestants fanned the flames of religious intolerance, repeating Restorationist Catholics' own criticisms of the religion of northeastern "fanatical mobs" and sertanejan "ignorant masses." In the end Protestantism's fight to eradicate religious fanaticism aided the Catholic Restoration's campaign against religious heterodoxy, thereby weakening Protestants' own position in the northeastern interior.

And yet, because local authorities and justice systems had utterly failed to provide Protestants with any protection or recourse, the cases of Catolé do Rocha and Cuité make clear that Protestant leaders had little choice but to appeal to the TSN by arguing that Catholics represented national security threats. It is often difficult for historians to investigate absences, as there are rarely records of police investigations not undertaken, persons not interviewed, or punishments not imposed. TSN cases, however, contain a notable amount of detail about just such holes in the evidentiary record. The case documents from Catolé do Rocha and Cuité are full of instances in which federal authorities express their frustration and anger at how local officials had mishandled, overlooked, not investigated, or simply claimed to have lost crucial evidence relating to crimes committed against Protestants, and they make clear that had these crimes not been brought to the attention of the TSN they never would have been prosecuted. The cases thus provide rare insight into how Protestants normally experienced the Brazilian justice system, proving that accountability for religious persecution of Protestants was the exception, not the rule.

Protestant Growth and Catholic Restorationism in Catolé do Rocha and Cuité

Religious conflict came to Catolé do Rocha and Cuité as Protestant growth collided with Catholic Restorationism in both towns. In the late 1920s the British missionary Harry G. Briault began to travel throughout the far interior of Paraíba, preaching and founding Congregationalist communities across the sertão. Reverend Briault was affiliated with the Evangelical Union of South America (EUSA), an interdenominational missionary society based in Great Britain. He and his wife, Frieda Winifred Briault, had arrived in Brazil in 1921 and immediately gone to the Northeast, originally settling in Recife, Pernambuco.[3] Soon thereafter they were sent to the "untapped" field of Paraíba, where they made Campina Grande their missionary base. The Briaults were ardent, committed evangelizers and church builders, and it was not long before they founded a church in Catolé do Rocha. The exact date the Briaults arrived in Catolé do Rocha is unknown, but records indicate they founded a congregation in the nearby town of Patos in 1928. Presumably they appeared in Catolé do Rocha around the same time since the congregations were both geographically and administratively connected. The Catolé do Rocha congregation grew rapidly, and by 1934 its leaders were sending their own evangelizers to the more isolated areas of the municipality, distributing Bibles, preaching sermons, and organizing small satellite congregations.[4] By 1935 the Catolense church was led by a Brazilian pastor, Rev. Josué Alves, rather than a EUSA missionary. Reverend Alves was a rising star in the Congregational church and the first Brazilian pastor appointed to lead the congregation. He was determined to convert Catolé do Rocha into a center of evangelical activity in the Northeast. In his first month as Catolé's pastor Reverend Alves founded new lay organizations such as the Women's Society and worked to expand the number of deacons who were serving both the main church in Catolé and the smaller surrounding congregations.[5] Reverend Alves's pastorate was so successful that he was soon asked to lead the Congregational church's Biblical Institute in nearby Patos, and his replacement, Rev. Lindonio de Almeida, proved to be no less zealous in his efforts to strengthen and expand Protestantism in Catolé. Reverend Almeida was a native son of Catolé do Rocha, and his ordination was living proof of the strength of the Catolense Congregational church. As pastor, Almeida imposed strict discipline on church members, ensuring that they refrained from smoking, drinking, working on Sunday, and marrying Catholics.[6] By 1938 Protestants were a visible, dynamic presence in Catolé do Rocha, having built no fewer than three new temples in the area.

The Congregationalists were the first Protestants to arrive in Catolé do Rocha, but they were not the only Protestants there, as by the mid-1930s a fledgling Pentecostal Assembléia de Deus congregation had established its presence in the sertanejan town. There are few extant records of early Catolense Pentecostals, but it is possible that, like many Pentecostal churches in the 1920s and 1930s, the first Pentecostal congregation in Catolé do Rocha was formed by disaffected Congregationalists who were either expelled from or voluntarily left the Congregational church as a result of believing in certain Pentecostal precepts like Spirit baptism. Congregational records indicate that in 1934 a man named Manoel Vieira Lima went before the Congregational church's leadership to "present Pentecostal ideas," perhaps with the intent of bringing the church into the Pentecostal fold. Congregational leaders were not impressed with the presentation and immediately suspended Lima and later expelled him from church membership.[7] The next two decades would see the two denominations clashing frequently as they competed for adherents, oftentimes drawing converts from each other's congregations.[8] The competition would push both churches to heighten their efforts to draw new members, resulting in an uptick in the public Protestant presence in the town.

Cuité's introduction to Protestantism was remarkably similar to that of Catolé do Rocha: a fledgling movement that began in the late 1920s strengthened and revitalized itself in the mid-1930s. In the case of Cuité it was the Pentecostal Assembléia de Deus that led the way. During its early years in Cuité the AD struggled to attract and keep members, and more than once the new religion found itself on the edge of extinction. This would change with the arrival of a Pentecostal man named José Ferreira da Silva.[9] When Silva came to Cuité in 1935 he encountered a discouraging situation: the Pentecostal congregation was demoralized and stagnant, having largely given up on expanding its evangelization efforts after it encountered the "indifference and cruelty of the people, who, led by the town priest, had set in motion a campaign of persecution" against them.[10] At first Silva did not want to lead the congregation, and he "refused to talk of celestial things," but he later felt that the "Lord demanded that [he] speak," so he began to preach.[11] The leadership of Silva revitalized the downtrodden congregation, and its members began to evangelize with more vigor and passion than ever before. The church soon was gaining new adherents at a rapid pace, and in just five years its membership had grown from "a few believers" to over eighty-two individuals.[12] With these new members came more funds and greater prominence in Cuitense society. Pentecostals were still a minor and marginalized presence in the regional community, but it was clear that they were taking major steps toward establishing themselves as legitimate actors in the local religious scene.

At the same time that Protestants were growing in strength and vitality in Catolé do Rocha and Cuité, Catholic Restorationists were transforming the way their coreligionists experienced their faith. Both Padre Joaquim, the priest of Catolé do Rocha, and Padre Luiz, the priest of Cuité, had been trained at the Romanized archdiocesan seminary in the capital city of Paraíba, João Pessoa, and they were committed to enacting Restorationist reform projects in their parishes.[13] During the 1930s they had both sought to revitalize lay involvement in local religious life by founding lay associations such as Marian Congregations, Daughters of Mary, Catholic Workers' Circles, and Eucharistic Crusades, and they had both undertaken building projects that would enhance Catholicism's physical and social presence in their respective towns.[14] In Catolé do Rocha Padre Joaquim completed a top-to-bottom remodeling of the main parish church, transforming the crumbling, decrepit building into a "modern temple" that would be able to support the greater number of people and activities the church now expected to host on a regular basis.[15] In Cuité Padre Luiz not only enlarged and renovated the main parish church and rectory but also oversaw the construction of smaller chapels in rural areas of the municipality that had previously been removed from parish life, both geographically and spiritually.[16] In just seven years he oversaw the construction of six chapels.

Padre Joaquim also transformed the Catolense church into a leading provider of education. In 1937 Padre Joaquim founded and became the first director of the Colégio Diocesano Leão XIII, a primary and secondary school that would educate the children of the town's elite. That same year construction began on the Escola Normal Dona Francisca Henriques Mendes, a primary school for girls. The school was the brainchild of Padre Joaquim,

who had aggressively lobbied Coronel Antônio Mendes Ribeiro, a Catolense real estate magnate who had moved to João Pessoa at a young age but
had a soft spot for the town of his youth (and that of his wife, Dona Francisca
Henriques, the namesake of the new school), to finance the initiative. The
following year Padre Joaquim arranged for four Franciscan nuns to come to
the town and teach at the girls' school.[17]

Similarly, Padre Luiz participated in some of the Catholic elite's most urgent projects. When the Catholic Church in Recife and João Pessoa waged
a campaign against practitioners of Afro-Brazilian religions in the early
1930s Padre Luiz gained statewide notoriety for aiding in the persecution
and arrest of an Afro-Brazilian religious leader labeled a witch doctor by Padre Luiz and local authorities. The so-called *macumbeiro* had gained influence and followers among workers at a fazenda in Cuité, and Padre Luiz
was hailed for ridding his town of the man's "diabolical operations."[18] When
the National Eucharistic Congresses became the centerpiece of Catholic
Restorationist pageantry and power, Padre Luiz not only enthusiastically attended the congresses but also brought delegations from Cuité and the surrounding villages to both the 1939 congress in Recife and the 1936 congress
in Belo Horizonte.[19]

Protestants Confront Persecution

By 1938 Catholics and Protestants were on a collision course in Catolé do
Rocha and Cuité, as Restorationist efforts to dominate the public sphere
came into conflict with Protestant leaders who were successfully revitaliz-
ing their churches' public activities. In Catolé do Rocha priests had attempted to quell the growth of Protestantism throughout the early 1930s but
had little success. It was not for lack of trying: in the parish's livro de tombo
each successive priest gave detailed documentation of his efforts to combat
the "pernicious sect." The priests tried to wrest from the Congregational
church legal control of land the church had bought for the site of a future
church building, they preached passionate sermons against Protestants, and
they tried to convince Protestants to see the errors of their ways and return
to the Catholic fold.[20] In 1933 Catholics dedicated the Marian month of

May to combating Protestants because, as the correspondent for the Catholic newspaper A *Imprensa* stated, "Protestants are horrified by the Most Virgin Mary."[21] The Catolense priest took part in debates with local Protestants, hoping to show the community the superiority of Catholic doctrine.[22] Prominent Catolense Catholics even wrote letters to the federally appointed Paraíban interventor, accusing Reverend Briault of being a spy for the United States and asking the government to expel him from the country. After accusing Briault and other Protestants of "taking pictures of the area [of Catolé do Rocha] and sending them to the Ministry of War in the United States," Otávio de Sá Leitão, a prominent lawyer and intellectual in Catolé do Rocha, insisted it was Catholics' right to harass and attack Protestants. "Freedom of religion doesn't give [Protestants] the right to perpetrate such scams," he wrote to the interventor. "These men ... ask for protection [against Catholic violence] and pretend to be victims, when they should really be in jail!" he exclaimed.[23] The letters failed to persuade the government to take action, and Reverend Briault and all other Protestants were allowed to stay in the Northeast and continue evangelizing.

Even when their campaigns failed, Catholics were convinced that the battle must not be abandoned. This was especially true of priests. With enough zeal and effort, they believed, their successors would be able to accomplish what they themselves could not. This feeling was fervently expressed by Padre Manuel Octaviano de Moura Lima, who served as the priest of Catolé do Rocha from 1932 to 1934. Although he waged a campaign against Protestants so fierce that he was accused of being a revolutionary separatist and was briefly detained by local police, he believed he had ultimately failed in his duty to extinguish the Protestant threat.[24] On departing, Padre Manuel made a rather unusual entry in the parish's livro de tombo. He directed a plea to his immediate successor, employing forceful Restorationist–nationalist language:

> The priest who will substitute me must not cease to fight the Protestants, who are the enemies of our faith and of our nation, and the puppets of corrupt foreigners—the North Americans—who work against Brazil's future. Pray with your parishioners and put

them into action against the perverse foreigner who tries to turn unsuspecting Brazilians against their own homeland and their own country, stealing away their faith. I must now leave for another parish that God has placed in my hands, and perhaps there my fight against the Protestants will be more effective. Leaving these parishioners, I pray for the triumph of my successor in directing his flock towards the true fold of our Holy Church.[25]

Padre Joaquim de Assis Ferreira would prove to be up to the task. He took the Protestant threat in Catolé do Rocha seriously, and on taking possession of Nossa Senhora dos Remédios he "preached constantly" against Protestants.[26] In this respect he was much like his predecessors, giving sermons that employed militant and violent language to implore parishioners not only to avoid Protestantism (and the Bibles its adherents were known to distribute) but also to actively and forcefully campaign against Protestant institutions and individuals.[27] His sermons won him fame throughout the region, and he was soon known as "one of the best religious orators in the Northeast."[28] But unlike previous priests of Catolé do Rocha, Padre Joaquim had fostered a religious and political climate that allowed his anti-Protestant campaign to be substantially more effective than those of his predecessors. The heightened prestige of the Catholic Church, along with the presence of new religious associations that promoted lay activism and militancy, encouraged Catolenses to participate more frequently and with greater commitment in Padre Joaquim's campaigns against Protestantism. Moreover, the renewed political support for the Catholic Church and its activities created an environment of impunity in which Catholics could rest assured that their attacks on Protestants would go unpunished.

Protestants did not allow the organized intolerance of local Catholics to diminish their evangelization activities. The Congregational pastor in Catolé do Rocha, Rev. Lindonio de Almeida, was determined to continue to hold public events and religious services, even if he knew they would likely attract the ire of Catolense Restorationists. Thus in June 1938, when Rev. Almeida announced an upcoming public lecture by Rev. Josué Alves, Catolé do Rocha's former pastor, who was now a pastor in Patos and the leader of the

Biblical Institute, Catolense Protestants were aware of the potential persecution that could result from such an event. The lecture was to be held in the newly built Congregational church in the center of town, across the street from the local tavern. Reverends Almeida and Alves were hoping the lecture would attract curious Catholics and win converts for the Congregationalists. Word of the arrival of the new pastor and his planned lecture had spread quickly throughout Catolé do Rocha, and Padre Joaquim immediately denounced the pastor's visit as a provocation to the town's Catholics. There was talk of the Catholic townspeople, under the leadership of Padre Joaquim, planning an action—perhaps a demonstration, procession, or attack—that would coincide with Alves's lecture. In the days leading up to the big event rumors flew at an ever-faster rate, especially within the Catolense Protestant community. "Protestants will never preach here again" was the refrain Protestants heard repeated throughout the streets of Catolé do Rocha. Tensions were so high that Reverend Almeida tried to secure police protection for the event, but he was informed that no such service could be provided. The police unhelpfully suggested that if the Congregationalists were worried about their safety they should cancel the event and keep a lower profile in the town.[29] Almeida refused to allow Catholic intimidation to prevent his church from holding the event, and Alves arrived in Catolé as planned.

On June 18, the night before the conference, Reverends Almeida and Alves were in the church with four other Congregationalists preparing the space and practicing the hymns for the religious service that would be held the next day, immediately following the pastor's lecture. Suddenly the sound of yells and screams filtered into the church, and soon the walls echoed from the stones pelting the building's walls. Minutes later the power went out, and the building was cloaked in darkness.[30] More and more people arrived at the church, and soon it was surrounded by men and women yelling violent threats, throwing rocks, and banging away at the windows and door. Fearing the building would be set on fire, the pastors and their coreligionists fled out the only door in the church. They were immediately hit with rocks and clubs. Articles of clothing, including shirts, jackets, and hats, were ripped off and shredded by the crowd. Fortunately for the Protestants the crowd's attention soon shifted to the church itself. Men and women entered and began destroying the pews, pulpit, organ, and books. Once the church had been sufficiently torn apart, the group proceeded to the neighboring settlements of Brejo dos Cavalos and Cajazeirinhas, where attacks on Protestant churches were repeated.[31]

Reverend Almeida had known the public lecture might elicit a negative reaction from Catolense Catholics, but he had no idea it would set off a months-long "brutal and diabolical [campaign of] persecution" that would strike fear into Protestants in Catolé do Rocha and in all of the towns and villages in the region.[32] Protestants reported that Catholics had threatened to burn Reverend Briault's car and beat up and even kill Reverend Almeida.[33] The Congregationalists implored state authorities to intervene in order to both prevent further persecution of Protestants and to bring the original perpetrators of violence to justice. They received no such help. Local police did not appear to conduct any investigation of the church destruction or personal assaults. Years later, when a federal judge requested the original documentation relating to the 1938 attacks, local police and prosecutors would state that all records had mysteriously disappeared.[34] Reverends Almeida and Briault brought the case to the attention of the state's secretary of the interior, but his only response was to tell them, "You, sirs, came to break the spiritual unity of Brazil."[35] He would offer them neither support nor protection.

Feeling abandoned by Brazilian authorities who refused to guarantee the safety of Protestant worshippers in the area, Reverend Almeida believed he would put his entire congregation in danger if he continued to preach and keep up a visible Protestant presence in Catolé do Rocha. After a period of painful deliberation the Congregational church in Catolé do Rocha decided to suspend all operations. Reverend Almeida, who left the area and found safe haven in João Pessoa, had no hope or expectation of being able to return to Catolé in the near future. In the Catolense region no Protestant dared attend religious services for fear of being attacked, and all evangelization work ground to a halt. Numerous Congregationalists left town, most of whom crossed the border into Ceará.[36] Others, either out of fear or genuine religious feeling, converted to Catholicism.[37] The Congregational Church in Catolé do Rocha, for all intents and purposes, ceased to exist. The church remained in its damaged state, as no one was able to raise the funds (or even dare to speak of raising the funds) to restore it.

Even the empty, nonfunctioning Congregationalist structures would prove to be too much of a provocation for Catholics in the Catolé do Rocha area. In Brejo dos Cavalos, a small agricultural hamlet of Catolé, a once-new church that the Congregationalists had been forced to abandon soon after its construction sat unused. Although the few families of Congregationalists who still lived in the area did not dare enter the church after 1938, the structure nevertheless remained as a reminder of the Protestants' presence. Moreover, it seemed that some Congregationalists, ever defiant in the face of continued Catholic persecution, had been quietly but determinedly raising funds to repair the Catolense churches in hopes of resuming religious activities.[38] Then, on the evening of May 31, 1939, a large group of Catholics, after organizing a novena in the nearby Catholic chapel in Brejo dos Cavalos, tore down the Congregational building and assaulted José Alves da Silva, the Congregationalist man who attempted to stop the destruction and defend the temple.[39]

In the initial weeks following the incident it seemed the perpetrators of the 1939 attack would operate with the same impunity as those of the 1938 one. The police interviewed forty-nine individuals over ten days, none of whom admitted to taking an active role in the destruction of the church, although numerous people admitted to being present at the scene of the attack. The witnesses said the attack on the church was a completely spontaneous act, inspired by intense feelings of piety and religious fervor that resulted from the holy experience of the novena. As for the beating of Alves da Silva, they claimed that a mysterious man by the name of Aprígio Grande, a drifter who was not from Catolé do Rocha and who had left town immediately after the incident, had committed the crime.[40] Only one witness told a notably different story: Zacarias Saldanha, an illiterate Catholic farm-worker, told the police that the destruction of the Congregational church had been planned long before the night of the novena and that Padre Joaquim's lay assistant, Eliziario Luiz da Costa, had organized the attack with the permission of the town's ecclesiastical and civil authorities.[41] Saldanha's testimony was largely ignored by the police and local prosecutor, who concluded that the only proven perpetrator of the destruction and violence was Aprígio Grande. But since he had left Catolé do Rocha after the attack, the authorities declared the case closed. No further steps were taken to investigate either Grande's whereabouts or the identities of the other fifty or sixty suspects, nor did the authorities question Padre Joaquim or any of the other town elites who were accused of having organized and authorized the attack.[42] A judge would later express anger at the extent to which "the police investigation was poorly executed," pointing to the fact that police asked no questions of the accused, and the local prosecutor never even bothered to reinterview witnesses.[43] "No one wanted to help solve the crime, no one knew anything, and no one recognized the perpetrators, even though they witnessed the crime and lived in a small town with few people," the judge wrote in frustration and disbelief.

Protestant activity in Catolé do Rocha would not resume for four years, when the Congregational church met again for the first time in June 1942, the same month and year Padre Joaquim left the Catolense Catholic parish for his promotion to the larger city of Patos.[44] But much damage had already been done. When the Congregational church resumed operations, it was greatly reduced in size and influence. Its first meetings were consumed by the slow process of rebuilding its leadership and institutional structures. A new pastor needed to be inaugurated, new church officials needed to be elected, and new plans for reevangelization needed to be put into action.[45] Sunday school classes, the Women's Auxiliary Society, youth groups—in the post-1942 years all of these organizations, which had been operating at full capacity in 1938, took months or even years to function again at even a minimal level. There is evidence to suggest that the Pentecostal church too suffered setbacks in the wake of the attacks. In 1940 members of the Assembléia de Deus would describe a trip to Catolé do Rocha in which they were unable to preach due to the persecution and extreme hostility they encountered. They gave no indication there was an active AD congregation in town, even though Congregationalists had described a flourishing Pentecostal congregation that existed pre-1938.[46] Presumably the Pentecostals, like the Congregationalists, had shut their church down in 1938 and had not yet resumed activities when evangelists attempted to visit in 1940.

In Cuité religious conflict followed a timeline remarkably similar to that of Catolé do Rocha. As the Pentecostal pastor José Ferreira da Silva worked to expand the Assembléia de Deus's presence in Cuité, Padre Luiz Santiago considered such an expansion to be a direct threat to everything he valued most: his Catholic Restorationist mission, his moral authority, his political capital, and the traditional Catholic culture of his town. Padre Luiz decided to take action. Throughout Cuité, from the main town church to the recently erected rural Catholic chapels, he gave impassioned sermons against Protestantism and its adherents. In these speeches he revealed this thinking to be influenced by northeastern anti-Protestant traditions as well as the supposedly modern Restorationist anti-Protestant ideology. As was common practice throughout the Northeast, Padre Luiz declared that Catholics were not to have any contact or transact any commerce with Pentecostals. Catholics were even to deny Pentecostals bread and water should they be in need.[47] Some of the extreme measures Padre Luiz felt the need to employ were violent. By 1940 his sermons had begun to sound eerily like how-to seminars on the best ways to commit violent crimes against Protestants. Moving about in groups of ten or more, he allegedly remarked more than once, would decrease the possibility of individuals being held responsible for any violent acts.[48] Moreover, he argued, crimes against Protestants were not crimes at all, even if they involved murder. In an infamous sermon given in 1940 Padre Luiz said to his parishioners, "Killing a Protestant is the same as killing an animal. It is not a crime."[49] It was not long before violent words were translated into violent actions. In the early years of the AD's existence Padre Luiz himself was said to have gone to the home of the town chauffeur to confront him about his conversion, physically assaulting him and destroying AD church documents, pamphlets, and Bibles in the process.[50] Some Cuitense residents said these home invasions became frequent occurrences oftentimes directed at the home of Pastor Silva.[51]

Nevertheless, Pastor Silva refused to be intimidated by Padre Santiago's actions, and he continued to work toward strengthening and expanding the AD's presence in Cuité. Most important, Pastor Silva raised funds for the construction of an official church and, in 1939, he began looking for land on which to build the temple. Since its founding, one of the AD's central goals had been the construction of the church. The building would not only give them a permanent place in which to hold religious services (previously they had been holding them in the homes of congregants) but also serve as physical proof of their newly obtained prominence in Cuitense society. Padre Luiz reacted with alarm and animosity at the idea and tried to prevent any land or building from being sold to the AD. His efforts at obstruction were unsuccessful, and construction of the new church began in February 1940. Padre Luiz was furious. Numerous people reported that he was threatening to take revenge on the Pentecostals and to "bring the [AD] church to the ground in broad daylight."[52]

Before long the threat was carried out. On March 14, 1940, Francisca Taveira do Nascimento, a twenty-two-year-old Pentecostal domestic servant, was awoken at midnight by the sound of bricks crashing to the ground and men yelling. As she peered out of the doorway of her house she saw a large group of men crowded around the nearly completed Pentecostal church across the street. The men had broken down the church door and were in the process of destroying the building's interior. Nascimento ran outside with the intention of assembling her coreligionists to defend the church, but as soon as she stepped out her door she was met by a group of armed men who blocked her path and told her to return to her home or they would shoot her. Having no choice, Nascimento did as she was told, and she was forced to watch helplessly as the group finished destroying the church's interior and moved on to the exterior. They began to tear down large sections of the back and side walls of the church, a tall order given that the walls were made of bricks. Part of the roof was destroyed as well.[53] Unsurprisingly, members of the Assembléia de Deus believed that Padre Luiz and his Catholic parishioners were behind the attack. While eyewitnesses confirmed that he was visiting sick parishioners on one of the rural fazendas, far from the Pentecostal church, his previous threats to bring down the church as well as the broader anti-Protestant campaign taking place in Cuité fueled the idea that Catholics, under the orders of Padre Luiz, were the perpetrators of the destruction.[54]

The most serious problems for the Pentecostals were yet to come. Just five months after the assault on the church a more devastating attack was carried out against AD church members themselves: the fatal shooting of AD member Severino Amaro.[55] Members of the Pentecostal church had no doubt as to who had perpetrated the fatal attack. They immediately went to the police station and accused Padre Luiz of organizing and possibly carry-

ing out the assassination. In their statements to authorities Pentecostals detailed the escalating violence against their church members that had taken
place over the past years, stressing that the persecution had been encouraged and organized by Padre Luiz. But as was the case in the March 1940
attack on the church, Padre Luiz had an alibi for the night of August 15: he
was in the Paraíban capital of João Pessoa attending the inauguration of the
new state interventor, Rui Carneiro.[56] In the absence of firm knowledge
about who had actually fired on the Pentecostal group, it was impossible to
know whether or not Padre Luiz had collaborated with or directly ordered
the attack. Initial witness testimony placed suspicion on a man known as
Joca Sapateiro, a so-called criminal associate of Padre Luiz who had been
accused of playing a central role in the March 1940 incident. Joca Sapateiro
was described as Padre Luiz's *jagunço*, a bodyguard or enforcer who was
commonly employed by northeastern *coronéis*. If Padre Luiz ordered the
murder of Protestants, the Pentecostals surmised, he most certainly would
have hired Sapateiro to complete the gruesome task. Yet when the police attempted to interview Sapateiro he was nowhere to be found. Cuitense residents said he had left town a few days after the attack. The police appeared
to have little interest in finding him. Just as in Catolé do Rocha, Cajazeiras,
Guarabira, Esperança, Areia Branca, Mossoró, Flores, Pesqueira, Arcoverde, and all of the other northeastern towns in which crimes against Protestants were committed, the police in Cuité made only a perfunctory show
of investigating the murder. They never interviewed Padre Luiz nor did they
attempt to find witnesses who might have seen the killer arriving at or leaving the scene of the crime. After two weeks the police sent their official (in-
conclusive) findings to the local judge, and no charges were made. The
case was, for all intents and purposes, closed.[57] Authorities did not seem
interested in bringing the perpetrators to justice.

Local Politics and Changing Religious Alliances in Paraíba

Protestants were hardly surprised by the official indifference and hostility
they encountered, as this was how supposed investigations into crimes
against Protestants had taken place throughout the Northeast for much

of the early twentieth century. And yet even when success seemed impossible Brazilian Protestant leaders had never stopped demanding justice. Such persistence would finally bear fruit in the cases of Catolé do Rocha and Cuité when the confluence of a complex array of local, regional, and national political events gave Protestants the ability to make their voices heard at the highest levels of the Vargas government. Throughout much of the northeastern interior the Vargas era was a period of upheaval and transition as traditional oligarchical families adjusted to and realigned themselves with the new centralizing power of the federal state.[58] Within this process the last years of the 1930s marked a moment of intense political conflict and uncertainty for Paraíba. One of the most powerful political figures in the state, José Américo de Almeida, found himself in conflict with the Vargas regime, as his candidacy for the presidency was cut short by the 1937 coup and the establishment of the Estado Novo dictatorship. This meant that many of Paraíba's most powerful families who had supported Almeida's campaign would fall out of favor with Vargas officials during the Estado Novo. Moreover, during the final years of the 1930s the state interventor, Argemiro de Figueiredo, would become involved in a political dispute with a powerful Paraíban family, the Pessoas—specifically, with Epitácio Pessoa Cavalcanti de Albuquerque, the son of the deceased revolutionary hero João Pessoa. He was known popularly as Epitacinho in order to distinguish him from his famous great-uncle Epitácio da Silva Pessoa, a former president of the country.[59] In the face of incessant attacks by the Pessoa family and their allies, which culminated in the publication of a damning book by Epitacinho in which he accused the Figueiredo administration of financial irregularities, gross administrative mismanagement, violent persecutions of political opponents, and general "tyrannical" behavior, Argemiro de Figueiredo began to lose his grip on power in Paraíba.[60] In August 1940 he was finally expelled from the state government, and a new interventor, Rui Carneiro, was appointed. The political fallout from Figueiredo's expulsion had a dramatic effect at the local level. All local mayors were removed from office and replaced with individuals loyal to Rui Carneiro.[61] Power dynamics in local towns were thus upended, as former allies of Figueiredo were now vulnerable to attacks from their political adversaries, many of whom were now in positions of power in their municipalities.

The political realignment in Paraíba would present opportunities for Protestant activists and dangers for Catholic leaders. Both Padre Joaquim and Padre Luiz had forged positive relationships with political authorities during the Argemiro de Figueiredo regime, and they suffered when he fell out of favor. In Catolé do Rocha Padre Joaquim had gained the trust of the powerful Maia family, who had controlled local politics for most of the 1930s.[62] But he also had enlisted the support of local intellectuals and *bach-aréis* such as Octávio de Sá Leitão, the town lawyer who is credited with bringing to town the first radio, telegraph, and films.[63] Like a good Restora-tionist, Padre Joaquim did not himself become involved in partisan politics but instead built up a widespread foundation of political goodwill that would provide the Catholic Church with support when it needed it most: when the diocesan school required certification and recognition from the government, when funds were needed for the expansion of religious asso-ciations and Catholic social programs, and, perhaps most of all, when Prot-estantism threatened the church's religious hegemony over the town.

Unfortunately for Padre Joaquim, his chief ally, the powerful Maia fam-ily, was a supporter of both José Américo de Almeida and Argemiro de Figueiredo.[64] To make matters worse, the family was a longtime political ad-versary of Rui Carneiro, who hailed from the rival town of Pombal.[65] When Carneiro came to power in 1940 he immediately replaced then mayor Na-tanael Maia Filho with one of his compatriots from Pombal, Aristeu For-miga. To residents of Catolé do Rocha, the appointment of Formiga was a humiliation in which Catolenses were "once more put under the yoke of the Pombal municipality."[66] To Padre Joaquim, the rise of Carneiro and the appointment of Formiga represented a considerable setback for the Catho-lic Church's projects in Catolé do Rocha. One of Padre Joaquim's most im-portant achievements, the founding of the Colégio Leão XIII, a Catholic school for the children of local elites, was put in jeopardy by the state's re-fusal to continue contributing funding to the institution. The refusal was said to be motivated by "Carneiro's political opposition to the Maia fam-ily."[67] By 1942 the school closed down for lack of funds amidst a bitter feud between the school director, Padre Américo Sergio Maia, and the Carneiro government.[68]

To Padre Luiz in Cuité, the fallout from the political upheaval was much more detrimental. At first glance it seemed that Padre Luiz, like Padre Joaquim, had done what any Restorationist priest would do, namely, foster positive relationships with local political officials.

He had such good relationships with local Cuitense politicians during the pre-Carneiro era that when Dom Adauto Aurélio de Miranda Henriques, the archbishop of Paraíba, came to Cuité for a pastoral visit in 1934, he singled out Padre Luiz's political connections as being especially beneficial to the Cuitense church: "Above all, our heart was gladdened to see the moral support and harmonious relationship maintained [between the civil authorities] and the Parish Priest, and we hope that this relationship continues to deepen. . . . Now we can clearly see how in our Catholic country, close relationships between the two powers—spiritual and civil—can contribute to the achievement of our people's moral and material progress."[69]

In a basic sense the archbishop's assessment was correct. Padre Luiz did indeed foster excellent relationships with key political leaders in Cuité. However, what Dom Adauto did not yet realize, or perhaps did not want to point out, was that the nature of Padre Luiz's political activity differed greatly from what was expected and desired from a model Restorationist priest. Unlike Padre Joaquim in Catolé do Rocha, Padre Luiz had not merely cultivated strong relationships with Cuitense political authorities; he himself had become active in local politics, becoming deeply involved in factional disputes and electoral campaigns. The political and economic life of Cuité, like that of Catolé do Rocha, was dominated by a few powerful families who were constantly competing with one another for political and economic power. Padre Luiz used these divisions to his advantage. He allied himself with certain factions, most notably the faction led by the powerful Pereira family, and, in doing so, increased his own political influence.[70] His quick wit and literary flair made him an able satirist, and he anonymously wrote or helped write many scathing critiques of the Pereira family's political opponents. In one tract called "The ABCs of João Venâncio" he called the former mayor "the king of the idiots" and an "imitator of Satan."[71] He campaigned

openly and forcefully for his chosen candidates, delivering eloquent and impassioned speeches at rallies, all the while conspicuously carrying an auto-
matic rifle under his cassock.[72] The rifle was, in fact, an important part of his
identity. It represented his secular power in Cuitense society, which was becoming equal to or even greater than his moral and religious authority.
When residents described Padre Luiz they rarely failed to remark that he
"always carried a gun" with him in public.[73] The weapons he possessed,
which included not only the rifle but also a walking stick whose hilt hid a
dagger that could be brandished in seconds, defined his place in society and
signaled to others that his authority extended beyond the religious sphere.
As the Cuitense historian Crisólito Marques has argued, Padre Luiz "became a type of *coronel* of the region, using all of his prestige and social status
to take a position of leadership" in Cuité.[74] He was a political power broker,
a man both respected and feared by the residents of Cuité. He even became
an important economic force in the town after he bought a large fazenda
and began to plant sisal, a species of agave plant used to make rope, twine,
cloth, paper, and other fibrous products.[75] His business dealings could also
lead to conflict: some people in Cuité and the surrounding area believed he
behaved less than honorably in his economic transactions, charging unfair
prices and cheating them out of money and goods.[76]

Padre Luiz was a curious mix of a modern Restorationist reformer and an
antiquated relic of the First Republic. On the one hand, his commitment to
the Restorationist reform of his parish was genuine. He was, by all accounts,
passionate about his pastoral duties and serious in his intentions to modernize the religious life of Cuité. Yet, at the same time, he adopted methods
and practices that harked back to an earlier era. He was what Eul-Soo Pang
has called an "activist priest-politician," an all-too-worldly priest who was involved in secular intrigues, partisan infighting, and economic rivalries and
who oftentimes aspired to hold public office himself.[77] The sertão had a
long tradition of priests becoming political and economic powerbrokers,
and Padre Luiz was not the first, nor would he be the last. However, it was
precisely these types of worldly strongmen that both the Catholic Church
and the Vargas government were intent on eradicating. Restorationist Catholics had declared themselves "above partisan politics" and committed to a

more dignified, lobbying-based form of advocacy, while the Vargas government was intent on breaking the power of local *coronéis* in order to implement a more modern style of politics that looked to federal, not local, authority as the ultimate arbiter of political and economic life. The 1930s would thus see the rise of the "lobbyist priest," who, like Padre Joaquim, would advocate for church privileges, concessions, and moral authority in the public sphere, all while remaining officially unaffiliated with any single party or oligarchical alliance.[78]

Padre Luiz's political activism put his status as a true Restorationist reformer in doubt, but, perhaps more important, it made him extremely vulnerable to the whims of political change. From the beginning of Argemiro de Figueiredo's tenure in 1935 Padre Luiz had become one of the interventor's staunchest supporters. He actively supported a major mining project promoted by Figueiredo in the town of Picuí, adjacent to Cuité and, for two years, under the pastoral care of Padre Luiz. He wrote numerous newspaper articles in which he marveled over the richness of the copper, beryl, and columbite reserves in the region, and he argued that exploiting these resources would bring progress and wealth to both the local region and the state.[79] Figueiredo and Padre Luiz also collaborated in the effort to grant Cuité municipal independence. Cuité had been an autonomous municipality in the nineteenth century, but in 1904 it was annexed by the neighboring town of Picuí, and it had remained subordinated to Picuí's municipal authority ever since. For much of his pastorate Padre Luiz had campaigned passionately for the emancipation of Cuité.[80] He was a leading member of the Comissão Pró-Autonomia de Cuité (Pro-Autonomy Commission of Cuité), and he even wrote a book, *Serra do Cuité: sua história, seu progresso, suas possibilidades* (The history of Cuité: its history, its progress, its possibilities), that served as a testament to Cuité's independent political, economic, and religious history.[81] Figueiredo was a key ally in the pro-autonomy campaign, having visited the city in the early 1930s, before he became interventor, and promised to help Cuité obtain its independence.[82] When municipal autonomy was finally granted in 1937 the Pro-Autonomy Committee made sure to give credit to Figueiredo, erecting an arch at the entrance to the town that read, "The People of Cuité Give Thanks to Dr. Argemiro de Figueiredo."[83]

Unsurprisingly, Figueiredo's fall from power in Paraíba would signal Padre Luiz's fall from power in Cuité.

Protestant Leaders and the Tribunal de Segurança Nacional

Protestant leaders in Catolé do Rocha and Cuité knew that the diminishing political power of local priests was a rare opportunity to obtain justice for their persecuted brethren. Ever since the attack in Catolé do Rocha in 1938 Rev. Lindonio de Almeida had been working ceaselessly to gain protections for members of his congregation. His forced exile dealt a devastating blow to Catolense Congregationalism, but Reverend Almeida's presence in the Paraíban capital of João Pessoa allowed him to network with important political and social actors who could champion his community's cause. Together with Reverend Briault, who at the time was the pastor of the prominent sertanejan Patos church, Reverend Almeida did what so many other Brazilian Protestants had done throughout the past decades: he made as many appeals to as many individuals, authorities, and organizations as he could, asking them to push for protections for the Catolense Congregational church. He enlisted the help of the Confederação Evangélica do Brasil, the nationwide ecumenical Protestant organization, to send telegrams to the Paraíban interventor, the minister of justice, and even President Vargas demanding action.[84] "We beseech Your Excellency, in the name of the evangelicals of Brazil, to take immediate action to protect lives and guarantee the free exercise of religion," wrote Nemesio de Almeida, the president of the confederação, to the Paraíban interventor.[85] Reverends Almeida and Briault made connections with the editors of prominent Protestant newspapers, convincing them to feature articles detailing the persecution taking place in Catolé do Rocha and making sure that citizens throughout Brazil knew of the "indescribable barbarism" of the Catholics who had attacked the Protestant faithful.[86]

Although government authorities largely ignored the pleas of Reverend Almeida and his Protestant allies for nearly a year, the Catolense leader did not give up, continuing to enlist the help of prominent Brazilians to champion his cause. Reverend Almeida's luck started to turn when Reverend Briault convinced Horácio de Almeida, an up-and-coming lawyer, public intellec-tual, and cousin (albeit estranged) of the powerful José Américo de Almeida, to join their crusade against Catholic persecution.[87] On the surface Horácio de Almeida and the Congregationalist pastors seemed to make an unlikely team. Horácio de Almeida was associated with Spiritism, and Congregation-alists, along with Presbyterians, Baptists, and Methodists, had long declared Spiritism to be a religious plague on par with Pentecostalism, Catholicism, and Afro-Brazilian religions.[88] Neither party wanted the other's religion to prosper, and they could frequently be found criticizing each other's theology and philosophy. However, they had a common enemy. Much like his Protes-tant counterparts, Horácio was a fierce promoter of religious liberty, which meant that he detested Restorationist Catholicism's anti-Protestant and anti-Spiritist campaigns and was wary of the Catholic Church's new alliance with the Vargas regime.[89] He was one of the founders of the state's Liga Pró-Estado Leigo (League for the secular state), which had acquired much of its mem-bership and financial support from northeastern Protestants. To Horácio and the Congregationalists, it made sense for them to unite in the common cause against the Catholic Church and attempt to deal a blow to religious intoler-ance in the interior.

The Congregationalist alliance with Horácio de Almeida occurred just as the political winds were dramatically shifting in Paraíba, allowing the group's protests to find a sympathetic ear. By November 1939 the attacks against the government of Argemiro Figueiredo had intensified. The inter-ventor found himself on the defensive, as one by one his former allies be-gan to distance themselves from his administration. It was then that Reverend Almeida, Reverend Briault, and Horácio de Almeida were granted an interview with Rômulo de Almeida, an official working for the Paraíba branch of the Estado Novo's secret police, DEOPS.[90] During the interview Reverends Briault and Almeida recounted the history of the Catolé do Ro-cha congregation, including its struggles to gain funding and recognition, the hostility of the local Catholic population, the vicious attacks of June 1938 and the subsequent need to suspend all public religious services and evangelization efforts, and the recent attack on the Brejo dos Cavalos church.[91] Instead of dismissing their claims, Investigator Almeida decided that the case had merit, and formal charges were brought against the accused Catholics. It was an impressive display of state power, as charges were brought not only against the supposed ringleaders of the attack, the lay assistant Elizario Luiz da Costa and the mysterious Aprígio Grande, but also against nearly every individual who admitted taking part in the May 1939 novena. In all, forty-two people were charged with perpetrating a "religious motivated attack" on persons and property.[92] All of the accused were agricultural laborers or small-time merchants, the town authorities who supposedly supported and encouraged the attack being left out of the indictment. Padre Joaquim de Assis Ferreira was also not charged with any crime. Once DEOPS decided to take on the case events moved very quickly. In December 1939 the case was forwarded to the Tribunal de Segurança Nacional (TSN) based in Rio de Janeiro.[93]

The TSN was originally created as a temporary tribunal to be used in the prosecution of the individuals involved in the Intentona Comunista, the failed communist uprising of 1935. In 1936 the Vargas regime decided to make the TSN a permanent court to be used in prosecuting all crimes that threatened the national security of Brazil. The court mostly targeted communists, Integralists, and other "political subversives" who threatened the Estado Novo's monopoly on power.[94] However, lesser-known crimes also fell under the TSN's jurisdiction. The court prosecuted people who committed "crimes against the popular economy," that is, price gouging or fee fixing, as well as those who "spread false rumors" or interfered with the nomination of a public official.[95] To Padre Joaquim and Padre Luiz as well as all Catholics who engaged in anti-Protestant activities, the central article in the TSN statutes was number 3.16, which prohibited individuals or groups from "inciting or preparing an attack on persons or possessions for ideological, political, or religious motives."[96] But while the TSN has often been thought of as an all-powerful repressive arm of the state that "helped maintain the power of dictators," its actions regarding the minor, nonpolitical crimes reveal the limitations of its power.[97] Like most judicial bodies the TSN was not an active agent in the prosecution process and did not and could not seek out cases of religious violence. Instead, it relied on local and state police, prosecutors, and judges to refer cases to the TSN prosecutor.

Thus the TSN's adjudication of cases could be heavily influenced by the interests of local and state actors, both civil and religious, who oftentimes had personal and political motivations for wanting to see the accused prosecuted to the fullest extent of the law.

Political and personal motives were especially relevant in the case of Padre Luiz Santiago. As in the Catolé do Rocha case, Padre Luiz's troubles began when Interventor Argemiro de Figueiredo was rapidly losing his grip on power in Paraíba. In March 1940 Cuitense authorities opened an investigation into the attack on the Pentecostal church. At first, the actions of local authorities had seemed like business as usual. Pastor José Ferreira da Silva and his Pentecostal church members told the police that Padre Luiz Santiago and his followers had organized the destruction of the church, and Padre Luiz and Cuitense Catholics vehemently denied having any knowledge of or taking part in the attack. But Ulisses Pereira da Costa, a prominent businessman in Cuité, testified against Padre Luiz, saying that the priest had "declared that if the Evangelicals tried to build a church, he was going to tear it down in broad daylight, but only after the church was already built, in order to cause the most damage."[98] However, given the fact that there was only one supposedly unreliable eyewitness to the crime—a young Pentecostal domestic worker with little social status or credibility to back up her claim—and there were numerous contradictory reports regarding which individuals had specifically participated in the church destruction, the case seemed destined to remain one of the many abandoned, unsolved cases of anti-Protestant violence. But the investigation soon took a sudden turn. Ten days after the original witness statements had been given, the sacristan of the Cuité parish, João Bezerra Montenegro, went to the police station to change his story. He had originally testified that he knew nothing of any organized plot to destroy the Pentecostal church.[99] Now he was admitting that he had overheard Padre Luiz and two of his right-hand men, João Dozio and Joca Sapateiro (the man who would later be accused of murdering Severino Amaro), organizing the attack.[100] The investigating police officer, Lt. Severino Cesarino da Nóbrega, immediately sent a report of his findings to the local judge, stating that Padre Luiz Santiago had conspired with João Dozio and Joca Sapateiro to destroy the Pentecostal church. What his report did not mention was that Montenegro and another witness who had testified against Padre Luiz had both recanted their statements and accused the police lieutenant of kidnapping them, taking them to a remote location on the outskirts of town, and torturing them until they agreed to implicate Padre Luiz in the church destruction.[101] The actions of the local authorities were so egregious that TSN officials, though not necessarily believing Padre Luiz was innocent, were forced to dismiss the charges because "[the] testimonial proof was obtained through inappropriate and reprehensible means."[102] Even the TSN prosecutor, whose job it was to present the case against the accused, admitted that the "authorship of the crime was uncertain" owing to the violence and intimidation used against the witnesses. Not only had powerful officials in Cuité not protected Padre Luiz, it seemed as if they had targeted him, going so far as to violently coerce witnesses into testifying against him.

While Padre Luiz was found innocent of the charges in the vandalism case, his problems were far from over. The August 1940 murder of Severino Amaro had never been solved, and in April 1941, nearly eight months after the original witnesses had testified, the police reopened the investigation under the command of a newly appointed police lieutenant, Antonio Correa Brasil.[103] Padre Luiz was the first suspect to be interrogated. He flatly denied any involvement in the murder and accused the authorities of continuing to persecute him because of his political affiliations.[104] Once again concrete evidence against Padre Luiz was hard to uncover. The most immediate issue was that he had an airtight alibi for the night of the murder: he had been in João Pessoa attending the inauguration of the new interventor, Rui Carneiro. His presence at the inaugural ceremonies was attested to by numerous Paraíban eyewitnesses and noted by the state-run newspaper, A União.[105] Officials decided they would thus need to argue that he was the "intellectual author" of the crime and that he had ordered the killer to do the deed. The problem with this theory was that the police could not find the person who had actually committed the murder. The original suspect named in the August investigation, Joca Sapateiro, had fled town, and there was little to no hard evidence connecting him, or anyone, for that matter, to the killing. The lack of a true suspect did not prevent the police from pointing the finger at an illiterate farmhand named Venâncio Alves de Lima, who was said to have expressed support for Padre Luiz's campaign against the Pentecostals. The only evidence against Lima was the third-party testimony of his cousin, Antonio Barbosa dos Santos, who claimed to have heard someone say that they had seen him walking toward the assassination site on the night of the murder.[106] When that person was interviewed, however, he denied having ever told Barbosa that he had seen Alves de Lima, instead accusing another man, Francisco Negrinho, of having committed the crime.[107] Throughout the investigation Padre Luiz repeatedly argued that his arrest was motivated by political animosities and that local and state officials, particularly Manuel Casado de Oliveira Nobre, the local judge who had been appointed just five months before the case was reopened, were leading a concerted campaign to undermine his political and ecclesiastical position in the town. Nevertheless, both Padre Luiz and Venâncio Alves de Lima were charged with murder, and local officials forwarded the case to the TSN.

Religious Fanatics, Protestants, and the Brazilian State

In the space of eighteen months the cases of anti-Protestant violence in both Catolé do Rocha and Cuité were sent to the TSN. The circumstances leading to the cases being transferred were likely influenced by local and state politics, but another element would prove to be central to the court's decision-making process, namely, the supposed cultural backwardness and inherent violence of the northeastern backlands. In the eyes of the TSN the cases of persecution against Protestants were not merely violations of the constitutionally protected freedom of religion but a manifestation of a deeper, more worrisome evil: religious fanaticism. At the time, the term "fanaticism" was loaded with meaning in Brazil. It was most often used to describe the religious culture of the northeastern sertão, which was thought to be mystical, penitential, and strongly influenced by messianic and apocalyptic discourses and traditions, particularly Sebastianism.[108] This connotation was especially true in the 1920s and 1930s, when, as Durval Muniz de Albuquerque Júnior has argued, the idea of the impoverished, violent, fanatical Northeast was first invented.[109] Elite views of northeastern fanatics were heavily shaped by the era's journalistic and literary depictions of religious millenarian movements, in which charismatic leaders claiming to have special knowledge of the imminent arrival of the End Times gained large followings throughout the rural interior of Brazil. Many of the most famous movements were regarded as threats to the security of the newly created Republic and were repressed in acts that produced incredible violence and bloodshed.[110] By far the most famous depiction of one such movement is that in Euclides da Cunha's *Os Sertões* (*Rebellion in the Backlands*), which portrayed the members of the millenarian Canudos community as ignorant, impoverished, and superstitious individuals who were victims of their own atavism and backwardness.[111] As Maria Cristina Pompa has noted, urban Brazilians, above all, those residing in the southeastern states of Rio de Janeiro and São Paulo, came to "identify the sertanejan man by his fanaticism," and they believed that at any moment he could be incited to violence.[112] As a result, to many Brazilian elites, nearly all displays of popular religiosity in the northeastern interior were believed to be inherently in danger of morphing into millenarian uprisings.

Protestants were aware of and perhaps even shared this wariness of northeastern religious culture among the elite, and they used it to their advantage. Whenever Protestants, whether Presbyterian, Baptist, Congregationalist, or Pentecostal, wrote or spoke about Catholic persecution of their congregations they almost always called the persecutors fanatics, and they often made references to their relationship, whether real or imagined, with regional millenarian movements. A favorite target was Padre Cícero Romão Batista, the leader of a large community of supposedly ignorant and fanatical followers in the town of Juazeiro.[113] Protestants frequently referred to priests who spearheaded anti-Protestant campaigns as "the new Padre Cícero." In the Baptist newspaper *Jornal Batista* pastors called Padre Manoel Marques, the leader of the anti-Protestant campaign in Flores, Pernambuco, "the second Padre Cícero, in terms of fanaticism."[114] When Catholic leaders boasted that Ceará was the "most Catholic state in Brazil," Protestants seized on the opportunity to remind Brazilians that Ceará was the home state of Padre Cícero and that "Ceará, the most Catholic State in Brazil, is where there is the greatest percentage of illiterate individuals, of crude superstitions, of savage fanatics; and where we have verified all sorts of persecutions against evangelical Protestants, many times with the collaboration of certain intolerant authorities, who are no less fanatical."[115] Thus Protestants invariably portrayed their Catholic persecutors as being ignorant, superstitious, illogical, and easily manipulable by priests and friars who may or may not have been fanatics themselves. When the Catholic priest of Mogeiro, Paraíba, "vomited diatribes from the pulpit against [the town's Protestant pastor]," the Presbyterian newspaper, O Norte Evangélico, declared that the cleric "deserved the title of . . . the representative of intolerance and fanaticism."[116] The Catholics who were accused of destroying Protestants' property and invading their homes in Leopoldina, Alagoas, were deemed to be "fanatical threats to order," and Catholics in Flores were said to be "lacking education," "fanaticized by Catholic idolatry," and so loyal to their priest and superstitious devotions that their highest desire was to "die at the foot of the sacristy."[117] According to Protestants, all Catholics in the northeastern interior, by virtue of being members of a religion that promoted magical understandings of the cult of the saints, the transubstantiation of the Eucharist, the sacrament of confession, and numerous other idolatrous beliefs and practices, were susceptible to outpourings of fanatical behavior.

In the specific cases of Catolé do Rocha and Cuité, Protestant leaders again utilized the language of fanaticism when attempting to convince the public and, specifically, civil authorities, to intervene on their behalf. When the Catholics of Cuité began to commit acts of violence against the Pentecostal community, Pastor José Ferreira da Silva immediately declared that the persecutors of his church "had been fanaticized" by the "famous priest, Luiz Santiago."[118] The pastor opined that the intolerance and fanaticism of the inhabitants of Cuité had made them impervious to all reason and appeals for peace and, worse still, had eliminated "all respect for laws and established authorities."[119] Pastor José portrayed Cuitense Catholics as not only backward fanatics who refused to conform to the modern standards of the new Brazil but also as a group that was dangerously defiant of the forces of law and order. The greatest threat was posed not by the Catholic community itself but by Padre Luiz, who was taking advantage of the ignorance and

simplicity of his flock in order to enlist them in his messianic quest to annihilate Cuité's Pentecostal inhabitants. Whether the focus on Padre Luiz
was part of a broader political strategy that sought to gain the support of the
priest's enemies or whether it sprang from genuine alarm over his sermons
and actions, which, by all authoritative accounts, were truly violent in nature, Pastor Ferreira da Silva's description of events was ultimately meant
to warn authorities that it was only a matter of time before Padre Luiz and
his followers turned into a more serious threat to the order and stability of
Brazilian society.

In Catolé do Rocha Pastors Almeida and Briault depicted a similarly
aggressive image of Catholic fanaticism. Their statements to DEOPS authorities described the attack on the Congregational church in Brejo dos
Cavalos as having been carried out by a "hoard of fanatics" who themselves
were a product of the "violence that comes from the religious fanaticism
that is dominant in that zone of the state."[120] The language used by the Protestants in their official complaint to the TSN was even more intent on depicting Catholics as irrational, fanatical beings. Their description of the
events that had taken place in 1939 stated to the TSN that

> in the village of Brejo dos Cavalos, in the municipality of Catolé
> do Rocha, Paraíba, the Evangelical Congregational Church built
> a chapel for religious services to be attended by the Protestants liv-
> ing in the area. This was enough for the neighboring Catholics to
> become furious [assanhados], and, with calculated intent, erect a
> neighboring chapel for their own parishioners. The objective of
> the Catholics, organized and led by the parish priest, was not to
> foster their own religious life, but rather to crush Protestantism,
> which they considered to be a sect that needed to be fought with
> fire and sword. As the Protestants gained new adherents, the intol-
> erance of the Catholics grew, culminating in the attack men-
> tioned in the police investigation. The ignorant mass of Catholics,
> manipulated by prestigious elements in Catolé society, did not
> hesitate to attack the small evangelical church, violently tearing it
> down in an almost savage act of intolerance.[121]

Much like the Catholics in Cuité, Catolense Catholics were rhetorically transformed into a violent hoard of savage extremists, subject to manipulation by both Padre Joaquim and the town's political elites. The words "furious," "fighting with fire and sword," "ignorant masses," and "savagery" all served to paint a picture of an out-of-control movement whose assaults on peaceful members of Brazilian society would only grow in frequency and intensity.

When lobbying on behalf of their Catolense brethren, Congregational leaders in Rio de Janeiro were eager to separate northeastern Protestants from the "banditry" that supposedly pervaded nordestino culture, arguing that nordestinos' conversion to Protestantism purified and stripped them of their backward, violent customs. Protestant leaders writing in the Rio-based *O Christão* made sure readers knew that Catolense Congregationalists were good nordestinos, as opposed to the bandits that surrounded them: "Inoffensive evangelical believers, men and women who do their duty and respect the laws of the Country, peaceful citizens who do not give trouble to authorities, because they have a way of life that is shaped by the eternal principles of the Gospel, which renews their lives and modifies their customs . . . [these evangelicals] are defenseless victims of the religious banditry that reigns in some parts of that Northeastern state."[122] Evangelical elites argued that Protestantism was providing a service to nordestino authorities by "modifying the customs" of the common people and thus creating a new citizenry that would be peaceful, law-abiding, and free of the backward bandit culture that purportedly reigned in the sertão.

When the religious persecution cases went to trial, the TSN largely agreed with the Protestants' arguments. The TSN prosecutor, Eduardo Jara, described the Catholics who attacked the Brejo dos Cavalos church as fanatics who were terrorizing the inhabitants of Catolé do Rocha and leaving destruction, fear, and disorder in their wake.[123] Even Octávio Sá de Leitão, the defense lawyer who represented all forty-two defendants except for the outsider, Aprígio Grande, did not dispute the interpretation that the attack on the Congregational church was perpetrated by ignorant and savage elements. He instead argued that there was no way to definitively prove that his clients had taken part in the criminal act, given the contradictory nature of the testimony and the lack of eyewitnesses who were willing to testify. Jailing the accused, he concluded, would only have the negative consequence of "punishing humble, poor agricultural workers whose only crime was attending a religious celebration" and "causing material hardship to the State and Municipality, who would be deprived of the labor of these field workers."[124]

While the TSN repeated many of the well-worn tropes of the backland religious fanatic in describing the violence in Catolé do Rocha, its judges went beyond connecting Catolense Catholics to generalized images of religious fervor and superstitious practices. In fact, the TSN was relating anti-Protestant violence to a very specific millenarian movement that had violently clashed with government forces in the same year the first attack on Catolé do Rocha's Congregational church occurred. In the latter half of the 1930s there was a period of heightened concern among state authorities over the violent and potentially revolutionary tendencies of backland religious movements. Much of the anxiety stemmed from the death in 1934 of Padre Cícero, whose entry into the political and economic culture of the region had caused him to be viewed by many elites as a paternalistic redeemer of his fanatical followers, capable of containing their more extreme beliefs and tendencies.[125] In the absence of Padre Cícero's mediating and pacifying presence in the sertão, officials worried that religious movements would spiral out of control. Events in the post-1934 years seemed to confirm such fears. In 1936 the small Pernambucan town of Panelas was host to João Cícero, a man claiming to be inhabited by the departed spirit of Padre Cícero. João Cícero amassed a devoted group of followers who, in an attempt to free one of their group from a nearby prison, killed the local police chief and injured three others during a forty-minute firefight.[126] That same year authorities in Ceará would enter into a bitter conflict with the followers of the *beato* José Lourenço, a popular religious leader who had previously been closely affiliated with Juazeiro and Padre Cícero. Having formed his own community of followers in a place called Caldeirão de Santa Cruz do Deserto, authorities became suspicious of his movement's intentions and beliefs, which they viewed as being simultaneously fanatical and communist. In 1936 military forces expelled the group from Caldeirão, burning their homes and possessions. When the group reformed, the minister of war and the state government of Ceará joined forces to annihilate the entire community, invading the encampment with two hundred soldiers while bombing the area with two airplanes from the federal air force. The events were widely reported in regional and national newspapers, with journalists calling the episode "a new Canudos."[127]

Yet perhaps even more violent and disturbing than the events in Panelas and Caldeirão was the movement that arose in Pau de Colher, a hamlet on the border of the states of Bahia, Pernambuco, and Piauí. Pau de Colher had close cultural ties to Juazeiro and Caldeirão, and for years the town had been a center of millenarian beliefs.[128] In 1937 a man named Quinzeiro arrived and proclaimed himself the new leader of the nascent millenarian movement. Under his leadership the group grew and evolved, giving up their possessions and living in a communal space under strict rules that prohibited them from having sexual relations, even among spouses, and eating certain types of food, such as meat. But their plans turned violent when they were told to proselytize the surrounding area and win converts for their cause. At some point, evangelizers began to kill those who would not join or support the Pau de Colher community. Entire families, men, women, children, and even animals, were beaten to death. In what Felipe Pinto Monteiro has identified as the increasing "demonophobia" of the movement, outsiders came to be seen as vessels for evil spirits who could be exorcized only through the death of those they possessed.[129] Quinzeiro and his followers called their victims infidels, and the number of victims began to rise precipitously. In an act reminiscent of the so-called sacrifices made during the Pedra Bonita movement in the nineteenth century, the Pau de Colher community even turned on its own members, killing those who broke the strict rules of the community.[130] When state and federal authorities learned of the movement, they again responded with intense violence. They attacked Pau de Colher with military battalions and, after an initial armed clash with Quinzeiro's followers compelled them to retreat, they returned to the site and used overwhelming force to subdue the town's inhabitants. Over four hundred men, women, and children were killed.[131]

The Pau de Colher movement would have direct consequences on the anti-Protestant cases brought before the national security court. In the eyes of the TSN groups of Catholic backlanders being intolerant of other religions took on a more sinister meaning when placed in the context of the late 1930s millenarian movements. The prosecutor in the Catolé do Rocha case, Eduardo Jara, explicitly connected the violence in Brejo dos Cavalos to that in Pau de Colher, using the "case of the fanatic Quinzeiro" to illustrate the danger posed by religious movements that were hostile to those who did not share their views and beliefs. Quoting from the transcripts of the trial of Quinzeiro in the Supremo Tribunal Federal, he declared, "When [these attacks] against people of a different creed are repeated, they foster hatred between groups of differing opinions and thus divide the nation; these conflicts seriously compromise public peace and are true harbingers of future civil discord—and even civil war."[132]

Taken in isolation, the attack on the Protestant churches in Catolé do Rocha would seem to be extremely unlikely to lead to civil war. Yet when viewed from the perspective of Brazilian elites like Jara, any spark of religious unrest in the fanatical environment of the northeastern sertão had the potential to ignite a regionwide conflagration. At a time when millenarian movements seemed to be forming as quickly as the government could send troops to repress them, Jara argued that all religious conflicts, whether explicitly millenarian or not, must be viewed as harbingers of future violence. The judge in the case, Alfredo Miranda Rodrigues, agreed. He averred that "the religious intransigence [of Catolé do Rocha], already manifesting itself in criminal acts, could generate an unstable situation with unforeseeable outcomes in the interior of Paraíba."[133] It was the duty of the government, Rodrigues continued, to avoid such a disaster. He therefore decided to look past the relative lack of evidence against the defendants and hand down guilty verdicts to all those who had openly admitted during their interrogations to being present during, but not participating in, the attack on the Congregationalist church. Padre Joaquim's lay assistant Elizario Luiz da Costa, José Apolonio, Manoel Batista de Queiroz, José Conrado, Aristides Pinheiro, Zacarias Alves Saldanha, the only person to admit that the attack on the church was premeditated, and Aprígio Grande were all sentenced to one year in prison and were each fined 10 percent of the monetary damages caused to the church.[134] The sentences, while not extremely harsh, were symbolically momentous in that they were rare official punishments of perpetrators of anti-Protestant violence.

In its case against Padre Luiz Santiago the TSN placed the murder of Severino Amaro in the same fanatical and potentially millenarian context as Catolé do Rocha. The tribunal's prosecutor made an explicit connection between the cases, calling the anti-Protestant violence in Cuité "nothing less than a repetition, with much more grave consequences, of the events that occurred on July 18, 1938, when the Congregational church of Catolé do Rocha was destroyed, and again on May 31, 1939, when the Evangelical temple in Brejo dos Cavalos was attacked. All of these events were motivated by the religious intransigence that is being cultivated in the interior of the State of Paraíba."[135]

Nonetheless, there was one key difference in how the state approached the two cases: whereas the Catolé do Rocha defendants had been portrayed as ignorant peasants who could be easily controlled by outside forces and charismatic individuals, Padre Luiz was cast as the crazed, yet manipulative millenarian leader himself. In the eyes of the TSN Padre Luiz had fallen victim to an irrational hatred of non-Catholics that bordered on the obsessive. Even worse, he had used his position as parish priest to foment unrest among his parishioners and amass a group of loyal followers who, by virtue of their status as backlanders, were presumed to harbor latent fanatical and violent attitudes. The TSN took particular issue with Padre Luiz's sermons, in which he famously declared that laws against murder did not apply when the victim was Protestant: "Considering that a priest's influence is inversely proportional to the cultural level of his parishioners, the expression used by the accused, 'IT IS NOT A CRIME TO KILL THE INFIDEL,' which would not have had any effect in the civilized culture of the city, represents an incitation, or even an order, in the fanatical environment in which it was spoken."[136]

Padre Luiz's crime was thus not that he was preaching violent sermons against Protestantism but that he was doing so within an already fanaticized popular religious culture. This transformed the priest from a lone crusader against a religious sect into a fanatical leader in his own right. In this sense the judge's use of the term "infidel" is revealing. In their original testimonies, witnesses routinely said they heard Padre Luiz say, "It is not a crime to kill a *Protestant.*" There were variations on how the phrase was thought to have been said; many people added that he had compared killing a Protestant to killing an animal, some said that he had used the words "it is not a *sin* to kill a Protestant," while others claimed he had called the Protestants evangelicals or, erroneously, Lutherans. No one, however, claimed he had used the word "infidel"—this was a creation of the judge. If his substitution of "Protestant" for "infidel" was a mistake, it was a highly meaningful one. The word "infidel" was closely associated with millenarian movements. King Sebastian of Portugal, the object of many messianic hopes, had disappeared in the sixteenth century while fighting Muslim infidels, and millenarian leaders often used the term to describe their movements' many enemies: the police, the government, and anyone who opposed them. Quinzeiro and his followers in Pau de Colher had similarly justified their massacres by calling their victims infidels. To claim that Padre Luiz had directed his parishioners to kill infidels was to give his violent anti-Protestant rhetoric a distinctly millenarian bent. The TSN believed that the violence fomented by Padre Luiz "should serve as a severe warning to the local authorities of Cuité and the State of Paraíba," who needed to take urgent action in order to preserve order in the Northeast.[37]

By transforming Padre Luiz into a quasi-messianic leader intent on instigating violent unrest in the northeastern interior the TSN changed the judicial nature of the case itself. The question at hand was no longer whether Padre Luiz had directly ordered the murder of Amaro—in fact, Amaro's death was rarely mentioned in the court proceedings—but whether he had created a more general "environment of fanaticism" that had allowed the assassination to take place. While this did not, as Padre Luiz's lawyer forcefully argued, fit the definition of an "intellectual author" of a crime, the judge overlooked this fact in his effort to bring order and security back to the Northeast. In the end he sentenced Padre Luiz to twelve years in prison, even while acquitting the supposed "material author" of the crime, Venâncio Alves de Lima.[38]

A prison term of twelve years was an extremely harsh punishment for a priest, and one might expect the Catholic Church to have been outraged by the verdict, especially given the scarcity of hard evidence connecting Padre Luiz to the crime.[39] This is not what happened. There was no formal protest, and the Catholic newspapers did not print indignant articles lamenting the injustice of the authorities. This response was a departure from the church's reaction in the previous case against the priest, in which the statewide Catholic Paraíban newspaper, A *Imprensa*, strongly denounced the savagery of the local authorities who had unjustly persecuted Padre Luiz and tortured his allies in Cuité.[140] Just a year later there was no indication that the church was prepared to support Padre Luiz further. Not only did Catholic leaders not speak in his defense, they defrocked him, expelling him permanently from the priesthood.[141] The removal of priestly orders was a serious penalty, one reserved for the gravest of cases. Even more revealing of the church's attitude toward Padre Luiz was the fact that ecclesiastical officials removed his priestly orders *before* the guilty verdict was announced, not after. To the Catholic Church, once the facts about Padre Luiz were publicly exposed he ceased to be the model priest who had been so highly lauded in the archbishop's 1934 pastoral visit. Restorationist Catholics were just as opposed to the supposed fanaticism of northeastern religiosity as the Brazilian government was. Whereas civil authorities viewed fanaticism as a threat to national security, religious authorities viewed it as a threat to doctrinal orthodoxy. Moreover, the TSN case had revealed Padre Luiz's deep involvement in the type of factional partisan politics that were rejected by the Restorationist Church, which believed that Catholics should be above all party politics. Such conduct was reminiscent as well of the old way of doing politics, which supposedly had been superseded by the new postpartisan politics of the Vargas era. Taken together, Padre Luiz's fanaticism and political involvement smacked of the very backwardness the Catholic Restoration was trying so hard to eradicate. The church had little choice but to remove him as an official representative of its institution.

In December 1941, in a startling turn of events, the Court of Appeals reversed the TSN decision, holding that the letter of the law required that the intellectual author of a crime must be proved to have directly communicated with the material author of said crime. In the absence of a known material author, the intellectual author could not be determined with legal certainty.[142] Yet again the Catholic Church did not demand that Padre Luiz be proven guilty in order to punish him for his unorthodoxy. Padre Luiz was now absolved of his crimes by civil authorities, but his expulsion from the priesthood was permanent.

The Catholic Church's attitude toward Padre Luiz contrasted sharply with that toward Padre Joaquim de Assis Ferreira. Padre Joaquim not only retained his position as Catolé do Rocha's parish priest but also was apparently able to reassert much of his power and prestige within the Catolense community, so much so that he was able to continue his anti-Protestant campaign. As noted above, the Congregational Church did not feel safe enough to return to Catolé do Rocha and restart their church after the judicial victory of 1940. They waited until 1942, which happened to be right after Padre Joaquim had left Catolé do Rocha to take up a position in the diocesan administration of Bishop Henrique Gelain in Cajazeiras.[143] Only in light of Padre Joaquim's absence did Congregationalists believe that their persecution would lessen, if not completely cease. In the eyes of the Catholic Church this was the optimal outcome for an anti-Protestant campaign: instilling fear in the hearts of the enemy while sustaining a working relationship with local and state officials, even those who were not natural allies of Padre Joaquim. Upon Padre Joaquim's exit from the parish his successor, the young Américo Sérgio Maia, would praise his "profound and brilliant administration" that "dealt serious blows [to the Protestants], extremely reducing their membership."[144]

Elusive Victories

The cases of Catolé do Rocha and Cuité shed light on the contradictory impulses within Catholic Restorationism, the church–state alliance, and Protestant activism in the early twentieth century. Both church and state were anxious to assert the primacy of the Catholic faith in Brazilian society, but they did so in service of a mission to unify, modernize, and stabilize the country, subordinating regional and local forces to centralized national authority. Anti-Protestant discourses and even anti-Protestant violence were useful when they were part of Restorationist projects undertaken by so-called civilized individuals, such as Catholic bishops and sufficiently obedient and Romanized priests. However, when they were taken up by individuals whose profile did not fall comfortably within the narrow confines of orthodox Restorationist Catholicism, civil and religious authorities alike sought to punish and suppress the leaders of the religious campaigns, now declared to be a threat to national security. Actions that in one context might have been deemed a legitimate "religious defense of Brazilian national values" were now seen as an illegitimate expression of religious fanaticism. Protestants, for their part, understandably seized on any weakness in official support of Catholic persecutors and attempted to use the stereotypes of uncivilized nordestino religiosity to convince authorities to take action against them. Protestants hoped that by uncovering the fanatical roots of nordestino religious persecution, they would expose all Catholic anti-Protestant campaigns for what they really were and always had been: violent, backward, and unconstitutional expressions of religious intolerance. Nevertheless, by creating a dichotomy between fanatical, rebellious Catholic nordestino culture and law-abiding, peaceful Protestant culture stripped of the supposedly bad nordestino elements, Protestant leaders bolstered, albeit indirectly, the idea that the illegitimacy of religious violence was dependent on the perpetrators' cultural fanaticism.

And yet Catolé do Rocha and Cuité threw into doubt the very idea that Catholic Restorationists and government officials could successfully punish perpetrators of anti-Protestant violence, illegitimate or otherwise. In June 1941, over a year after the Catholics in Catolé do Rocha were sentenced to prison, the TSN received word from officials in João Pessoa that the convicted individuals had never, in fact, served their time. Authorities in Catolé do Rocha claimed that all of the men had fled the town and were nowhere to be found, but coastal officials suspected that not much effort had been expended in attempting to discover their whereabouts. In November 1942, after repeated demands to find the men, the local police finally took action but were able to imprison only three of the seven convicts. Moreover, the three individuals whom authorities had the luck to find were those who had the least social prestige and, as in the case of the farmworker Zacarias Alves Saldanha, had informed on their fellow Catholics in their testimonies and thus could be considered to have been at least partly responsible for the trouble in which the group had found itself. Due to what was called a clerical accident the three men would serve more time in prison than they should have, one year and seven months instead of one year. The other four men would not spend a day in jail. Even when justice was supposedly done and anti-Protestantism deemed unacceptable, concrete consequences for the perpetrators were difficult to enforce.[145]

A similar situation would occur with Padre Luiz in Cuité. Although the Catholic Church had taken away his priestly orders, they did not succeed in diluting his influence in Cuité. In fact, they essentially created a parallel religious authority in the town. After his expulsion from the priesthood in 1941, Padre Luiz continued living in Cuité and for all intents and purposes acted as both priest and *coronel*. Until the day he died he wore his cassock, insisted on being addressed as Padre, carried his rifle and dagger/walking stick around with him, and remained involved in local and state politics. For decades to come residents of Cuité continued to consult Padre Luiz on religious matters, listened to his lectures and the sermons he gave in the private chapel he built on his fazenda, and brought their children to be blessed by him—although only after being baptized in the official church. If Catholic leaders' intentions were to eliminate backward sources of religious authority and unify the church under Romanized orthodoxy, they were utterly unsuccessful.

Ultimately, the cases of Catolé do Rocha and Cuité speak to the failure of the efforts of the Vargas state, the Brazilian Catholic Church, and Brazilian Protestantism to impose their national visions of the new Brazil in the local context of the Northeast. Protestants, to whom the new Brazil meant a secular state in which the freedom of religion reigned supreme, saw their government attempt to assert an even more narrow definition of "acceptable religiosity," all while maintaining Romanized Catholicism as the desired norm. The Catholic Church, for its part, proved unable to suppress the influence of the rogue priest in Cuité and instead watched its authority become further diluted as the defrocked cleric continued to claim the allegiance and loyalty of the town's parishioners. And while the Estado Novo regime had employed one of its most authoritarian institutions, the TSN, to assert control over anti-Protestant fanatics, it not only was unable to make its convictions and sentences stick but also found itself, whether knowingly or not, deepening local political struggles and fortifying oligarchical authority in Catolé do Rocha and Cuité. Local actors in the interior strategically engaged reformist ideals in order to advance their own goals and agendas. In doing so, they often strengthened the very religious and political traditions that central authorities were working to eradicate.

Not all encounters between northeastern religious culture and reformist Restorationist ideals were inherently confrontational. Some religious actors, such as the Capuchin leaders of santas missões populares, were able to integrate the modern Restorationist mission and anti-Protestant religious traditions that were in danger of being labeled fanatical. In this way, they were able to promote an anti-Protestant cultural project that was legible to and celebrated by Brazilian civil and ecclesiastical leaders. Protestants would find that no matter how strongly they argued that santas missões and their leaders were representative of dangerous fanatical millenarianism, they could do little to stop the missões and their harmful effects on Protestant communities.

FIVE

Fire, Brimstone, and the War
against the Heretics

Santas missões, Protestants, and
Religious Conflict in the Northeast

In April 1937 two Congregational pastors, Synesio Lyra and Artur de Barros, traveled to Guarabira, a town in the interior of Paraíba. They were attending a celebration for the inauguration of a new evangelical temple, and they planned to preach at a special service to mark the occasion. Before Reverends Lyra and Barros arrived they heard that local Catholics had learned about the event and were planning a "terrible persecution" meant to intimidate the Congregationalists and demonstrate that Protestants and their new temple were not welcome in Guarabira. On the evening of the event the church was packed to the brim with Congregationalist worshippers, many of whom had traveled from the surrounding towns to show their support for the Guarabira Protestant community. Just as the choir began to sing hymns to open the service "a large mob of fanatics gave a great whoop . . . [and] thus began the cruel venture." The Catholics cut off the electricity to the church and began throwing rocks at the building. Afraid to go outside, the congregants sat in the darkness as a "hailstorm" of stones bounced off the walls, smashed through the windows, and rained on the roof. When it became clear that no authority figures were willing or able to stop the assault, Reverends Lyra and Barros suspended the service and sent the congregation home. The next day, to avoid further conflict, the pastors returned to João Pessoa.[1]

The events of Guarabira were reported in the Presbyterian newspaper, *O Puritano*, which highlighted one fact above others: as members of the crowd outside the temple threw stones they were yelling, "Long live Frei Damião!" According to *O Puritano*, such statements were yet another example of how a "dangerous agitator," the Capuchin missionary Frei Damião de Bozzano, was sowing fear and hatred among Catholic communities in the Northeast.[2] Weeks before, Frei Damião had visited Guarabira, and, as reported in *O Puritano*, the friar had known about the temple inauguration and wanted the local community to prevent the event from happening. In his sermons Frei Damião was said to have "publicly attacked [Reverend Lyra], saying that [he] was a great enemy of the Church. He made it so that the fanaticized people were ready to assassinate the pastor."[3] Protestants believed that when the crowd gathered around the temple that April evening they were carrying out the direct orders of Frei Damião.

The article in *O Puritano* was not the first to single out Frei Damião as an instigator of persecution of Protestants. Throughout the 1930s and 1940s the Capuchin friar was linked with increasing frequency and intensity to some of the most virulent episodes of anti-Protestant agitation in the Northeast. As he traveled through the vast expanses of the northeastern interior to preach revival-like santas missões populares he was said to have left behind a trail of burned churches, injured pastors, and frightened believers. Frei Damião and his ecclesiastical superiors insisted that he neither instigated nor condoned such violence in his itinerant missions, but Protestant observers thought otherwise. They argued that Frei Damião was leading a "holy war" against Brazilian Protestants, "subverting public order, fomenting anarchy, pitting brother against brother, families against families, Brazilians against Brazilians, and even Catholics against Catholics."[4] Throughout the early and mid-twentieth century Frei Damião served as the public face and voice of religious conflict in the Northeast: he was lauded by many Catholics and despised by most Protestants.

Frei Damião was not the first or the last Capuchin missionary to turn the space of the santa missão into a battlefield against Protestant communities. Many of the anti-Protestant rites common to campaigns against Protestants—the processions, commercial bans, book burnings, etc.—were expanded, systematized, and spread by missionary preachers like Frei Damião who had made the fight against Protestantism central to their religious message. Santas missões were a fundamental part of northeastern religiosity, and anti-Protestantism came to be woven into their fabric. Catholic parishioners, the ordinary men and women of the sertão, were thus motivated to be party to acts of persecution against Protestants that went beyond loyalty to their priest or bishop. The strong emotions associated with the missionary experience became linked to the intense antipathy felt toward the presence and growth of Protestant churches.

Protestants did not sit idly by as santas missões threatened the integrity and safety of their communities. In the face of growing persecution Protestant leaders developed new evangelization strategies to combat the negative images of Protestants being promulgated in missionary sermons and protect the spiritual and physical health of congregants. In doing so, they increased the level of ecumenical cooperation between different denominations and developed novel ways to communicate their ideals and beliefs to broad audiences. While they were largely unsuccessful in their attempts to prevent acts of persecution or hold perpetrators accountable, they did make it more likely that vulnerable congregations would be able to withstand the pressures and conflicts that frequently accompanied santas missões.

Protestants and the Capuchin Order in the Northeast

The conflict between Capuchins and Protestants had a long history in both Brazil and the wider world. The Capuchin Order was founded in the midst of the Protestant Reformation, and one of the order's most important initial activities was preaching against the "new heresy" and seeking to reconvert individuals and families who had turned away from the Catholic Church.[5] The history of the Capuchin Order in Brazil was similarly steeped in confessional conflict. The first Capuchins to set foot in the Land of the Holy Cross arrived in Recife in 1642 not as missionaries but as prisoners of the (Protestant) Dutch West India Company, which occupied northeastern Brazil from 1630 to 1654. Originally from Brittany, the three imprisoned friars had been en route to the mission field of Africa when they were captured by the

Dutch on the island of São Tomé.[6] To Capuchin authorities as well as to many subsequent Capuchin historians of the order, this turn of events seemed providential. Members of their order had arrived in Brazil under treacherous circumstances to find themselves in an ideal position to contribute to what they believed was one of the most important tasks of the era: fighting against the Protestantism of the Dutch Calvinists, whom Capuchins viewed as both political and religious oppressors.[7] According to the Capuchin historian Pietro Vittorino Regni, the mission in Dutch-controlled Brazil had two main objectives, both rooted in combating Protestantism: to provide "opposition to the proselytism of Calvinist preachers and numerous Jewish people who had come to Pernambuco during the religiously tolerant regime of Maurício de Nassau; and to offer "assiduous spiritual guidance to the Catholics threatened by heresy."[8] When Portuguese colonists rose against the Dutch in 1645 the Capuchins actively supported the rebellion, portraying the war as a "battle in defense of the faith," a holy war meant to free the Catholics from the heresies of the oppressors.[9] When the Portuguese and therefore the Capuchins proved victorious in their war against the Dutch the missionaries rejoiced in the victory, viewing it as a triumph for the Catholic Church as much as for the Portuguese Crown. The Capuchins' presence in the Northeast, however, was short-lived. By 1687 political disputes between Portugal, France, and the Holy See meant that new French missionaries were no longer allowed to enter Brazil, and by 1702 the Portuguese Crown had officially expelled them from the colony.[10] The French would later be replaced, in fits and starts, by Italian missionaries who would establish a permanent presence in the region in 1840.

The reemergence of Italian Capuchins in the Northeast paved the way for the ascension of one of the most famous Brazilian Capuchins of all time, Dom Frei Vital Maria Gonçalves de Oliveira. While Dom Vital is most well-known for his opposition to Masonry and his involvement in the 1870s-era Questão Religiosa, he was also a critical voice in opposition to the Protestant missionaries who had arrived in Brazil in the decades before his rise to the episcopate.[11] Dom Vital believed that these Protestants, most of whom were from the United States, were intimately involved in a grand Masonic conspiracy against the Brazilian Catholic Church. As a native son of Pernambuco and the archbishop of the preeminent episcopal see of the Northeast, the Archdiocese of Olinda and Recife, Dom Vital's anti-Protestant influence was felt keenly throughout the region. The media outlets controlled by his archdiocese produced a constant stream of polemical articles that attacked the Protestant religion and defended the archbishop against the counterattacks inevitably appearing in the liberal press. Moreover, Dom Vital went out of his way to put up roadblocks to the few Protestants who dared come to Recife to distribute Bibles and give conferences, imploring the police to break up their meetings and prevent their preaching. While his main concern was combating Masons and their Catholic supporters, he saw his opposition to Protestantism as part and parcel of his larger goal. Like all Romanized Catholics, Dom Vital believed that Masons, positivists, and Protestants represented an evil fruit from the same tree, namely, the liberal individualism that had overtaken the world from the moment Luther nailed his ninety-five theses to the door of a Wittenberg church.[12]

Dom Vital's battle against Protestantism was largely ideological; he believed that the ideas being spread by Protestants and their liberal allies were harmful to the spiritual integrity of the Catholic Church. Yet there was another Capuchin who believed that the "religions of Luther" posed a more immediate and practical challenge to Catholic hegemony in the region. Frei Celestino de Pedavoli was a Calabrian friar who had arrived in Recife in 1876, just a year after Dom Vital had been released from prison for having opposed Masonry during the Questão Religiosa.[13] In many ways Frei Celestino was ahead of his time. In the late 1800s and early 1900s, before Protestants had established a forceful presence in the northeastern interior and before the advent of the Catholic Restoration, Frei Celestino began to work furiously to spread the word about the dangers of heresy. He argued that the conversion of masses of supposedly ignorant, uneducated Brazilians who did not understand the destructive nature of Protestantism and thus could not protect themselves from the wiles and seductions of Protestant heresies would bring about the downfall of the Catholic institution. To warn his fellow Catholic elites of the potential ruin that awaited their church, he wrote editorials in Recife newspapers attacking Protestantism and published anti-Protestant tracts with titles like *Combate ao Protestantismo* (Battling Protestantism). He sent out a "cry of alarm" to his fellow Catholics, urging them to reject the "dark, disgraceful, and dreadful insidiousness that is plotting against [Brazilian Catholics]" and attempting to replace the One True Faith with the "sorry synagogue of their errors, blasphemies, and heresies!"[14] In 1902, with the support of the bishop of Olinda, Dom Luiz Raimundo da Silva Brito, Frei Celestino founded the Liga Contra o Protestantismo, a zealous but short-lived group that sought to enlist the support of elite Recifenses in the campaign against Protestantism.[15] The liga had few real members beyond Frei Celestino and his Capuchin brethren, but it nevertheless succeeded in raising the public's awareness of the "pernicious Protestant threat" by organizing dramatic theatrical demonstrations of what they proclaimed to be victories against Protestantism. Liga members organized Bible drives in an effort to get Recifenses to turn in their illicit Protestant Bibles, which Capuchins would then burn in dramatic bonfires outside of their convent. They also held lavish so-called conversion ceremonies in which ex-Protestants formally renounced their religion, swearing fealty to the Catholic Church and cursing the religion that had seduced them into sinning against the True Faith.[16] Capuchins invited local politicians and dignitaries to these events as a way to both convince elites of the worthiness of their cause and to show the rest of the community that the liga had the power of the authorities on its side.

Early Protestant missionaries did not hesitate to confront Frei Celestino and the liga at every turn. They used the liberal press of the First Republic to their advantage, publishing articles in secular newspapers that undermined Frei Celestino's credibility and accused the Catholic Church of fomenting irrational, antirepublican, unpatriotic, and dangerously intolerant religious fervor. John Rockwell Smith, a Presbyterian missionary in Recife, took to the pages of the *Jornal do Recife* to condemn Frei Celestino's attacks on Protestantism and apologies for Catholicism as "dim-witted adulation and vile servility . . . [that] reeks of papist slavery and has nothing, nothing of the spirit of religious and civil liberty of the historic Calvin of the sixteenth-century Reformation. Every intelligent man," Smith continued, "recognizes that this spirit of vileness comes from the same lips that kiss the infallible feet [of the pope]."[17] In his articles defending his faith Reverend Smith strove to show that Frei Celestino and his incessant attacks on Protestants were merely further proof that the future of liberal Brazil lay with the rational and enlightened Protestants rather than the backward and monarchical Catholics. Similarly, the Baptist missionary Solomon Ginsburg understood that the Liga Contra o Protestantismo, and especially its Bible-burning ceremonies, represented an opportunity rather than a setback for Brazilian Protestantism. "[The Catholics] are getting mad and losing their heads," Reverend Ginsburg wrote to the Baptist mission board in 1903. "[The Bible burning] has roused the public more than anything else. Today I published an article calling the attention of the people to that fact and it is producing wonders. The priests are losing ground every day."[18] Reverend Ginsburg's many articles calling attention to the Bible-burning ceremonies were an attempt to stir up outrage among Brazil's liberal and secular leaders. He described the burned Bibles as evidence of a "new Inquisition" being spearheaded by the "new Torquemada," Frei Celestino.[19] Reverend Ginsburg's articles did not immediately put an end to the Bible burnings or other liga ceremonies, which would go on for another three years, until 1906, but they did succeed in stirring liberal antipathy toward Frei Celestino and the liga. Prominent secular Brazilians would soon engage in their own print war with the friar.[20] The result was a blow to the popularity and credibility of Frei Celestino and his Bible-burning ceremonies. When Frei Celestino died in 1910 the Liga Contra o Protestantismo effectively ceased to exist, and for at least a few years it seemed as though Protestants and Capuchins would cease to lock horns in Recife. Yet the relative quiet that followed the death of Frei Celestino was misleading, for while conflict may have been decreasing in the pages of Recifense newspapers and the pulpit of the Capuchin Convento da Penha, it was increasing in another key space: the santas missões populares, the itinerant missions that represented one of the most important spaces for popular religiosity in the Brazilian Northeast.

Santas Missões Populares in the Brazilian Northeast

Itinerant missions have deep roots in Brazil and the rest of the Catholic world. While scholars can find traces of their traditions and methods going as far back as the Middle Ages, santas missões took on their official, organized form in the sixteenth century. Undertaken primarily by Capuchins and Jesuits, the missions sought to reawaken the Catholic faith of the "humble countryfolk" of Europe and thereby provide a bulwark against the growing threat of Protestantism. At the same time, they were meant to bring the presence of the institutional Catholic Church and the doctrinal orthodoxy that came with it to the formerly superstitious towns of rural Europe.[21] In Italy Capuchin missions soon became "one of the strongest links, both spiritually and physically, between the city and the countryside." The urban-based Capuchins, many of whom hailed from the very same countryside towns they visited on their missions, both shaped and were shaped by the popular religiosity of rural villages.[22] Capuchins became famous for their close identification with the everyday, so-called simple people of Italian society, providing solace during the hard times of drought and disease and bringing thanksgiving and happiness during times of celebration and local religious festivities. The popular missions enabled and deepened this relationship and quickly became central to Italian Capuchin identity. When Italian Capuchins arrived in Brazil as missionaries in the eighteenth and nineteenth centuries, they brought with them their commitment to preaching missions. Capuchin friars as well as Franciscans, Jesuits, and, later, Vicentians and Redemptorists traveled extensively throughout the Brazilian backlands celebrating Mass, overseeing catechism instruction, performing marriages, and hearing confessions.[23] As Kenneth Serbin has noted, by the nineteenth century the missions had become key elements in the church's Romanization campaign, allowing even the most remote communities to be influenced by the European and therefore, in the eyes of ecclesial leaders, inherently more orthodox and disciplined sensibilities of foreign missionaries.[24] Yet the missions were not as orthodox and disciplined as their description might indicate or as Catholic leaders might have hoped. In reality Capuchin missions were theatrical, emotional, even mystical events designed to elicit a great amount of religious fervor in a short period of time. In the words of the religious scholar Cândido da Costa e Silva, "The internal dynamic of a mission is a crescendo, which will eventually reach a climax of dramatic expressiveness that generates strong emotions, rash decisions, and unpredictable generosities."[25]

The event was preceded by weeks of anticipation and preparation, as Catholics from the surrounding region made plans to go to the "mission town," often traveling long distances that imposed sizable physical and material costs. For many, the journey to the mission town was part of the mission itself, a type of pilgrimage that contributed to the salvific effects of the overall experience. In the words of one observer, as the mission drew near, "the wave of faithful Catholics flooding the town grew. Traveling great distances, overcoming difficulties, taking step after step on hard, uneven soil, suffering the twin plagues of the intense heat and material poverty, the people came to the Font of Holy Grace in order to quench a thirst that had been devouring their souls—souls which for many years had been denied the salutary water of penitential regeneration."[26]

The days and weeks leading up to the mission also saw an increase in commercial activities as traveling merchants arrived and began to sell their wares. As more and more individuals and families streamed into the mission town, small tent cities arose and improvised markets sprang up. In the meantime parish buildings were cleaned and public spaces were prepared for the large gatherings and processions that were the hallmarks of the mission experience. By the time the mission began, the town would be nearly unrecognizable to its inhabitants. Such a transformation was ideal for the mission experience, which was intended to disrupt worldly routines and realities, replacing them with the traditions of the santa missão.

The friars usually traveled in pairs, and upon their arrival they would be met on the outskirts of the town or at the train station by thousands of members of the faithful, including local dignitaries and regional politicians. The Capuchins rarely failed to make a first impression. Their long, flowing beards and simple homespun robes gave them an ascetic, holy appearance, and their severe demeanors imbued all missionary activities with a somber and reverent atmosphere. After a few words of welcome from the town priest or mayor the large crowd would solemnly process, oftentimes while singing hymns or reciting prayers, to the town church. If the church was not large enough to accommodate the crowd, the church steps or even an outdoor stage constructed especially for the occasion served the purpose. After giving a brief overview of the schedule for the following days, one of the friars would preach an inaugural sermon in which he would "declare the objective of [the mission]: the salvation of souls and the betterment of parish."[27] And with that, the mission would officially begin.

During the mission, the days began as early as four in the morning with an "invitational procession" in which the missionaries and a small group of local Catholics would walk through the streets of the town, waking the inhabitants by singing such hymns as "Come Mothers, come Fathers, and Bless this Mission."[28] As the march progressed, more and more people would emerge from their houses and join the procession, which ended at the local church, where a Mass was held at five o'clock.[29] After Mass the mission activities would begin. Throughout the week a number of functions were carried out. Large-scale catechism classes in which the missionaries examined the preparedness of the town's inhabitants and gave detailed lessons on the finer points of Christian doctrine were a central activity. The instilling of the immutable Truths of the catechism was thought to be essential to warding off backland superstitions and, later, the heresies supposedly being spread by Protestants. Another central function of the mission was to perform as many sacraments as possible. Attendees were encouraged to perform their annual obligation of receiving Communion during one of the daily Masses, and hundreds of parents brought their children to be baptized. Of special import was the marriage of couples who had been "living in scandal," that is, living together without having been married, or, perhaps worse, who had had a civil marriage without also having been married in the church. Even the couples that "did not want to marry" were made to feel "so ashamed of their deplorable scandal" that they "went to the feet of the anointed [missionary] to be absolved of their recognized and enormous sins."[30]

When not attending catechism instruction or receiving sacraments, mission participants could be found doing physical labor: repairing or building a chapel or church, building or refurbishing the stone walls that surrounded the local cemetery, or even constructing what would be considered public works for the common good of the town, like roads, bridges, irrigation and sanitary systems, and other such projects.[31] While such work may not have been as obviously sacred as the other mission activities, it served as a way for the sinners to perform penance for their many offenses. The sinners were a

group which, in missionaries' eyes, comprised nearly all individuals by virtue of their contact with the sinful material world. The labor campaigns also
served as a potent example of the Capuchins' desire to be one with the people: rather than simply organizing and directing the projects, missionaries
worked alongside their congregants, performing the same backbreaking
physical labor and enduring the same harsh environmental conditions. At
times the work projects were performed at the behest of the missionaries. If
they arrived in a town and saw that a chapel was in need of repair or a cemetery wall was collapsing, they would organize a labor team accordingly.[32]
Many of the projects, however, were done in response to specific requests
from the parish priest or the townspeople. The requests were usually made
before the arrival of the Capuchins, as a side request that the priest or town
leader made when requesting the mission itself. At times santas missões
were portrayed by outsiders as little more than a means by which to accomplish material goals: a town needed a new church or bridge or cemetery or
other labor-intensive project and thus contacted the Capuchins in the hope
that the mission would provide the influx of persons and resources necessary to accomplish the task.[33] The missionaries themselves would never describe the objective of their missions in these terms, but the buildings,
bridges, and walls constructed during their stay were often the most visibly
long-lasting effects of the mission.

The most memorable and dramatic moment of the mission would not
occur until the evening, when the missionaries preached their famous sermons. More than anything else, the Capuchins were known for their zealous,
passionate, fire-and-brimstone preaching style. They railed against the god-
lessness of the modern world, demanded congregants repent their sins and
reform their errant ways, and warned of the eternal consequences of refusing
to heed their words. The sermons were often preached outdoors at night, the
only source of light coming from the candles held by the thousands of spectators who stood silently in the dark. This was the atmosphere in which the
Capuchins gave graphic, fear-inspiring depictions of the Hellfire that
awaited all unrepentant sinners: "In Hell there burns a vast and terrible fire
that is enclosed on all sides, with no way to escape it. The damned are forced
to swim in this lake of fire, without any hope of respite. The fire soaks

through their skin and blood, streaming through their veins and arteries, tearing apart their hearts. ... It torments all their body parts, entering through the eyes, ears, nose, and mouth, all the while burning like a furnace. ... The ordinary fire with which we are familiar here on earth is only a weak dream [compared to the strength of the Hellfire]."[34]

Missionaries constantly stressed the fact that anyone, at any time, could die a sudden and unexpected death, and if that person had not reconciled him or herself with the Lord by receiving the requisite sacraments from the church, eternal damnation was the inevitable result. In pamphlets they distributed to mission-goers, Capuchins warned that "death approaches quickly, and may be closer than you think!" and that "Hell is full of sinners who wanted to repent their sins, but never truly converted!"[35] In order to avoid being caught unprepared, Catholics were exhorted to always keep in mind "the Last Things: DEATH — JUDGEMENT — HELL AND HEAVEN — remember these, and you will never sin again!" Many sermons and pamphlets ended with the ominous question: "Who knows if this will be your last invitation and opportunity [to repent your sins]?"[36] Understandably, evening sermons provoked an emotional response in listeners, causing many to cry out, sob uncontrollably, and even faint. This was entirely by design, as missions were structured in such a way as to make the most dramatic and lasting impression possible in the hope that the spiritual influence of the mission would continue to reverberate among the public long after the missionaries left the town.[37] Only when attendees viscerally understood the horrific ramifications of a godless, unrepentant life would the mission be viewed as a success.

How, then, did congregants express their repentance? Here the sacrament of confession was central. The mission was, in many ways, structured entirely around the desire to elicit as many confessions, and absolutions, as possible. After days hearing about sin, eternal damnation, and the horrors of Hell, attendees would line up by the thousands to confess their sins to the friar and reconcile themselves with God and the church. Some of the most memorable scenes of the mission were the long, snaking queues of Catholics that would appear outside of the church as the multitudes patiently waited to give their confession to the Capuchin friars. Such images made a lasting impression on participants and observers alike. Catholic journalists marveled at how, during a single mission, "thousands of believers partook in the sacrament of penitence and holy communion, even people who had refused them for thirty, forty, or fifty years—for some, it was their first time."[38] Missionaries were frequently compelled to stay up all night in order to hear the confessions of all those awaiting absolution.

And yet the confession itself was oftentimes not enough to fulfill the penance needed for absolution. As mentioned above, many people took part in communal labor projects as acts of penitence. However, the most common way to truly and dramatically repent one's sins was to walk in a penitential procession. Normally held on the second-to-last day of the mission, the processions featured men and women trudging slowly through the village streets carrying a cross (or two crosses if they were young, able-bodied men) on their backs and at times flagellating themselves in order to demonstrate their repentance for their sins.[39] Like much of the rest of the mission, the penitential procession was an emotionally charged event for participants and spectators alike.

Yet the Capuchins did not end the missions on such a somber note. The last day of the mission almost always featured a triumphal procession in which the friars, holding a large cross triumphantly in the air, led all of the mission attendees through the streets of the town, singing hymns and shouting vivas! to the Virgin Mary, the Sacred Heart of Christ, and the Most Holy Pope.[40] The triumphal procession celebrated not only the concrete fruits of the mission, that is, the large number of marriages and baptisms performed, holy communions given, and confessions made, but also the more general "triumph over sin" the entire community had achieved by taking part in the purifying rituals of the mission, both sacramental and otherwise. After the procession had ended, either the same day or the next, the mission would officially be closed. When the missionaries packed up their belongings and left the town, commonly accompanied by a large crowd of singing and chanting believers, they were confident they were leaving behind a community that was more faithful, more orthodox, more obedient to ecclesial leaders, and more likely to be welcomed into the Kingdom of Heaven.

Religious Conflict, Fanaticism, and the Rise of
Restorationist Santa Missões

Ever since the arrival of the first Protestants in the interior of the Northeast in the late nineteenth century santas missões had represented a space of conflict and contestation between the two faiths. To Protestants, the transformation of an ordinary town into a mission town posed an immediate threat to their spiritual and physical well-being, as their very presence disrupted the mission's overarching objective of communal purification. They were a constant reminder of the presence of persistent sin and the inability of the town to truly be triumphant in the face of so-called heresy and apostasy. Protestants could choose to leave the area or minimize their public presence during a santa missão, and some did. But many Protestant leaders believed that santas missões represented opportunities to both witness their faith in front of large audiences and combat the supposed fanaticism and backwardness of the santas missões' popular Catholic traditions.

U.S. Protestant missionaries especially reacted in this way, their unease regarding northeastern santas missões deriving in part from the low opinion they held of nordestinos themselves. Like many Brazilian Catholic leaders of their time, Protestant missionaries believed northeasterners to be inherently violent and easily manipulable by outside forces. Protestant missionaries like Eliza Reed, a Presbyterian in Recife, viewed the gathering thousands of northeasterners in a single place as an manifest threat to the peace and safety of the community. "[Capuchin leaders of santas missões] have called in from the country, for miles around, all the ignorant, fanatical people for confession and mass," wrote Reed, describing a santa missão to a U.S. audience in 1896. "Women and men come barefoot from great distances, and carry stone and wood to the place where the new building is to be erected. Most of these men are armed with long, daggar-like [sic] knives and great clubs. They come by thousands, thronging the streets and largos of the city—an excitable, superstitious crowd."[41] An unidentified Baptist believed Catholic leaders had purposefully fanaticized nordestinos in the hope they would persecute non-Catholics in their communities. "The purpose of their missions," this person wrote in 1904, "is not to teach the people God's commandments, or Man's need to love God, obey his holy precepts, and love his neighbor, but rather to sow discord between Brazilians and give weapons to people fanaticized by [Catholic] missionaries so that those fanatics go on to injure their neighbors who were born under the same skies, under the same flag, and upon the same terrain."[42]

Protestants were not the only people raising concerns about the supposed fanaticism and backwardness of santas missões in the late nineteenth and early twentieth centuries. The very elements that made Capuchins such effective missionaries—their fiery preaching, ascetic personality, and ability to evoke intensely emotional responses from those who heard their message—were the same ones that had the potential to make Catholic leaders uncomfortable. They smacked of the type of unorthodox, potentially fanatical religiosity thought to be prevalent among the supposedly ignorant communities of the northeastern backlands.

The fact that Capuchins were so "close to the people" could be a double-edged sword. On the one hand it helped the Capuchins promote the distribution of sacraments, but on the other it exposed them to accusations of being too close to those they were meant to evangelize and reform. Such ambivalence was especially true in the nineteenth and early twentieth centuries, when Capuchins were appreciated for their role as religious and political pacifiers even as they were being simultaneously denigrated for allegedly being just as uneducated, rude, and fanatical as their flock.[43] For this reason, every so often calls to put an end to the missions sounded, as "concerned Brazilians" contended that "it is very bad . . . to congregate large groups of uncivilized people, far from the eyes of authorities, and fanaticize them with miracles of salvation and talk of eternal life."[44] Capuchin missionaries' emphasis on catechism and the distribution of sacraments had always been an effective counterweight to such accusations: in speaking of salvation and eternal life, the friars were also making clear that the only way to obtain such benefits was to participate in the official sacraments of the Catholic Church, whose distribution was tightly controlled by ecclesiastical authorities.

Yet this fact alone could not eliminate elites' suspicion of missionary endeavors. As Lúcia de Fátima Guerra Ferreira has shown, when the bishop of Paraíba wanted to Romanize and modernize his diocese at the beginning of the twentieth century, he favored the Jesuits and his own pastoral visits over

Capuchin-led activities. The bishop did not prevent Capuchins from conducting santas missões, but he could not prevent journalists and politicians from accusing Capuchin missions of promoting fanaticism.[45] In 1903, after Frei Celestino and his Capuchin brethren began burning Bibles in public ceremonies during santas missões, an outcry arose among liberal members of the Recifense and national Brazilian elite who condemned the Capuchins as religious fanatics promoting antiquated religious traditions. That same year the federal representative Germano Hasslocher declared on the floor of Congress that the actions of the Capuchins were an embarrassment to modern Brazilians and were "compromising the name of our country" by making foreigners "believe that we are a savage people who haven't lived up to the cultural standards that are enshrined in our Constitution."[46] After Representative Hasslocher and many other prominent Brazilians condemned the Bible burnings, the bishop of Olinda and Recife, Dom Luíz da Silva Brito, decided to take action. Noting that anyone could burn their private property, the bishop warranted that the actions of the Capuchins were legal, but he distanced himself from the Bible burnings themselves, saying he gave neither permission nor directions for them to take place. He demanded that in the future Capuchins perform Bible burnings indoors, in the privacy of the convent sanctuary, so they would not provoke criticism.[47] Dom Luíz's decision demonstrated the unease many Catholic leaders felt about Capuchin projects in the early twentieth century. Before the advent of the Restoration, Capuchins and their santas missões occupied a liminal space in the Catholic world, blurring the line between the reformers and the communities that were the objects of that reform.

The Catholic Restoration marked a shift in the relationship between Capuchins and Catholic Church leaders. As the twentieth century progressed, the identity and agendas of missionary Capuchins and Restorationist leaders became more closely aligned. By the 1930s small but crucial changes had been made to the missionary experience that gave them an air of cultured, educated events. Although penitence was still central to the missionary experience, increasingly missions were not solely focused on penitential ceremonies but instead put more emphasis on the Eucharist and the sacrament of communion. The more extreme activities of nineteenth- and

early twentieth-century missions, such as flagellating processions and penitential common works projects, were soon phased out and replaced with activities that were supposedly more educated and that displayed the public
power of the august institution of the Catholic Church. Thus catechism instruction and the regularization of Catholics' sacramental relationship with
the church were still vital elements of the missions, but they had been deem-
phasized in favor of the mass, rally-like gatherings that displayed the public
power and numerical strength of the Catholic Church in the Northeast.

One of the most important activities of the mission now was a Eucharistic
march in which thousands—even tens of thousands—of Catholics walked
solemnly behind the Holy Host displayed in an ornate monstrance. The procession reflected both the importance the Romanized Catholic Restoration
gave to the Eucharist as well as the church's desire to assert its newfound
power in the Brazilian public sphere. When Frei Damião led a Eucharistic
procession of more than ten thousand people during his mission in Alagoa
Nova, a local Catholic journalist described it as "the most dazzling and cap-
tivating event that this land has ever seen in its history."[48] By the 1930s missions had become less about the practical need to distribute sacraments to
pastorally underserved communities than about providing a space in which
to publicly demonstrate a town's commitment to defending its identity as a
singularly Catholic town. When Capuchin missionaries came to the Pernambucan town of Timbauba the event was hailed as a dramatic demonstration of the town's Catholic militancy. "TIMBAUBA AFFIRMS ITS CREDENTIALS
AS A CATHOLIC CITY," read the headline of the Catholic newspaper based
in Nazaré da Mata. The days of the mission were declared to be "days of
Faith in which the Catholic spirit and the profound religious sentiments of
the Timbaubense population were made evident in a manner never seen before."[49] Also on display was the presence in the processions of "the most representative figures of Timbaubense society," including politicians and the
local business elite. Missions, then, became akin to small Eucharistic Congresses, vehicles through which Catholics proved the power of the Catholic
Church in the social and political spheres.[50]

This new objective of the santas missões, that is, the display of Catholic
social and political prowess, greatly expanded the targeted audience of the

missions. While missionaries still spent the vast majority of their time in the rural interior of the Northeast, they began to establish a regular presence in urban areas. This was especially true in João Pessoa, the capital city of Paraíba, where, in 1933, the archbishop expressed a desire to have Capuchins preach an annual mission in the city during the Christmas season.[51] The annual missions in the city were evidence of the increasingly close relationship between Capuchins and urban parishes like João Pessoa that wanted to become centers of Restorationist activity. The missions were undoubtedly a success, as observers marveled at the dramatic displays of religious fervor. When the missionary Frei Damião gave a sermon in João Pessoa's cathedral in the middle of the afternoon, inhabitants of the city were amazed to see that "the cathedral and its courtyard were literally full, with crowds of people spilling out into the surrounding areas."[52] It was, the newspaper declared, "a multitude of people never before seen gathered on a weekday, when commerce and office buildings were still supposed to be functioning."[53]

On an even more practical level, santas missões became a convenient way to advertise and promote lay participation in the nationwide Catholic Action movement. During the height of the missions the local diocesan priest would often make an announcement "about Social Assistance and other issues related to Catholic Action, taking advantage of the large number of people who had shown up for the Santas Missões, a number that normally would have been very hard to gather all together at the same time."[54] Missionaries' rhetorical prowess thus became valued not only for its ability to elicit feelings of fear and repentance in the hearts of listeners but also for the sheer number of people it would inspire to gather in public spaces, thereby allowing the Catholic Church to both demonstrate its public prominence and recruit more soldiers for its militant Restorationist campaign.

Capuchin missionaries began to recognize that their lay orders could be integrated into the broader Restorationist goal of increasing the number and influence of lay associations that cultivated a Catholic spiritual elite in both urban and rural areas. To this end, Capuchins began heavily promoting the creation of Franciscan Third Order associations. These groups were made up of lay Catholics who desired a more militant and committed religious life guided by Franciscan spirituality and led by Franciscan and Capuchin friars. The activities and functions of Third Orders as well as the social status of their membership were very similar to those of Catholic Action associations. Third Order sisters and brothers were often members of the local elite, and they participated in such activities as organizing local religious celebrations, going on spiritual retreats led by Capuchin friars, supporting charity work and other campaigns to aid the less fortunate, and holding weekly or monthly meetings in which they discussed theological, spiritual, institutional, or social issues.[55] Third Orders would not displace Catholic Action nor vice versa. Capuchins argued that Third Orders were themselves indispensable elements of the Catholic Action movement: they served as "schools of Catholic Action" and prepared local Catholics to become more involved in the lay apostolate.[56] In a city like Gravatá, where local elites were deeply involved in Catholic Church life and Restorationist organizations, it was common to hear people remark, "Catholic Action in this city, in its essence and majority, is composed of members of the Third Order."[57]

Third Orders were thus a way for the Capuchin Order, famous for its closeness to the poor and humble masses, to branch out and move nearer in prestige to the Restorationist elites who were increasingly gaining influence in the national church. Throughout the 1930s Capuchins were committed to cultivating these dual relationships. In the words of Frei Otavio de Terrinca, one of the leaders of the Capuchin Order in Recife in the 1930s, a Capuchin friar should be proud of his ability to "walk between worlds": "The Capuchin is a friar of the people, a friar that knows how to rise to the level of the aristocracy and converse with them with dignity, but who also has the humility to lower himself to the democratic classes and live as the people live; his life is mixed in this way, taking on both the ministry of Martha and the ministry of Mary."[58]

It was no surprise, then, that the second half of the 1930s proved to be the great age of expansion for Third Order Franciscans in the Northeast. Before 1936 only three active Third Orders, all in the Pernambucan cities of Recife, Garanhuns, and Gravatá, were led by Capuchins in the northeastern province, which covered all of Pernambuco, Paraíba, Rio Grande do Norte, Paraíba, and Alagoas.[59] In 1935 and 1941 no fewer than forty-seven additional fraternities came into existence, the vast majority of which were founded in 1937 and 1938.[60] Santas missões played a central role in promoting the spread of the fraternities: whenever Capuchins preached a mission in a town in the northeastern interior with a sufficiently advanced local elite, they would endeavor to organize a chapter. Subsequent missions also afforded opportunities for Capuchins to host spiritual retreats for the orders' members, thus ensuring that the groups remained active and orthodox.[61] The retreats allowed well-off locals to become more actively involved in the planning and execution of the missions, but they also created an increasingly compartmentalized religious experience in which private retreats were held for the benefit of the elites while the santas missões were increasingly reserved for *o povo*, the poor, humble, and decidedly nonelite members of local society. Nevertheless, that development allowed Capuchin missionaries to move more comfortably throughout a variety of Catholic communities while assuaging the worries and suspicions that they were too close to any one group.

The 1930s and 1940s saw the Capuchins attempt to unite their missionary endeavors with broader nationalist sentiments that more clearly aligned with Restorationist goals. Their santas missões were no longer merely a means by which to sanitize the faith of the rural inhabitants of the interior; now they were patriotic campaigns to restore Catholicism's rightful place in the Brazilian public sphere and protect the nation from insidious foreign religious influences. Rather than view these developments as forming part of a new or innovative phase of their activism, Capuchins interpreted their new nationalist mission as being a retrieval of their long-standing identity as the "protectors of the True Faith" in Brazil and, specifically, in the Northeast. The 1930s saw a revival of interest in the Capuchins' role in the seventeenth-century Dutch occupation of Pernambuco, when, according to the Capuchins themselves, "they performed their apostolic ministry among the Pernambucan Catholics, fighting so that these Catholics would not be infected with the Dutch heresy."[62] Capuchins highlighted the daring and heroic nature of their history, depicting the anti-Dutch campaign as a sacrificial struggle to save the soul of the nation: "It was a time of devastation and terror, when Catholics were prohibited under threat of capital punishment to receive the sacraments; Catholic churches were profaned, destroyed, and burned, and priests were sent into exile. . . . In this emergency, French Capuchins rose to the highest reaches of their evangelical ministry, giving advice, comfort, and encouragement to our countrymen, who were the target of the most atrocious Calvinist persecutions. In doing so, they guaranteed the survival of Catholicism upon the blessed soil of our nation, our homeland."[63]

Capuchins were not the only ones to laud the crusade against the Calvinists of the seventeenth century. In the late 1930s national Restorationist leaders also began to rediscover the heroic resistance of the Capuchins and Catholic laymen in Pernambuco. This anti-Protestant history was one of the principal reasons Pernambuco was chosen as the site of the 1939 Eucharistic Congress, which, in many ways, became a weeklong commemoration of the long-ago "war against the heretics." Speaker after speaker cited the role played by the "Lion of the North" in saving the Catholic soul of the nation. "The soul of the superhuman resistance of Pernambucans [to the Dutch Calvinists] was the Catholic faith," declared Francisco Barretto Campello, a law professor and prominent member of elite society in Recife. Pernambucans may have had economic and political motivations for their revolt against the Dutch, the professor explained, but the true source of their ability to unify in opposition to their oppressors was their religious fervor. "Above all," he declared, "there was resistance to the Dutch people's insulting profanation of sacred images and hatred toward the Holy Host."[64] Northeastern Catholics, led by the zealous anti-Protestantism of their Capuchin missionaries, defended their nation by coming together under their common Catholic faith.

Frei Damião and the Rise of Anti-Protestant Rites in Restorationist Santas Missões

Nowhere could the Restorationist potential of Capuchin missionaries be more clearly seen than in the santas missões populares and their contribution to the Restorationist campaign against Protestants in the Northeast. Just as Frei Celestino had been the public face of Capuchin anti-Protestantism at the beginning of the twentieth century, so a newly arrived missionary,

Frei Damião, would become the standard-bearer for religious intolerance during and after the period of the Catholic Restoration. Born Pio Giannotti in 1898 in Bozzano, a small town in the northern Italian province of Lucca, he came from an extremely pious family. His brother was a diocesan priest, and his sister was a nun in the recently created Oblate Sisters of the Holy Spirit. The young Frei Damião entered the convent of the Capuchins in Villa Basilica in 1914, when he was sixteen years old. Like many priests and friars of his time, he served in World War I fighting in the trenches along-side his secular comrades. When the war ended, Frei Damião returned to his convent in Tuscany, where his ecclesiastical superiors took note of his expanding intellectual abilities. He was soon sent to Rome to continue his religious studies, going on to complete a doctorate in dogmatic theology at the Gregorian University in 1925. After completing his education, Frei Dam-ião returned to northern Italy and spent the next five years moving among various convents in Tuscany where he taught theology to young Capuchin novices. At the time Frei Damião seemed destined for a life as a theology instructor, preparing the next generation of northern Italian Capuchin fri-ars and missionaries. Yet something about Frei Damião's nature—perhaps his oratorical aptitude or his penchant for wandering about from convent to convent and region to region—convinced his superiors he would be best suited for missionary life. And so in 1931 he embarked for Brazil, prepared to become a missionary in the Capuchin province of Nossa Senhora da Penha, the provincial seat in the heart of the Brazilian Northeast.[65]

Examining the first decade of Frei Damião's missionary activity in the Northeast, one can only conclude that he was sent to Brazil with a single task: to preach as many missions with as much passion and zeal as was hu-manly possible. While other Capuchins made only occasional missionary trips, treating them as brief absences from their regular religious duties in Recife, Frei Damião was truly a full-time missionary. He essentially lived in the northeastern interior, traveling from town to town without returning to Recife for long periods of time. From 1931 to 1939 Frei Damião preached 223 missions, an almost shockingly high number. To place it in the broader con-text of Capuchin missionary activity, the second most active missionary, Frei Antonio, preached 62 missions during the same time period.[66] Given Frei

Damião's frenetic missionary schedule, he surely spent nearly all of his time traveling throughout the interior. In 1935, for example, he spent 313 days, or more than 85 percent of the year, either preaching a mission or traveling between missions.[67] Frei Damião thus had immense influence over an extensive geographical space. The friar was constantly interacting with new rural communities and accruing admiration and recognition for his unparalleled oratorical skills as well as his unique ability to establish emotional connections with everyday Brazilians. A Catholic newspaper explained Frei Damião's facility for creating intimate relationships with the common man: "During each [encounter with a group of believers], he gave a sermon that was relevant to the circumstances of the moment and that conformed to the spiritual necessities of [those listening]."[68] It was for this reason, observers surmised, that he was greeted with flowers and "vivas!" when he arrived in a town and bade farewell with tears and melancholy when he left.

Frei Damião was an instant success as a preacher, and he soon began to gain fame for his spiritual strength and eloquence. People traveled from far and wide to attend his missions, which rarely failed to disappoint. His sermons were even more fiery and emotional than those of his Capuchin colleagues, and they produced instant responses from listeners. A typical sermon by Frei Damião was described in the following terms:

> Thousands and thousands of the faithful came to the Mission, traveling distances of ten, fifteen, and even more leagues, crossing rivers and forests, spurred on by the desire to see the Missionary sent by God. They listened to the words of the Missionary with the most pious attention and wept for their sins, begging for the forgiveness and mercy of God. During the sermons, more than once the crowd parted and the most hardened sinners made their way through the multitudes and, moved by the inflamed words of the Missionary, threw themselves at his feet and renounced once and for all their evil ways. Those who were living in sin got married, and those who had previously rejected the sacraments now partook in them. After receiving the blessing from the priest with the comforting knowledge that it was the blessing of God, the

multitudes returned to their humble homes, overflowing with joy and *saudades*.[69]

Throughout the 1930s Frei Damião's missionary sermons increasingly came to address the evils of Protestantism, as he connected the sinfulness of the modern world and the hardships of the sertão with the infiltration of heretics into the region, arguing that the rise of Protestant believers was proof that the Devil had found fertile ground in the sinful backlands. In time Frei Damião became known for "always ending his sermons with violent words against Protestantism," as he exhorted the faithful to reject Protestants, whom he called seducers, and repent for the societal weaknesses that had allowed evangelical churches to gain a foothold in Brazil.[70] In these sermons Frei Damião called Protestants liars and hypocrites, saying they were "denying the divinity of Christ" while at the same time purporting to derive all Truth from the Bible, which clearly demonstrated that Christ was both fully human and fully divine.[71] The Capuchin friar incorporated his campaign against Protestantism into the mission's sessions of doctrinal instruction. As early as 1934 Frei Damião began to regularly give a talk titled "Which is the TRUE Church of Christ?"[72] The speech was most likely a simplified, popularized version of an article by the same title published in the Capuchin monthly journal, in which Frei Damião systematically presented scriptural evidence that "(1) Jesus founded his Church and then entrusted its government to Peter; (2) that it was Jesus's intention that Peter transfer that government to his successors; and (3) that those successors are the Popes." Anyone who said otherwise was "taunting the Sacred Scriptures" and setting themselves against the will of Christ.[73] Observers regularly marveled at how Frei Damião translated complex theological arguments into more relatable formulas and lessons, using "simple and accessible language familiar to all, committed immediately to one's memory and heart, and understood by the masses" in order to defend the dogma of the Church.[74]

Frei Damião incorporated his battle against Protestantism into the traditions and rituals of his santas missões, reinforcing the common set of the anti-Protestant rites (see chapter 3). The large-scale processions that were at the heart of the missionary experience became sites of anti-Protestant solidarity in which attendees expressed their rejection of the Protestant interlopers and pledged to fight against them. Baptists in Arcoverde recalled one such procession in which Catholics, waving white flags, sang the following song:

O Santo Padre triunfará	The Holy Father will triumph
E o protestantismo se derrotará	And Protestantism will be defeated
Levanta o povo a bandeira branca	The people raise the white flag
bandeira branca, bandeira branca!	white flag, white flag![75]

The "white flag" was a reference not to the flag of surrender but to the "white flag of Christ" that was used as a symbol of militant Catholicism.[76] Baptist leaders claimed that the procession ended with chants of "Death to Protestants! Death to Protestants!" and they denounced the processions as "truly Carnivalesque displays full of threats and enraged yelling against evangelicals."[77] Protestants held that these marches promoted confrontation and violence between religions, whether in the immediate or near future. The Baptist minister in Arcoverde said that "after the aforementioned Italian friar left, the [local] priest sustained the hatred that [Frei Damião] had been preaching, and [Arcoverde] lived interminable days of agitation that did not end until authorities from the Capital intervened."[78] As was so often the case, none of the Catholic agitators were punished by state authorities, and the cycle of rituals and persecution was left open, to be repeated over the following months and years.

During his missions Frei Damião worked to promote the ban on Catholic commercial transactions with Protestants. The friar continually told mission-goers that it was a betrayal of Christ and the Catholic Church to buy, sell, or barter goods with Protestants of any denomination. Frei Damião integrated the prohibition into his mission rituals through ceremonies in which Catholics solemnly swore to avoid contact with any and all Protestants. In a mission he preached in Esperança in 1936 Frei Damião held a special ceremony on the final night in which, to make them more effective, he blessed the rosaries, candles, and medals of the faithful. After the ceremony he spoke to the fifteen thousand people gathered in the plaza, telling them to cut off any and all commercial activity with Protestants. To ensure that they complied, he led them all in a "solemn oath to the Most Holy Virgin," who, he reminded the crowd, was the avowed enemy of the Protestants because they continuously denied her sanctity.[79] The crowd obeyed, "promising the eminent Virgin that they would flee from all commercial contact with the followers of the Devil."[80] Judging by Protestant accounts, it appears that many of them did so: Protestants related countless stories of being unable to sell their wares after Frei Damião visited their town, and other Protestants spoke of being unable to buy even basic goods for their families.[81]

Frei Damião incorporated Frei Celestino's conversion ceremonies, called abjurations of faith, into his santas missões, turning them into what was called a *fruto de missão* ("missionary harvest" or "fruit of the mission"). The frutos de missão were the baptisms, marriages, confirmations, confessions, and communions distributed or performed during the mission, all of which were closely counted and tracked. At the end of each visit the missionary would send a report to his superior detailing the precise statistics of each category.[82] These numbers were the metric by which the mission was judged: the higher the number of frutos, the greater the mission's success. In the 1930s, likely owing to the preaching of Frei Damião, abjurations of faith became especially coveted missionary fruits. They were proof that the weeklong events had the power to bring about a "conversion of the heart" in Catholics who wanted to renew and recommit to their faith. They could also quite literally bring about religious conversions and convince those living in the ultimate state of sin—that is, those who were consciously rejecting communion with the Catholic Church, which Frei Damião had repeatedly declared to be the True Church of Christ—to repent their heresies and rejoin the Catholic community. The mission-related conversions, though intensely reported and celebrated in the Catholic press, were in reality small affairs. Most of the conversion ceremonies that took place during Frei Damião's missions involved one person or a small group of two or three, often members of the same family. Many times Frei Damião's missions prompted no conversions at all. Yet the heightened focus on Protestant-to-Catholic conversions as frutos de missão—thus possessing the same importance as the number of Communions, marriages, and confessions made—contributed to the growing impression that the battle against Protestantism was a central objective of the santas missões.[83]

Ultimately, Catholics came to explicitly identify Frei Damião's missions with the Restorationist campaign against Protestantism. The two were inextricably intertwined, as the missãos were celebrated as a highly effective means of promoting the Restoration. In São José de Mipibú Catholic leaders described Frei Damião's mission as an opportunity to mount "a great demonstration of faith, showing that [the residents of the town] do not want the Protestant invasion."[84] In Macaíba Catholic authorities issued an "orientation message" to the mission-goers, advising them on proper conduct while there and describing the event's goals and desired outcome. In addition to promoting the sacraments of baptism, confirmation, confession, communion, and marriage, the mission aimed to allow the faithful to "listen to and learn the truth" about the "evils strung together" by Protestants, who denied the efficacy of good works and the all-important sacrament of confession.[85] Under Frei Damião santas missões were no longer "meant only for Catholics, but also for Protestants, Spiritists, the indifferent, and even atheists."[86] Simultaneously deepening and transcending their original goal of instructing and Romanizing the Catholic populace, Frei Damião's missions were now self-consciously outward projections of Catholicism's public power and the centrality of anti-Protestantism to the Romanizing project.

Proof That We Will Be Victorious: Protestants Confront Frei Damião

By the mid-1930s Protestants were beginning to see Frei Damião as a serious threat to their well-being in the Northeast, as more and more congregations reported incidents of persecution and conflict occurring at Frei Damião's missions. While the secular press largely ignored the episodes, Protestant newspapers increasingly sounded the alarm about the increase in violent crimes being committed against their coreligionists. After their abovementioned experience at the temple inauguration in Guarabira, Revs. Synesio Lyra and Artur de Barros accused Frei Damião of being a "dangerous agitator" whose sermons had specifically advocated violence against the pastors.[87] Protestants' warnings grew louder as scenes similar to the one in Guarabira were repeated throughout the sertão. In Gravatá, a midsize city in Pernambuco, Frei

Damião was accused of starting a holy war between Protestants and Catholics.[88] In Santa Rita, a small town on the outskirts of João Pessoa, he was said to have started an anti-Protestant riot.[89] In Esperança a U.S. missionary reported that after he left the town "two believers were horribly beaten up as they returned from a Sunday night service."[90] In the small town of Boi Velho on the Atlantic coast in Rio Grande do Norte there were unconfirmed rumors of Protestants being forced to perform manual labor—hoeing and weeding the gardens being planted in front of the municipal jail—with Bibles hanging from a cord around their necks.[91] By publicizing these incidents in the regional and national religious press, Protestants were signaling their refusal to suffer in silence, and they were promoting a narrative that highlighted Catholic fanaticism and Protestant faithfulness in the face of persecution.

Protestants were determined to push back against Frei Damião's attacks, and when santas missões came to their towns they adopted a variety of strategies to resist and respond to the friar's campaign. In the early years of Frei Damião's ministry Protestants faced a steep learning curve as they sought to improvise tactics and learn from their setbacks. The case of Apolonio Marinho Falcão is representative of some of the complex decisions faced by Protestant leaders when first confronted with Frei Damião's santas missões. In April 1934 Falcão was the pastor of a small but growing congregation of Baptists in the village of Itambé, located on the border between Pernambuco and Paraíba. Frei Damião was only just becoming known among Protestants in the Northeast as a "little, shriveled-up Italian monk with deep-set eyes and a sparse, shaggy beard" whose "appeal is to the ignorant masses and he shows a master's art in preaching to them."[92] Frei Damião arrived in Itambé on October 7 to preach a ten-day mission, and Pastor Falcão was caught somewhat off guard when the friar began "insulting the evangelicals and asking for a pastor to debate with him."[93] There was immense pressure on Pastor Falcão to defend Protestantism in a public venue against the attacks of Frei Damião, and the pastor decided "without hesitation" to debate Frei Damião that very day. The pastor soon came to regret having accepted the invitation because the debate was an unmitigated disaster for the Baptists. Pastor Falcão had not thought to negotiate the topics, rules, and location of the debate, and Frei Damião was able to dictate terms that would be most favorable to his own cause. According to Pastor Falcão, Frei Damião spoke most of the time, constantly interrupted the pastor during the short time he was allowed to speak, and filled the audience with supposedly fanatical and ignorant supporters who would not tolerate any words from the pastor. "I found myself facing a dilemma," Falcão wrote. "Retreat or venture forward." After attempting for some time to carry on, he decided that retreat was the wisest course of action. "Seeing that there was nothing more to be done," he wrote, "I accused the friar of being a liar, sophist, and anarchist" and left the stage, "descending into the ferocious crowd." He wrote that he worried for his physical safety, believing that Frei Damião was trying to incite violence against him, but he left the debate unharmed. Although he had tried his best, Pastor Falcão knew that the debate had been a failure for his cause, and he was "disheartened" that "he had missed the opportunity to let the people know the Truth."[94] Frei Damião's mission had been an undeniable success for the Restorationist cause in Itambé, intensifying local Catholic militancy and striking a blow against Catholic tolerance for religious pluralism.

Pastor Falcão's encounter with Frei Damião also had positive results for Protestants, however, allowing them to address weaknesses in their evangelization strategies and strengthen their ability to withstand the pressures and dangers that accompanied the friar's visits. Over time Protestants developed three main strategies for confronting Frei Damião and his santas missões. First, they realized that, alone, local pastors often did not have the means to counteract the intensity of Frei Damião's missionary activity. They decided that pastors from nearby locales should travel to the mission town to bolster Protestant activism and give the community spiritual and material support.

In the aftermath of Frei Damião's visit to Itambé, for example, Pastor Falcão traveled to Recife and met with the Baptist leaders Munguba Sobrinho, Orlando Falcão, and Firmino Silva. Together, they decided to send Reverend Silva to Itambé to help Pastor Falcão conduct intense preaching sessions that would refute Frei Damião's condemnations of Protestantism and restore their faith's reputation in the town. The men collaborated in writing and publishing a formal condemnation of Frei Damião's actions and distributed the pamphlet to all the residents of Itambé. They hoped to give Itambenses the opportunity to hear the arguments Pastor Falcão would have made at the debate had he been allowed to take part on his own terms. Pastor Falcão found the strategy to be successful. "The proof that we will be victorious," he wrote, "is that many people expressed their disgust with the conduct of the friar; some of these people already joined our congregation, while others have decided to not attend Catholic Church services anymore."[95]

While the pastors at Itambé did not arrive until after the mission had concluded, future preaching efforts would frequently occur during Frei Damião's mission. When Frei Damião arrived in Bezerros, a small town in Pernambuco, in 1938 the local Baptist pastor, Miguel Archanjo Vieira, knew he could not contest the mission's message on his own. As the leader of a "very small church" with few congregation members he did not have the resources to provide a Protestant counterweight to the Catholic event. He therefore asked the Baptist pastor of the neighboring town of Gravatá, Rosalino da Costa Lima, to come to Bezerros and help him give "a series of conferences to attract some curious [Catholics] who had become tired of listening to the long tirades in [Frei Damião's] sermons."[96] Such conferences, meant both to appeal to disillusioned Catholics and to boost the morale of local Protestants, became standard features of evangelical responses to santas missões.

Protestants' second approach to subduing Frei Damião was to strengthen their strategies of interdenominational cooperation, as Baptists, Presbyterians, and Congregationalists realized they needed to put aside their differences and work together to counteract Frei Damião's missions. Such unity was called for especially when they took part in high-profile events like theological debates. To the Baptist missionary Charles Stapp, the debate in Itambé was a wake-up call for northeastern Protestants, for it showed how it was "more zealous than wise" to agree to a debate with Frei Damião without first consulting other Protestants, including those of other denominations.

In the months after the October 1934 meeting in Itambé Frei Damião continued to challenge Protestants to debate in nearly every town he visited throughout the Northeast. But he found there were few who would accept without first consulting with wider Protestant networks. In Itabaiana, Paraíba, the Baptist pastor Firmino Silva told the Capuchin friar that he would debate only if he first went to João Pessoa to consult with other Protestants and create rules and security protections for the event.[97] Frei Damião did not stay in Itabaiana long enough for such a consultation to take place, and the occasion never materialized. In Esperança the Congregationalist missionary Charles Mathews teamed up with the Presbyterian leader Israel Gueiros in order to respond to Frei Damião's challenge. Together, the two men decided not to go through with the event when Frei Damião appeared to be breaking the rules previously agreed to.[98] Catholics seized on these cancellations as proof that Protestants were attempting to flee from opportunities to defend their religion. "Cowards. Spineless men. Liars," declared one Catholic observer from Esperança.[99]

But Protestants stood their ground, determined to engage with Frei Damião's missions only when they would have the best possible chance of success. When a debate finally took place in the larger and more Protestant-friendly city of Campina Grande, it was again an interdenominational affair, with Baptists, Presbyterians, and Congregationalists included in the planning and preparations. Together, they negotiated with Catholics regarding the debate topics, audience composition, moderator, speech lengths, security, and debate format. They chose as their representative Synesio Lyra, a respected Congregational pastor from Recife who would champion all Protestant denominations and who they believed would be best able to compete with Frei Damião's theological expertise. The highly anticipated debate was a lively affair, breathlessly covered by both religious and secular newspapers in the Northeast. There were reports of clubs, knives, and guns being found on members of the crowd, but despite Protestants' last-minute worries that the "fanatical hordes" in the audience were planning to start a riot and assassinate Reverend Lyra, the debate proceeded in a largely peaceful, orderly manner. Protestants were pleased by the outcome.

Although Catholics declared that "the great Christian mystery was affirmed by the Catholics and was diminished and ridiculed by our separated brothers," Protestants clearly believed they had redeemed themselves and their faith after the disastrous affair in Itambé. They were especially proud of their ability to work across denominational lines to showcase the strengths of their common doctrines.[100] Protestant leaders in Recife went so far as to organize an Interecclesiastical Thanksgiving Celebration to commemorate the performance in Campina Grande of Reverend Lyra, who was henceforth deemed a "hero of the faith." Also celebrated was the cooperation the diverse faith leaders exhibited in confronting their common foe.[101]

The third Protestant stratagem was to take security precautions before the arrival of a santa missão. Shaken by the specter of violence they believed pervaded Frei Damião's visit to Itambé and other northeastern towns, Protestants resolved to ask local and state authorities to guarantee their protection before, during, and after every santa missão. In Bezerros Protestants had been in contact with the chief of police for the duration of the mission, and Pastor Rosalino da Costa Lima expressed his relief that the chief was able to "see the side of reason," "serv[ing] as an instrument in God's hands to free us from those hyenas in cassocks," Frei Damião and his Capuchin partner.[102] However, as was the case in many instances of violence toward and intimidation of Protestants, simply asking for police protection did not mean it would be provided. Protestants would contact local authorities in advance of nearly every visit from Frei Damião, but they frequently were met with indifference, hostility, or simple incompetence. As Josebias Fialho Marinho, a leader of the Presbyterian church in João Pessoa, wrote, it was not rare for "the local authorities [to be] powerless to contain the excesses of the fanatical hordes who were brutalized and blinded by the hatred that was made to run through their veins by the inquisitorial preaching of Frei Damião."[103]

Moreover, even when Protestants found local authorities who were willing to intervene on their behalf there was always danger that the efforts would backfire, causing negative repercussions for police and Protestants alike. During Frei Damião's santa missão in Cajazeiras in 1936 Protestants went to the police and issued formal complaints against him and his Catholic supporters. They accused Frei Damião of encouraging physical attacks on Protestants, which resulted in a group of Catholics invading the home of a Protestant pastor and threatening him with violence unless he left town. According to the accounts of Protestants and Catholics alike, the police in Cajazeiras acted forcefully in order to ensure Protestants' safety, and they opened investigations of Catholics for their offenses against Protestants. After the home invasion the police chief sent a group of officers armed with bayonets to protect the Protestants who had been threatened.[104] Protestants spoke of how police officers personally broke the commercial boycott Frei Damião had promoted, "managing, with difficulty, to buy some milk in the street and bring it to the family of our evangelist, thereby saving the life of his small child, who was crying out of hunger."[105] It finally looked as though Protestants would be afforded the police protection and justice they had failed to obtain in so many cases.

However, Catholic leaders in Cajazeiras, both ecclesiastical and lay, were "stupefied" and furious that Brazilian security forces would protect their enemies. They pushed back forcefully against the local police, gaining the support of the police chief's superiors in the hope of overturning his orders. They accused the police of allowing Protestants to slander the Catholic Church with impunity, claiming that "under the protection of the police, Protestants redoubled their insults against the Catholic community."[106] The bishop, whose seat was in Cajazeiras, organized a massive rally in support of Frei Damião and, more generally, the Catholic Church that was attended by the most prominent regional authorities, all of whom wanted to show their "absolute solidarity with the Diocesan Bishop." Thousands of Catholics filled the main square in a "boisterous demonstration of faith," putting the power of the Catholic Church on full display.[107] Catholic newspapers reported that the police chief, Severino Cordeiro, came to the rally himself and publicly came to an understanding with the bishop, thereby recanting police support for Protestants. He said that the government had been insufficiently informed of the reality of the events in Cajazeiras. Even so, Cordeiro's reputation among Catholics and the reputation of his police force was permanently tarnished. A Catholic journalist wrote, "[Chief Cordeiro], being unfamiliar with the community [of Cajazeiras], perhaps fell under the criminal influence of certain leftist elements who were trying to take advantage of the incident."[108] During a time when the government was cracking down on Communists throughout Brazil, connecting Protestants and the local authorities who supported them to "leftist elements" was a strategy that frequently proved successful for northeastern Catholics.

While Cordeiro's apology and renewed support for the bishop allowed state authorities to forgive the police for being duped by Protestants and leftists, it may not have been enough to save the chief's job. According to Padre Fernando Gomes, the priest of the Cajazeiras parish, the police chief was fired for having dared oppose the church and Frei Damião.[109] Gomes reported as well that the Protestant pastor who had made the initial complaint to the police had been forced to leave town. To many Protestants, the victory of Frei Damião and the Catholic Church in Cajazeiras highlighted the fleeting nature of Protestant victories and the seemingly insurmountable barriers they faced in attempting to confront the power of the santas missões. "The laws of the nation are trampled to the ground [by the Catholic Church]," lamented Pastor Firmino Silva, "and any authorities who dare condemn [it] incur its wrath and suffer the consequences."[110] At the end of the controversy, Silva and his fellow Protestants in Cajazeiras realized it was not enough to have either police backing or that of individual representatives of authority. If Frei Damião enjoyed the support of the wider networks of power, Protestants could do little to prevent or punish religious persecution.

By 1940 santas missões were among the most frequent sites of religious conflict in the Brazilian Northeast: where missionaries went, conflict often followed. Protestants argued that religious persecution was the primary goal of the santas missões from the beginning. The Baptist leader J. Fialho Marinho spoke for many Protestants when he declared that the Catholic missionaries who traveled throughout the Northeast were nothing less than "offensive artillery units against the evangelicals" that had been sent by ultramontane Catholic leaders intent on reversing the gains Protestants had made in the Northeast in the first half of the twentieth century.[111] Catholics saw santas missões as part of the fabric of popular religiosity in the Northeast, and the conflicts that arose during the missions were the natural result of Catholic communities that were offended by outsiders' disrespect for their local religious culture. Catholic leaders believed that, if anything, the contention proved that santas missões could be successfully integrated into the modern Restorationist project by ensuring that rural communities became active participants in promoting and defending Catholicism in the face of Protestant growth. Much like the triumphal processions and the foundation of associations of Third Order Franciscans, the displays of anti-Protestantism were yet another way old traditions of santas missões could support new Restorationist objectives.

In this way Frei Damião proved himself to be a valuable member of the Restorationist movement. The Capuchin friar had gained a reputation as someone uniquely able to translate Restorationist goals, particularly anti-Protestant goals, into a ritual language that was legible to the supposedly backward populations of the interior. He preached a message that was as consistent as it was passionate, repeating the same denunciations and proscriptions over and over again: Protestants were bringing the wrath of God upon the sertão. Protestants were mocking the Holy Virgin and the communion of saints. Protestants needed to be barred from buying and selling with Catholics. Protestants needed to be expelled from their communities. These discourses and ideas were adopted by local Catholics and spread throughout towns in the northeastern interior (see chapters 3 and 4). Frei Damião was thus promoting a universal anti-Protestant project whose words and actions were attractive to and adopted by Restorationist priests and sertanejan parishioners alike. His singular commitment to preaching as many missions as humanly possible meant that this anti-Protestant message traveled far and wide throughout the Brazilian Northeast.

Protestants, for their part, neither passively accepted nor automatically fled from the hostility they encountered during the missions. They both recognized the dangers inherent in publicly challenging the missionary project and understood the opportunities such confrontations presented. By creating new evangelization strategies that relied on ecumenical networks of support for Protestant activism around mission activities, evangelical workers could reach larger audiences and spread their ideas in ways not previously possible. While their preaching tours and debates did not often result in many conversions, they allowed Protestants to defend their religion from the verbal attacks of missionaries, and there was always hope that Catholic attendees would reflect on the Protestant messages they heard and seek out more information and perhaps conversion in the future. But, perhaps most important, Protestant counterevangelization strategies aimed to strengthen the spirits and build solidarity among the local Protestants who were present in the mission town. Knowing they had support and protection from their coreligionists, local congregations were more likely to stand strong in their faith and refuse to flee their communities in the face of the missões.

In one area Protestant efforts failed to succeed. Their attempts to hold Frei Damião accountable for the persecution that often resulted from his missions were thwarted by the unflagging support ecclesiastical and state authorities showed him. On the one hand, the impunity enjoyed by Frei Damião was hardly surprising, since most Catholic actors went similarly unpunished for their anti-Protestant actions. Yet there was reason for Protestants to think that both state and ecclesiastical authorities might be hesitant to encourage Frei Damião's missionary activities. With every year that passed Frei Damião was showing increasing signs that he embodied one of the identities that both church and state feared most: the popular saint.

SIX

Saint, Fanatic, or Restorationist Hero?

Frei Damião's Otherworldly Mission

In June 1939 the Baptist pastor Silas Falcão wrote an article for the *Jornal Batista* in which he sounded the alarm regarding a Capuchin friar named Frei Damião who "for many years has been fanaticizing the most backward populations in the Northeast, preaching the most horrifying hatred against Protestants."[1] Reverend Falcão was living in Arcoverde, a town in the Pernambucan sertão where Frei Damião had recently conducted a santa missão. Much like his fellow Protestants had done in the past, Reverend Falcão painstakingly described the religious intolerance his congregation had faced during and after Frei Damião's visit. He wrote of processions in which Catholics sang anti-Protestant hymns, sermons that accused Protestants of being adulterous liars, ceremonies in which Catholics promised to refrain from conducting any commercial exchanges with Protestants, and even bonfires in which evangelical pamphlets were incinerated. In his description of Frei Damião's santas missões Reverend Falcão seemed less worried about these concrete acts of religious intolerance than about what he believed were the fanatical beliefs motivating such acts. "The backward people of the Northeast are increasingly venerating [Frei Damião]" as a saintly figure, he wrote. "[Many Catholics] are even saying that Frei Damião is Padre Cícero of Juazeiro, Ceará." Reverend Falcão was sure that Frei Damião himself was encouraging these beliefs: "Frei Damião has hinted to people, in various places, that they should call him Saint Damião!" The Baptist pastor could not understand why the authorities did not step in and put an end to such fanaticism. "Isn't this an embarrassment for the Northeast, and maybe even for Brazil? . . ." he asked. "Since local authorities remain silent,

I ask God for the President of the Republic to pay attention and put an end to this shameful situation."[2]

While Reverend Falcão was clearly not a disinterested observer of northeastern religious culture, he was correct in his observation that an important shift was occurring in popular perceptions of Frei Damião's spiritual identity. By the mid-1930s nordestinos had indeed come to see Frei Damião as more than just a charismatic Capuchin missionary. To many he was a popular saint who was endowed with special, even miraculous, spiritual powers. And his fame would only grow as years passed. Today, Frei Damião is one of the best-known religious figures in Brazil. His sanctuary attracts tens of thousands of *romeiros*, or pilgrims, every year, his statues can be found throughout the sertão, and the Vatican has given him the title Venerable, the first step leading to beatification and eventual sainthood. Many scholars and journalists have directed their attention at Frei Damião's activities during the 1970s, 1980s, and 1990s, when his saintly status was at its height.[3] Missing from the literature is an in-depth analysis of Frei Damião's early anti-Protestant campaigns and how they impacted Catholic and Protestant communities in the Northeast. In what Patricia Pessar has called the "sacralizing process," lay Catholics in the northeast made Frei Damião into a holy figure.[4] They found in his personality, features, and actions elements that connected him to a lineage of popular Brazilian saints and *conselheiros* such as Padre Ibiapina, Antônio Conselheiro, and, most important, Padre Cícero.[5] Frei Damião was increasingly portrayed as an individual who was different from regular Capuchin monks. He was said to possess special faculties, like the capacity to deny himself food and drink, a gift for transfixing his listeners with his deep voice and divinely inspired sermons and compel them to convert, and, most important, the power to perform miracles, make prophecies, and give divine and supernatural protection to those who believed in him. In this context Frei Damião's actions against Protestants increased his fame as a popular saint in that he was seen as having a special ability to combat the rise of evangelicalism in the Northeast. His reputation as a popular saint fueled the potency of his anti-Protestant campaigns, as his missions drew larger crowds and his words carried greater weight.

Protestants believed that Frei Damião's saintly reputation figured as both a danger and an opportunity. They worried that the emergence of a popular saint who counseled his followers to reject religious pluralism seriously threatened the tranquility and safety of their communities, and they believed their strategies for combating the negative effects of santas missões would become less effective as the Capuchin's fame grew. However, many Protestant leaders also understood that Frei Damião's popular sainthood made him vulnerable to accusations of religious fanaticism. Some thought that if they exposed a prominent Capuchin leader of santas missões as a fanatical charlatan who was taking advantage of the popular masses, they could fight back against Catholic persecution of northeastern evangelicals as well as gain ammunition for broader Protestant arguments regarding the backwardness of the Catholic religion and the need for modern Protestant reforms. As they had in Catolé do Rocha and Cuité, Protestants sought to appeal to elites' anxieties surrounding popular religiosity and millenarianism in the Northeast, portraying Frei Damião as a dangerous threat to public order and an embarrassing relic of a Brazilian past that modern civic leaders were attempting to leave behind.

Protestant accusations of fanaticism may have contributed to the arrest and punishment of Catholics in Catolé do Rocha and Cuité, but their arguments with respect to Frei Damião were largely ineffective, as ecclesiastical and civil authorities allowed him to continue his ministry. Such tolerance did not mean that northeastern elites were not unsettled by the friar's growing celebrity as a popular saint. Bishops issued strident denials of the rumors of Frei Damião's miracles and prophecies, calling them "groundless popular superstitions, utter foolishness, and laughable nonsense" that represented nothing more than the "gross exploitation of ignorant people."[6] Yet in the end Catholic leaders directed their ire not at Frei Damião but at his followers, who were accused of trying to sully the orthodox friar's identity with their unorthodox beliefs and practices. Romanized Restorationists would simply need work harder, they believed, to cleanse these communities of their heterodox beliefs.

Catholic leaders thus vigorously defended Frei Damião against accusations of fanaticism throughout the 1930s and 1940s, championing him in a way they did not the Catholic activists in Catolé do Rocha or Padre Luiz Santiago in Cuité, who arguably had weaker ties to millenarian movements and fanatical identities than Frei Damião. The friar received this support because, unlike Padre Luiz, he had transformed himself into the ideal Restorationist agent. He was well educated, eloquent, an expert in church doctrine and theology, and committed to instilling respect for sacraments and the institutional church among the supposedly ignorant and superstitious masses. Perhaps most important, he had integrated his missionary and his anti-Protestant activities into the broader agenda of church leaders in the Northeast. As priests and bishops became determined to combat the growth of Protestantism, Frei Damião and his missions were in more demand than ever. Rather than traveling throughout the Northeast in pursuit of his own spiritual agenda, Frei Damião was preaching missions in parishes and dioceses whose leaders had invited him specifically to take part in their own anti-Protestant campaigns, which they had often initiated well before Frei Damião arrived. Restorationist priests and bishops knew that a visit from Frei Damião could help their cause, and they viewed his missions as tools to help them implement their own Restorationist initiatives better.

The relationship forged between Frei Damião and Restorationist clergymen did not mean, however, that he acted merely as their puppet. The friar's anti-Protestantism was not imposed on him from above but sprang forth from the well-established traditions of the santas missões. The highly emotional, even mystical, atmosphere fostered by the popular missions enabled the missionary to form a unique bond with the people to whom he preached. Bonds like this were crucial to missionaries' ability to address unorthodox religiosities and promote reforms, giving missionaries an identity distinct from that of the priests and bishops championing the same agenda of purification and reform. Frei Damião, deemed a prophet and miracle worker by nordestinos and an effective reformer by his hierarchical superiors, developed a dual identity, part popular saint, part Restorationist agent.

Padre Cícero, Padre Pio, and . . . Frei Damião?

Frei Damião had been in Brazil for less than three years when rumors began to circulate about his otherworldly identity. The first signs of the sacralizing process could be found in newspaper accounts of his missions. In the early years of his missionary career Frei Damião had clearly made a strong impression on the communities of the northeastern interior. Local journalists and Catholic observers rarely failed to remark on his extreme ascetic and penitential personality, claiming that the friar barely ate or drank anything, only slept three hours a night, and wore a hair shirt and other penitential devices when he was awake.[7] People were immediately curious about this mysterious man who spoke with an Italian accent so thick as to be almost unintelligible and who seemed to be completely removed from the passions and needs that dominated most people's lives. As was true of all Capuchin missionaries, he lived a life of poverty, wearing only his simple robes and sandals as he traveled throughout the Northeast. It was said that Frei Damião was so devoted to praying all-night vigils and abstaining from food and drink that when he was not preaching he appeared to be physically weak, "with a waxlike paleness to his countenance, and eyes that shone only in the rare instances that he looked directly at a person."[8] He was unusually quiet and pensive, "almost never speaking, never conversing, and laughing only rarely and discreetly."[9] Yet this weak, reserved manner disappeared completely when Frei Damião began to preach his famous sermons. As soon as he rose to the pulpit, he "transformed . . . into a passionate preacher of the faith, full of energy, enthusiastic, demanding conversions from the people who stood in awe, transfixed, even moved to tears, just from listening to [Frei Damião's] words."[10] After he finished his long, seemingly exhaustive sermons he would not retire or rest but invite the repentant crowd to line up behind the confessional, where he would sit for hours upon end hearing confessions and dispensing advice, counsel, and forgiveness.[11] When the mission came to an end and Frei Damião prepared to leave, he would be surrounded by the multitude of the faithful, at which time he would give a rousing, almost enrapturing speech. As one observer described the scene, "Frei Damião, carried away by enthusiasm as a hero of the faith, transfigured and divinely inspired like a saint, gave a speech that elicited from the hearts of the people the purest feelings of love for Jesus, and garnered their most ardent ovations."[12]

Descriptions like this were published in coastal newspapers and usually represented the voices of the Catholic social elite. While they implied that

Frei Damião was a special preacher and alluded to his holy, even saintlike qualities, they stopped short of declaring the Capuchin himself to be a saint or to have supernatural abilities. Other northeastern Catholics were not as circumspect. Many residents of the interior saw Frei Damião as being more than a passionate, effective missionary preacher: he was, they were convinced, endowed with otherworldly powers. Rumors of Frei Damião's supposed saintly status spread quickly. One way was through *cordéis*, small pamphlets or chapbooks that served as a means of circulating popular news and soon-to-be-legends throughout the sertão. As Pessar has argued, cordel literature often played a key role in the saint-making process, for it facilitated the development and dissemination of popular narratives regarding the holiness of the popular saint.[13] Called "literature on a string" because they were pegged to a cord in order to be displayed for sale, the *folhetos* were composed by popular *cantadores*, or "singers," and were written in verse form so as to be more easily read aloud to groups and passed along orally. Given that they were created and consumed by nordestinos, their subject matter could be seen as mirroring the beliefs and opinions of those same people, and, as Candace Slater has written, "New developments in the *cordel* therefore suggest important shifts in the way ordinary people think."[14] Hence it was telling when, in the mid-1930s, folhetos that spoke of Frei Damião as a prophet and miracle worker began to appear in local markets. In 1936 a local Paraíban newspaper reported that a cordel titled *The Prophecy of Frei Damião* was being sold to Catholics throughout the Northeast.[15] Multiple versions of this cordel were likely circulating in the interior, all declaring that the friar had a special relationship with the Divine that had given him the ability to predict the future.[16] In 1939 reports in Rio Grande do Norte cited a folheto called *News of the Miracle of Frei Damião*.[17] While the reports did not contain transcriptions of the folheto, they made clear that *News of the Miracle of Frei Damião* portrayed the Capuchin missionary as a supernatural and saintly figure.

Frei Damião's identity as a popular saint was reinforced by the production of miraculous prayer cards that began to be sold in Pernambuco, Paraíba, and Rio Grande do Norte in the thirties and forties. Prayer cards, common in the Catholic world, typically depicted the image of a saint on the front, while printed on the back was a special prayer usually associated with the saint. The prayer cards depicting Frei Damião's image were different. They were miraculous prayer cards, also called strong prayer cards (*orações fortes*), and purported to have special powers that would protect the bearer of the card from illness, incarceration, and even death. In an oração forte, the prayer itself was usually short and addressed to the Virgin Mary or, in rare cases, to other saints or even the Holy Cross.[18] The card had a transcription of the prayer followed by a miraculous origin story in which the prayer was proven to be effective when tested by a persecuted individual. For example, a "strong prayer card" for Our Lady of Exile that was linked to Frei Damião claimed that the first person to come upon the written prayer (which was found, said the card, in the Holy Sepulcher in Jerusalem) had tied it around his neck and subsequently survived a knife fight. Anyone who carried the card on their person, the text said, would be protected. They would not die a sudden death "in the middle of the street" or be attacked by their enemies. Women who possessed the card would not die during childbirth or even feel pain. Dogs and snakes would not be able to bite the card holder.[19] To get the best results from the prayer card, holders were encouraged to send the cards to a certain number of other people.[20] The text of the prayer card was important, but the image was equally expressive. Putting Frei Damião's picture on the card gave the prayer an extra layer of protection; it was his blessing, though, that ultimately gave the prayer its effectiveness. A report by the Diocese of Mossoró stated that people buying the cards believed that the miraculous promises made would not come to pass unless the card had been personally blessed by Frei Damião.[21]

As early as 1936 Frei Damião was being explicitly connected to Padre Cícero, the towering leader of a large millenarian community in the Cearense town of Juazeiro.[22] When Frei Damião arrived in Recife in 1931, Padre Cícero was the most influential religious figure in the Northeast, viewed by many nordestino Catholics not only as their ultimate patron and benefactor but also as a man endowed with miraculous powers. When Padre Cícero died in 1934 the region was left with a power vacuum in the popular religious sphere. Various new religious movements emerged in the years after Padre Cícero's death, many of their leaders alleging they were the successors to or even reincarnations of the popular saint of Juazeiro. Not surprisingly, then, Frei Damião, too, came to be seen by many as having received his saintly powers from Padre Cícero himself, thus becoming the recently deceased saint's designated successor. He had arrived in the Northeast just a few years before Padre Cícero's death. Many believed that this was no coincidence and that Frei Damião had been sent by God or perhaps by Padre Cícero himself to grant the region a new spiritual leader. The divine connection between Padre Cícero and Frei Damião could be seen in the 1930s cordel *News of the Miracle of Frei Damião*, which was said to describe Frei Damião as "the substitute or messenger of Padre Cícero."[23] The idea that Padre Cícero's prophecies, miracles, and messages would now be relayed to his people by Frei Damião subsequently became a central theme of cordel literature inspired by Frei Damião.[24] In later years, one could find folhetos like José Francisco Borges's *The True Warning of Frei Damião about the Punishments That Are to Come*, which included the following stanza:

> [Jesus Christ] left for every nation
> A Counselor
> And for our Brazil
> That counselor came to Holy Juazeiro
> Padre Cícero Romão
> died and Frei Damião
> Joyously assumed his place.[25]

The transformation of Frei Damião into the successor of Padre Cícero was a vital moment in the sacralization process. As Pessar has argued, connecting a popular religious leader to Padre Cícero "placed him within that divine pantheon" and directly linked Frei Damião to the mystical lineage of those popular saints who had come before him.[26] Suddenly, Frei Damião became a potentially millenarian figure with the power to influence an untold number of followers who viewed him as a miraculous, all-powerful saint.

Padre Cícero was certainly the frame of reference that the majority of nordestinos used when interpreting the saintly nature and acts of Frei Damião, but for many Italian Capuchins living in Recife the more immediate comparison was Padre Pio. A fellow Italian Capuchin, Padre Pio, at the same

time Frei Damião was gaining a reputation for possessing miraculous qualities, was already known throughout Italy and much of the rest of the Catholic world for being a "living saint." In September 1918 Padre Pio had received
what appeared to be the wounds of Jesus's stigmata on his hands, feet, and
side. Soon pilgrims were flocking to the hamlet of San Giovanni Rotondo in
southern Italy, and news of miracles associated with Padre Pio's saintliness—
cures, the capacity to read minds and souls, and the ability to be in two
places at once—spread quickly throughout the globe.[27] It is not far-fetched to
believe that Frei Damião, having spent his formative years as a Capuchin in
Italy during the very period that Padre Pio was becoming famous for his status as a supposed living saint, was influenced, either positively or negatively,
by the stories of Padre Pio and his miracles.

The Italian Capuchins in the Convento de Nossa Senhora da Penha in
Recife were undoubtedly aware of Padre Pio and his miracles. In 1919 or 1920
one of the friars from the convent clipped an article in a Brazilian newspaper
that described Padre Pio and how he had "put everyone in ecstasy with the
extraordinary miracles" he had been performing. "We give thanks," the article continued, "that in these times that are so lacking in faith, [God] deigns
to reveal his mercy and his power in the humble son of Saint Francis, Pio de
Pietra-Elcina."[28] Initially, the Capuchins of Nossa Senhora da Penha shared
the opinion of the article's author, believing wholeheartedly in the miracles
of Padre Pio. In 1920 at least one friar was in direct contact with Padre Pio's
secretary, Padre Ignazio. This friar had specifically asked that Padre Pio pray
for the healing of a woman who was ill, perhaps a relative, a nun, or an ac-
quaintance of the friar. The secretary had responded that Padre Pio would
indeed pray for the woman as well as the rest of the friars of the Brazil Mission. He even included two "blessed images" of Padre Pio, both of which
had been personally signed by the saintly Capuchin himself.[29]

By the 1930s Padre Pio's story had become even more famous in the
Catholic world, but it had also become more complicated and conflict rid-
den. The historian Sergio Luzzato has written that from 1923 to 1933 "the
going [had gotten] tough for the friar with the stigmata," as forces within the
Vatican seemed to turn against him.[30] Over the next ten years Padre Pio's
movements and responsibilities were restricted and his access to the outside

world curtailed. In 1931, at the height of the Vatican's campaign against him, he was "relieved of almost all his faculties as priest."[31] How much the Capuchins of Nossa Senhora da Penha knew about Padre Pio's problems with the Vatican is unclear, but likely they were informed by their Capuchin superiors of the limits being placed on devotions related to him. They were probably instructed to ensure that their friars and parishioners were not engaging in similar activities. While such restrictions were gradually loosened after 1933, in the early years of Frei Damião's preaching some unease surrounding Padre Pio and his miracles surely lingered.

Protestants, Catholics, and Religious Fanaticism

As Frei Damião's saintly reputation grew in the Northeast, Protestants embarked on a campaign to prohibit Frei Damião's missionary work, using his supposed fanaticism as a central reason why religious and civil authorities should be worried about his santas missões. They pointed with distaste to the way Frei Damião "was followed by the people who were kissing his garment and pulling out threads for adoration," which they saw as evidence of an unhealthy obsession with the friar that could quickly spiral out of control.[32] In their descriptions of the persecution that occurred during Frei Damião's missions, Protestants consistently called him and his followers fanatics, organized into mobs and hordes whose very nature threatened violence and destruction.[33] Describing missions as simultaneously regimented and unruly, Protestants depicted nordestino Catholics as prepared to follow Frei Damião's every order while being constantly on the edge of uninhibited and unstoppable violence.

Frei Damião was not just a fanatic himself, Protestants argued, but a vector through which fanaticism spread and intensified. His true mission was to "fanaticize the multitudes" of simple nordestinos and cause potential political upheavals through his "revolutioniz[ing]" language.[34] They warned authorities of his relationship to present and past millenarian figures, especially Padre Cícero and Antônio Conselheiro. In 1938 Pastor João Rodrigues witnessed Frei Damião preaching missions against Protestants during the Presbyterian Council in Fortaleza. He demanded that government officials pay more attention to the growing "savage fanaticism, stirred up [in Ceará] by beatos who emulate Padre Cícero." Pastor Rodrigues accused Frei Damião of "wanting to install a new Canudos in the Cearense capital" and proclaimed that the friar's missions "humiliated us in the eyes of those who visit our city [of Fortaleza]."[35] In his opinion Frei Damião was dangerous not only because he was fanning the flames of fanaticism in the sertão but also because he was "reproducing these [fanatical] scenes in the capital." Such delirium, Pastor Rodrigues avowed, was infecting the supposedly more civilized parts of Brazilian society with the beliefs of so-called backward sertanejans already infected by the beliefs of Padre Cícero and Antônio Conselheiro.[36] In their descriptions of the persecution that occurred during Frei Damião's missions, Protestants consistently pointed to Frei Damião's fanaticism.

Protestants warranted that while the Vargas government was working to modernize Brazil, Frei Damião was working to undermine the values of "Ordem e Progesso" that the federal government sought to uphold. Though Protestants praised the Estado Novo for "making Brazil stronger [and] more modern," they blamed Frei Damião for the fact that "there still exist in Brazil things that are shameful to civilized men."[37] The Baptist pastor Rosalino da Costa Lima celebrated Brazil's modernity, stating that "it cannot be denied that Brazil is marching on the road of progress," but he also underlined the continuing presence of "backward elements" in the Northeast who, "if it were possible, would return Brazil to colonial times, since they do everything they can to dim the shining light of civilization we have attained."[38] The backward element Pastor Costa was describing was Frei Damião, whom the pastor accused of "leaving Italy to come and rob the purses of the faithful."[39] Protestants repeatedly emphasized Frei Damião's identity as a foreigner who did not have the best interests of modern Brazil at heart. They claimed he preached against the laws of the nation, and they emphasized that he promoted unconstitutional religious marriages, implying that Frei Damião, like Antônio Conselheiro before him, rejected the law of civil marriage.[40] Many sources, including those in the secular press, confirmed that Frei Damião condemned those who had *only* a civil marriage, saying that a civil marriage by itself was akin to a marriage "between a male cat and a female cat."[41] Yet there is little evidence that Frei Damião rejected the law of civil marriage or knowingly performed illegal religious marriages of people who had not received civil licenses. Rather, he wanted to make sure those who entered into civil marriages also participated in the Catholic sacrament. Nevertheless, Protestants seized on Frei Damião's position, especially his statement regarding male and female cats, as evidence of his similarity to fanatical, Conselheiro-like crusaders against the Brazilian government. Protestants held that if authorities saw Frei Damião in action in the Northeast, "they would be astonished to know how a foreigner is disrespecting our Constitution and making the backward people [of the Northeast] do the same. Frei Damião's work is not only anti-Christian but also antipatriotic because it exploits our backward compatriots."[42] The Baptist pastor Silas Falcão wrote that he had brought together a group of "evangelicals, non-Catholics, and liberal Catholics who don't agree with these shameful actions of a foreign friar" and who were "raising their voices, throughout these immense northeastern lands in protest against these calamities [of Frei Damião]."[43] The failure of local authorities to suppress Frei Damião's activities was a "betrayal to the Fatherland" and to the "[federal] government that has put its trust" in local officials to uphold the constitution.[44] Protestants were hoping the Estado Novo government, perhaps in the form of the Tribunal de Segurança Nacional, would intervene and punish Frei Damião or compel him to return to Italy.

Protestants were not alone in their condemnation of the perceived fanaticism surrounding Frei Damião's missions. Catholic leaders themselves were greatly worried about his growing fame as a popular saint and tirelessly warred against the growing cult surrounding his person. In 1939 Dom Jaime de Barros Câmara sent a missive to the priests in the Mossoró diocese that scathingly condemned the cordéis that were spreading stories of Frei Damião's miracles. He called them vehicles of "gross exploitation of ignorant people" who were spouting lies and nonsense, and verses "so completely incoherent as to render them ridiculous."[45] The folhetos not only took advantage of the ignorance and superstition of the Catholic masses, Dom Jaime wrote, but also "could not fail to cause great irritation to enlightened Catholics" who had worked hard to rid their religion of its backward reputation. Moreover, such publications furnished ample fodder to the church's non-Catholic enemies, who would view them with "derision . . . perhaps believing that all of us [Catholics] are equally gullible, superstitious, and ridiculous." Dom Jaime was attempting to defend the church against these types of attacks, which were not all that different from Romanized Catholics' own critique of Brazilian Catholicism. At the end of his missive Dom Jaime instructed all priests to do their best to educate their parishioners about the malicious untruths being spread through such means.[46]

Dom Jaime's pastoral advisory was seemingly not very successful at stemming the tide of rumors regarding the miracles of Frei Damião because priests and bishops continued to warn their parishioners against the flood of popular religious items being sold in interior towns of the Northeast. In an "orientation pamphlet" meant to prepare Catholics for the upcoming mission of Frei Damião, the local priest of Macaíba, Padre Alexandrino Suassuna de Alencar, concluded with an "IMPORTANT WARNING" telling his parishioners to "flee from the exploitation of certain vendors of *religious pamphlets, verses, strong prayers, etc.* These exploiters of the people go about spreading *superstition and fanaticism* throughout the region. They are abusing the name of the Capuchin Missionaries of the Convento da Penha of Recife! This can also be said of those who sell *portraits of Frei Damião* and *medals and portraits of the deceased Padre Cícero.* . . . Be careful! Be careful! Be very careful! There are many people who don't know the harm they are doing!"[47]

Even Dom Jaime found himself needing to send another letter to his priests, just a year after his previous missive. This time he condemned the *orações fortes* that featured Frei Damião and, in the opinion of Dom Jaime, were making a mockery of the church's official, canonized saints. Judging by the tone of Dom Jaime's letter these so-called superstitions had become a problem for his diocese, perhaps even gaining a certain following among diocesan priests. They were wasting Dom Jaime's time and exhausting his resources. "While we have already sent you many exhortations and warnings to not fall prey to superstition and unfounded beliefs," he complained, "once again we find ourselves obliged to denounce, dear sons, the passing through—or perhaps even the permanence of—bad elements in our midst."[48] These "bad elements" had once again taken advantage of the ignorance and "credulous simplicity" of the good people of the diocese, and the bishop expressed irritation and frustration that his multiple attempts at eradicating these backward beliefs had gone largely ignored. The real blame, he declared, lay with the "lack of religious education" of parishioners, which allowed them to believe in these "groundless popular superstitions, utter foolishness, and laughable nonsense."[49] The only solution was to educate parishioners in religious doctrine and catechism, a task which, perhaps ironically, was central to the missions of Capuchin friars such as Frei Damião.

Capuchin friars were worried as well about Frei Damião's growing saintly reputation, perhaps fearful he would run into the same trouble encountered by Padre Pio. It was in this context that a warning was published in the Recife-based Capuchin journal *Revista Dom Vital* regarding the "miraculous prayers about Frei Damião that have been circulating in Paraíba and other states."[50] The short article, printed in December 1937, declared such prayers and the prayer cards that promoted them to be "absurd, condemned by the Catholic Church, and banned." Moreover, the author of the warning, most likely a member of the Capuchin leadership in Recife, asserted that such cards were not being peddled by local Catholic merchants, which was true of most popular Catholic paraphernalia, but instead were part of a larger "Judeo-Protestant exploitation scheme" designed to "take money from simple country people."[51] In advancing such a theory the Capuchins were furthering Catholic stereotypes of Jews and Protestants by asserting they were duplicitous and obsessed with money. They were also illustrating a common fear of Catholic leaders, namely, that the backward Catholicism of the rural interior would be used by Protestants to attack the church and convince more enlightened Brazilians to defect to the Protestant faith. The revitalization of Catholic intellectual life, elite lay associations, and nonpartisan political groups would be all for naught if the Catholic Church were to be unable to rid itself of the reputation for being the religion of the ignorant and superstitious.

Even Frei Damião himself was compelled, either by his religious superiors or by his own concerns, to publicly condemn the rumors surrounding him and his missions. On December 6, 1936, the following notice appeared in the Paraíban Catholic newspaper *A Imprensa*:

THE PROPHECY OF FREI DAMIÃO
Against an exploitation
In this capital [João Pessoa] and in various places in the
interior a pamphlet titled THE PROPHECY OF FREI DAMIÃO
has been circulating. I believe it is an opportune time to warn
the public that such absurdity is not coming from me, but
rather from people who want to take advantage of the good
faith of the people, making use of my name.[52]

The notice was signed "Frei Damião de Bozzano." Such a strong disavowal
of rumors of prophecies and saintliness coming from the supposed prophet
himself would have had a major impact on readers of the newspaper. It is
unclear whether similar pronouncements were made to the audiences not
accustomed to reading João Pessoa–based newspapers and to those among
whom his reputation for saintliness had most credence, that is, the crowds
of people who attended his santas missões. Even if he had made such statements during his missions it is unlikely they put much of a damper on people's belief in his holiness—after all, it was often said that saintly men were
the first to deny their own sainthood.[53] What is known, however, is that in
the years following the 1936 and 1937 condemnations belief in Frei Damião's sainthood continued to grow, regardless of whether such beliefs were
disavowed by the saint himself.

A Safe Saint and a Restorationist Leader:
Frei Damião Escapes Condemnation

Given Protestants' efforts to publicize the so-called fanaticism surrounding
Frei Damião as well as the fear and frustration Catholic authorities expressed about pamphlets and prayer cards containing themes related to
the friar, one would assume that the friar would have been sanctioned and
perhaps removed from missionary work in an effort to dilute his influence
over nordestino Catholics. However, apart from a brief transfer to the Maceió convent to serve as the director of moral theology and canon law, a post
which lasted for less than a year, after which he returned to active missionary work, Frei Damião was not removed from his missionary position.[54]

Moreover, Frei Damião became a religious figure who was increasingly celebrated by the Catholic leadership in the Northeast. The more missions he preached, the more priests and bishops clamored to have him preach santas missões in their parishes and dioceses. By the late 1930s Frei Damião's missionary schedule was busier than ever.

Even when Catholic Church authorities were condemning the superstitions and rumors that surrounded his person, they went out of their way to emphasize that Frei Damião himself was not responsible for the excesses of those who admired him. Indeed, they often portrayed Frei Damião as the ultimate victim of such excesses. In Dom Jaime's missive condemning the pamphlet *News of the Miracle of Frei Damião*, he lamented the possible negative effects such folhetos would have on Frei Damião's reputation. "What truly causes me sadness," the bishop wrote, "is that such a dignified and virtuous priest with so much theological knowledge, a model of religious life and inexhaustible apostolic services, would see his honored name disgraced in folhetos of such [lowly] origin."[55] This sentiment was echoed by nearly all religious leaders who expressed their misgivings over the popular rumors of Frei Damião's saintliness. Frei Damião was not the problem, they argued; the ignorance of the people, the fanaticism of the culture, or, as the Capuchin authorities had declared, the conspiracies of "Judeo-Protestant" enemies were to blame for the unfortunate development.

The Catholic leaders' reaction to Frei Damião differed measurably from the reaction to other post-Padre Cícero popular religious movements. The leaders of popular religious communities like those formed in Caldeirão, Pau de Colher, and Santa Brígida as well as the anti-Protestant movements in Catolé do Rocha and Cuité were directly condemned by both ecclesiastical and civil authorities, accused of deliberately fanaticizing the populace for their own benefit. Frei Damião, on the other hand, was protected and celebrated by institutional church leaders. Why? First, Frei Damião was seen as being markedly different from other popular saints and millenarian leaders. In many ways he represented less of a threat to church authority and discipline in the northeastern backlands. As a Capuchin missionary he was fully integrated into a hierarchical and disciplinary ecclesiastical structure, and he had shown himself to be obedient and responsive to his hierarchical superiors when he publicly disavowed the popular rumors of his prophecies.

Furthermore, Frei Damião's missionary identity allowed his person and actions to be legible to church leaders. Elements of his missionary work that potentially might be associated with millenarian movements—his zealous preaching about Judgment and the End Times, his long beard and simple dress, his asceticism, his dedication to hearing confession, and even his anti-Protestantism—were normalized by the fact that all could be seen as forming part of the Capuchin tradition in Brazil. Moreover, while his constant travel throughout the Northeast increased the geographical scope of his influence and message, it also prevented him from establishing a territorial base of operations to which pilgrims could flock and in which a New Jerusalem could be founded. For Frei Damião there was no space like Juazeiro, Canudos, or Santa Brígida that would allow him to exercise earthly authority and distribute material goods and wealth. As Pessar has argued, becoming "the ideal patron" for one's followers was central to the identity of northeastern millenarian leaders, and it formed a key element of the sacralizing process.[56] Patron-leaders, however, could also attract negative attention from both civil and ecclesiastical authorities, who often felt threatened by the competing political or religious power structures that such patronage represented. Frei Damião, by remaining firmly rooted within the Capuchin hierarchy and detached from any single territorial or material base of support, posed less of a danger to his superiors.

More important, Frei Damião worked hard to transform himself into an ideal Restorationist agent in the Northeast and demonstrate that he could help Catholic leaders achieve their pastoral goals. The Capuchin friar was mostly known for his special ability to connect with the poor and humble residents of the northeastern interior, but he was also comfortable with the intellectual culture of Restorationist Catholicism. Frei Damião took pride in his education. He had received a doctorate from the Gregorian University in Rome in an age in which a Romanized education was highly prized in the Brazilian church. He embraced opportunities to display his educated status to elite audiences, making sure they knew he had a sophisticated understanding of Catholic theology and church doctrine. This was especially evident in his anti-Protestant campaign. Though his santas missões were the setting of his most passionate and influential sermons, he wrote a series of apologetic articles in which he laid out theological, historical, and philosophical arguments against Protestantism. In these articles he covered a wide variety of issues, including the primacy of Peter, the infallibility of the pope, Purgatory, the Real Presence of the Eucharist, and the sinfulness of divorce.[57] He gave public talks on the subject of Protestantism in coastal capitals such as Recife, Natal, and Maceió, eliciting glowing reviews in Catholic newspapers. "His polemics," a writer for Natal's elite Catholic newspaper A Ordem declared, were "based solely in the inexhaustible sources of his theological and exegetical wisdom," and they were capable of "liberating innumerable souls from the swamps of sin, from the prisons of heresy and ridiculous superstitions."[58] In Maceió Frei Damião was praised for "analyzing the religion of Luther with elegant scholarly knowledge, making crushing arguments [against the Protestants]."[59] Catholic elites were always quick to emphasize Frei Damião's calm, collected, polite, and educated demeanor, perhaps to counterbalance the fiery, passionate, and supposedly uneducated atmosphere of his santas missões.

In public debates with Protestants Frei Damião demonstrated his intellectual prowess, and Catholic leaders combated rumors of fanaticism by highlighting the friar's erudite performances. After the 1935 debate between Frei Damião and Synesio Lyra in Campina Grande Catholic observers stressed that "the contest proceeded serenely, within an environment of perfect order and complete silence." They portrayed the event as a demonstration of the Catholic Church's role as an "institution of order" and a refutation of Protestant accusations of Catholic fanaticism. They marveled at the educated performance of the Capuchin friar, emphasizing that Frei Damião had followed the "classical forms of dogmatic Catholic expositions" and that his extensive knowledge of scripture, logic, and philosophy had enabled him to gain the upper hand in the debate. Catholic journalists were particularly proud of Frei Damião's "unmasking" of Rev. Synesio Lyra's lack of philosophical knowledge, gleefully reporting that the Protestant pastor "was unfamiliar with even the most universal concepts and accomplishments of philosophy."[60] Frei Damião was hailed as a heroic defender of Catholic truths, showing that "in two great and memorable hours, the great Christian mystery was affirmed by the Catholics, and was diminished and ridiculed by our separated brothers."[61] Word of the debate spread beyond urban newspapers, reaching northeastern Catholics through cordel folhetos that gave detailed descriptions of the arguments and of Frei Damião's "splendid victory" over Protestants.[62] Via his erudite performance in the debate, Frei Damião had shown Catholic leaders that he was a successful agent of the Catholic Restoration in the northeastern interior.

Above all, it was Frei Damião's campaign against Protestants that made the most direct contribution to the Restorationist cause. The message of the santas missões certainly reinforced the general anti-Protestant message being adduced by Restorationist leaders. But a closer examination of the religious conflict surrounding Frei Damião's santas missões reveals that it also helped sustain the local anti-Protestant campaigns already present in the dioceses and towns the friar visited. When priests and bishops wanted to mount an aggressive campaign to rid their parish of Protestants, they frequently called on Frei Damião to come and preach missions specifically intended to inspire anti-Protestant sentiments. Thus when the Presbyterian Church held its Supreme Council in Fortaleza in 1938, Archbishop Dom Manoel da Silva Gomes asked Frei Damião to preach missions throughout the congress to encourage Catholics to "extinguish the great evil" of Protestantism in their midst.[63] Protestants reported that the friar incited Fortalezan Catholics to such a degree that they threatened Protestants, yelled "Death to Protestantism," and very nearly stormed the conference hall with the supposed intention of "throwing people out the second-floor windows."[64]

This is not to say that anti-Protestant disturbances were planned or desired by the Catholic authorities who invited Frei Damião but that the friar's fiery, emotional anti-Protestant rhetoric had a destabilizing and violent effect in areas where sustained anti-Protestant campaigns were already under way. It was not the inherent "fanaticism" of either Frei Damião or the people to whom he preached that determined the nature of the local anti-Protestant response to missions; it was, rather, the nature of the supposedly civilized anti-Protestant movement being promoted by local and regional church leaders. Frei Damião ultimately became a valuable resource for Restorationist priests and bishops who were looking to enhance the reach and intensity of their local anti-Protestant campaigns.

Nowhere can the mutually beneficial relationship between Restorationist priests and Frei Damião be seen more clearly than in the religious controversy of Cajazeiras, one of the earliest, most widely reported violent encounters between Catholics and Protestants that occurred during a mission led by Frei Damião. Cajazeiras was a city on the border between Paraíba and Ceará, in the far interior of the northeastern sertão. Throughout the 1930s Cajazeiras prided itself on two of its most salient characteristics: its dedication to education and elite culture and the devout religiosity of its Catholics. The city's leaders proudly proclaimed it to be a beacon of culture in an otherwise backward region, the "center of sertanejan civilization" and the "city of light that shined brightly in the northeastern hinterland."[65] Cajazeiras celebrated the Catholic identity of its founder, Padre Inácio de Souza Rolim, who was deemed the "father of sertanejan education," as he had established the first secondary school in the region.[66] For nearly one hundred years children of the regional elite, including the first Latin American cardinal Joaquim Arcoverde, the eminent historian Capistrano de Abreu, and, perhaps most famously, the popular saint Padre Cícero, had been sent to Cajazeiras to receive a strict Salesian education. By the 1930s the city was on the rise, touted as a rare success story of material and cultural progress in the rural backlands. It had been connected to the coastal city of Fortaleza by train since 1926, and its cotton-based economy was booming. One observer remarked that "economically, no city in the sertão offers such prosperity as the invincible city of Padre Rolim."[67] Moreover, Cajazeiras's residents were quick to note that the city had not succumbed to the secularist evils that often accompanied economic progress but had maintained its traditional Catholic values. "The material opulence that Cajazeiras enjoys today is far from being the center of its social system," Dom João da Mata Amaral, Cajazeiras's second bishop, declared in 1934. "The force of its people lies in their fondness for their intimate traditions . . . in the penetration of Christ in the sertanejan soul."[68] In recognition of Cajazeiras's intense Catholic faith the city had been made the seat of a new diocese created in 1915, and the diocese's first bishop, Dom Moisés Coelho, was a native son of Cajazeiras.[69] In the thirties the city's powerful combination of traditional religious piety and economic, cultural, and ecclesiastical power made it an ideal entry point for Catholic Restorationist reforms in the far northeastern interior. The city's main parish, Nossa Senhora da Piedade, had some of the most active and enthusiastic religious associations in all of Paraíba, having organized one of the first Paraíban Círculos Operários in the sertão and founded five Catholic Action organizations.[70] Much of this Restorationist zeal was due to the influence of Hildebrando Leal, a prominent Catholic intellectual and the mayor of Cajazeiras in the late twenties and early thirties.[71] As the national secretary of Brazilian Catholic Action and personal friend of Alceu Amoroso Lima, Leal represented the ideal Cajazeirense Catholic: highly educated, devoutly religious, politically active, and closely connected to the Restorationist leaders in Rio de Janeiro.[72]

Cajazeiras's status as a model Catholic society did not prevent Protestants from attempting to establish a presence in the town. Protestant preachers had visited Cajazeiras throughout the first two decades of the twentieth century, but not until the early 1930s did they start to found permanent, albeit small, congregations in the city. In the first years of the decade a Cajazeirense man had converted to the Baptist faith and "risked his life by letting it be known that he was a 'Protestante' in that town."[73] In 1935 the city was visited for the first time by an ordained Protestant pastor, a U.S. Baptist missionary by the name of Charles Stapp. Just a year later he sent glowing reports on the evangelization progress being made in Cajazeiras. "Things are so changed now," Reverend Stapp excitedly wrote, "that we preached to large crowds and talked the Gospel to anxious people in the hotel and on the street corners."[74] In less than nine months a twelve-member congregation of Baptists had formed.

The Baptists were not the only Protestants in Cajazeiras. The Congregationalist church in Catolé do Rocha supported two evangelizing missionaries who had worked in Cajazeiras from the beginning of the decade, and by 1938 the Cajazeiras evangelical community had its own deacon, José Lezario.[75] In March 1936 Reverend Stapp wrote, in a tone at once dismissive and alarmed, that "a Holy Roller [Pentecostal] missionary has moved in and set up shop" in Cajazeiras.[76] In reality, the Assembly of God had been in Cajazeiras since 1934, led by a returning migrant who had converted while working for the rubber industry in Pará.[77] Thus in less than five years the "land of Padre Rolim" had gone from having no Protestant congregations to having three: Baptist, Congregationalist, and Pentecostal. As was so often the case, the majority of the new converts represented the poorer and humbler members of Cajazeirense society, living on the outskirts of the city or in nearby satellite towns.[78] None of the three religious denominations had a permanent pastor or an official church temple in Cajazeiras, but the mere existence of three new Protestant congregations in a town that previously boasted of having none was enough to effect profound and contentious changes to its religious culture.

The Catholic Church was not at all pleased with the growth of Protestantism in the purported "beacon of Catholic civilization" in the sertão. With the support of Dom João da Mata Amaral, the diocesan bishop, Padre Fernando Gomes, the local parish priest, began an intense campaign to warn his parishioners about the "Protestant propaganda" being spread by "masked enemies who cause great harm" to the unity and stability of the Cajazeiras community.[79] In February 1936, in an effort to "curb the destructive Protestant propaganda being spread in the parish," Padre Fernando embarked on an anti-Protestant "preaching tour" throughout the poor neighborhoods on the periphery of the city. In many ways Padre Fernando's campaign closely resembled a prolonged santa missão: for an entire month he and his parish assistants gave sermons, conducted adult catechism lessons, organized anti-Protestant processions and demonstrations, and led special anti-Protestant Masses both in the city center and in suburban communities.[80] Padre Fernando was widely praised for his efforts, the local correspondent of a Catholic newspaper reporting, "The indoctrination and activity that Padre Fernando Gomes has developed among his flock has been eliciting widespread approval and congratulations" from the population.[81] The public campaign was "the reliable sign that in Cajazeiras only one religion is professed—the religion of Christ, proclaimed and followed by the absolute majority of the Brazilian population." It was directly responsible for the fact that the "Protestant sect that wanted to penetrate the gates of [Cajazeiras] is retreating, bit by bit."[82] Observers were quick to emphasize the orderliness and efficiency of the campaign as well as the "peaceful and disciplined" nature of the Catholics who attended the events.[83] Protestants would later claim that the campaign had been full of violent language and ominous threats, but at the time there were no reports of physical attacks on Protestants or their property.

It was in this environment that Frei Damião's mission took place. On March 30, just over one month after Padre Fernando's anti-Protestant preaching tour had commenced, Frei Damião arrived in Cajazeiras prepared to conduct a special mission. The santa missão would last for two weeks and include the preparation for and celebration of Holy Week liturgical festivities. Having come directly from Esperança, where he had given a sermon in which he led a crowd of fifteen thousand people in a solemn oath against buying from, selling to, or having any personal or professional relationships with Protestants, Frei Damião was on something of an anti-Protestant tour of the Paraíban countryside.[84] When he arrived in Cajazeiras he found the city overflowing with Catholic pilgrims who had come from neighboring towns near the border between Paraíba and Ceará. Frei Damião immediately began the work of the mission, giving passionate and emotional sermons, organizing catechism courses, leading processions, and performing the sacraments of baptism, marriage, and reconciliation. Since his mission overlapped with Holy Week, he also participated in the festivities and solemnities associated with Palm Sunday, Holy Thursday, Good Friday, and Easter.[85]

In his customary fashion, Frei Damião offered a fiery rebuke of Protestantism and its presence in Cajazeiras. While there is no extant description of the sermons Frei Damião preached in Cajazeiras, the reactions of the Catholics in attendance as well as Catholic observers' broader descriptions of the mission make clear that all the hallmarks of the friar's anti-Protestant campaigns were on full display: fiery condemnations of Protestants' so-called blasphemies against the most sacred doctrines of the church, such as the Immaculate Conception of the Virgin Mary; calls for a militant campaign of spiritual renewal that demonstrated Catholicism's privileged position in the Brazilian public sphere; demands that Catholics refuse to conduct any commercial transactions with their Protestant neighbors; and denunciations of (figurative) attacks by Protestants on the Catholic clergy and the Brazilian family.[86] Throughout the two weeks of the mission Frei Damião gave no fewer than forty-five sermons, and, given the events that transpired, it is safe to assume that a great number of them contained the aforementioned anti-Protestant sentiments.

The effect of Frei Damião's sermons was immediate. Even as the mission was still in progress Catholics began an "extreme boycott" of all commerce with Protestants, refusing to sell even basic alimentary goods to Protestant families.[87] The boycott brought tensions in Cajazeiras to a new high, and U.S. Baptist missionaries began to report that Catholic mobs were threatening to kill any and all Protestants in Cajazeiras.[88] The final straw came toward the end of Frei Damião's mission, when a group of men broke into the home of a Protestant church leader and threatened his life as well as the lives of his family members and his fellow Protestants.[89] The attackers gave the church leader an ultimatum: leave town or face more violence. Protestants claimed that the church leader was also physically assaulted by the group of men, but Catholics disputed that claim. Catholics did not, however, dispute the fact that the attack had occurred or that threats were made and ultimatums were given. The Catholic newspaper A Imprensa admitted as much, stating that the attack was the work of "some working-class men [who], outraged over the blasphemies being said against the doctrine of the Immaculate Conception," had then "invaded the house of a Pastor, telling him to leave town."[90] In the end the attack bore its intended fruits: at least one of the Protestant leaders in Cajazeiras, the Brazilian Baptist missionary, left town, and all Baptist evangelization efforts in the city and surrounding areas ceased.[91] Protestants had no doubt about who was ultimately responsible for the attack: Frei Damião, who had entered the town in a "total state of war" and had proceeded to "subvert the public order and promote anarchy, pitting brothers against brothers and impeding Brazilians from exercising their religion."[92] One Protestant observer argued that the people of Cajazeiras were "by their nature calm and respectful," but that Frei Damião's fanaticism had been so strong and his reputation as a popular saint so potent that he had convinced otherwise reasonable people to commit fanatical acts.[93]

There is no doubt that Frei Damião bore much of the responsibility for the violence that occurred during his missions. The emotion, fury, and intensity he brought to his anti-Protestant campaign had few parallels in the Brazilian Catholic world. Yet to dwell solely on him as the cause of the violence in places like Cajazeiras is to overlook the complex interreligious dynamics that were in place both before and after Frei Damião preached his mission. Padre Fernando Gomes, with the support of Dom João da Mata Amaral, had not only initiated his own anti-Protestant campaign in Cajazeiras before Frei Damião had arrived but also continued to do battle with Protestants even after Frei Damião left. In August 1936 Padre Fernando held a lavish ceremony to break ground on a chapel to be built in Santo Antônio, the very neighborhood that had been home to the largest grouping of Protestants in Cajazeiras. The symbolic meaning of the gesture was transparent: Padre Fernando explicitly declared the chapel to be "a sign of the victory that we won against the Protestants, who tried to make their lair in our parish."[94] The victory chapel became a public manifestation of the church's reoccupation of the public sphere in Cajazeiras, a victory made possible by the work of both Frei Damião and Padre Fernando.

Frei Damião and Capuchin anti-Protestantism were not the *cause* of anti-Protestant violence in the interior of the Northeast. Santas missões served to intensify and shape the religious conflicts already present in the towns missionaries visited. They influenced the words, feelings, and even specific actions that were associated with these conflicts, tying them to the rituals and traditions of the santas missões. More often than not, however, campaigns against Protestants were under way before the arrival of Frei Damião, and they continued after he left. Bishops and priests valued the friar's missions not because they brought anti-Protestant campaigns to places where there previously had been none but precisely because they could support the anti-Protestant projects these leaders had already undertaken.

Catholic leaders' unqualified support of Frei Damião would not last forever. Decades later, in the 1960s and 1970s, numerous bishops in the Northeast banned Frei Damião from preaching missions in their dioceses, accusing him of fanaticizing believers there and promoting an antiquated version of

Catholicism that was not in line with the new teachings of the Second Vatican Council.[95] By that time Frei Damião's saintly status was well established, and the prohibitions engendered considerable controversy and scandal. Numerous prominent Catholics, including politicians, denounced the ban as unjust and defamatory. More important, it did little to diminish popular support for Frei Damião, whose fame and miraculous identity only grew stronger in the years to come. Eventually the prohibitions were dropped, and Frei Damião continued his missionary work until his death in 1997 at the age of ninety-eight.

Today, Frei Damião is one of the most well-known and beloved religious figures in the Northeast, second in fame only to Padre Cícero. The evidence of Frei Damião's continued status as a powerful religious authority in the Northeast can be seen everywhere: in the hundreds of chapels dedicated to his memory, the enormous statues of his person scattered throughout the northeastern countryside, and the hundreds of thousands of pilgrims who travel to his shrines every year. What is more, the support of the people has nearly been matched by the support of Catholic Church authorities. On January 31, 2003, the Capuchin Order, with the backing of officials from the Archdiocese of Olinda and Recife, submitted the cause for the beatification and canonization of Frei Damião to the Vatican's Congregation for the Causes of Saints, and an official case was opened. Since his death the Catholic Church has promoted Frei Damião as the true representative of northeastern popular religious culture, the official "people's saint." Every year on the anniversary of his death the Capuchin convent of Recife holds a three-day festival in his honor, which is attended by cardinals, archbishops, and tens of thousands of the Catholic faithful. Even the more informal pilgrimages to various shrines dedicated to Frei Damião throughout the Northeast, such as those in Guarabira (PB) and São Joaquim do Monte (PE), enjoy the official sponsorship of church authorities. Although the people of the Northeast canonized the friar long before the Vatican took up his case, Catholic leaders have also embraced the missionary as their own. In 2019 the Vatican declared that Frei Damião was Venerable, one of the first steps toward declaring him a saint.

Ultimately, Frei Damião was able to do what few before him have done: walk the thin line between being a holy member of the institutional church who inspires the faithful and a dangerous religious radical who foments fanaticism. In the 1930s and 1940s Frei Damião accomplished this feat by successfully integrating himself into the Restorationist project in the Northeast while maintaining his intimate connection to the everyday faithful. He was able to show Catholic Church authorities how both his intellectual prowess and his saintly status could contribute to official church goals, particularly those that involved the expulsion of Protestants from the public sphere. Such capability allowed Frei Damião and his saintly identity to avoid censure during the crucial first decades of the sacralization process.

Church(es) Divided

The Polarization of Brazilian Religious Life and the Transformation of Protestant–Catholic Relations

Religious conflict between Catholics and Protestants did not disappear with the end of the first Vargas regime in 1945. For the next two decades Protestants would continue to decry acts of "Catholic intolerance" that were occurring in the Northeast, albeit with decreasing frequency.[1] Yet the nature and reception of anti-Protestant attacks were unlike those of earlier decades, as the national religious and political context in which these acts occurred underwent major changes. Between 1945 and 1960 the Catholic Restoration ceased to be a universal project of the Brazilian church, as new, more progressive Catholic movements emerged, challenging the conservative corporatist model championed by Dom Sebastião Leme and the Catholic activists of the first half of the twentieth century. Catholic anti-Protestantism therefore became an ideological position associated with a single faction of an increasingly polarized religious culture. More Catholic bishops and priests than ever were advocating ecumenism and tolerance, thereby redefining what it meant to be a good priest in their dioceses. However, at the same time that many Catholics were beginning to reach out across denominational divides, the leadership of many Protestant churches began to move sharply in the opposite direction, opting for fundamentalism and isolationism rather than pluralism and ecumenism. At a time when political tensions were rising and fears of a perceived communist menace were becoming more acute, Catholics and Protestants alike came increasingly to define Brazilian national identity in political as well as religious terms. While divisions within both denominations prevented Catholics and

Protestants from being each other's primary enemies, they also stymied any meaningful efforts to promote reconciliation or build alliances.

The Fracturing of the Catholic Restoration

The disappearance of a unified anti-Protestant project in the Brazilian Catholic Church was the result of the decline of the Catholic Restoration, which would not outlast the fall of the Estado Novo and the transition to democracy in 1945. The Restorationist downfall was partly due to the fact that with the disappearance of the Estado Novo the Catholic Church lost one of its most reliable allies, the corporatist and authoritarian Brazilian state. Brazil fought on the side of the Allies in World War II, and as a result the anti-democratic, anti–United States, xenophobic ideals that had underpinned much of Catholic Restorationism and Catholic anti-Protestantism were no longer in favor among Brazilian political and social leaders. Following Brazil's transition to democracy the Catholic Church found it difficult to exert influence over a larger, more unwieldy political system that was less dependent on the unified support of the church.

However, the decline of the Catholic Restoration was mostly caused by factors internal to Brazilian Catholicism itself. As Ralph Della Cava has argued, the late 1940s and early 1950s were marked by "the profound decentralization of Brazilian Catholicism," as Restorationist consensus fractured and multiple voices and organizations competed to put forth their own visions of a new Catholic future.[2] Three factors contributed to the Catholic Restoration's decline. First, new theological and religious movements that anticipated the reforms of the Second Vatican Council began to gain influence among certain Catholic leaders in Brazil. As early as the mid to late 1930s Alceu Amoroso Lima and many of his colleagues at the Centro Dom Vital were beginning to promote the liturgical movement, which aimed to make the Catholic Mass more accessible to the laity so that they would rediscover its power and vitality. Supporters of the movement promoted liturgical reforms that would eventually be adopted by the Second Vatican Council, among which were conducting the Mass in the vernacular language and having the priest face the congregation.[3] Lima and other reform-minded

Catholics were especially dedicated to the ideas of Jacques Maritain, who had developed new ways of thinking about the relationship between the Catholic Church, the state, and religious freedom.[4] Maritain advocated the construction of a Christian society that, while not allowing unlimited moral and theological license, did allow for the development of a pluralistic community that was inclusive rather than defensive and that looked to collaborate with diverse religions, groups, and ideas in order to promote the common good. Careful to praise the Syllabus of Errors and other antimodernist repressions as necessary means of "purifying the domain of thought and eliminating error," Maritain nevertheless concluded that the Catholic Church needed "[to] be setting its course in the direction of new cultural types."[5] This new course would accept different ideas and different religions. "The Christian world," he declared, "is not the Church."[6] Liberal democracy and the separation of church and state were now considered to be not only compatible with but also ideally suited to Catholic and Christian society. These ideas were problematic for a Restorationist movement founded on the desire to reunite the church with a corporatist state and promote a reactionary vision of Brazilian Catholic nationalism. They were even more problematic for a movement determined to advance anti-Protestant initiatives. Lima, who in 1932 had called Protestants one of the "most dangerous enemies" of the Catholic Church, was, by 1946, calling on Catholics to collaborate with non-Catholics in an effort to improve society, declaring that "many of the ideals for which they are fighting . . . are also [Catholic] ideals."[7] Foreshadowing the ecumenical language used in later years, above all, after the Second Vatican Council, he called on Catholics and non-Catholics "to unite [them] selves in every way that [they] can be united."[8]

Yet the ideas espoused by *liturgistas* and *maritainistas* were not especially revolutionary; indeed, many who supported the liturgical movement and Maritain in the 1930s and 1940s would become fervent opponents of the progressive Catholic movements of the 1960s and 1970s. Activists like Lima might well have remained under the Restorationist umbrella if not for the second blow to the movement: the death of Dom Sebastião Leme in October 1942 and the subsequent decentralization of Catholic leadership. Dom Leme had been the guiding hand and propelling force behind the Catholic

Restoration, and while he was cardinal-archbishop of Rio de Janeiro he skillfully balanced the various competing ideologies and interests that existed within his constituencies. In doing so, he concentrated power in his office and ensured that the Catholic Church spoke with one voice. Dom Leme's death created an immense power vacuum in the Brazilian church, as his successor, Dom Jaime de Barros Câmara, did not have the charisma or the political expertise necessary to exert his predecessor's level of control over the national church. Dom Jaime was a staunch supporter of Restorationist ideals. He had, after all, encouraged and rewarded anti-Protestant campaigns throughout his diocese when he was bishop of Mossoró. However, his heavy-handed suppression of the liturgistas and maritainistas—he removed Lima as head of Catholic Action soon after assuming his post as archbishop—meant that he pushed out rather than reined in emerging progressive Catholic movements. These movements would find alternative means by which to exert influence in the Brazilian church. In particular, the founding of the Conferência Nacional dos Bispos do Brasil in 1952 represented a turning point in Brazilian Catholic Church leadership, shifting power away from Rio de Janeiro. Now, bishops from all dioceses were able to wield more power over the direction of the national church. Although Dom Jaime worked hard to continue the Restorationist project, he no longer spoke for all Brazilian Catholics.

The final blow to the Catholic Restoration came from the Catholic faithful themselves, particularly young lay Catholics who, faced with an increasingly modernizing, urbanizing, and mobilizing society, believed that the church should actively address the social and economic problems of the contemporary world. This turn was most evident in the development of Catholic Action. While Catholic Action had begun as a Restorationist project aimed at creating an active, obedient, and Romanized laity, in the late forties and fifties it increasingly became a site for the expression of an alternative Catholic agenda, one concerned more with social justice and economic equality than dogmatic apologetics and Catholic nationalism. In the early 1940s conservative Catholic leaders were already worried about the direction in which Lima and others were taking Catholic Action, arguing that the groups were becoming too independent, too accepting of religious and ideological pluralism, and focused more on worldly activities than interior spirituality.[9] And while it seemed as though the innovation in Catholic Action would cease when Dom Jaime expelled Lima as director of the organization in 1945, the opposite occurred. Brazilian Catholic Action moved further and further away from its top-down, hierarchy-focused roots in Italian Catholic Action and ever closer to the more independent, laity-centered model of French and Belgian Catholic Action. Emphasizing a new ground-up methodology known as See–Judge–Act, Catholic Action devoted energy to studying and attempting to resolve the problems it identified in Brazilian society. By 1950, with Padre Hélder Câmara at the helm, Catholic Action officially embraced its new orientation, reorganizing in order to emphasize the goals or specialization of Catholic Action groups rather than the status of its members. Whereas previously Catholic Action groups had determined their membership on the basis of age and/or marital status, they now organized themselves around occupations, for example, Young Catholic (Urban) Workers (JOC), Young Catholic University Students (JUC), Young Catholic Rural Workers (JAC). These specialist groups had existed before 1950, but they gained new prominence and support as they became the principal representatives of the Brazilian national Catholic Action strategy. By recognizing Catholics' identities as factory workers, agricultural laborers, and students, Catholic Action began to encourage its members to see themselves and their faith in relation to wider social and economic concerns.[10]

As these Catholics paid more attention to how the church should confront Brazilian social and economic challenges, they became less concerned with confronting the growth of Protestantism in their midst. Most did not yet specifically advocate ecumenical activism, but many did see anti-Protestantism as a vestige of the old Catholic activism that was no longer relevant to the modern Catholic agenda. In this context, the Protestant Question receded into the background. Significantly, the anti-Protestant and antipluralist Catholic Action Departamento Nacional de Defesa da Fé e da Moral (DNDFM) was discontinued in 1950.[11] Rather than fighting against the church's enemies, Protestantism, liberalism, and communism, Catholic Action was fighting for social equality and economic justice. For this new generation of Catholic activists Brazilian identity was no longer strictly tied to the Catholic faith; to be

Brazilian was to believe in the ideals of a more just Brazilian future, one in which diverse groups could come together to advance social and political goals to benefit all members of society.

Not all Catholics agreed with the progressive Catholic reformers. At the same time that Catholic Action members and maritainistas were opening up to ecumenical ideas and movements, others were strengthening their stance against religious pluralism, essentially doubling down on the anti-Protestant ideological campaigns of the twenties and thirties. Such resistance is most clearly visible in the case of the Secretariado Nacional de Defesa da Fé (SNDF). As discussed above, the SNDF was founded in the 1930s with the mission of waging an official, coordinated campaign to impede the spread of non-Catholic religions, particularly Protestantism and Spiritism. In light of the redemocratization of Brazil and the rise of progressive Catholics committed to religious pluralism, one might assume that the SNDF would decrease in prominence. However, the opposite occurred: in the 1950s, after a period of relative dormancy in the late 1940s, the SNDF expanded its anti-Protestant and anti-Spiritist activities, garnering funds and the backing of prominent Catholic clerics and intellectuals. In essence the SNDF took over activities that had lapsed when Catholic Action discontinued the DNDFM in 1950. In 1953 the SNDF launched an intense campaign against Protestants, Spiritists, Afro-Brazilian religions, and Masonry. Their most notable and long-lasting project was the curation and publication of "Vozes em Defesa da Fé" (Voices in defense of the faith), a series of more than thirty apologetic volumes meant to help both priests and laypeople understand and oppose the errors of so-called heretical sects. Some were translations of Anglo and European Catholic polemicists, and others were written by members of the SNDF. In the Vozes series each Protestant denomination was treated and refuted in a separate work that outlined the denomination's history and beliefs as well as the dangers associated with those beliefs and the ways in which Catholics could disprove them.[12] The volume *Assembléias de Deus e outras Igrejas Pentecostais* compared Pentecostal revivals to the "insanity of the 1956 rock 'n' roll craze that nearly became an epidemic" in which impressionable individuals came together to experience an emotional release that was akin to a "contagious disease."[13] Catholics were warned to inoculate themselves against such a disease by rejecting all invitations to such meetings, redoubling their commitment to the Catholic sacraments, and advising others of the dangers associated with such a fanatical expression of religious faith.

The anti-Protestantism of the SNDF was one element of a larger set of oppositional positions—antiliberalism, anti-Spiritism, anti-Masonry, and especially anticommunism—that distinguished conservative Brazilian Catholics from their more progressive counterparts. They believed that instead of discarding the defensive posture of the Restorationist movement, the church should enhance and intensify its battle against its religious and ideological enemies. To conservative Catholics, Protestantism and pluralism represented the eroding of traditional Brazilian values, themselves the ultimate bulwark against communism. Anti-Protestantism and anticommunism were therefore intimately connected. Many SNDF leaders would become central figures in the emerging conservative Catholic movement and its fight against communism. Frei Boaventura Kloppenburg, a Franciscan friar and later a bishop, was the editor of Vozes em Defesa da Fé and wrote many of the tracts, particularly those relating to Spiritism and Afro-Brazilian religions, which he singled out for intense criticism.[14] After Vatican II and the Medellín Conference Kloppenburg would become one of the leading opponents of liberation theology in Brazil, accusing many liberationists of being sympathetic to communism and insufficiently obedient to the Catholic hierarchy. Eurípides Cardoso Menezes, the general secretary of the SNDF in the 1940s, would become one of the foremost Catholic anticommunist politicians of the 1950s, while continuing to travel throughout Brazil to "attend to the many requests of bishops and priests to give conferences on the defense of the Faith" and serve as the president of the Catholic Confederation of the Archdiocese of Rio de Janeiro. A former Protestant himself, Menezes published books addressed to his "separated brothers" of the Protestant faith in an effort to show that Protestants were being intransigent and anti-Brazilian in their insistence on remaining outside the Catholic Church.[15] He also published books warning Catholics of the dangers that communism posed to people of faith.[16] Supported by the Catholic leadership of Rio de Janeiro, including Dom Jaime de Barros Câmara, Menezes became a spokesperson for nationalist Catholicism and a constant critic of his Protestant, left-leaning colleagues in the Congress. In 1958, when Menezes was running for reelection as a federal deputy, Catholics were told that it was a "question of honor" to vote for him, since he was "always alert in his defense of Brazil and the Church."[17]

Thus by the 1950s the Brazilian Catholic Church was a church divided, with progressive and conservative Catholics articulating different visions of Brazilian Catholic identity and mission in the postwar world. In this way Catholic anti-Protestantism was transformed from a universal project of the national Brazilian church into an ideological position associated with a single faction of an increasingly polarized religious culture. No longer was it true that being a good priest or a good Catholic required adopting a confrontational stance toward Protestantism. With the diversification of Catholic theological and social positions in Brazil came the emergence of new ways to be a good priest, many of which did not include taking a defensive posture against Protestantism.

The Decline, but Not the Fall, of Anti-Protestant Campaigns in the Northeast

The varied approaches to anti-Protestantism could be seen on the ground in the Northeast, where Catholic Action groups and regional bishops were among the earliest voices to speak out in favor of the new social agenda but also where the ingrained anti-Protestantism of the santas missões continued to push against pluralism. In 1950 Dom Jerônimo de Sá Cavalcante, a Benedictine monk who was the director of the JUC in Garanhuns (PE) and Fortaleza (CE) wrote, "The primary purpose [of the JUC] is not to combat communism, throw stones at [apedrejar] Protestant churches, or paint Catholic slogans on the sidewalks, but rather to form the Christian personality of each student." He went on to write that the church should reject "the scandal of a self-righteous religion, with an intransigent and petty spirit and a retrograde and stolid mentality. The presence of the JUC is the presence of the Church. And the Church is Life, Dynamism, and the strong wind of the Spirit, renewing the face of the earth and transforming the soul of the student."[18]

To Dom Jerônimo and his students in the JUC, Catholic Action was not about apologetics, and it was "much more than defending [the faith]."[19] Anti-Protestant campaigns, especially the local anti-Protestant attacks often characterized by the stoning of Protestant churches, were no longer seen as an appropriate use of Catholic activists' time. Instead, Catholic Action activists needed to understand "the apostasy of the workers." Why, Dom Jerônimo asked, were the common people abandoning their Catholic faith and choosing alternate religions or ideologies? Only if the church provided *positive* reasons to convince workers (and students) that they should retain their Catholic faith would it be a growing, vital institution of the postwar age.[20] And while Dom Jerônimo promoted the creation of a Catholic nation, he wanted to redefine what it meant for a nation to be truly Catholic. A Catholic nation, he argued, was not one in which Catholics had a mere numerical majority or retained special rights and privileges. Instead, he wrote, "Catholic government is that which above all defends the human person and gives him all his rights and privileges. Can one speak of a Christian government in a country where there is no social justice, . . . where workers are oppressed, that allows for the extortion of the humble, and where men openly exploit other men? . . . The Church must fight against these policies and the people who preach them."[21]

For progressive nordestino Catholics like Dom Jerônimo Catholic nationalism was rooted not in opposition to Protestantism and religious pluralism but in its desire to aid the poor and vulnerable in society. Thus in places like Garanhuns, where Benedictines like Dom Jerônimo held great influence, anti-Protestant campaigns receded into the background. But for other northeastern Catholic leaders the fight against Protestantism remained central to their activities and message. In Fortaleza, where Dom Jerônimo had founded a JUC chapter, the Capuchin friar David de Miritiba founded an organization that promoted traditional Restorationist ideals, including anti-Protestantism. The group began as a journalistic endeavor centered on the distribution of Frei David's conservative Catholic newspaper, *Âncora*. However, it soon morphed into a stand-alone youth movement aimed at recruiting students and workers who did not "find Catholic Action to be a suitable environment" for them and their beliefs, presumably because of Catholic

Action's progressive trajectory.[22] As Frei David traveled throughout Ceará, Piauí, and Pernambuco to conduct santas missões he founded blocs of youths who were committed to disseminating *Âncora* and advancing the newspaper's causes and ideas.[23] A central pursuit was the campaign against Protestantism, which Frei David promoted in the towns and cities he visited. In 1951 he traveled to Esperantina, Piauí, to headline an anti-Protestant campaign that was taking place over the course of two days. "The apostolic zeal of the young Capuchin," an observer wrote, "allowed him to immediately perceive how Protestantism had infiltrated our beloved land, and he made sure to jolt the people into action and warn them about the grave danger to our Faith."[24] While he was criticized by Protestants and progressive Catholics for his aggressive tactics, the Catholic writers of *Âncora* congratulated him for his courage and militancy, celebrating the anti-Protestant event on the front page of the newspaper. "ESPERANTINA AGAINST PROTESTANTISM" read the banner headline of the article, which praised the demonstration as "yet another apostolic gesture of the impassioned soul of our beloved Founder."[25] The campaign was also lauded by civil and military officials from the area, such as Lieutenant Adail de Araújo Melo, a leader in the state military police, who gave a speech at the Esperantina event in which he registered his "most vehement protest against the diabolical Sect that is Protestantism" and thanked the Capuchin friar for having defended the town against it.[26]

Indeed, Capuchin friars were one of the most consistent sources of messages and movements against Protestantism throughout the 1950s. For the most famous anti-Protestant Capuchin, Frei Damião, the 1950s constituted a period of intensifying, rather than waning, anti-Protestant activity. In this period he published his first and only book, *Em Defesa da Fé* (In defense of the faith), which his Capuchin superior described as "a keepsake from [Frei Damião's] innumerous and fruitful santas missões ... dedicated to erecting an impassible dike to hold back the overpowering wave of corruption with which the heresy of Luther threatens the most splendid traditions of Catholic Brazil."[27] In the book the reader could "hear the prophetic tone of his stirring speeches to sinners, unmarried lovers, adulterers, Protestants, and Spiritists, using his vibrant voice to show them the inevitable consequence of their perverted lives: Hell."[28]

As Frei Damião's reputation as a popular saint continued to grow, so too did the passions inflamed by his anti-Protestant sermons in the towns and cities he visited throughout the Northeast. The most extreme case of mission-associated religious conflict occurred in 1958, when Frei Damião visited Patos, a town in the interior of Paraíba, to conduct a santa missão. As was so often the case, Frei Damião's visit represented the culmination, rather than the beginning, of an anti-Protestant campaign. According to Protestants, months before Frei Damião arrived, the priest of Patos, Padre Manoel Dutra, had begun to organize frequent religious processions whose purpose was to intimidate local Protestants. The crowds often stopped in front of Protestant homes and churches, yelling threats and insults and, at times, throwing stones.[29] When Frei Damião arrived to conduct santas missões in June of that year, tensions were already high. After a day of processions and sermons by the Capuchin friar, groups of Catholics attacked the Presbyterian and Baptist churches, smashing furniture, ripping up Bibles, and creating bonfires in front of the churches in which they burned sacred possessions. The violence continued throughout the following day, until police arrived and dispersed the crowds.[30]

Although no one was arrested or held responsible for the damages, there were signs that Brazilian attitudes toward the type of religious intolerance displayed in Patos were changing. In the past such actions would not have elicited much notice from the wider public, Catholic or otherwise. But by the 1950s attacks on Protestants were increasingly seen as representing extremist religious views, and more voices than ever before were raised in objection to the violence. Even before Frei Damião had arrived the newspaper O Correio da Paraíba based in João Pessoa had condemned the anti-Protestant campaign of Padre Dutra, asking, "Why can [Padre Dutra] not understand that the battle for Christ must be fought on the field of ideas and persuasion, not violence and disrespect?"[31] After Frei Damião's mission the situation in Patos was labeled a crisis by both civil and religious authorities, and the governor of Paraíba traveled to the town in an effort to promote reconciliation between the religions and promote peace. The bishop of Cajazeiras, in whose diocese Patos was located, also went to the town for discussions with the governor, town officials, and religious leaders.[32] While neither Frei Damião nor Padre

Dutra was punished or publicly criticized by civil or ecclesiastical authorities, the fact that leaders traveled to the sertanejan town in order to put an end to the conflict highlights that it was no longer considered desirable or normal for such anti-Protestant displays to take place.

Moreover, the career trajectory of Frei Damião illustrates how his message was no longer universally accepted by Brazilian Catholic leadership. While he was not punished for his role in the 1958 events, as the years passed he became an increasingly controversial presence in northeastern parishes and dioceses, no longer universally lauded for his holiness and apostolic zeal. This change was especially true after the Second Vatican Council, whose commitment to ecumenism and reform made northeastern bishops and priests who endorsed the council wary of the effects of Frei Damião's missions in their dioceses and parishes.[33] Frei Damião's fire-and-brimstone sermons, his reputation as a miracle worker and popular saint, and his anti-Protestantism made some pro–Vatican II reformers view his missions as antiquated and backward. Certain bishops began to regard them as an obstacle to modernizing their dioceses' pastoral strategies. In 1968 the bishop of Crato, Dom Vicente de Paulo Araújo Matos, prohibited Frei Damião from preaching missions in his diocese in order to "avoid accentuating the fanaticism that exists in [the diocese of Crato]."[34] Over the next two decades more northeastern bishops adopted similar prohibitions. Yet throughout the era of the dictatorship Frei Damião enjoyed the favor of bishops, priests, and politicians who saw him as a champion of traditional Catholic morality and a bulwark against the excesses of Vatican II reformers. Thus, while his attitudes and message changed very little, his status as a representative of official or orthodox Catholicism depended on the theological, ideological, or political identity of the observer.

Anti-Ecumenism and the Rise of Fundamentalism in Brazilian Protestantism

Protestant churches in Brazil also experienced a great deal of change and division in the postwar period. As Antonio Gouvêa Mendonça has argued, the 1950s saw the emergence of "a host of new theologies" and new religious movements among historical Protestant congregations. The redirection can be attributed partly to young students who were seeking to reconcile their Christian beliefs with the modern world and make a commitment to advancing progressive social and political causes. Much as Catholic Action transformed from an organization that assisted the Catholic hierarchy in enforcing orthodoxy and Romanizing reforms into a vehicle through which young Catholic activists promoted social and economic justice, so Brazilian Protestant organizations like the Christian Union of Students (UCEB), whose original goals consisted primarily in proselytizing and promoting conversions, turned their attention to issues of social justice. Influential in this process was Richard Shaull, a young missionary who arrived at the Seminário Presbiteriano do Sul in 1952 and began encouraging seminarians to read new theological texts that called for Christians to challenge any injustice they saw in the world around them. This new progressive Protestant generation was inspired by the rise of the global ecumenical movement and the establishment of the World Council of Churches, which allowed diverse denominations to find common theological ground and to work together to confront the problems of the modern era.[35]

Yet not unlike the Catholic Church, historical Protestant denominations in Brazil in the 1950s and 1960s were riven by profound divisions both between and within their churches. Many conservative Protestant leaders disagreed with the new theological movements arising in the seminaries, and disputes and even schisms erupted as a result. This was especially the case in the Northeast, where the Presbyterian Church underwent a period of great turmoil and eventually schism owing to disagreements over ecumenism and accusations of modernism and heresy. While such disagreements dated back to the 1930s, they boiled over in 1956, when a leader of one of the most prominent families of Brazilian Presbyterian pastors, Rev. Israel Gueiros, forcefully objected to what he saw as the infiltration of theological modernism into the Presbyterian Seminary of the North. Influenced by the fundamentalist movement of Carl McIntire and his International Council of Christian Churches, Reverend Gueiros believed that the future orthodoxy of the Brazilian Presbyterian Church was in danger. Its seminaries, he contended, were teaching dangerous ideas of ecumenism and advocating affiliation with the World Council of Churches. When he attempted to

found a rival Presbyterian seminary in Recife, raising funds among fundamentalist supporters in the United States, the Presbyterian Church expelled
him from his position in the ministry and leadership of the Pernambucan
church. In response, Reverend Gueiros founded his own church, called the
Fundamentalist Presbyterian Church of Brazil.[36]

The departure of Reverend Gueiros and his fundamentalist followers
did not resolve the internal tensions that plagued historical Protestant
churches. Although the 1960s were a period of progressive innovation and
growth, as exemplified in the Confederação Evangélica's convening of
the Conference of the Northeast in 1962 under the theme "Christ and the
Brazilian Revolutionary Process," it was also a period of conservative backlash to the changes of the past decade.[37] In his iconic work *Protestantismo e
repressão* (Protestantism and repression), Rubem Alves identified the sixties,
seventies, and eighties as a period of repression within Protestantism, as
church leaders rejected ecumenical dialogue and moved away from prophetic calls for social justice.[38] Alves argued that whereas Protestantism had
been a "force of renewal" in its early years, fighting for personal freedoms
and rejecting political authoritarianism, during the postwar period "talk
about freedom of conscience gave way to talk about obedience and con-
formity to the thinking inherited from the past."[39] During this period theological conservativism was mirrored by social and political conservatism, as
anticommunism began to define Protestant churches' stances on issues of
social justice. Anticommunism had always been central to Brazilian Protestantism, especially during the Vargas era, but not until the onset of the Cold
War did fears of communism begin to define internal as well as external theological divisions and debates. Many Protestant leaders began to see certain
theological movements, especially ecumenical movements, as being linked
with social and political forces that were fostering communism and unrest
in Brazil and the rest of the world. Thus a divide formed between young students involved in national and international ecumenical organizations like
the UCEB and the leadership of Protestant churches themselves, which
were increasingly moving toward conservativism and fundamentalism.

In their rejection of ecumenism and stalwart opposition to left-leaning political positions, many Protestant leaders moved closer to their conservative

counterparts in the Catholic Church. Both sides promoted a national political vision based on anticommunism and the repression of progressive religious movements. For a brief period in the 1950s it seemed as though anticommunism might be the common ground that would bring conservative Protestants and conservative Catholics together. Each side praised the other for its interdenominational condemnations of the Soviet Union and its atheistic ethos. Catholics in the Brazilian Northeast frequently cited and praised the united front against communism being formed by leaders of multiple faiths. "To fight back against the red advances, Catholics, Protestants, and Jews are, for once, organizing a defense," wrote a journalist in A *Ordem*. "Protestant pastors, as well as rabbis and other Jewish dignitaries, do not miss an opportunity to denounce any red ploy, wherever it might be."[40]

Early enthusiasm for the united front, however, was shallow and sporadic, as conservative Catholics and Protestants were more likely to attack each other for alleged links to communism than propose alliances to combat its influence. In 1953 Monsignor Agnelo Rossi angered the Confederação Evangélica by publicly accusing various Brazilian Protestants, particularly those affiliated with the Presbyterian Seminary of the South, of being communist sympathizers.[41] Protestants, in their turn, were quick to criticize Catholic Action's newfound focus on social justice as a mere cover for dangerous communist plots. As Alves has noted, the Catholic Church remained "the first enemy" of conservative Protestants in the 1960s and 1970s, as they believed "their conflict with Catholicism must be radical and total."[42] This outlook was especially true in the Northeast, where fundamentalism found fertile ground and memories of Catholic persecution remained fresh. Indeed, anti-Catholicism was so entrenched in Protestant churches in the Northeast that when a Catholic lawyer in Recife wrote an article praising the recently deceased Presbyterian leader Jerônimo Gueiros for his willingness to reach out to Catholics and maintain positive relationships between the two faiths, Protestants in the city treated the article as a calumnious attack on Reverend Gueiros's orthodoxy and character.[43] Conservative Protestants felt the need to respond and defend Reverend Gueiros's good name, and a Baptist pastor, Munguba Sobrinho, even published a pamphlet with the letters he had written to the Catholic lawyer refuting his article. Reverend Sobrinho hoped to publicize "the opinions and judgments of Rev. Gueiros regarding the tremendous errors, the aggressive heresies, and the repugnant superstitions of the Roman Church as it has progressively separated itself from Jesus and the Bible."[44] While progressive Protestant organizations like the UCEB increased their collaboration with progressive Catholic organizations in the fifties and sixties, conservative Protestants were largely avoided establishing the same kind of relationships due to their entrenched anti-Catholic views.

But Catholics and historical Protestants could agree on one thing: Pentecostalism was an ever-growing threat to the success and survival of their respective institutions. The 1950s and early 1960s marked the beginning of what Paul Freston has called the second wave of Pentecostalism. It was characterized by the expansion, diversification, and proliferation of new Pentecostal denominations, setting off a Pentecostal boom that would propel charismatic Christianity to the forefront of Brazilian religious culture.[45] The fifties saw the founding of new Pentecostal churches that would find great success, among them the Church of the Four-Square Gospel (Igreja do Evangelho Quadrangular) and Brasil Para Cristo (Brazil for Christ). These churches evangelized mass urban audiences, attracting thousands of people to religious services and revivals held in circus tents, cinemas, and even stadiums. They put an even greater emphasis on healing than ever before, as their religious services were meant to bring relief from both the physical and mental challenges of everyday life. These Pentecostal leaders did not dwell on sin and damnation when speaking to their congregations but spoke of the transformative power of spiritual healing and how it could change one's life for the better. The new Pentecostal churches saw themselves as very much part of the modern world and thus did not demand that their followers isolate or separate themselves from secular society. The strict moral and behavioral codes that had characterized first-wave Pentecostal churches were largely discarded in favor of a more open membership model that did not demand dramatic lifestyle changes from potential converts.[46]

The rise of new Pentecostal churches proved a challenge not only to Catholic and historical Protestant churches but also to first-wave Pentecostal churches like the Assembléia de Deus. Much as conservative Catholics and fundamentalist Protestants intensified their rejection of modernist movements in the 1950s, first-wave Pentecostal churches like the Assembléia de Deus began to reinforce their own prohibitions on worldly activities and beliefs during this period, thus defining themselves by what they were not. As Gedeon Freire de Alencar has argued, the period between 1946 and 1988 was marked by the institutionalization and the "traditionalization" of the Assembléia de Deus, as the church's "identity was marked by *discipline*."[47] Hierarchies became more rigid, and boundaries between the AD and other charismatic movements became more fixed. Ecumenism was an enemy that represented a profound danger to the AD's future: the blurring of denominational lines and the proliferation of new and competing Pentecostal churches.

Legacies of Religious Conflict

Ultimately, the twentieth century witnessed the struggle of multiple religious denominations, both Catholic and Protestant, to come to terms with the modern era—and, in particular, the religious and political pluralism that inevitably accompanied it. In this context Catholic campaigns against Protestantism in the 1920s, 1930s, and 1940s were not isolated outbursts of reactionary rage but part of a longer and broader process through which religious groups defined their relationship with Brazilian society and articulated their vision for Brazil's national future. As Dom Sebastião Leme and Catholic Restorationists sought to reenter the Brazilian public sphere and reassert the church's influence over the moral and political soul of the nation, they attempted to put Catholic faith at the heart of Brazilian citizenship. The Catholic corporatism that reigned during the first Vargas regime left little room for religious diversity, as the unity of the national body was dependent on its uniformity. Thus the Catholic Restoration was defined by both its triumphalism and its anxieties, for its exclusive claim to Brazilian identity created a fragile supremacy whose existence was inherently threatened by alternative religiosities and ideologies.

To a great extent the Northeast was the point at which all of the Catholic Restoration's greatest anxieties converged. To Restorationists, the Northeast represented the heart of Brazilian Catholicism, the sacred deposit of national Catholic culture that needed to be protected at all costs. For this

reason the growth of Protestantism in the interior of the Northeast represented a grave threat not only to northeastern Catholicism but also to national Catholic identity. The emergence of anti-Protestant campaigns
therefore evidenced not the Northeast's backward religious and social culture but nordestinos' engagement with national Restorationist discourses
and projects. This did not mean that anti-Protestant campaigns were simply
imported by or imposed upon the Northeast. Local expressions of anti-
Protestantism drew on the religious culture and traditions of the towns in
which they emerged, facilitating the creation of anti-Protestant rites meant
to protect the spiritual and material health of the local community.

Yet the local traditions that enabled the campaigns against Protestantism
in the Northeast had the potential to intensify another anxiety of the Catholic Restorationists, religious fanaticism. For while church leaders believed
the Northeast represented the traditional heart of Catholicism, they also
thought that the Northeast represented the legacy of the church's supposed
failure to fully catechize and Romanize the Brazilian faithful. That defi-
ciency resulted in heterodoxies and superstitions that continually threatened
to morph into fanatical millenarianism. In the eyes of Catholic Restorationists northeastern religious culture needed to be simultaneously protected
and policed. Anti-Protestant leaders like Frei Damião who proved adept at
doing both were celebrated as courageous defenders of the faith. Those who
were seen as privileging popular religiosity over Restorationist reforms, such
as Padre Luiz Santiago, were labeled as dangerous religious fanatics representative of a backward past that needed to be superseded by the modern
Restorationist project. The process of distinguishing between legitimate and
illegitimate anti-Protestant actors highlighted the tension inherent in the
Catholic Restoration, which saw itself pulled between a desire to construct a
modern, lawful, and unified Catholic nation and the need to use violent, un-
lawful means to achieve such unity. In many ways the Romanized Catholic
Church's move away from and rejection of religious pluralism and Latin
American popular religiosity, both Catholic and Protestant, opened up
space for religious actors like Pentecostals to offer Brazilians a direct connection to the spiritual world that Romanized Catholicism rejected, thus making the Catholic Church one of the architects of its own decline.

What, then, did the legacy of Restorationist anti-Protestantism in the Northeast mean to Protestants themselves? On the one hand, violence and persecution against Protestant congregations had the potential to slow or even stop the growth of Protestantism in certain areas of the Northeast. In such towns as Catolé do Rocha, Cajazeiras, and Pesqueira anti-Protestantism led to the exodus of Protestants from the town or region, which in turn led to the collapse and disappearance of numerous formerly thriving Protestant congregations. Many churches would see their congregations reestablished and their temples rebuilt, but the loss of time, money, and members represented a serious setback for the Protestant cause in the region.

On the other hand, many Protestants who have spoken of their churches' persecution have viewed its legacy in a more providential light, depicting their survival in the face of adversity as proof of both God's support and the resilience of their faith. A member of the Assembléia de Deus in Rio Tinto, Paraíba, described the persecution of his congregation:

> In spite of great opposition, and of the persecutions that have been directed against us, the word of the Lord has not come up empty. The Lord Himself said that we would be despised and insulted because of His Word; but He nevertheless gave us the promise that we would be victorious in all of our battles; He promised to be with us, until the end of the ages.
>
> We give thanks to God, because even when faced with the greatest persecutions, He has blessed us; and the proof of his blessing is that even with all of the opposition that has been directed toward the Gospel of Christ, we have still managed to perform eleven water baptisms, and there are five more people whom we hope to baptize soon.
>
> It brings us joy to see how the Lord does his work, preparing the people for His arrival.[48]

Today, the Assembléia de Deus in Rio Tinto is thriving, having just built a new temple so grand that local tourist shops feature its photo on postcards. Protestantism, and especially Pentecostalism, is alive and well in Rio Tinto.

Indeed, throughout the Northeast new congregations are being founded and new temples are being raised in an explosion of religious diversity and dynamism that is constantly changing the face of Brazilian religiosity in the region. Although Catholic Restorationism may have won many battles in the 1920s, 1930s, and 1940s, they ultimately lost the war.

The triumph of Protestantism and Pentecostalism over Catholic persecution did not represent the final triumph of religious pluralism over religious intolerance. While one battle was won, others were yet to be fought. Promoting and protecting religious pluralism in any society, including Brazilian society, is a job that never ends. Today, when one speaks of religious intolerance in Brazil, one is more likely to be speaking of acts of intolerance perpetrated by rather than perpetrated against members of the Pentecostal faithful. As Milton Bortoleto has argued, the holy war taking place in Brazil today is not between Catholics and Protestants but between Pentecostals and members of Afro-Brazilian religions, as evangelical persecution of members of Candomblé, Umbanda, and Spiritist religions rises.[49] The methods of persecution used by Pentecostals are haunting echoes of the same methods used against them many decades ago: stonings, invasions of religious temples and destruction of religious objects, threats of bodily harm, and demands that their religious opponents leave the community. Clearly, the memory of past torments does not always prevent the persecuted from becoming the persecutors. In fact, the providential lens through which Pentecostals have viewed their persecution — "He nevertheless gave us the promise that we would be victorious in all of our battles" — can merely set the stage for further acts of intolerance. For this reason discussions and debates surrounding religious freedom, religious pluralism, and national identity will continue to be painfully relevant and necessary, and individuals and communities will continue to take action to protect their beliefs. On September 17, 2017, the tenth annual March in Defense of Religious Freedom was held in Rio de Janeiro, and fifty thousand people representing members of Candomblé, Umbanda, Spiritist, Jewish, Muslim, Catholic, and Protestant faiths came together to demand that Brazilian authorities protect their right to openly practice their religion. "We don't want just tolerance," they chanted. "We want RESPECT."[50]

NOTES

Introduction

1. A *Questão Protestante no Brasil: Semana de Estudos sobre "O Protestantismo no Brasil,"* realizado no Seminário Central de Ipiranga, de 19 a 23–8–1940 (São Paulo: Tipografia Orfanato Cristovão Colombo, 1940), 11.
2. Arlindo Vieira, S.J., "A ameaça comunista é uma realidade," *Estrela do Mar* (September 1942): 18.
3. Cunha, *Os Sertões*.
4. Albuquerque Júnior, *The Invention of the Brazilian Northeast*.
5. Rolim, *Pentecostais no Brasil*, 28. Rolim names one other outlier of low Protestant numbers: the state of Minas Gerais, which also was considered to be a stronghold of traditional Catholicism. Minas Gerais, too, experienced a relatively high rate of conflict between Catholics and Protestants in the 1920s and 1930s, although the violence was not as frequent and widespread as in the Northeast.
6. Rolim, *Pentecostais no Brasil*, 27; Marcelo Côrtes Neri, *Novo Mapa das Religiões* (Rio de Janeiro: Fundação Getúlio Vargas, 2011), 61.
7. Antonio Gouvêa Mendônça, "Evolução histórica e configuração atual do protestantismo no Brasil," in *Introdução ao Protestantismo no Brasil*, ed. Mendônça and Filho.
8. For more on missionary Protestantism, see Mendônça, "Evolução histórica," 31–46.
9. For an examination of the history and religious life of the São Paulo Confederados, as they came to be called, see Dawsey and Dawsey, eds., *The* Confederados. For the authoritative book on Confederados in the Amazon, see Guilhon, *Confederados em Santarém*.
10. For more on the history of the Congregação Cristã, see Monteiro, "Congregação Cristã no Brasil."
11. The most authoritative work to date on the history of the Assembléia de Deus is Alencar, *Matriz Pentecostal Brasileira* and *Assembléias de Deus*.

12. Mendonça, *O celeste porvir*, 97.
13. Mendonça, "O protestantismo brasileiro e suas encruzilhadas," *Revista USP* 67 (September–November 2005): 48–67, 55. Mendonça points to four major periods in Protestant history: (1) "implantation" of Protestantism in Brazil, from 1824 to 1916; (2) unionism and cooperation, from 1916 to 1952; (3) religious and political crisis, from 1952 to 1962; and (4) internal repression within Protestantism and the rise of neo-Pentecostalism, from 1962 to 1983.
14. "Anotações: Confederação evangélica," *Unum Corpus* 2.7 (October 1934): 1.
15. Bishops in Brazil are addressed with the honorific title "Dom." Many were known by their first names (i.e., Dom + first name), but Dom Sebastião Leme was usually addressed by his last name: Dom Leme.
16. Sebastião Leme da Silveira Cintra, *A carta pastoral de S. Em. Sr. Cardeal D. Leme quando Arcebispo de Olinda, saudando os seus diocesanos* (Petrópolis: Editora Vozes, n/d [1916]), 18.
17. For a discussion of religious orders in nineteenth-century Brazil, see Azzi and Beozzo, *Os religiosos no Brasil*, 5–25.
18. For a discussion of the decline of church authority as well as the history of celibacy among priests in nineteenth-century Brazil, see Serbin, *Needs of the Heart*, 19–53.
19. For general overviews of the institutional church and popular religiosity during the Brazilian Empire, see Azzi, *O estado leigo e o projeto ultramontano*; Vieira, *O processo de reforma e reorganização da Igreja no Brasil*; De Groot, *Brazilian Catholicism and the Ultramontane Reform*; Hauck et al., eds., *História da Igreja no Brasil*; Bruneau, *The Political Transformation of the Brazilian Catholic Church*, 11–37.
20. For the classic and most comprehensive accounts of the Questão Religiosa, see Villaça, *História da Questão Religiosa*; Guerra, *A Questão Religiosa do Segundo Império Brasileiro*; De Groot, *Brazilian Catholicism and the Ultramontane Reform*; Pereira, *Dom Vital e a Questão Religiosa no Brasil*.
21. Serbin, *Needs of the Heart*, 74–75.
22. For more on the Collegio Pio Latinoamericano, see Edwards, *Roman Virtues*.
23. Leme, *A carta pastoral*, 12.
24. Ibid., 61.
25. Adroaldo Mesquita da Costa, "A Acção Catholica, defesa social da familia christã," Arquivo do Centro de Documentação e Informação Científica (CEDIC), Publicações Não-Periódicas, Grupo Secretariado Nacional, Subgrupo 2: Ampliação de Quadros e Formação de Militantes,.
26. Episcopado do Brasil, "Estatutos da Ação Católica Brasileira," in *A Ação Católica: documentos fundamentais*, ed. Romeu Dale, O.P., 27–31 (São Paulo: Edições Loyola, 1985), 30.
27. Catholic Action was not officially founded in Brazil until 1935, when it was canonically approved by Pope Pius XI. However, throughout the 1920s and early 1930s the term was used loosely in Brazilian Catholic circles to refer to the general

promotion of lay Catholic activism in the broader public sphere. Many of the organizations founded during this period, such as the Ação Universitária Católica (Catholic University Action) and the Círculos Operários Católicos (Catholic Worker Circles), would become the basis for future official Catholic Action groups (in these cases the Juventude Universitária Católica (JUC) and the Juventude Operária Católica (JOC), respectively).

28. Perillo Gomes, "Defesa da sociedade," in A Ordem 2.13 (August 1922): 4.

29. Lima, A contra-revolução espiritual, 11.

30. Ibid., 14.

31. For more on the Centro Dom Vital and the rise of Catholic Action, see Bruneau, *The Political Transformation of the Brazilian Catholic Church*, 38–51; Bandeira, *A Igreja Católica na virada da questão social*; Costa, *Um itinerário no século*; Della Cava, "Catholicism and Society in Twentieth-Century Brazil," 7–50; De Groot, *Brazilian Catholicism and the Ultramontane Reform*; Mainwaring, *The Catholic Church and Politics in Brazil*; Serbin, *Needs of the Heart*, 54–109; Souza, *Os círculos operários*; Azzi, *A Neo-Cristandade*; and Azzi, *Os pioneiros do Centro Dom Vital*.

32. P. C. de Mello and J. A. Leonardi, "Idéas sobre a Acção Catholica," in A Ordem 14.57 (November 1934): 355–69, 363, 355.

33. *Acção Catholica: Pequeno Catecismo: Principios e Disposições Gerais*, Publicações Não-Periódicas, Grupo Secretariado Nacional, Subgrupo 2: Ampliação de Quadros e Formação de Militantes, Arquivo CEDIC.

34. Della Cava, "Catholicism and Society in Twentieth-Century Brazil," 13.

35. An account of Dom Leme's role in Washington Luís's capitulation can be found in Laurita Pessoa Raja Gabaglia's hagiographical biography, *O Cardeal Leme (1882–1942)*, 216–26. See also Azzi, *A Neo-Cristandade*, 19; and Della Cava, "Catholicism and Society in Twentieth-Century Brazil."

36. "Em acção de graças pela pacificação do Brasil," *O Jornal*, November 29, 1930, 1.

37. Ibid.

38. The pioneering work on the relationship between Integralism and the Catholic Church is Margaret Todaro, "Pastors, Prophets, and Politicians: A Study of the Brazilian Catholic Church, 1916–1945" (PhD diss., Columbia University, 1971). An article based on her dissertation was published as "Integralism and the Brazilian Catholic Church," *Hispanic American Historical Review* 54.3 (August 1974): 431–52.

39. Although Dom Hélder clashed with Protestants in the early 1930s over the issue of religious instruction in public schools ("Intolerância em Fortaleza," *O Escudo*, March 10, 1934, 4), he should not be considered an active participant in the anti-Protestant movement in the Northeast. Moreover, just four years later, in 1938, he would receive the extremely rare distinction of being a Catholic leader who was praised by Protestants for his tolerance and moderation. A Baptist leader published one of his speeches in the *Jornal Batista*, saying, "This thesis [of Padre Hélder] was written with such impartiality and with such a noble Christian spirit to which we

are unaccustomed when dealing with Catholic publications, that we cannot resist the temptation of publishing parts of it here, with the regret that our limited space does not allow us to publish it in full" ("O ensino religioso em face do protestantismo," *O Jornal Batista*, December 5, 1938, 11). Protestant Integralists formed a small minority of both the Integralist movement and Protestantism in general, but they did exist. Many were German Lutherans who were attracted to the fascist ideology of the movement. Trindade, *Integralismo*.

40. Eduardo Góes de Castro has shown that in São Paulo agents of the local secret police, DEOPS-SP (Departamento Estadual de Ordem Política de São Paulo) conducted surveillance on Protestants because they were concerned that Protestants had subversive leanings. Góes also argues that DEOPS officials were complicit with Catholic persecution of Protestants, supporting them when they accused Protestants of supposedly provoking confrontations. Castro, *Os 'quebra-santos'*, 57–97. While no evidence in the DEOPS-Pernambuco archive suggests that officials in the Northeast conducted these types of surveillance on regional Protestant churches, there was a similar complicity of nearly all regional officials who were made aware of anti-Protestant persecution. They frequently ensured that Catholics, especially Catholic priests and bishops, were not punished for the violent outcomes of their anti-Protestant campaigns.

41. While by no means a comprehensive list, the following are some representative studies: Camargo, ed., *Católicos, Protestantes, Espíritas*; Corten, *Pentecostalism in Brazil*; Mariz, *Coping with Poverty*; Sanchis, *Catolicismo: modernidade e tradição*; Sanchis, *Catolicismo: cotidiano e movimentos*; Sanchis, *Catolicismo: unidade religiosa e pluralsimo cultural*; Mafra, *Na Posse da Palavra*; Chesnut, *Born Again in Brazil*; Chesnut, *Competitive Spirits: Latin America's New Religious Economy*; Burdick, *Looking for God in Brazil*; Campos, "El campo religioso brasileño: Pluralismo y cambios sociales.

42. For a classic analysis of nineteenth-century ideological conflicts between Catholics and Protestants, see Vieira, *O protestantismo, a maçonaria, e a Questão Religiosa no Brasil*. The most famous confessional history of religious persecution is Tarsier, *História das perseguições religiosas no Brasil*. Boanerges Ribeiro, a pastor of the Presbyterian Church, also wrote of religious persecution in his work *O padre protestan*, and Émile G. Léonard referenced cases of persecution in *O protestantismo brasileiro*, as did Carl Joseph Hahn in *História do culto protestante no Brasil*. None of these studies, however, analyzed persecution extensively, mostly limiting their accounts of violence to those that occurred during the pioneer years of the nineteenth century.

43. Mendonça, *O celeste porvir*, 239.

44. For works that have noted anti-Protestant discourses, see Azzi, *A Neo-Cristandade*; Azzi and Klaus van der Grijp, *História de Igreja no Brasil*; Bruneau, *The Political Transformation of the Brazilian Catholic Church*; Mainwaring, *The Catholic Church and Politics in Brazil*.

45. Almost all of these studies are theses or dissertations: Simões, "O Rebanho de Pedro e os Filhos de Lutero"; Souza, "Vaqueiros de Deus"; Santos, "A ordem social em crise"; Silva, "Práticas e representações hagiológicas: a devoção a Frei Damião de Bozzano"; Oliveira, "Bodes, hereges, irmãos"; and Edilson Souza, "Cristãos em confronto." Maria de Lourdes Porfirio Ramos Trindade dos Anjos and Carlos Henrique de Carvalho have published an article on the Protestant–Catholic conflict over religious education: "Católicos e protestantes no Nordeste brasileiro no século XX: a educação em questão," *Saeculum* 22 (January/June 2010): 51–68. Only one published work deals directly with the issue of religious persecution in Brazil: Rev. Zaqueu Moreira de Oliveira, *Perseguidos, mas não desamparados: 90 anos de perseguição religiosa contra os batistas brasileiros (1880–1970)* (Rio de Janeiro: JUERP, 1999), a largely narrative rather than analytical account of the persecution experienced by Baptists throughout Brazil. Like many accounts of Protestant history, it focuses primarily on the nineteenth century, devoting only one chapter to the period 1907–70.
46. Freyre, *The Masters and the Slaves*, 41.
47. Mariz and Campos, "Pentecostalism and 'National Culture,'" 107.
48. Alencar, *Matriz Pentecostal Brasileira*, 50–59; Premack, "'The Holy Rollers Are Invading Our Territory': Southern Baptist Missionaries and the Early Years of Pentecostalism in Brazil"; Freston, "Protestantes e política no Brasil."
49. Bellotti, "Pluralismo protestante na América Latina."
50. Ramírez, *Migrating Faith*, 27–29.
51. Premack, "The Holy Rollers Are Invading Our Territory."
52. Zemon Davis, "The Rites of Violence: Religious Riot in Sixteenth-Century France."
53. Nesvig, ed., *Religious Culture in Modern Mexico*; Butler, ed., *Faith and Impiety in Revolutionary Mexico*; Butler, *Popular Piety and Political Identity in Mexico's Cristero Rebellion*; Wright-Rios, *Revolutions in Mexican Catholicism*; Voekel, *Alone before God*; Fallaw, *Religion and State Formation in Postrevolutionary Mexico*; Gilbert Joseph, "Some Final Thoughts on Regional History and the Encounter with Modernity at Mexico's Periphery," in *Peripheral Visions: Politics, Society, and the Challenges of Modernity in Yucatan*, ed. Edward D. Terry et al., 254–66 (Tuscaloosa: University of Alabama Press, 2010); and Overmyer-Velásquez, *Visions of the Emerald City*. While the term "popular religion" is widely used, scholars have begun to note its shortcomings. As Carlos Eire has argued, historians have tended to view religious experiences in terms of dichotomies like popular/elite, lay/clerical, below/above, piety/theology, or superstition/religion, but the reality of religious experiences defies such stark divisions. Eire, "The Concept of Popular Religion." I will use the term "popular religiosity" sparingly in this book, and when I do I will take care to convey the complexities of its application to northeastern religious life.
54. Pessar, *From Fanatics to Folk*, 11.
55. For more on Romanization in Brazil and Latin America, see De Groot, *Brazilian Catholicism and the Ultramontane Reform, 1850–1930*; Serbin, *Needs of the Heart*,

54–109; Oliveira, *Religião e dominação de classe*; Vásquez, *The Brazilian Popular Church and the Crisis of Modernity*, 104; Klaiber, *The Catholic Church in Peru, 1825–1985*, 45–47; Fitzpatrick-Behrens, *The Maryknoll Catholic Mission in Peru, 1943–1989*, 5–13; Bautista García, "Hacia la romanización de la Iglesia mexicana a fines del siglo XIX"; Wright-Rios, *Revolutions in Mexican Catholicism*, 43–72.

56. For more on the cultural aspects of the Brazilian Romanization project, see De Groot, *Brazilian Catholicism and the Ultramontane Reform*; Della Cava, "Catholicism and Society in Twentieth-Century Brazil," 7–50; and Pessar, *From Fanatics to Folk*. For more on the devotional movements in nineteenth- and twentieth-century Europe, see Kselman, *Miracles and Prophecies in Nineteenth-Century France*, Blackbourn, *Marpingen: Apparitions of the Virgin Mary in Bismarckian Germany*; and Ivereigh, ed., *The Politics of Religion in an Age of Revival*.

57. Kenneth Serbin declares the Romanizing reforms of the nineteenth and early twentieth centuries to be the moment when "Trent comes to Brazil"—a delayed moment of reform and renewal in the Brazilian Catholic Church. *Needs of the Heart*, 54.

58. Serbin, *Needs of the Heart*, 57; Wright-Rios, *Revolutions in Mexican Catholicism*, 43–72.

59. The archive of the Convento da Penha in Recife, which served as the provincial headquarters of the Capuchin Order for much of the northeastern region in the 1920s, 1930s, and 1940s, contains a wealth of information about the *santas missões populares* (holy popular missions) that were conducted throughout the interior of the Northeast. It is an excellent source for the study of sertanejan religious culture.

60. Premack, "The Holy Rollers Are Invading Our Territory."

1 Quem Não Crê, Brasileiro Não É

1. *Anais do III Congresso Eucharístico Nacional* (Recife: Jornal do Commercio, 1940), 36–37, Arquivo da Arquidiocese de Olinda e Recife (AAOR).

2. For more on Eucharistic Congresses, see Serbin, "Church–State Reciprocity in Contemporary Brazil."

3. *Anais do III Congresso Eucharístico Nacional*, 351–52, AAOR.

4. Vieira, *O protestantismo, a maçonaria*, chaps. 3–5.

5. Pereira, *O problema religioso na América Latina*. For an analysis of Pereira's place in the broader history of Brazilian Protestant polemics, see Mendonça, *O celeste porvir*, 130–35.

6. Pereira, *O problema religioso*, iii.

7. Ibid., 418.

8. Franca, *A Igreja, a Reforma, e a civilização*, 286, 288.

9. Ibid., 301.

10. Ibid., 457.

11. Ibid., 452.

12. Ibid., 456.

13. Mendonça, *O celeste porvir*, 134.

14. The three responders were Ernesto Luiz de Oliveira, Lisânias de Cerqueira Leite, and Otoniel Mota. Oliveira published the first response as *Roma, a Egreja, e o Anticristo* in 1931. Leonel Franca published a response in 1933, *Catolicismo e Protestantismo*. This was followed by Lisânias de Cerqueira Leite's *Protestantismo e romanismo* in 1936 as well as by the work of Otoniel Mota, who, using the pseudonym Frederico Hansen, published a number of pamphlets and articles disputing Franca's work. Franca then published a response to the Protestants' works, *O protestantismo no Brasil*, in 1937. Leite then published a second volume of his *Protestantismo e romanismo* in 1938, which continued to focus mostly on *A Igreja* but also took into account Franca's new response, *O protestantismo*.

15. "Letras nacionaes e extraneiras: Pe. Leonel Franca, SJ: O protestantismo no Brasil," *O Legionário*, May 1, 1938, 8.

16. "Uma reivindicação oportuna," *O Puritano*, September 25, 1936, 3.

17. "Roma, a Igreja, e o Anticristo," *A Imprensa*, August 14, 1931, 2.

18. "Curso apologético," *A Defesa*, October 11, 1934, 4.

19. Simões, "O Rebanho de Pedro e os Filhos de Lutero." Padre Júlio Maria de Lombaerde should not be confused with another famous Padre Júlio Maria, Júlio César Morais Carneiro, the Redemptorist priest who became an advocate for Catholic social reform at the beginning of the twentieth century.

20. Simões, "O Rebanho de Pedro e os Filhos de Lutero," 43.

21. Júlio Maria de Lombaerde, *Luz nas Trevas, ou respostas irrefutáveis às objeções protestantes* (Petrópolis: Editora Vozes, 1945), 148, quoted in Simões, "O Rebanho de Pedro e os Filhos de Lutero," 105.

22. "Aviso no. 200: Associação Cristão de Moços," *A Cruz*, June 8, 1930, 1.

23. Ibid.

24. Lima, "A offensiva protestante," *O Jornal*, July 19, 1932, Centro Alceu Amoroso Lima para a Liberdade (CAALL).

25. Ibid.

26. Agnelo Rossi, *O Diretório Protestante no Brasil* (Campinas: Tipografia Paulista, 1939), 39.

27. Lima, "A offensiva protestante."

28. Ibid.

29. Vieira, *O protestantismo, a maçonaria*.

30. "A Egreja Presbyteriana do Brasil e o Novo Governo," *O Puritano*, December 30, 1930, 5–6, 5.

31. Ibid., 5.

32. Ibid., 5–6.

33. Ibid., 6.

34. Campos, "O protestantismo de missão no Brasil," 81.

35. "O ensino religioso nas escolas: Estatutos do Comité Central Pró-Estado Leigo," *O Jornal Baptista*, May 21, 1931, 3.

36. Rev. Mattathias Gomes dos Santos, the pastor of the First Presbyerian Church in Rio, was a founding member and the vice president of the National Central Committee of the LPEL. "O ensino religioso nas escolas," 3.

37. "Manifesto-Programa das Ligas do Pensamento Livre e Pró-Estado Leigo: Ao eleitorado Livre de Pernambuco," *O Escudo*, April 22, 1933, 1.

38. "O movimento Pró-Estado Leigo," *O Escudo*, June 11, 1934, 1; "Manifesto da Liga Pró-Estado Leigo aos Laicistas de Todos os Cleros," *A Defesa*, October 11, 1934, 1.

39. The other demands were freedom to form religious trade unions; exemption of clergy from military service; labor legislation based on Catholic corporatist principles; protection of individual property rights; support of "national security laws" that would target "subversive activities," such as those of Communists: and rejection of any and all legislation contrary, either explicitly or implicitly, to Catholic doctrine. "O programa de 1933 da LEC," in Lustosa, *A Igreja e a política no Brasil*, 106.

40. "Estatutos da Liga Eleitoral Católica," in *A Igreja e a política no Brasil*, 102–3.

41. While Alceu Amoroso Lima and other Restorationist leaders had pushed for LEC to be affiliated primarily with Catholic Action, the reality was that older religious associations such as Marian Congregations, Daughters of Mary, Catholic Youth Union, etc. were often more developed and thus more prepared to provide LEC activists. In their self-consciously renewed role of social activists, these associations saw themselves, in the words of Plínio Corrêa de Oliveira, as "forming the front lines of combat during the May 3rd election." "É necessario," *O Legionário*, August 6, 1933, 1.

42. Telegram from Oswaldo Aranha to Alceu Amoroso Lima, April 4, 1933, Pasta 05/1, Correspondência, CAALL.

43. "Vitoriosos na Assembléia Constitutional, os Postulados Católicos: o 'Te Deum' na Catedral amanhã," *A Imprensa*, June 2, 1934, 1.

44. Tristão de Athayde [Alceu Amoroso Lima], "Os perigos da victoria," *A Ordem* 48 (July 1934): 3–11, 4.

45. Athayde [Lima], "Os perigos da victoria," *A Gazeta*, September 9, 1934.

46. Guaraci Silveira, "Prestando contas à Igreja Evangélica," *A Defesa*, August 8, 1934, 4.

47. "Está tardando," *O Norte Evangélico*, May 15, 1934, 1.

48. "Primicias do fruto do ensino religioso nas escolas," *O Jornal Batista*, June 25, 1931, 10.

49. "Veja o Sr. Francisco de Campos!" *O Jornal Batista*, July 23, 1931, 3.

50. "Movimenta-se a juventude católica de nossa cidade, Pia União do Colegio de Nossa Senhora das Neves," *A Imprensa*, February 14, 1933.

51. *O Legionário*, January 29, 1933; *A Imprensa*, March 18, 1933.

52. Oliveira, "Liga Eleitoral Catholica: A postos!" *O Legionário*, January 15, 1933, 1.

53. Souza, "Liga Eleitoral Catholica," *O Legionário*, November 20, 1932, 1.

54. Telegram from Alceu Amoroso Lima to Oswaldo Aranha, April 22, 1933, Pasta 05/1, Correspondência, CAALL.

55. "A Constituição de 91 e a Liga Paraibana Pró-Estado Leigo," *O Norte Evangélico*, April 1, 1934, 4-5; "Atitudes reacionarias," *A Imprensa*, May 19, 1933, 1; "Manifesto da Liga Eleitoral Catolica: orientação eleitoral aos catolicos," *A Imprensa*, April 27, 1933, 1; Andrade Bezerra, "Sobre o pensamento livre," *A Imprensa*, March 18, 1933, 1.

56. *Arquivo da Congregação Mariana da Mocidade Académica*, 210, Arquivo da Arquidiocese de Olinda e Recife (AAOR).

57. Cruzada Nacional da Educação to Delegado da Ordem Política e Social de Pernambuco, June 26, 1939, Arquivo Público Estadual Jordão Emerenciano (APEJE), Acervo do Departamento de Ordem e Política (DOPS), 558/0368. See also "Secretariado Nacional da Defesa da Fé," *O Puritano*, June 25, 1941, 2; and "Cruzada Nacional da Educação," *O Legionário*, May 30, 1943.

58. Pope Pius XII's letter to Dom Leme was published in newspapers throughout Brazil. Examples of such republication can be found in "Concilio Plenario Nacional: realizada, hontem, a sessão preparatoria da magna assembléia," *A Batalha*, July 2, 1939, 1, 5; "A solenissima instalação do Primeiro Concílio Plenário Brasileiro," *A Cruz*, July 9, 1939, 14.

59. "Crônica eclesiástica do Brasil: Secretariado Nacional de Defesa da Fé," *Revista Eclesiástica Brasileira* 1.3 (September 1941): 609.

60. Strictly speaking, Marian Congregations were not supposed to compete for members with Catholic Action organizations but instead complement and assist Catholic Action groups in their mission. However, in practice the introduction of Catholic Action into a parish usually instigated a drop in Marian Congregation membership, as the more activist members migrated to Catholic Action, thereby taking on a reduced role in their congregation or leaving it completely.

61. Dainese, "Nossas reuniões de dezembro: formação e trabalho: nosso apostolado 'ofensivo,'" *Estrela do Mar* 32.327 (December 1941): 295-99.

62. This was especially true of *O Legionário*, a Catholic newspaper in São Paulo. *O Legionário* was originally the newspaper of the local Marian Congregation in São Paulo. Plínio Corrêa de Oliveira, its future director, became involved in the journal through his membership in the congregation. It was not until 1933 that the newspaper stopped putting "Official Organ of the Marian Congregation of the Parish of Santa Cecília" on its cover. Even then the periodical retained its Marian identity, routinely publishing articles relating to congregational issues and mission. *O Legionário* not only reprinted almost all SNDF-related articles and pronouncements but also became the mouthpiece of many prominent anti-Protestant writers, such as Padre Agnelo Rossi.

63. This embrace of intolerance was not unique to José de Azeredo Santos. It was also practiced by other Congregationists and Restorationist leaders, such as Benedicto

Vaz and Jackson de Figueiredo. See Vaz, "Intolerancia," *O Legionário*, December 18, 1932, 1, 4.

64. José de Azeredo Santos, "A proposito da queima de livros," *O Legionário*, July 6, 1941, 2.

65. "Protestanda," *O Legionário*, April 13, 1941, 2; "Na escola de nossos inimigos," *O Legionário*, August 10, 1941, 2.

66. Even before LEC was formed in Rio, Marian Congregations in Recife had formed the *União Nacional Catolica por Deus e pela Patria* (National Catholic Union for God and Country), which essentially had the same mission as LEC: to promote political candidates and parties that adhered to Catholic values and demands. See *Arquivo da Congregação Mariana da Mocidade Académica*, 210. Located in the AAOR.

67. Armando Más Leite, "Espirito das Congregações Marianas," *A Imprensa*, January 12, 1937, 1.

68. Ibid.

69. "Nosso movimento: Pernambuco," *Estrela do Mar* 36.410 (June 1944): 173; "Nosso movimento: Pernambuco," *Estrela do Mar* 36.416 (December 1944): 412; "Em Pernambuco: Nobre reação dos marianos contra os blasphemadores da Nossa Senhora," *Estrela do Mar* 34.384 (January–February 1942): 17.

70. "A Congregação Mariana matou o templo protestante," *Estrela do Mar* 37.420 (May 1945): 141.

71. "Preparando a futura Congregação Mariana de Paparí," *A Ordem*, August 8, 1939, 1–2, 2.

72. Ibid., 2.

73. "Crônica eclesiástica do Brasil: Secretariado Nacional de Defesa da Fé," 609.

74. For more on Menezes and his activities as editor of *Anauê!*, see Rogério Souza Silva, "A política como espetáculo: a reinvenção da história brasileira e a consolidação dos discursos e das imagens integralistas na revista *Anauê!*," *Revista Brasileira de História* 25.50 (July–December 2005): 61–95.

75. The first three pamphlets published by the SNDF—*Unidade protestante, Imagens e escultura*, and *A Seita pentecostal*—were all written by Menezes. "Diretório Protestante," *Estrela do Mar* 32.364 (March 1940): 62.

76. Menezes, "Igreja Cristã Evangélica (carta a um pastor presbiteriano)," *Estrela do Mar* 31.360 (October 1939): 269–72; "O culto das imagens (carta a um protestante 'reformado')," *Estrela do Mar* 31.361 (November 1939): 306–9; "A seita pentecostal," *Estrela do Mar* 31.362 (December 1939): 337–39; "Seitas de todos os matizes," *Estrela do Mar* 32.363 (January–February 1940): 27.

77. Cônego Emilio José Salim, "Prefacio," in *O Diretório Protestante no Brasil*, Agnelo Rossi (Campinas: Tipografia Paulista, 1939), 4–5. Crivelli's magnum opus, titled *Directorio Protestante de la América Latina* (Liri: Tipografia Macioce e Pisani, 1933), was a towering overview (over eight hundred pages long) of all the Protestant

churches operating in Latin America. He catalogued their history, activity, beliefs, and locations in which they operated.

78. Crivelli, *Directorio Protestante de la América Latina*.
79. According to Padre Rossi, he would have received a doctorate from the Gregorian had his ecclesiastical superiors, "fearing [he] would become a Jesuit," not ordered him to return to Brazil before he could submit his thesis for approval. Agnelo Rossi, *Flores em meus 50 anos de sacerdócio*.
80. Salim, "Prefacio," in *O Diretório Protestante no Brasil*, 5.
81. Dom Francisco de Campos Barreto, "Introduction," *O Diretório Protestante*, 3. When Agnelo Rossi returned to Brazil he became Dom Francisco's personal secretary and enlisted his aid in combating Protestantism in São Paulo state.
82. Barreto, "Introduction," *O Diretório Protestante*.
83. Rossi, *O Diretório Protestante*, 8, 12.
84. Ibid., 43–44.
85. Agnelo Rossi, "D. Barreto e a Defesa da Fé," *O Legionário*, September 7, 1941, 7.
86. For an example of Agnelo Rossi's book series, see "Apreciações," *Revista Eclesiástica Brasileira* 3.3 (September 1943): 822–23.
87. Agnelo Rossi, "História do Pentecostismo," *O Legionário*, October 5, 1941, 3; Rossi, "Adventistas do Sétimo Dia," *O Legionário*, August 17, 1941, 3.
88. "I Semana de Estudos de Acção Catholica para o clero de Taubaté," *O Legionário*, April 27, 1941, 8; "Exposição de imprensa protestante," *O Legionário*, September 1, 1940, 1.
89. Agnelo Rossi, "A Ação Católica e a opinião dos protestantes no Brasil," *Revista Eclesiástica Brasileira* 3.3 (September 1943): 619–32.
90. "Ação Católica Brasileira: Departamento Nacional de Defesa da Fé e da Moral," *A Cruz*, September 29, 1946, 2.
91. *A Questão Protestante no Brasil*, 17.
92. Ibid., 32–42.
93. Rossi, *O Diretório Protestante*, 43.
94. Ibid., 44.
95. Ibid., 12.
96. Rossi, "Perseguições religiosas no Brasil," *O Legionário*, May 18, 1941, 5. A version of this article was also published in the official journal of Brazilian Marian Congregations, *A Estrela do Mar*. "Diretório protestante: perseguições religiosas no Brasil," *A Estrela do Mar* 33.382 (November 1941): 322–24.
97. Rossi, "Perseguições religiosas no Brasil."
98. Rossi, *O Diretório Protestante*, 31.

2 Toward a Sertanejan Church

1. João Passos Cabral, "A invasão protestante," *A Cruz*, June 25, 1939, 1.

2. See Rolim, *Pentecostais no Brasil*, 24–29.

3. The PCUS, originally called the Presbyterian Church in the Confederate States of America, resulted from the split between the northern and southern Presbyterian churches during the Civil War. The Presbyterian churches that remained loyal to the federal government, mostly those in northern states, were known as the Presbyterian Church in the United States of America (PCUSA). Both the PCUS and the PCUSA did missionary work in Brazil, but the PCUS was active in the Northeast whereas the PCUSA limited its activities to the southern and central regions of the country.

4. At the time, Reverend Henderlite was working in the area around the Pernambucan-Paraíba border that included the towns of Triunfo, Flores, Rio Branco (present-day Arcoverde), Afogados de Ingazeira, Serra Talhada, Princesa, and São José do Egito.

5. Langdon M. Henderlite, "The Tale of an Itinerant Missionary," *Presbyterian Survey* (November 1932): 671–72.

6. Ibid., 672.

7. W. C. Taylor, "North Brazil Mission: Annual Report," presented at the seventy-fifth session of the Southern Baptist Convention, May 14–18, 1930, and published in the *Annual of the Southern Baptist Convention, 1930*, Southern Baptist Historical Library and Archive (SBHLA).

8. Livro de Atas do Presbitério de Pernambuco, 1930–1942, ff. 19, 54, Arquivo do Seminário Presbiteriano do Norte (SPN).

9. Premack, "The Holy Rollers Are Invading Our Territory," 18–19.

10. In the 1920s and 1930s the city of Arcoverde was known as Rio Branco. It was renamed in 1943 in honor of the late Cardinal Arcoverde, a native of the city.

11. For more on the activities of Joel Rocha, see "Livro de Atas do Presbitério de Pernambuco, 1930–1935," ff. 2–84, SPN. For more on the work of Feitosa and Jacintho, see *O Jornal Baptista*, various articles, 1930–35, and L. L. Johnson Correspondence, SBHLA, Foreign Mission Correspondence, AR 551–2, box 73, folder: Ex. Secretary.

12. George W. Taylor, "The 'Cut' in Northern Brazil," *Presbyterian Survey* (January 1932): 21.

13. Robert B. Smith, "Some Developments in North Brazil," *Presbyterian Survey* (November 1942): 727.

14. Harold Cook, "An Open Air Market in Brazil," *Presbyterian Survey* (December 1936): 726–27, 727.

15. Charles F. Stapp to Jessie R. Ford, February 20, 1939, AR 551–2, box 113, folder: Charles F. Stapp, Ex. Secretary, 1931–1939, SBHLA. Reverend Stapp, like many of his U.S. colleagues, expressed his lack of esteem for Brazilian leaders even when attempting to praise them. When he began working with Reverend Elias Ramalho, a Baptist pastor in Campina Grande, he expressed surprise that "[Ramalho's] work would stand with that of an American evangelist." Stapp to Everett Gill, January 28, 1944, AR 551–2, box 113, folder: Charles F. Stapp, Ex. Secretary, 1940–56, SBHLA.

16. Premack, "The Holy Rollers Are Invading Our Territory," 18–19.

17. Egbert W. Smith, "Call upon Me in the Day of Trouble and I Will Deliver Thee," *Presbyterian Survey* (December 1930): 22.
18. "I Want to Know," *Presbyterian Survey* (June 1932): 378. In response to the question, "Why has North Brazil fewer missionaries today than it had years ago?" the editor answered, "Unfortunately, our work in North Brazil has, for some unknown reason, not been so challenging to the young people of our Church, and there have been fewer volunteers interested in this field than the others."
19. "Editor's Column," *Letters Home* 5.3 (1933): 6,AR 551–1, box 217, folder: Brazil Mission: Letters Home, 1928–, SBHLA.
20. Taylor, "The 'Cut' in Northern Brazil," 20.
21. Erik A. Nelson, "What Must We Do?" *Letters Home* 5.2 (1932): 7–8, 7; AR 551–1, box 217, folder: Brazil Mission: Letters Home, 1928–, SBHLA.
22. The Seminário Presbiteriano do Norte, which also served as the seminary for the Congregationalists in the Northeast, was officially established in 1924, and the Seminário Teológico Batista do Norte do Brasil was founded in 1918. Both denominations had been training pastors on an informal basis since the early 1900s, but it was not until their "officialization" that the seminaries began to receive recognition and funding from their churches' national leadership, thereby greatly expanding their significance and capacity. But their earlier iterations also contributed to a rise in Brazilian pastors. Robério Américo do Carmo Souza has noted the link between early incarnations of the Seminário Presbiteriano de Pernambuco and the formation of Brazilian Presbyterian pastors like Natanael Cortez, who would evangelize much of Ceará in the early twentieth century. Souza, "Vaqueiros de Deus."
23. The Congregationalist situation was unique in that, as Émile Léonard has written, "While for other denominations, Brazilian congregations were founded by foreign Missions, here [in the case of the Congregationalists] it is the Brazilian Church that creates the foreign Mission," in the form of "Help for Brazil." Léonard, *Protestantismo brasileiro*, 77–79.
24. Léonard, *Protestantismo brasileiro*, 136–60.
25. Paul Everett Pierson, *A Younger Church in Search of Maturity: Presbyterianism in Brazil from 1910 to 1959* (Philadelphia: Temple University Press, 1974), 74–93.
26. In the Pernambucan Presbytery's Livro de Atas there are numerous references to invitations that the Presbytery leadership extended to U.S. missionaries, enabling the latter to carry out evangelization work in the region. Livro de Atas do Presbitério de Pernambuco, SPN.
27. Executive Board of the Regional Baptist Convention [of the North] (signed by A. N. Mesquita, A. O. Bernardo, and Manoel C. F. da Paz) to the Foreign Mission Board of the Southern Baptist Convention, n/d [est. 1923], Correspondence with Nationals, AR 551–1, box 216, folder: Brazil: Letters from Nationals, 1913–1914 and 1923–1924, SBHLA.
28. Many Baptist confessional histories avoid discussing the "unfortunate Radical incident" in depth. For example, see Crabtree, *Baptists in Brazil*. A more detailed

examination of the conflict can be found in Martins, "O radicalismo batista brasileiro"; and Léonard, *Protestantismo brasileiro*, 172–89.

29. Regional Baptist Convention to Foreign Board of Missions.

30. Ibid.

31. These accusations were especially directed against Antônio Mesquita, one of the
leaders of the supposed revolt who had studied in the Baptist seminary in Fort
Worth, Texas. U.S. Baptists called Mesquita "an ungrateful foreigner" for believing
that he "owed the Americans nothing" after they helped him acquire an education
in the United States. L. D. Johnson to the Baptist Standard, n/d [est. 1923], Correspondence with Nationals, AR 551–1, box 216, folder: Brazil: Letters from Nationals,
1913–1914 and 1923–1924, SBHLA.

32. Some nationalist churches decided to return to the missionary fold in 1925. But
when the Foreign Missionary Board modified their Bases of Cooperation in order
to make some concessions demanded by the nationalist cause, a large number of
noncooperating churches remained. At times the number was equal to or greater
than the number of cooperating churches, until, in 1938, the missionaries again
updated their cooperation agreement with Brazilian churches. Yet the agreement
of 1938 did not put an end to the dispute, as in 1940 a conflict arose over control of
Baptist educational institutions. The discord resulted in another revision of the
Bases of Cooperation and a second, albeit smaller, schism that would last until
1973. See Martins, "O radicalismo batista"; Léonard, *Protestantismo brasileiro*,
184–85; Mesquita, *História dos Batistas no Brasil*, 305.

33. Souza has argued that while the IPI did not have a presence in Ceará in the early
twentieth century, the experience of the schism pushed the IPB to place greater
value on Brazilian leaders. "Vaqueiros de Deus," 31.

34. As noted above, the number of Brazilian pastors tripled between 1920 and 1930.
W. C. Taylor, "North Brazil Mission: Annual Report," presented at the seventy-fifth
session of the Southern Baptist Convention, May 14–18, 1930, and published in the
Annual of the Southern Baptist Convention, 1930, SBHLA.

35. Arnold E. Hayes to T. S. Ray, January 2, 1932, A. E. Hayes Correspondence, AR
551–2, box 319, folder: Ex-Secretary, 1931–1939, SBHLA.

36. Ibid.

37. "Circular 2: Pela União dos Católicos e Conservação da Fé," September 12, 1936,
D. Jaime de Barros Câmara (Circulares e Correspondência), box 2.1, Arquivo da
Diocese de Mossoró (ADM).

38. "Circular Recebido," Livro de Tombo da Paróquia de Flores, f. 38, Arquivo da
Paróquia de Flores (APF).

39. Oliveira, "Bodes, hereges, irmãos," 71.

40. Presbyterian missionaries often repeated the story of Reverend Ferreira's illiteracy,
using it as proof of the transformative and civilizing power of Protestant conversion.
See Julia Pratt Taylor, "In North Brazil," *Presbyterian Survey* (May 1934): 303;

Langdon H. Henderlite, "The Evangelistic Work of the North Brazil Presbyterian Mission," *Presbyterian Survey* (November 1934): 669. While it is unclear if the "literacy-as-conversion" story is true, there is no reason to suspect that Reverend Ferreira did not come from a working-class background.

41. Charles F. Stapp to Jessie R. Ford, November 6, 1939, Charles F. Stapp Correspondence, AR 551–2, box 113, folder: Ex. Secretary, 1931–1939, SBHLA.

42. Ibid.

43. Charles F. Stapp to Jessie R. Ford, July 13, 1944, Charles F. Stapp Correspondence, AR 551–2, box 113, folder: Ex. Secretary, 1940–56, SBHLA.

44. Arnold E. Hayes, "Letters Home," undated [1935?], Brazil Mission: Letters Home, AR 551–1, box 217, folder: 1928–, SBHLA.

45. Charles F. Stapp to Jessie R. Ford, March 30, 1934, Charles F. Stapp Correspondence, AR 551–2, box 113, folder: Ex. Secretary, 1931–1939, SBHLA.

46. Henderlite, "The Tale of an Itinerant Missionary," 669.

47. Bear, *Mission to Brazil*, 54.

48. Ibid.

49. Regional Baptist Convention to Foreign Board of Missions.

50. Ibid.

51. Pierson, *A Younger Church in Search of Maturity*, 132.

52. "Campina Grande," *A Imprensa*, April 25, 1934.

53. Ibid.

54. Olympio de Mello, "Uma propaganda patriotica," *Jornal do Brasil*, August 11, 1931, 5.

55. Ibid.

56. For more on the evangelization work of Feitosa, see *O Jornal Baptista*, various articles, 1930–35, and L. L. Johnson Correspondence, Foreign Mission Correspondence, AR 551–2, box 73, folder: Ex. Secretary, 1915–1934, SBHLA.

57. Rev. Walter Swetnam, "Carregando Pedras," *Presbyterian Survey* (October 1942): 461–64.

58. "Numero dedicado ao Jubileu da Igreja P. de João Pessoa," *O Norte Evangélico*, December 21, 1934, 1.

59. The hometowns of pastors can be found in the records of the Protestant ecumenical seminary in Recife: Livro das inscrições do seminário, STPN.

60. "Rio Branco—Pernambuco," *O Jornal Batista*, January 8, 1931.

61. Francisco Bonato, "Os batistas de Pernambuco recordam 1923 e 1973," *O Batista Pernambucano* (June 2013): 4.

62. Ibid., 5.

63. Bear, *Mission to Brazil*, 82.

64. Livro de Atas do Presbitério de Pernambuco 1920–1929, f. 141, SPN.

65. Bear, *Mission to Brazil*, 84–85.

66. Livro de Atas do Presbitério de Pernambuco, 1930–1942, ff. 28–29, SPN.

67. According to *Moody Monthly*, Reverend Briault and his wife, Frieda, arrived in Pernambuco in 1921. "Personalia," *Moody Monthly* (December 1921): 739. After spending a year learning Portuguese, they went to Campina Grande (PB), leading the first Congregationalist congregation in that town in 1922. In 1927 Reverend Briault journeyed even farther into the sertão, becoming the pastor to numerous congregations such as Patos, Catolé do Rocha, and Brejo da Cruz from the late 1920s to the mid-1930s. See Livro de Atas da Igreja Evangélica Congregacional de Catolé do Rocha, AIECCR.

68. Reverend Mathews was originally described by Baptist missionaries as being Congregationalist. Charles Stapp to Unknown, April 24, 1935, FMB: Missionary Correspondence, AR 551–2, box 113, folder: Charles Stapp Ex. Secretary, 1931–1939, SBHLA. But by the 1940s he was listed as a member of the Brazilian Baptist Convention. "Nomes e Endereços de Pastores," AR 214–20, folder: Brazil Baptist Convention: Misc. Information, 1940–1976, SBHLA. It is possible he switched denominations yet remained affiliated with the same missionary society, but he may have changed his society affiliation as well. It is known that he was representing the Gospel Furtherance Band in 1938, most likely as a Baptist, when he gave a presentation about his missionary work at a Baptist church in Pennsylvania. "Pictures Shown at Blanchard Church by Missionary to Brazil," *The Express*, March 24, 1938, 13.

69. "O protestante Mateus anda a distribuir, pelo interior, boletins hereticos," *A Ordem (Natal)*, February 3, 1941, 1.

70. Fernando de Oliveira, "Conversando com Mateus," *A Ordem (Natal)*, March 22, 1941, 1–2.

71. Ibid., 2.

72. Untitled article from *Letters Home*, vol. 4, no. 1 [1930s], Brazil Mission: Letters Home, AR 551–2, box 217, folder 21, SBHLA.

73. Rossi, *O diretório protestante no Brasil*, 127.

74. Ibid.

75. Paul Freston, "Protestantes e política no Brasil," 1–2. Other denominations, such as the Methodists, would also be included in this category, but the historical denominations of the Presbyterians, Congregationalists, and Baptists were the only ones that had an evangelistic presence in the Northeast during the 1920s, 1930s, and 1940s.

76. Berg and Vingren had immigrated to the United States at the beginning of the twentieth century. According to official AD history, while in Chicago the two Swedes received a prophetic vision that told them to go to Pará. Paul Freston has argued they were also likely encouraged to come, either directly or indirectly, by the Baptist missionary already stationed in the state. There they began to promote Pentecostal ideas, provoking a conflict with local Baptist leaders that caused them to start their own church. Although the AD would share a name with the U.S.-based Assembly of God Church, it began and developed as a completely independent organization, having more connections to fellow Pentecostals in Sweden than to AG members in the United States. For a more detailed account of the Amazo-

nian origins of the AD, see Alencar, *Matriz pentecostal brasileira;* Alencar, *Assembléias de Deus* Chesnut, *Born Again in Brazil,* chap.1; Freston, "Protestantes e política; Freston, "Pentecostalism in Brazil: A Brief History,"; Rolim, *Pentecostais no Brasil;* and Conde, *História das Assembléias de Deus no Brasil.*

77. For more on the social status of Berg and Vingren and its impact on the development of the AD movement in Brazil, see Freston, "Protestantes e política," 68–71.

78. Chesnut, *Born Again in Brazil,* 32.

79. For more on how these factors influenced the higher growth rate of the AD vis-à-vis historical denominations such as the Baptists, see Premack, "The Holy Rollers Are Invading Our Territory."

80. Alencar, *Assembléias de Deus,* 69.

81. Conde, *História das Assembléias de Deus,* 113.

82. Ibid., 148–50.

83. Alencar, *Assembléias de Deus,* 69.

84. José Raimundo de Lucena, "Como achei Jesus," *Mensageiro da Paz* 11.10 (May 1941): 3.

85. Alencar has argued that the origins of the AD were so firmly rooted in the small towns of the interior as to create a "rural ethos" that would affect the structure, organization, and theology of the AD for decades to come, even after the urban Pentecostal boom of the 1950s and 1960s. Alencar, *Matriz pentecostal brasileira,* 88–90. The rural ethos described by Alencar complements the "Swedish-cum-North-Eastern ethos" described by Paul Freston, who argued that the political and social culture of the Northeast had a lasting effect on the religious culture of the ADs throughout Brazil. Freston, "Protestantes e política."

86. Agnelo Rossi, "Práticas pentecostistas," *A Ordem (Natal),* September 15, 1942, 3.

87. Ibid.

88. Eurípedes de Menezes, "A seita pentecostal," *Estrela do Mar* 31.362 (December 1939): 339.

89. Ibid.

90. In some cases entire churches became Pentecostal. For an analysis of Baptists' conversions to Pentecostalism, see Premack, "The Holy Rollers Are Invading Our Territory." For a broader view of the relationship between Pentecostals and historical Protestant denominations, see Alencar, *Matriz Pentecostal Brasileira.*

91. Pedro Tarsier, "O Pentecostismo, ou reflexões versus algumas reflexões," *O Jornal Batista,* January 14, 1932, 9.

92. Livro de Atas do Presbitério de Pernambuco, 1920–1929, f. 95, SPN.

93. Jeronimo Gueiros, "O pentecostismo no Brasil," *O Escudo,* October 7, 1933, 1.

94. Ibid.

95. Agnelo Rossi, "Pentecostistas e protestantes," *A Ordem (Natal),* December 3, 1941, 3.

96. Processo Luiz Santiago, Acervo Judiciário, Fundo Tribunal de Segurança Nacional, C8.0.APL.0851, Arquivo Nacional (NA).

97. Livro de Tombo da Paróquia de Flores, f. 69, APF.

98. "Correspondência: Estado de Pernambuco: I.B. de Espinheiro," *Jornal Batista*, July 19, 1934.

99. "Operações Evangélicas no Campo de Souza Paraíba," *O Cristão*, January 15, 1944.

100. "Villa Nova—Rio Grande do Norte," *Mensageiro da Paz* 2.9 (May 1932): 7.

101. "Campina Grande, Parahyba do Norte," *Jornal Batista*, September 29, 1932.

102. Ramírez, *Migrating Faith*.

103. Henderlite, "The Tale of an Itinerant Missionary," 670.

104. Charles F. Stapp to Charles E. Maddry, December 28, 1932, FBM: Missionary Correspondence, AR 551–2, box 113, Charles F. Maddry Correspondence Ex. Secretary, 1931–1939, SBHLA.

105. Margaret Douglas, "Margarida of Brazil," *Presbyterian Survey* (June 1931): 374.

106. Manoel Francisco de Almeida, "Campo Maior—E. do Piauí," *Mensageiro da Paz* 7.2 (January 1942): 8.

107. Ana Alves, "Testemunhos: Testificando do Senhor," *Mensageiro da Paz* 5.9 (May 1935): 3.

108. Steigenga and Cleary, "Understanding Conversion in the Americas," 7.

109. Ibid.

110. "Três vezes salvado," *Mensageiro da Paz* 10.20 (October 1940): 3.

111. "Minha conversão," *Mensageiro da Paz* 5.1 (January 1935): 3.

112. "Se pedires, eu o fares," *Mensageiro da Paz* 12.15 (August 1942): 3.

113. "Aleluia," *Mensageiro da Paz* 12.5 (March 1942): 3.

114. "Na seára do Senhor—Fortalecida—Castelo Novo—Ilheus," *Mensageiro da Paz* 12.16 (August 1942): 7.

115. "Salvo, abençoado, e batizado no Espírito Santo," *Mensageiro da Paz* 5.2 (January 1935): 3.

116. "Long Distance Call," June 1937, AR-551–2, FMB: Missionary Correspondence, W. C. Taylor, box 124, folder: W. C. Taylor Newsletters, SBHLA.

117. L. L. Johnson to T. B. Ray, January 9, 1930, FMB: Missionary Correspondence, AR 551–2, box 73, folder: L. L. Johnson Ex-Sec, 1915–1934, SBHLA.

118. Katherine Cozzens, "North Brazil Mission: Annual Report," presented at the eighty-eighth session of the Southern Baptist Convention and published in the *Annual of the Southern Baptist Convention, 1944*, SBHLA; "Antenor Novarro," *Mensageiro da Paz* 12.22 (November 1942): 8.

119. Arnold E. Hayes to T. B. Ray, January 2, 1932, FMB Correspondence, AR 551–2, box 319, folder: Arnold E. Hayes and Ex-Secretary, 1931–1939, SBHLA.

120. "'Maravilhas' do Protestantismo," *A Imprensa*, July 4, 1931.

121. "O protestantismo, fabrica de negações e de loucuras," *A Imprensa*, July 18, 1931.

122. "A unidade religiosa do Brasil: Catolicismo e protestantismo," *O Norte Evangélico*, July 15, 1942, 1.

123. J. Adelino, "Enfrentemos a offensiva protestante," *A Ordem*, February 26, 1941.

3 To Be a "Good Priest"

1. In 1939 the town of Nísia Floresta was known as Paparí. In 1948 it changed its name to honor the writer Dionísia Gonçalves Pinto, whose pen name was Nísia Floresta Brasileira Augusta.
2. "O caso de Paparí: demonstrações de solidariedade ao vigario, por parte do clero e das forças católicas," A *Ordem*, May 11, 1939, 1; "A solidariedade do clero regular e secular e associações religiosas ao vigario de Paparí," A *Ordem*, May 12, 1939, 1.
3. "A volta do Pe. João Verberck a Paparí: as grandes festas naquela cidade," A *Ordem*, May 20, 1939, 1, 4. The Natal-based A *Ordem* should not be confused with the Rio-based Catholic journal of the same name.
4. "Preparando a futura Congregação Mariana de Paparí," A *Ordem*, August 8, 1939, 2.
5. When Dom José was appointed bishop in 1915 the seat of the Pesqueira Diocese was in the nearby town of Floresta and was called the Floresta Diocese. The seat of the diocese, along with its name, was changed to Pesqueira in 1918, when the latter town's industrial growth and subsequent population boom made it the premier urban center of the region.
6. Livro de Tombo da Diocese de Pesqueira, f. 33, Arquivo da Diocese de Pesqueira (ADPes).
7. Ibid., f. 45, ADPes.
8. Ibid., f. 40, ADPes. "Eucharistic adoration" refers to the act of worshiping a consecrated host that has been put in a tabernacle or monstrance and displayed on an altar. Like Eucharistic Congresses, Eucharistic adoration was a common Romanizing and Restorationist (and anti-Protestant) reform that was promoted in Brazilian dioceses and parishes.
9. Ibid., f. 99, ADPes.
10. Ibid.
11. Livro de Tombo da Paróquia de Pesqueira, f. 22, Arquivo da Paróquia de Pesqueira (APPes).
12. Circular, Livro de Tombo da Paróquia de Pesqueira, ff. 27–28, APPes.
13. Ibid., f. 27, APPes.
14. Ibid.
15. Ibid., f. 28, APPes.
16. Livro de Tombo da Diocese de Pesqueira, f. 180, ADPes.
17. Ibid., ff. 42–43, APPes.
18. "Por causa dos protestantes: o bispo de Pesqueira mandou os sinos a finados . . .," A *Noite*, July 16, 1931, 1.
19. "Dom José de Oliveira Lopes: O bispo de Pesqueira em visita a A NOITE," A *Noite*, August 5, 1931, 2.
20. J. O'Grady de Paiva, "O Sucessor de D. Leme e a sua primeira Diocese," *Revista Eclesiástica Brasileira* 3.3 (September 1943): 686–98.

21. "Santas missões em Mossoró, Areia Branca e Capellas," *O Mossorense*, June 15, 1928, found in the Livro de Tombo do Convento de Nossa Senhora da Penha, ACNSP.
22. Livro de Tombo da Paróquia de Areia Branca, f. 19, Arquivo da Paróquia de Areia Branca (APAB).
23. "Estado do Rio Grande do Norte," *O Jornal Batista*, February 25, 1932, 8.
24. Circular N. 2: Pela União dos Catholicos e Conservação da Fé, Coleção Bispo Jaime de B. Câmara, Estante 1, box 2.1, ADM.
25. Ibid.
26. "Diocese de Mossoró: contra-propaganda protestante," *A Ordem*, June 24, 1938, 2.
27. Termo de declaração necessária, Livro de Tombo da Paróquia de Catolé do Rocha, f. 39, Arquivo da Paróquia de Catolé do Rocha (APCR).
28. All priests were supposed to continuously update their parishes' livros de tombo, but the frequency and detail with which priests wrote in the books varied greatly depending on the individual. Some priests made almost daily entries, while others waited til the end of the year and merely gave a brief description of the past months' pastoral highlights. Some priests made few to no entries at all. However, even priests who made infrequent entries often provided special updates on anti-Protestant campaigns, which were considerably longer and more detailed than their other entries.
29. Livro de Tombo da Paróquia de Flores, f. 74, APF.
30. Livro de Tombo da Paróquia de Nossa Senhora da Piedade, f. 43, Arquivo da Paróquia de Nossa Senhora da Piedade (APNSP).
31. "D. José de Oliveira Lopes," *A Noite*.
32. Adelino, "Enfrentemos a offensiva protestante," 1.
33. "De Cajazeiras: notas religiosas," *A Imprensa*, February 24, 1937, 4.
34. There were two exceptions: Dom José de Oliveira Lopes and Padre João Verberck, who were both at an advanced age when they began their anti-Protestant campaigns. Dom José died and Padre Verberck retired before they had a chance to be promoted. For information regarding clerical appointments and promotions, I consulted a combination of parish and diocesan livros de tombo as well as various editions of *O Brasil Católico: sinopse da hierarquia eclesiástica brasileira, inclusive Ordens e Congregações Religiosas*, located in the Arquivo Metropolitano da Cúria de São Paulo (AMCSP).
35. "Eis a questão . . .," *O Nordeste*, August 20, 1943.
36. Circular N. 2: Pela União dos Catholicos e Conservação da Fé, ADM.
37. Livro de Tombo da Paróquia de Cajazeiras, f. 43, APC.
38. Padre Avila, "A propaganda protestante no Rio Grande do Norte e as verdadeiras tradições brasileiras," *A Ordem*, January 7, 1941.
39. Livro de Tombo da Paróquia de Flores, f. 73, APF.
40. In the 1930s Arcoverde was known by its original name, Rio Branco. In 1943 it was renamed in honor of its most famous inhabitant, Cardinal Joaquim Arcoverde de

Albuquerque Cavalcanti, the first prelate in all of Latin America to be elevated to cardinal.

41. Antonio Napoleão Arcoverde to Nelson C. Silva, May 8, 1937, Acervo DOPS, Fundo 4938: Ação Integralista Brasileira: Núcleo Eleitoral, APEJE.
42. Antonio Napoleão Arcoverde to Chefe Provincial, June 9, 1937, Acervo DOPS, Fundo 4938: Ação Integralista Brasileira: Núcleo Eleitoral, APEJE.
43. Antonio Napoleão Arcoverde, Of. Circular no. 34, July 24, 1937, Acervo DOPS, Fundo 4938: Ação Integralista Brasileira: Núcleo Eleitoral, APEJE.
44. Livro de Tombo da Diocese de Pesqueira, f. 288, ADPes.
45. Ibid.
46. Zemon Davis, "The Rites of Violence."
47. Rosalino da Costa Lima, "Frades turbulentos," O Jornal Batista, July 14, 1938, 11.
48. Leonard, O protestantismo brasileiro, 108–9.
49. Livro de Tombo da Diocese de Pesqueira, f. 180, ADPes.
50. Dom Jaime de Barros Câmara, Circular 2, ADM; "Combatendo o protestantismo," O Mossorense, August 17, 1930; "Pelo campo de ação: o evangelho no sertão," O Norte Evangélico, February 1, 1934, 5.
51. Livro de Tombo da Diocese de Pesqueira, f. 184, ADPes.
52. Zemon Davis, "The Rites of Violence," 59.
53. "Ipojuca, Pernambuco," O Jornal Batista, January 16, 1941, 7.
54. "Notícias de Guarabira," A Imprensa, June 2, 1935.
55. This story appears in two places: "For Righteousness' Sake," Brazilian Snapshot (March 1934): 2–4, and "Do sertão de Pernambuco," O Jornal Batista, November 2, 1933, 12.
56. "Os lamentáveis acontecimentos do sertão," O Jornal Batista, September 22, 1938, 9.
57. "Perseguição religiosa," O Puritano, June 10, 1936, 4.
58. Processo de Apelação, Luiz Santiago, f.12–13, C8.o.APL.851, AN.
59. Both santas missões and Frei Damião will be analyzed in further detail in chapters 5 and 6.
60. "Notícias de Esperança," A Imprensa, April 8, 1936.
61. Livro de Tombo da Diocese de Pesqueira, f. 195, ADPes.
62. "Jubileu sacerdota do Vigario do Assú," A Ordem, September 19, 1939, 2.
63. References to Saint Sebastian were clearly referencing the patron saint of the plague. But possibly there was a millenarian element to the ritual in the form of Sebastianism, which refers to King Sebastian of Portugal, who died in 1578 fighting Muslims in Morocco. Sebastianists believe that one day King Sebastian will return and inaugurate a millenarian age of justice on earth. For a discussion of Sebastianism in the Brazilian Northeast, see Pessar, From Fanatics to Folk; Silva, Roteiro da vida e da morte; and Myscofski, When Men Walk Dry.
64. Tarsier, História das perseguições religiosas no Brasil, tomo II, 37.

65. The most famous attacks on Protestant churches occurred in Itabaiana: "Os lamentáveis acontecimentos do sertão," *O Jornal Batista*, September 22, 1938, 9; Catolé do Rocha: Processo de Apelação, Agapito de Sousa e outros, AN C8.o.APL.467; Cuité: Processo de Apelação, Luiz Santiago, AN C8.o.APL.851; Salgado de São Felix: "Atentado à liberdade de cultos no interior da Paraíba," *A Defesa*, December 5, 1934, 1; Agua Preta: "O evangelho em Agua Preta," *O Norte Evangélico*, February 1, 1934, 5; and Esperança: Charles Stapp to Unknown, April 24, 1935, FMB: Missionary Correspondence, AR 551–2, box 113, folder: Charles Stapp Ex. Secretary, 1931–1939, SBHLA.
66. Livro de Tombo da Paróquia de Flores, f. 74, APF.
67. "O padre de Mogeiro em desespera de causa," *O Norte Evangélico*, May 15, 1935, 8.
68. Livro de Atas do Presbitério de Pernambuco, f. 60, SPN.
69. L. L. Johnson to Everett Gill, Jr., July 16, 1944, FMB: Missionary Correspondence, AR 551–2, box 73, folder: L. L. Johnson Ex-Sec, 1935–1949, SBHLA.
70. "Agua Preta," *O Norte Evangélico*, February 1, 1934, 5.
71. Abelardo Neves et al. to Interventor Agamemnon Magalhães, n/d [1942], Coleção Interventoria, Pasta 60, APEJE.
72. Livro de Tombo da Paróquia de Nossa Senhora da Piedade, f. 44, APNSP.
73. Livro de Tombo da Paróquia de Campina Grande, ff. 41–42, Arquivo da Paróquia de Campina Grande (APCG).
74. Ibid., f. 22.
75. Ibid., f. 43.
76. Ibid., ff. 42–43.
77. Livro de Tombo da Paróquia de Nossa Senhora da Piedade, f. 42, APNSP.
78. Processo Luiz Santiago, Tribunal de Segurança Nacional, C8.o.APL.0851, AN.
79. Livro de Tombo da Paróquia de Campina Grande, f. 81, APCG.
80. "Movimento religioso," *O Mossorense*, January 3, 1932.
81. Livro de Tombo da Paróquia de Areia Branca, f. 19, APAB.
82. "Dr. John R. Sampey as Missionary in North Brazil," article from "Letters Home," vol. 1 no. 1 [1930s], Brazil Mission: Letters Home, AR 551–2, box 217, folder 21, SBHLA.
83. Livro de Tombo da Diocese de Pesqueira, f. 344, ADPes.
84. "O que vai pelo interior: Alagoinha," *A Imprensa*, June 10, 1933.
85. Ibid.
86. "Notícias de Cajazeiras," *A Imprensa*, March 27, 1936; Gumercindo Medeiros, "Uma perseguição," *Mensageiro de Paz* 2.14–15 (July–August 1932): 10–11.
87. The religious identity of Gumercindo Medeiros, the pastor of Areia Branca, is complicated. In 1932, when this account was given, he was in the process of converting from the Baptist faith to Pentecostalism. Thus one can find accounts of Medeiros's plight both in Baptist publications ("Estado do Rio Grande do Norte: Mossoró," *O Jornal Batista*, February 25, 1932) and in Pentecostal publications ("Uma perseguição"). As was common among pastors, there was a period of time when Medeiros was essentially

a member of both faiths: he was officially a Baptist but believed in Pentecostal doctrine and thought it compatible with his Baptist religion. It seems that not long after 1932 Medeiros made a definitive break with the Baptist church and became exclusively a Pentecostal member of the Assembléia de Deus.

88. Adelino, "Enfrentemos a offensiva protestante," 1.
89. Livro de Tombo da Paróquia de Flores, ff. 73–74, APF.
90. Livro de Tombo da Diocese de Pesqueira, ff. 184–85, ADPes.
91. Livro de Tombo da Paróquia de Cajazeiras, f. 44, APC.

4 Punishing the Fanatics

1. Processo-Crime de Eliziario Luiz da Costa e outros, Fundo Tribunal de Segurança Nacional, C8.0.APL.0467, 21, AN.
2. Processo-Crime de Luiz Santiago e Venâncio Alves de Lima, Fundo Tribunal de Segurança Nacional, C8.0.APL.0851, AN.
3. "Personalia," Moody Monthly 22 (December 1921): 739.
4. Livro de Atas, Arquivo da Igreja Evangélica Congregacional de Catolé do Rocha (AICCR).
5. Livro de Atas, f. 12, AICCR.
6. Ibid., ff. 21–23, AICCR.
7. Ibid., f. 1, AICCR.
8. Ibid., ff. 1–33, AICCR.
9. José Ferreira da Silva, "Na Seára do Senhor: Serra do Cuité—Parahyba do Norte," Mensageiro da Paz 10.17 (September 1, 1940): 7.
10. Ibid.
11. José Ferreira da Silva, "A grande misericordia de Deus," Mensageiro da Paz 9.4 (February 1939): 3.
12. Silva, "Na Seará do Senhor."
13. For more on the Romanization of Paraíban religious institutions, see Lúcia de Fátima Guerra Ferreira, Igreja e Romanização: a implantação da Diocese da Paraíba (1894/1910) (João Pessoa: Editora UFPB, 2016).
14. For information on the founding of lay associations in Catolé do Rocha, see Livro de Tombo da Paróquia de Catolé do Rocha, f. 44–45, APCR. For Cuité, see Atas da Congregação Mariana, December 8, 1929, n.p., Personal Archive of Crisólito Marques (PACM), and Livro de Tombo, "Pedido de autorização para a Congregação Mariana," January 27, 1930, PACM.
15. Livro de Tombo, f. 44, APCR.
16. Livro de Tombo, "Objetos adquiridos pelo Pe. Luiz Santiago para a Matriz de Cuité e suas capelas," February 9, 1941, n.p., PACM.
17. Natércia Suassuna Dutra, Antônio Mendes Ribeiro—O Benemérito (Paraíba: n.a., 2009).

18. "O que vai pelo interior: Cuité," A *Imprensa*, March 7, 1934.
19. "Notícias de Picuí," A *Imprensa*, September 10, 1936; *Annais do III Congresso Eucharistico Nacional* (Recife: Jornal do Commercio, 1940).
20. Livro de Tombo, ff. 38–42, APCR.
21. "Catolé do Rocha," A *Imprensa*, June 20, 1933.
22. "O que vai pelo interior: Uma disputa publica entre catolicos e protestantes," A *Imprensa*, July 5, 1933.
23. Otávio de Sá Leitão to Gratuliano de Brito, June 7, 1932, Fundo Interventor Gratuliano de Brito, box 26, document 37, Arquivo Administrativo da Paraíba (AAP); Otávio de Sá Leitão to Gratuliano de Brito, August 29, 1932, Fundo Interventor Gratuliano de Brito, box 26, document 35, AAP.
24. "Intolerante! Um padre perrepista inimigo da liberdade de pensamento," A *União*, August 26, 1932, 6. Padre Manuel was accused of being sympathetic to the cause of José Pereira, who in 1930 led a rebellion against the then governor that would later be called the Revolt of Princesa. Having been a state deputy allied with Pereira and the powerful Catolense Suassuna family, Padre Octaviano had made powerful political enemies in Paraíba.
25. Livro de Tombo, "Termo de declaração necessária," f. 39, APCR. While it was common for priests to record an "exit inventory" in which they detailed the material and spiritual state in which they left the parish, these entries were usually dry, straightforward lists: of the lands they bought and sold, the church ornaments, furniture, and goods they acquired, the reforms and updates they made to church buildings, and any other significant spiritual or institutional advancements made during their tenure. They might include a more narrative description of the priest's accomplishments, including their anti-Protestant campaigns, but it was uncommon for them to directly address another individual, whether the newly appointed successor or the diocesan bishop (whose job it was to review the livros de tombo during pastoral visits).
26. Livro de Tombo, f. 45., APCR.
27. AN C8.0.APL.0467.
28. Natércia Suassuna Dutra, "Paróquia de Nossa Senhora dos Remédios (1773–2008)," 35, APCR.
29. Various accounts of the events of June 1938 appeared in Protestant periodicals. Some of the most detailed are "Perseguição religiosa," O *Puritano*, June 10, 1938, 4; "Violentas perseguições religiosas," O *Puritano*, September 10, 1938. The event was also described in the TSN proceedings for the 1939 attack on Brejo dos Cavalos: AN C8.0.APL.0467 as well as the Congregational church's own Livro de Atas, f. 28, AICCR.
30. The Congregationalists accused the Catholics of cutting the power intentionally, but it is not known for sure what happened. Electricity had arrived only recently in Catolé do Rocha, and blackouts were frequent. While the timing of the power

outage was suspicious, it could have been a coincidence. "Fiquem sientes de que há luz elétrica em Catolé do Rocha," *O Puritano*, November 25, 1938, 1.

31. Brejo dos Cavalos and Cajazeirinhas formed part of the municipality of Catolé do Rocha but were really more like satellite settlements, separated from the main town and containing their own Catholic chapels and, in this case, Congregational temples.
32. Livro de Atas, f. 28. AICCR.
33. "As perseguições continuam," *O Cristão*, March 15, 1939, 58.
34. AN C8.0.APL.0467, 13.
35. "As perseguições continuam."
36. "Perseguição religiosa," *O Puritano*; AN C8.0.APL.0467, 62.
37. When the Congregational Church resumed functions, it would need to officially expel six people for apostasy and "abandoning the Congregational church," and there were reports of others who temporarily attended Catholic services while secretly remaining faithful to their Congregational beliefs. Livro de Atas, f. 29, AICCR.
38. Harry G. Briault, "Catolé do Rocha," *O Christão*, June 15, 1939.
39. AN C8.0.APL.0467, 3–62.
40. Ibid., 19–55.
41. Ibid., 56–57.
42. Ibid., 61–62.
43. Ibid., 126.
44. Livro de Atas, f. 29, AICCR.
45. Ibid.
46. "Campina Grande—Paraíba do Norte," *Mensageiro da Paz* 10.2 (January 1940), 6–7.
47. Ibid., 13.
48. Ibid., 9.
49. Ibid., 11–12.
50. AN C8.APL.0577, 25.
51. Ibid., 24.
52. Ibid., 23.
53. Ibid., 13–14.
54. The parishioner whom Padre Luiz purportedly visited was one of his staunch political allies, so his testimony must be examined with a critical eye. However, Francisca Taveira do Nascimento, the witness who saw the destruction from her house, did not identify Padre Luiz as being physically present during the attack. This does not mean that Padre Luiz did not order or organize the attack, but it does indicate that the priest himself is unlikely to have contributed directly to its destruction.
55. AN C8.0.APL.0851, 13.
56. Ibid., 19.
57. Ibid., 1–16.

58. For a discussion of political transformations and oligarchical realignment in Paraíba during the Vargas era, see Carvalho and Santana, *Poder e intervenção estatal*; Gurjão, *Morte e vida das oligarquias*.

59. The dispute between Argemiro de Figueiredo and the Pessoa family has been documented in various regional histories of Paraíba: Almeida, *História de Campina Grande*; Sobrinho, *Anotações para a história da Paraíba, vol. 2*; Sylvestre, *Da revolução de 30 à queda do Estado Novo*. It has also been analyzed in studies on Paraíba's oligarchical familes. Carvalho and Santana, *Poder e intervenção estatal*; Gurjão, *Morte e vida das oligarquias*.

60. Albuquerque, *Desmascarando um mistificador*. When the Estado Novo came to an end an investigation into the alleged irregularities of Figueiredo's administration was opened, and he was cleared of all wrongdoing.

61. Rui Carneiro, *Rui Carneiro (depoimento, 1977)*. Fundação Getúlio Vargas (FGV), Acervo História Oral, Centro de Pesquisa e Documentação de História Contemporânea do Brasil (CPDOC).

62. Politics in Catolé do Rocha were dominated by two powerful families, the Maia family and the Suassuna family. The Maia family gained dominance in the 1930s after the Suassunas aligned themselves with José Pereira's failed 1930 attempt to rebel against the government of then governor and candidate for vice president João Pessoa in what would come to be known as the Princesa Revolt. For more on the Princesa Revolt, see Inojosa, *República de Princesa*; Procópio, *Meu Depoimento*; Caldas, *Porque João Dantas assassinou João Pessoa*; Rodrigues, *A revolta de Princesa: uma contribuição ao mandonismo local (Paraíba, 1930)*; Rodrigues, *A revolta de Princesa: poder privado-poder instituido*. The relationship between Padre Joaquim and the Maia family became so close that one of the family's sons, Américo Maia, would be ordained a priest and succeed Padre Joaquim in the pastorate of Catolé do Rocha in 1943 (Livro de Tombo, f. 46, APCR). For more information on the Maia family, see Ramos, *Agripino: o mago de Catolé*.

63. Otávio de Sá Leitão was known for his superb oratory skills, and he could be found making speeches at nearly all of the Catholic events throughout Padre Joaquim's pastorate (Livro de Tombo, ff. 44–46, APCR). He would also serve as the defense lawyer for the Catholics charged with the attack on the Congregationalist church (AN C8.0.APL.0467). Information on his life and achievements can be found in unpublished manuscript pages in the Biblioteca Municipal Augusto Maciel (BMAM) in Catolé do Rocha.

64. Ramos, *Agripino: Mago de Catolé*, 33.

65. Josivam Alves, "Notas históricas de Catolé do Rocha," manuscript, n/p, BMAM.

66. Ibid. The Maias would remain political outcasts until 1945, when democracy was restored and the position of the interventor was abolished—and along with it, the governorship of Rui Carneiro. Formiga remained in the mayor's office until 1943

and was succeeded by two more so-called outsiders: Eugênio Luiz de Oliveira from João Pessoa and Manoel Emílio de Sousa from Rio Grande do Norte.

67. Suassuna Dutra, "Paróquia de Nossa Senhora dos Remédios," 23, APCR. The Colégio did not immediately close down, however, as the instructors there continued to work without pay for a while.

68. "Fechou-se o Colégio Leão XIII de Catolé do Rocha," A Imprensa, May 31, 1942.

69. Termos de Visita Pastoral, AEP Chancelería 2.1 f/2.

70. See Marques, "Fé e poder andando juntos," 22. For an analysis of familial-based factional politics in the Brazilian Northeast, see Lewin, Politics and Parentela in Paraíba. For an analysis of Paraíban oligarchies during the Vargas era, see Carvalho and Santana, Poder e intervenção estatal, and Gurjão, Morte e vida das oligarquias.

71. "A.B.C. de João Venâncio," n/d, PACM. The tract was anonymous, but a draft in Padre Luiz's handwriting can be found his personal archive. Since Padre Luiz filed the document alongside other articles written under his name, and since there is no evidence to suggest he was given to writing out the works of other authors by hand, it can reasonably be concluded that Padre Luiz was either the sole author of "A.B.C. de João Venâncio" or he contributed substantially to the writing and editing of the tract.

72. Marques, "Fé e poder andando juntos," 22.

73. The fact that Padre Luiz carried a rifle was noted by numerous witnesses in the trials conducted by the Tribunal de Segurança Nacional (AN C8.APL.577; AN C8.APL.851); as well as people interviewed by Crisólito Marques in 2007 (PACM).

74. Marques, "Fé e poder andando juntos," 7.

75. As in many other things, Padre Luiz was a pioneer in sisal production. He was the first person in Cuité to begin cultivating the crop.

76. Pimenta, O diário de Vovô Pedro, 40–41.

77. Pang, "The Changing Roles of Priests in the Politics of Northeast Brazil, 1889–1964," 343.

78. For a discussion of the rise of the lobbyist priest during the Vargas era, see ibid., 357–59.

79. See his three-part series in the João Pessoa-based Catholic newspaper A Imprensa: "Uma visita às minas de Picuí," March, 2, 3, and 4, 1936.

80. Luiz Santiago, "Cuité e Barra de Santa Rosa querem constituir um município," A Imprensa, November 24, 1936.

81. Santiago, Serra do Cuité.

82. Ibid.

83. "Instalação do termo e município de Serra do Cuité," A Imprensa, February 11, 1937.

84. "Violentas perseguições religiosas," O Puritano, September 10, 1938, 3.

85. "Banditismo religioso no interior da Paraíba," O Christão, June 15, 1939, 126.

86. "Os lamentáveis acontecimentos do sertão," O Jornal Batista, September 22, 1938, 9.

87. Biographical information on Horácio de Almeida can be found in Nascimento, "Patrio-Biografia."
88. "Frutos do Espiritismo," *O Escudo*, January 11, 1934, 4; "Perigos dos Últimos Tempos," *O Norte Evangélico*, June 15, 1942, 4–5; L. O. Lima Filho, "O Espiritismo no Brasil," *O Puritano*, December 12, 1931, 4.
89. In 1944 Almeida got into a fierce and divisive debate with the prominent Paraíban priest Padre Hildon Bandeira over the latter's condemnation of Spiritism. A contemporary observer would later write that the conflict was the "most violent polemic ever to appear in the history of [Paraíban] journalism." Carlos Romero, quoted in Nascimento, "Patrio-Biografia," 32.
90. DEOPS stands for Departamento Estadual de Ordem Política e Social (State Department of Political and Social Order). Its name would later be shortened to DOPS, but much of its structure and mission would stay the same.
91. AN C8.0.APL.0467, 67–69.
92. Ibid., 3–4.
93. Ibid., 70–74. Although the case would be tried by the TSN in Rio de Janeiro, this did not mean the defendants would be transferred to Rio. The TSN did not require (and in some cases did not allow) defendants to be present during the hearing, and thus all of the court proceedings would take place while the accused men remained in Catolé do Rocha.
94. Very little scholarly work has been done on the TSN. The most authoritative account of its activities is Campos, *Repressão judicial no Estado Novo*. An account of the TSN's role in suppressing labor activists can be found in French, *Drowning in Laws*.
95. For a look at some of the *economia popular* cases, see Dulles, *Sobral Pinto, the Conscience of Brazil*, 103–31. For a full list of crimes that fell under the TSN jurisdiction, see: Decreto Lei n° 431/38.
96. Decreto Lei n° 431/38.
97. José Honório Rodrigues, "Apresentação," in *Repressão judicial no Estado Novo*, 9–10.
98. AN C8.APL.0577, 24–25.
99. Ibid., 27–28.
100. Ibid., 37–40.
101. Ibid., 83–84. The kidnapping and torture were also described in the Catholic newspaper *A Imprensa*: "Fatos lamentáveis em Cuité," *A Imprensa*, October 13, 1940.
102. AN C8.APL.0577, 97.
103. AN C8.0.APL.0851, 18.
104. Ibid., 19–20.
105. "Congratulações da representação campinense," *A União*, August 16, 1940, 3.
106. AN C8.0.APL.0851, 22–24.
107. Ibid.

108. Sebastianism is a type of millenarianism specific to Portuguese culture. It refers to the sixteenth-century King Sebastian of Portugal, who died fighting the Moors in Morocco. Sebastianists believe that one day King Sebastian will return and inaugurate an age of peace and justice on earth. For a discussion on mysticism, Sebastianism, beatos, and popular religiosity in the Brazilian sertão, see Pessar, *From Fanatics to Folk*; Silva, *Roteiro da vida e da morte*; and Myscofski, *When Men Walk Dry*.

109. Albuquerque Júnior, *The Invention of the Brazilian Northeast*.

110. For academic accounts of the millenarian movements in Canudos and the Contestado, see Levine, *Vale of Tears*; and Diacon, *Millenarian Vision, Capitalist Reality*.

111. Cunha, *Os Sertões*.

112. Pompa, "Leituras do 'fanatismo religioso' no sertão brasileiro," 73.

113. For an account of Padre Cícero and the movement in Juazeiro, see Della Cava, *Miracle at Joaseiro*. As Della Cava demonstrates, Padre Cícero and the Juazeiro community were far from being the isolated, fanatical, rebellious group so often associated with millenarian movements—they were in fact very much "integrated into the established and conservative political structures of the region, state, and nation"—but many coastal elites nevertheless continued to view Padre Cícero's followers as backward, superstitious, and illustrative of the irrationality inherent in the popular religiosity of the northeastern interior (3). This view extended beyond Protestant and secular circles, as northeastern Catholic elites, even those seemingly supportive of Padre Cícero's movement, did not hesitate to call Padre Cícero's followers fanatics and condemn the priest for "the great evil he perpetrated against the Catholic Church, fanaticizing our people!" "Padre Cícero Romão Batista," *A Tribuna*, August 8, 1934, 3.

114. "Do sertão de Pernambuco," *O Jornal Batista*, November 2, 1932, 12.

115. "Fanatismo truculento," *O Jornal Batista*, June 3, 1937, 12.

116. "Perseguição Religios," *O Norte Evangélico*, May 15, 1934.

117. "Perseguição religiosa em Alagoas!" *O Puritano*, January 23, 1932, 4; J. Feitosa, "O evangelho no sertão de Pernambuco," *O Jornal Baptista*, February 6, 1930.

118. Silva, "Serra do Cuité."

119. Ibid.

120. AN C8.0.APL.0467, 68–69.

121. Ibid., 10.

122. "Banditismo religioso no interior da Paraíba," 126.

123. AN C8.0.APL.0467, 5.

124. Ibid., 109.

125. Ralph Della Cava shows that in the 1910s and 1920s Padre Cícero's adviser, Floro Bartholomeu da Costa, was responsible for suppressing the more extreme manifestations of religious fervor, such as a society of penitential flagellants, the

sect of the "celestial hosts," and beliefs in the holiness of a bull that had arisen in the community founded by one of Padre Cícero's followers, the *beato* José Lourenço. Della Cava, *Miracle at Joaseiro*, 170–71.

126. Aquino et al., *Pernambuco em Chamas*, 263–66.

127. Gomes, "A destruição da terra sem males," 64. For a more extensive account of the Caldeirão movement, see Cordeiro, *Um Beato Líder*.

128. Severino Tavares, a member of the Caldeirão movement, had spent time in Pau de Colher and transmitted to inhabitants many of the ideas and practices of the Caldeirão community. Moreover, a key element of the Pau de Colher movement was a belief in the need to prepare for a future pilgrimage to Caldeirão. See Monteiro, "Peregrinação, violência e demonofobia."

129. Ibid.

130. Pedra Bonita was a movement that emerged in the interior of Pernambuco in the late 1830s in which a community lead by the *beato* João Ferreira offered "blood sacrifices" of over thirty people, all of whom were members of the millenarian community, in an attempt to bring about the return of King Sebastian. For an overview of the Pedra Bonita movement, see Levine, *Vale of Tears*, 218–19. The movement achieved an almost mythical status in northeastern culture through its depiction in cordel literature as well as in such novels as Rego, *Pedra Bonita* and Suassuna, *Romance d'A Pedra do Reino e o príncipe do sangue do vai-e-volta*.

131. For more on the Pau de Colher movement, see Pompa, "Memórias do fim do mundo"; Monteiro, "Peregrinação, violência e demonofobia"; Estrela, *Pau-de-colher*; Duarte, "Um movimento messiânico no interior da Bahia."

132. AN C8.o.APL.0467, 120.

133. Ibid., 127.

134. Ibid., 127–28.

135. Ibid., 125.

136. Ibid.

137. Ibid., 34.

138. Ibid., 126.

139. The only prominent Catholic to protest the verdict was Sobral Pinto, the famous lawyer who had defended numerous supposed subversives brought to trial under the TSN and was a frequent critic of the unjust actions of the court. Sobral Pinto, "A Igreja perante o Tribunal de Segurança Nacional," *A Ordem*, February 1942, 69–72.

140. "Fatos lamentáveis em Cuité," *A Imprensa*, October 13, 1940.

141. While I was not able to find the official decree that rescinded Padre Luiz's priestly orders, a great deal of evidence supports the conclusion that these orders were indeed taken away. The parish's livro de tombo indicates that Padre Luiz was removed from the parish and replaced by a new priest, Padre João Madruza, in July 1941. He never left Cuité, however, and therefore never took up a post as

priest of another parish. "Termo de posse de Padre João M. Madruza," Livro de Tombo, PACM. He also received a letter from church authorities in 1967 giving him "extraordinary powers" to celebrate baptisms and marriages in cases of grave necessity. "Provisão de Faculdades Especiais," December 31, 1967, PACM. An ordained priest would already possess these powers, and thus the fact that Luiz Santiago received them indicates that he did not have them prior to 1967.

142. AN C8.o.APL.0851, 130.
143. Padre Joaquim was also appointed parish priest of the prominent city of Patos, yet it seems he spent much of the 1940s in the even larger city of Cajazeiras. There, he helped administer the diocese both before and after the newly appointed bishop, Dom Henrique Gelain, officially took over the diocesan seat. Livro de Tombo, f. 45, APCR.
144. Padre Américo Sérgio Maia would himself become a model priest of the late Restoration. Having been trained at the prestigious Seminário Central de Ipiranga in São Paulo he would represent the conservative wing of the Catholic Church in the decades to come. Manuel de Silveira D'Elboux to Dom João da Matha de Andrade e Amaral, August 25, 1939, Arquivo Diocesano de Cajazeiras (ADC);Livro de Tombo, f. 45, APCR.
145. AN C8.o.APL.0467, 136–151.

5 Fire, Brimstone, and the War against the Heretics

1. "Perseguição religiosa no Norte!," *O Puritano*, June 25, 1937, 4.
2. Frei Damião's last name, de Bozzano, was not a last name at all but merely denoted the city where he was born. Upon their first profession of vows it was customary for Capuchin friars not only to receive a new first name but also to become known by their hometown.
3. "Perseguição religiosa no Norte!," 4.
4. Firmino Silva, "Perseguição religiosa," *Jornal do Commercio*, May 6, 1936.
5. In Europe Capuchin missions, especially in France and the Low Countries, served as the religious "occupying forces" that accompanied the Catholic monarchs' armies in their battles against Protestant foes. For more on the role of Capuchin missionaries during the Protestant Reformation in Europe, see Chatellier, *The Religion of the Poor*, 19–30.
6. The three Capuchins were Frei Colombino de Nantes, Frei Jorge de Comburg, and Boníco de Quimper (a Capuchin lay brother). They would later be joined by Frei Hugo de Ancenis, the only survivor of the initial mission to Guinea, as well as three other missionaries from Brittany. The most complete history of the Capuchin mission in Brazil is Nembro, *Storia dell'attività missionaria dei minori cappuccini nel Brasile.*
7. For a discussion of historians' providential view of Capuchin history in Brazil, see Regni, *Os capuchinhos na Bahia, vol. 1*, 47–48. Regni, a Capuchin friar, is himself

a providentialist, and he took the position that "the beneficial effects that paradoxically resulted from the freak episode [of the capture of the French Capuchins] fully justify the recourse to preternatural explanations in order to understand the event" (48).

8. Ibid., 71.

9. The contribution of the Capuchins to the war against the Dutch is chronicled in Faria, *Os barbidinhos franceses e a restauração pernambucana*. Descriptions and analyses can also be found in Nembro, *Storia dell'attività missionaria*; Regni, *Os capuchinhos na Bahia*, vol. 1; Zagonel, ed., *Capuchinhos no Brasil*; Gardelin and Stawinski, *Capuchinhos italianos e franceses no Brasil*.

10. For more on the political disputes that led to the expulsion of the French Capuchins, see Gabrielli, "Capuchinhos bretões no estado do Brasil."

11. As noted in the introduction, the Questão Religiosa arose when ultramontane bishops barred Masons from membership in lay Catholic sodalities, ultimately leading to a conflict that pitted the bishops against the Brazilian imperial government. In Brazilian Catholic history Dom Vital was seen as having taken a heroic stand against the forces of liberalism and anticlericalism, bravely going to prison in order to demonstrate the strength of his beliefs.

12. For Dom Vital's relationship with Protestantism, see Vieira, *O Protestantismo, a maçonaria*. The bibliography on the Questão Religiosa is extensive. For the classic and most comprehensive accounts, see Villaça, *História da Questão Religiosa*; Guerra, *A Questão Religiosa do Segundo Império Brasileiro*; Pereira, *Dom Vital e a Questão Religiosa no Brasil*.

13. Basic information about Frei Celestino's biography can be found in a series of articles published in the Capuchin journal *Dom Vital*: "Frei Celestino de Pedavoli," *Dom Vital* 8–9 (1940): 25–28; "Frei Celestino de Pedavoli, cont.," *Dom Vital* 9–10 (1940): 5–7; "Frei Celestino de Pedavoli, cont.," *Dom Vital* 11–12 (1940): 5–7.

14. Pedavoli, *Combate ao protestantismo*, 3–4.

15. Frei Celestino proposed and received approval for the creation of the Liga Contra o Protestantismo at the first Congresso Católico de Pernambuco (Catholic Congress of Pernambuco) in 1902, a meeting of elite Catholic clergy and lay leaders in Recife. For more information on the Congresso Católico and the founding of the Liga, see "Frei Celestino de Pedavoli," *Dom Vital* 8–9 (1940): 27–28.

16. For more on the organization of the Liga Contra o Protestantismo, see "Aniversario da liga anti-protestante," Livro de Tombo do Convento Nossa Senhora da Penha, ACNSP. For conversion ceremonies (*abjurações de fé*), see "Abjuração," "Abjuração na Penha," "Abjurações ainda," "Abjuração na Penha (II)," "Abjuração (II)," and "Abjuração (III)," Livro de Tombo do Convento Nossa Senhora da Penha, ACNSP. For more on Frei Celestino de Pedavoli and his relationship with the Protestants during the nineteenth century, see Santos, "A ordem social em crise," 169–74.

17. J. R. Smith, "À Illma. Redacção do Jornal do Recife: I," *Jornal do Recife*, August 25, 1880, 2. For more on the debate between Frei Celestino and Reverend Smith, see Santos, "A ordem social em crise."

18. Solomon Ginsburg to R. J. Willingham, February 21 1903, box 23, folder: Ex. Secretary 1902–1904, AR 551–2, SBHLA.

19. Solomon Ginsburg, "Nova quiema de Biblias," *Jornal do Recife*, September 22, 1903, 2.

20. See the series of articles by Symphonio Magalhães and João Barretto de Menezes published in *Jornal do Recife* and *Jornal Pequeno* from October to November 1903, for example, "São Pedro em Ceroulas," *Jornal do Recife*, October 24, 1903, 2; "Um Golias e dois Davids," *Jornal do Recife*, October 25, 1903, 1–2; "Ratos de opereta," *Jornal do Brasil*, November 10, 1903, 2; "Biblias em jogo," *Jornal Pequeno*, October 20, 1903, 2.

21. Chatellier, *Religion of the Poor*, 2. For a history of the Capuchin missions in Italy, see Samuele Giombi, "Predicazione e missioni popolari," in *I cappuccini in Emilia-Romagna: storia de una presenza*, ed. Paolo Prodi and Giovanni Pozzi, 472–515 (Bologna: Grafiche Deboniane, 2002).

22. Paolo Prodi, "I nuovi Ordini religiosi e l'identità cappuccina nella Chiesa dell'età moderna," *I cappuccini in Emilia-Romagna: storia di una presenza*, ed. Paolo Prodi and Giovanni Pozzi, 8–19 (Bologna: Grafiche Dehoniane, 2002), 8. An analysis of the role of Capuchin missions in the Italian spirituality in the countryside can be found in Pietro Zovatto, "Dalla spiritualità del settecento ai nostri giorni," in *Storia della spiritualità italiana*, ed. Pietro Zovatto, 445–708 (Rome: Città Nova, 2002).

23. The most comprehensive history of Italian Capuchins in Brazil is still Nembro, *Storia dell'attività missionaria*. For a study of the Capuchin presence in Bahia, see Regni, *Os capuchinhos na Bahia*. For province-by-province analysis of Capuchin history, see Zagonel, ed., *Capuchinhos no Brasil*. For Rio Grande do Sul, see Gardelin and Stawinski, *Capuchinhos italianos e franceses no Brasil*.

24. Ken Serbin gives an excellent analysis of the work of the Vicentian friars and their santas missões in Minas Gerais in *Needs of the Heart*, 54–109.

25. Silva, *Roteiro da vida e da morte*, 37.

26. "Itabayanna," *A União*. Transcribed in Livro de Missões do Convento da Penha, November 1906, ACNSP.

27. "Communicado: Traipú," *Jornal de Penedo*, ano 15, no. 1 (December 19, 1884). Transcribed in Livro de Missões do Convento da Penha, January 1885, ACNSP.

28. "Santas missões," *A Imprensa*, November 13, 1935.

29. Many times a second Mass was given directly after the first, at 6 a.m. "Santas missões," *A Imprensa*, October 24, 1935.

30. "Communicado: Traipú."

31. Cândido da Costa e Silva argues that these public labor initiatives represented a progressive redistribution of communal resources, as they disproportionately benefited

NOTES TO PAGES 173-177

the poor inhabitants of the sertão. Elite landowners were in the habit of constructing their own private chapels, cemeteries, roads, and bridges and were less in need of the services being provided by the mission campaigns. *Roteiro da vida e da morte*, 41.

32. Even when a mission would not have the time or resources to finish all of the necessary material projects, the missionaries would often take note of buildings or infrastructure in need of refurbishment, so that future missionaries could plan accordingly. "Visita missões," 1895–1924, ACNSP.

33. Such requests were especially common in the late nineteenth and early twentieth centuries, when the expansion of the railroads in the interior of the Northeast seemed to necessitate the construction of larger, grander churches that were "in proportion with [the town's] grandiose future." "A Igreja de Jabotá," *Diário de Pernambuco*, September 8, 1884. Transcribed in Livro de Missões do Convento da Penha, ACNSP.

34. Frei João Baptista Cingoli, "Sermões para as missões, AD 1900," Arquivo do Convento de Nossa Senhora da Piedade, Salvador, Bahia, quoted in Silva, *Roteiro da vida e da morte*, 48.

35. Unknown, *Lembrança das Santas Missões*, 38–39, ACNSP.

36. Ibid., 39.

37. Maria das Neves, "Impressões das Santas Missões," A *Imprensa*, September 30, 1934. For more on the emotional effects of santas missões, see Silva, *Roteiro da vida e da morte*.

38. "Noticias de Alagoa Grande," A *Imprensa*, April 30, 1935.

39. "As santas missões," Petrolina. Transcribed in Livro de Missões do Convento de Nossa Senhora da Penha, 1909, ACNSP.

40. "Missões em Bom Conselho," n/d. Transcribed in Livro de Missões do Convento da Nossa Senhora da Penha, n/d., ACNSP.

41. Eliza Reed, untitled, *The Missionary* (January 1896), quoted in Vieira, "A Historical Study of the Missionary Work of Dr. George W. Butler," 50.

42. "A obra dos frades," *O Jornal Batista*, June 20, 1904, 4.

43. Throughout its history in Brazil one of the Capuchin Order's central objectives was to make peace among all communities, on both an individual and societal level. In the nineteenth century, as Frei Hugo Fragoso has argued, this commitment to peace was transformed (and, in Fragoso's view, deformed) into a commitment to pacifying popular rebellions throughout the Northeast. In alliance with the Imperial and Republican governments, Capuchins participated in the pacification of a number of revolts, such as the Cabanada, the Praiera Revolt, the Guerra dos Moribondos, the Quebra–Quilos revolt, and, perhaps most famously, Canudos. Fragoso, "O apaziguamento do povo rebelado mediante as missões populares." For descriptions of criticisms of Capuchins' purported rude demeanors, see Julio Cezar de Moraes Carneiro (Padre Julio Maria), "O que é o Frade Capuchinho," in *Mais um triumpho do Catholicismo sobre o Protestantismo*, ed. Frei Celestino de Pedavoli, 200–204 (Recife: Empreza d'A Provincia, 1898).

44. João Brígido, quoted in Montenegro, *Historia do fanaticismo religioso no Ceará*, 7.
45. Ferreira, *Igreja e Romanização*, 170–73.
46. *Annaes da Camara dos Deputados* (Rio de Janeiro: Imprensa Nacional, 1903), 621.
47. Ferreira, "Cronica de Pernambuco: 1903," in *Almanach de Pernambuco para o ano 1909*, 76–77.
48. "Alagoa Nova," *A Imprensa*, November 23, 1934. Transcribed in Livro de Missões do Convento de Nossa Senhora da Penha, ACNSP.
49. "Timbauba afirma seus altos foros de cidade catolica," *Gazeta do Nazaret*, April 2, 1937. Transcribed in Livro de Missões de Nossa Senhora da Penha, ACNSP.
50. Ibid.
51. "Santas missões em Tambaú," *A Imprensa*, October 24, 1934. Transcribed in Livro de Missões de Nossa Senhora da Penha, ACNSP.
52. "As santas missões nesta Capital," *A Imprensa*, December 1, 1935. Transcribed in Livro de Missões do Convento de Nossa Senhora da Penha, ACNSP.
53. Ibid.
54. Ibid.
55. Quarterly reports of the activities of individual Third Order fraternities can be found in the *Revista Dom Vital* in a special section titled "Pelas nossas fraternidades."
56. Frei Agatângelo, "A Ordem Terceira: escola de Ação Católica," *Revista Dom Vital* (November 1942): 6–17.
57. "As Ordens Terceiras: Gravatá," *Revista Dom Vital* (November 1938): 17.
58. Frei Otavio de Terrinca, "Os PP. Capuchinhos da Penha e sua ação social," *Revista Dom Vital* (January 1939): 6.
59. "Quadro sinótico das Ven. Fraternidades Franciscanas da Custódia de Pernambuco," *Revista Dom Vital* (December 1941): special insert, n/p. The Third Orders in Recife and Garanhuns were both founded in the late nineteenth century: 1872 and 1884, respectively. The Third Order of Gravatá was not founded until 1932.
60. "Quadro sinótico." The Third Orders were founded in the following locations: Caruarú (1938), Paulista (1936), Cabo (1937), Alagôa de Baixo (1938), Rio Branco (present-day Arcoverde) (1938), Timbaúba (1937), Queimadas (1936), Carpina (1937), Aliança (1938), Correntes (1937), São Bento (1940), Canhotinho (1936), Petrolina (1937), São Gonçalo (1937), Ouricuri (1937), Barra de São Pedro (1937), Salgueiro (1939), Serrinha (1937), Bodocó (1937), Exú (1941), Natal (1937), Acari (1939), Nova Cruz (1937), Independência (1940), Macáu (1940), Angicos (1938), Santa Ana dos Matos (1938), Lages (1938), Caicó (1937), Santa Cruz (1938), Ceará-Mirim (1937), Baixa-Verde (1937), Santo Antônio (1938), Afonso Bezerra (1939), Areia Branca (1937), Santa Rita (1937), Serra Redonda (1936), Ingá (1939), Pirpirituba (1938), Monteiro (1939), Espirito Santo (1937), Umbuzeiro (1936), Queimadas (1937), Gurinhém (1939), Maceió (1936), Seminário do Arquidiocese de Maceió (1940), Fernão Velho (1940). These are only the officially established orders. In 1941

there were twenty-one additional groups that were classified as being orders "in formation," with anywhere between eight and forty-three documented members.

61. For a description of a Third Order retreat given by Frei Damião, see "Atraves das nossas fraternidades: Santa Rita," *Revista Dom Vital* (November 1941): 17.

62. "Nossa Senhora da Penha: resumo histórico da missão dos P.P. Capuchinhos em Pernambuco," *Revista Dom Vital* 3.8–9 (August–September 1939): 5.

63. Ibid.

64. *Anais do III Congresso Eucharístico Nacional* (Recife: Jornal do Commercio, 1940), 265.

65. While no comprehensive scholarly biography of Frei Damião yet exists, details about his early life can be found in various (largely hagiographical) publications as well as in scholarly analyses of elements of his works and legacy in the northeastern sertão: Moura, *Frei Damião e os impasses da religião popular*, 35–39; Neto, *Frei Damião: o missionário*; Maior, *Frei Damião: um santo?*; Vale, *Profeta da Paz: Frei Damião*; Silva, *Frei Damião*; Gomes, *Frei Damião: apóstolo do Nordeste, traços biográficos* (Recife: Causa de Beatificação e Canonização de Frei Damião, 2013).

66. Registro de Santas Missões, ACNSP. During the nine-year period there were eight Capuchin friars from the Northeastern Province who preached missions. Of those eight, only four, apart from Frei Damião, preached more than fifty missions. Moreover, many of the missions preached by other Capuchins, particularly by Frei Antonio, the friar with the second-highest number of missions, included numerous missions in which they were participating as Frei Damião's partner.

67. Registro de Santas Missões, ACNSP.

68. "Santas missões em Tambaú," *A Imprensa*, March 29, 1934.

69. "Missões em Petrolina (Pern.) e em Baixa-Verde e S. Bento (R.N.)," *Revista Dom Vital* (September–October 1941): 20.

70. "De Umbuzeiro: Santas missões na sede paroquial e capela de Aroeiras," *A Imprensa*, November 8, 1938.

71. "A proposito do Protestantismo," *O Semeador*, February 19, 1935. Transcribed in Livro de Missões do Convento da Penha, ACNSP; "O embarque de Frei Damião," *A Imprensa*, November 20, 1935; "Santas missões," *Jornal da Alagoas*, February 10, 1935. Transcribed in Livro de Missões do Convento da Penha, ACNSP; "Alagoa Nova," *A Imprensa*, November 23, 1934. Transcribed in Livro de Missões, ACNSP; "Santas missões na Catedral," *A Imprensa*, September 23, 1934.

72. "Missões em Alagoa Nova." *A Imprensa*, November 23, 1934. Transcribed in Livro de Missões do Convento da Penha, ACNSP.

73. Frei Damião de Bozzano, "Apologetica: Verdadeira Igreja," *Revista Dom Vital* 2.7 (November 1938): 4–9.

74. Speech by Luis da Câmara Cascudo, February 1, 1948, Natal, Livro de Ouro do Convento Santo Antônio, ACNSP.

75. Silas Falcão, "Uma vergonha para o Nordeste," *O Jornal Batista*, August 10, 1939, 12.

76. See, for example, "Os Ciculos Operarios na Parahyba," A *Ordem (Natal)*, March 27, 1938, 4.

77. Falcão, "Uma vergonha para o Nordeste."

78. Ibid.

79. "Notícias de Esperança," A *Imprensa*, April 8, 1936.

80. Ibid.

81. Firmino Silva, "Perseguição religiosa em Cajazeiras—Parahyba," *Jornal do Commercio*, May 5, 1936.

82. Registro de Santas Missões, ACNSP.

83. There are numerous accounts of Protestant conversions at missions. For a few of the earliest accounts, see "Santas missões em São José," A *Imprensa*, May 19, 1934; "Conversões durante as santas missões," A *Imprensa*, January 12, 1935; "Santas missões," A *Imprensa*, December 12, 1933; "Santas missões nesta Capital," A *Imprensa*, December 1, 1935; "Santas missões em Tambaú," A *Imprensa*, October 24, 1934.

84. "O exito das missões em S. José de Mipibú," A *Ordem (Natal)*, March 1, 1939, 1.

85. "Orientando o povo catolico para as Santas Missões na Freguezia de Macaíba," A *Ordem (Natal)*, December 7, 1939, 2.

86. "As Santas Missões em Natal," A *Ordem (Natal)*, November 7, 1937, 1.

87. "Perseguição religiosa no Norte!" O *Puritano*, June 25, 1937.

88. "Violentas perseguições religiosas," O *Norte Evangélico*, September 10, 1938.

89. Ibid.

90. Charles Stapp to Unknown, April 24, 1935, Charles F. Stapp Correspondence, FMB: Missionary Correspondence, AR 551–2, box 113, folder: Ex. Secretary, 1931–1939, SBHLA.

91. "Frei Damião, o 'Desenfreado,'" O *Puritano*, December 10, 1940, 3.

92. Charles Stapp to Unknown, April 24, 1935, 1.

93. Ibid.

94. Apolonio Marinho Falcão, "Movimento religioso de Itambé," O *Jornal Batista*, November 8, 1934, 13.

95. Ibid.

96. Rosalino da Costa Lima, "Frades turbulentos," O *Jornal Batista*, July 14, 1938, 11.

97. "Controversia Religiosa entre Frei Damião e o Rev. Prof. Synesio Lyra," A *Defesa*, May 18, 1935, 1.

98. Ibid.

99. "Notícias de Esperança," A *Imprensa*, April 4, 1935.

100. Severino Torres, "Em torno de uma controversia religiosa," A *Imprensa*, May 10, 1935.

101. "Movimento intereclesiastical de ação de graças pelos resultados da Conrroversia [*sic*] Religiosa em Campina Grande (Paraíba)," A *Defesa*, May 18, 1935.

102. Lima, "Frades turbulentos," 11.

103. J. Fialho Marinho, "Os lamentáveis acontecimentos do sertão," *O Jornal Batista*, September 22, 1938, 9.
104. "O 'caso' que o Protestantismo creou em Cajazeiras," *A Imprensa*, April 25, 1936.
105. "Perseguição religiosa," *O Puritano*, June 10, 1936, 4.
106. "O 'caso' que o Protestantismo creou."
107. "Ruidosa manifestação de Fé em Cajazeiras," *A Imprensa*, April 16, 1936.
108. "O 'caso' que o Protestantismo creou."
109. Livro de Tombo, f. 44, APC. I was unable to independently confirm Severino Cordeiro's firing.
110. "Perseguição religiosa," *O Puritano*, June 10, 1936, 4.
111. Marinho, "Os lamentáveis acontecimentos do sertão," *O Jornal Batista*, September 22, 1938, 9.

6 Saint, Fanatic, or Restorationist Hero?

1. Silas Falcão, "Uma vergonha para o Nordeste," *O Jornal Batista*, August 10, 1939, 12.
2. Ibid.
3. Silva's "Práticas e representações hagiológicas" contains an analysis of Frei Damião's early years, as does a subsequent article by Lêda Cristina Correia da Silva and Sylvana Maria Brandão de Aguiar, "Frei Damião: Trajetórias de vida, missões, carisma e poderes." Examinations of Frei Damião's role as a popular saint in later years can be found in Moura, *Frei Damião e os impasses da religião popular*; Oliveira and Cruz, "Frei Damião: a metamorfose do missionário"; Souto Maior, *Frei Damião: um santo?*; Vale, *Profeta da Paz*; Gomes, *Frei Damião: apóstolo do Nordeste*.
4. Pessar, *From Fanatics to Folk*, 37.
5. Oliveira and Cruz, "Frei Damião: a metamorfose do missionário." Some scholars use the terms *conselheiro* and *santo* (as well as *beato*, another word used to describe an itinerant preacher and holy man) interchangeably, but many make a distinction between them, arguing that there is a "spiritual hierarchy" of authority that places beatos at the bottom, conselheiros in the middle, and santos at the top. Oliveira and Cruz implicitly argue against such a strict hierarchy. Citing José Calasans Brandão Silva, the authors do make a distinction between beato and conselheiro/santo, arguing that conselheiros and santos both have more religious authority than beatos. However, the distinction they make between conselheiros and santos is functional rather than spiritual. To Oliveira and Cruz, a conselheiro is a *type* of saint rather than a lesser saint, one who gains much of his spiritual authority from his oratorical and counseling abilities and whose miracles and otherworldly powers are oftentimes related to the moral lessons and messages he wishes to convey— messages that will lead his followers to salvation.

6. "Diocese de Mossoró: Circular no. 29: February 24, 1939," box 2.1, A-B, Arquivo da Diocese de Mossoró (ADM); "Diocese de Mossoró: circular no. 51. March 3, 1940," box 2.1, A-B, ADM.

7. "Vida Paroquial: A santa missão em Macau," *Beira-Mar*, December 19, 1936. Transcribed in Livro de Missões do Convento de Nossa Senhora da Penha, ACNSP.

8. "Noticias do interior: Bezerros," *A Imprensa*, May 19, 1934.

9. Ibid.

10. Ibid.

11. "Santas missões em Tambaú," *A Imprensa*, October 24, 1934. Transcribed in Livro de Missões do Convento de Nossa Senhora da Penha, ACNSP.

12. "Alagoa Nova: santas missões," *A Imprensa*, November 11, 1934. Transcribed in Livro de Missões do Convento de Nossa Senhora da Penha, ACNSP.

13. Pessar, *From Fanatics to Folk*, 40–45.

14. Slater, *Stories on a String*, 2.

15. Frei Damião de Bozzano, "A profecia de Frei Damião: desfazendo uma exporação," *A Imprensa*, December 6, 1936.

16. Antônio Ferreira da Cruz, a well-known cantador who began writing folhetos in the 1930s, is also known to have written a cordel titled *A Grande Profecia de Frei Damião ao Povo Brasileiro*, although no extant copies remain. See Costa, *A presença de Frei Damião na literatura de cordel*, 111.

17. "Diocese de Mossoró: Circular no. 29," box 2.1, A-B, ADM.

18. A report by the bishop of Mossoró specifically mentions a Frei Damião-inspired prayer card that contains the "Oração do Santo Lenho." See "Diocese de Mossoró: circular no. 51. March 3, 1940." box 2.1, A-B, ADM.

19. Livro de Missões do Convento de Nossa Senhora da Penha (loose leaflet), ACNSP.

20. "Aviso interessante," *Revista Dom Vital* 1.6 (December 1937): 7.

21. "Diocese de Mossoró: circular no. 51. March 3, 1940," box 2.1, A-B, ADM.

22. The authoritative account of Padre Cícero and the movement in Juazeiro is in Della Cava, *Miracle at Joaseiro*.

23. "Diocese de Mossoró: Circular no. 29: February 24, 1939," box 2.1, A-B, ADM.

24. In his study of Frei Damião's presence in contemporary cordel literature—cordéis that were mostly written and published after 1960—Gutenberg Costa devotes an entire section to cordéis that depicted Frei Damião as the "new Padre Cícero." See Costa, *A presença de Frei Damião na literatura de cordel*, 49–56.

25. José Francisco Borges, *O verdadeiro aviso de Frei Damião—Sobre os castigos que vem* (Bezerros-PE: J. Borges, n.d.). Cited and transcribed in Costa, *A presença de Frei Damião na literatura de cordel*, 54.

26. Pessar, *From Fanatics to Folk*, 50.

27. One of the best academic biographies of Padre Pio is Luzzatto, *Padre Pio*.

28. "O Servo de Deus, P. Pio: milagres e dons extraordinarios do religioso capuch-
    inho," unknown periodical, c. 1920. Transcribed in Livro de Tombo do Convento
    de Nossa Senhora da Penha, ACNSP.
29. P. Ignazio, letter to [unknown Capuchin friar], June 24, 1920, box CE11, ACNSP.
30. Luzzatto, *Padre Pio*, 120.
31. Ibid., 176.
32. Charles Stapp to Unknown, April 24, 1935, Charles F. Stapp Correspondence,
    FMB: Missionary Correspondence, AR 551–2, box 113, folder: Ex. Secretary, 1931–
    1939, SBHLA.
33. C. Costa Duclerc, "De cá de Pernambuco," *O Jornal Batista*, June 15, 1939, 13.
34. Ibid.
35. João Rodrigues, "Um concilio presbiteriano e intolerância romanista," *O Jornal
    Batista*, March 17, 1938, 10.
36. Ibid.
37. Falcão, "Uma vergonha para o Nordeste," 12.
38. Rosalino da Costa Lima, "Frades turbulentos," *O Jornal Batista*, July 14, 1938, 11.
39. Ibid.
40. J. Fialho Marinho, "Os lamentáveis acontecimentos do sertão," *O Jornal Batista*,
    September 22, 1938, 9.
41. Octacilio Nobrega de Queiroz, "Reviva-se o mysticismo das populações do interior
    do Nordeste," *Diário de Pernambuco*, January 17, 1941, 3.
42. Falcão, "Uma vergonha para o Nordeste," 12.
43. Ibid.
44. Ibid.
45. "Diocese de Mossoró: Circular no. 29: February 24, 1939," box 2.1, A-B, ADM.
46. Ibid.
47. "Orientando o povo catolico para as Santas Missões na Freguezia de Macaíba," *A
    Ordem (Natal)*, December 7, 1939, 2.
48. "Diocese de Mossoró: circular no. 51. March 3, 1940," box 2.1, A-B, ADM.
49. Ibid.
50. "Aviso interessante," *Revista Dom Vital* 1.6 (December 1937): 7.
51. Ibid.
52. "A profecia de Frei Damião," *A Imprensa*, December 6, 1936.
53. Pessar, *From Fanatics to Folk*, 50.
54. Frei Damião was transferred to Maceió at the end of 1942 and returned to mission-
    ary duty in November 1943. See Cronaca do Convento Santo Antônio, f. 20. AC-
    NSP.
55. "Diocese de Mossoró: Circular no. 29: February 24, 1939," ADM.
56. Pessar, *From Fanatics to Folk*, 46, 51–55.
57. "Apologetica: Regra da Fé," *Dom Vital* 2.8 (July 1938): 12–14; "Apologetica: Verda-
    deira Igreja," *Dom Vital* 2.11 (November 1938): 4–9; "Apologetica: Perpetuidade do

Primado," *Dom Vital* 2.12 (December 1938): 8–10; "Apologetica: Infallibilidade do Papa," *Dom Vital* 3.8–9 (August–September 1939): 9–10; "Apologetica: Purgatorio," *Dom Vital* 3.11 (November 1939): 4, 6–8; "Apologetica: A Missa," *Dom Vital* 3.12 (December 1939): 8–10.

58. "Frei Damião de passagem por esta capital," *A Ordem (Natal)*, June 15, 1946. Transcribed in Livro de Ouro, f. 50, ACNSP.

59. "A proposito do Protestantismo," *O Semeador*, February 19, 1935.

60. Padre José Delgado, "Controversia Religiosa," *Diario da Manhã*, May 10, 1935.

61. Severino Torres, "Em torno de uma controversia religiosa," *A Imprensa*, May 10, 1935.

62. Manoel Fernandes Lopes, *Discussão religiosa do sabio missionario capuchinho Frei Damião de Bozzano e o pastor evangelico Synesio Lyra* (Esperança: Tipografia Beija-Flor, 1938), Fonds Raymond Cantel, Centre de Recherches Latino-Americaines, Université de Poitiers. Special thanks to Michel Riaudel and Sandra Teixeira for granting me access to this folheto.

63. "A invasão protestante," *A Ordem (Natal)*, February 19, 1938, 1.

64. "Um Concilio Presbyteriano e Intolerancia Romanista," *O Jornal Batista*, March 17, 1938, 9.

65. "Uma data histórica para o sertão paraibano," *A Imprensa*, June 29, 1934; "Cajazeiras: grande centro de civilização sertaneja," *A Imprensa*, June 29, 1934.

66. For more on Padre Rolim, see Deusdedit Leitão, "Padre Rolim: aproximações biográficas"; Francisco Cartaxo Rolim, "Padre-mestre Inácio de Souza Rolim, um retrato esquecido"; Eduardo Hoornaert, "Perspectivas históricas da obra educacional do padre-mestre Rolim." All in *A Igreja e o controle social nos sertões nordestinos*, ed. Severino Vicente da Silva (São Paulo: Edições Paulinas, 1988).

67. "A saudação dos eminentes prelados," *A Imprensa*, June 29, 1934.

68. Dom João da Mata Amaral, "A saudação dos eminentes prelados," *A Imprensa*, June 29, 1934.

69. Santos and Velôso, *O Ano Sacerdotal e o Clero da Arquidiocese da Paraíba*, 40.

70. At the parish level Catholic Action manifested itself in distinct groups that were organized according to age, gender, and occupation. Thus there were youth organizations for young men and women, organizations for married men and women, student organizations, workers organizations, and so on. In Cajazeiras, apart from the Círculo Operário, União de Moços Católicos (the equivalent of a young men's organization), and Ação Social Feminina—all of which predated the official national founding of Catholic Action—the parish founded the Juventude Católica Feminina, Liga das Senhoras Católicas, Liga dos Homens Católicos and Liga dos Estudantes Católicos. "Aspectos religiosos do Sertão Paraibano," *A Imprensa*, July 14, 1936.

71. Hildebrando Leal was one of the regional organizers of the Liga Eleitoral Católica (LEC) when it was first organized on a nationwide scale in 1931. When it resumed

operations in 1945 after a hiatus imposed by the Estado Novo he was named president of the national organization. See "Reunião: Setembro 1945," Livro de Tombo da Paróquia de Santana, Série Relatório Paroquial, Notação 036, Arquivo da Catedral Metropolitana do Rio de Janeiro (ACMRJ).

72. Alceu Amoroso Lima to o Diretor do Colégio Santa Rosa, January 10, 1936, Pasta 233, Arquivo 3, Gaveta 3, CAALL. See also "Atividades da Ação Católica Brasileira," *Ação Católica: orgão oficial da Ação Católica Brasileira* 6.5–6 (May–June 1943): 151–52.

73. C. F. Stapp to Charles E. Maddry [March 1936], Charles F. Stapp Correspondence, FMB: Missionary Correspondence, AR 551–2, box 113, folder: Ex. Secretary, 1931–1939, SBHLA.

74. Ibid.

75. Livro de Atas da Igreja Evangélica Congregacional de Catolé do Rocha, February 6, 1938, f. 22, AIECCR.

76. C. F. Stapp to Charles E. Maddry, [March 1936], SBHLA.

77. Duarte, "Antenor Navarro," 8.

78. The largest concentration of Protestants in Cajazeiras was in the Santo Antônio neighborhood, which was populated by poor and working-class families. It was located on what at that time was considered to be the periphery of the city.

79. "Visita à Paróquia," Livro de Tombo da Paróquia de Nossa Senhora da Piedade, f. 42, Arquivo da Paróquia de Nossa Senhora da Piedade (APNSP).

80. "Pregações nos bairros," Livro de Tombo da Paróquia de Nossa Senhora da Piedade, f. 43, APNSP.

81. "Notícias de Cajazeiras," *A Imprensa*, March 27, 1936.

82. Ibid.

83. Ibid.

84. Registro de Santas Missões, f. 13, ACNSP. For a description of the mission in Esperança, see "Notícias de Esperança," *A Imprensa*, April 8, 1936.

85. Capuchin missions were historically connected to Lent and Holy Week and to the devotions associated with them. As a result, they often were invited (or offered) to give their missions during Holy Week, and they had a special missionary program that incorporated the theme of repentance into the various Holy Week festivities and solemnities. For more on the historical association between Capuchins and Holy Week, see Giovanni Pozzi, "L'identità cappuccina e i suoi simboli: dal Cinquecento al Settecento," in *I Cappuccini in Emilia-Romagna: storia di una presenza*, ed. Giovanni Pozzi and Paolo Prodi, 48–77 (Bologna: Grafiche Dehoniane, 2002).

86. For Catholic accounts of the mission, see "Santas missões," Livro de Tombo, f. 43–44, APNSP; "Notícias de Cajazeiras: Uma renovação religiosa," *A Imprensa*, April 15, 1936; "Ruidosa manifestação de fé em Cajazeiras," *A Imprensa*, April 16, 1936; "O 'caso' que o Protestantismo creou em Cajazeiras," *A Imprensa*, April 25, 1936. For

Protestant accounts, see Firmino Silva, "Perseguição religiosa em Cajazeiras–Parahyba," *Jornal do Commercio*, May 5, 1936; "Perseguição religiosa," *O Puritano*, June 10, 1936.

87. Silva, "Perseguição religiosa em Cajazeiras–Parahyba," *Jornal do Commercio*, May 5, 1936.

88. "Annual of the Southern Baptist Convention: 1937," 183, Annual Reports, SBHLA.

89. It is surprisingly difficult to find information about the man attacked; not even his religious denomination is known for certain. However, when taken in their entirety the bits of evidence seem to point to the conclusion that the man and church attacked were Baptist. Firmino Silva, the Protestant who denounced the attack to the Recife-based newspaper *Jornal do Commercio*, was the leader of the First Baptist Church in João Pessoa, and in the Southern Baptist Convention's 1937 Annual Report there was mention of a "native missionary in the interior of Parahyba [who] was driven out because of persecution stirred up by a fanatical friar." Annual of the Southern Baptist Convention: 1937, 183, Annual Reports, SBHLA.

90. "O 'caso' que o Protestantismo creou em Cajazeiras," *A Imprensa*, April 25, 1936. The Catholic newspaper calls the church leader a pastor, but it is unlikely that the man was officially ordained. If he was indeed Baptist, then he would have been the "native missionary" to which the SBC Annual Report referred but who, according to the U.S. Baptist missionary Charles Stapp, was not ordained.

91. "Annual of the Southern Baptist Convention: 1937," 183.

92. "Perseguição religiosa," *O Puritano*, June 10, 1936.

93. Ibid.

94. "Bençam da Primeira Pedra da Capela Santo Antônio," Livro de Tombo, f. 44, APNSP.

95. Moura, *Frei Damião e os impasses da religião popular*, 45–49; Silva, "Práticas e representações hagiológicas," 58–69; Maior, *Frei Damião: um santo?*, 43–45.

Epilogue. Church(es) Divided

1. The two most prominent cases of anti-Protestant persecution in the post-1945 Northeast occurred in Patos, Paraíba, when two Pentecostal churches were partially torn down after a protracted anti-Protestant campaign and a visit from Frei Damião. "Evangélicos perseguidos!" *O Norte Evangélico*, July 1958, 1; and in the area surrounding Juazeiro, Ceará, where Protestants reported being threatened frequently by Catholics, and many of them were forced to leave the area. "Continuam as perseguições religiosas no Ceará," *O Jornal Batista*, September 28, 1950.

2. Della Cava, "Catholicism and Society in Twentieth-Century Brazil," 30.

3. For more on the Brazilian liturgical movement, see Silva, *O movimento litúrgico no Brasil*, 33, 40; Isnard, *Dom Martinho*. For the broader liturgical movement in Europe and the United States, see Fenwick and Spinks, *Worship in Transition*,

23–35; Reid, *The Organic Development of the Liturgy*, 63–89; Pecklers, *The Unread Vision*, 25–79.
4. Costa, *Um itinerário no século*; Azzi, *A neo-Cristandade*.
5. Maritain, *Freedom in the Modern World*, 101.
6. Ibid., 102.
7. Lima, *Pela Cristianização da Idade Nova*, vol. 1, 9.
8. Ibid.
9. These criticisms were most starkly put forth in Oliveira, *Em Defesa da Ação Católica*.
10. For more on the rise of specialist Catholic Action organizations, see Souza, *A JUC, os estudantes e a política*; Dale, *A ação católica brasileira: documentos*; "A Ação Católica: traços históricos," FACB, Grupo Secretariado Nacional, Subgrupo 2, Cx060001, Centro de Documentação e Informação Científica (CEDIC).
11. "A Ação Católica," CEDIC, 9.
12. In addition to a large number of works on Spiritism and Masonry there were pamphlets published on Lutherans, Presbyterians, Baptists, Congregationalists, Episcopalians, Methodists, Seventh-Day Adventists, Salvation Army, YMCA, Jehovah's Witnesses, Christian Scientists, Mormons, and Pentecostals.
13. L. Rumble, *Assembléias de Deus e outras Igrejas Pentecostais* (Petrópolis: Editora Vozes, 1959), 20.
14. The SDNF also published a separate book series called "Contra a Heresia Espírita" that focused exclusively on Spiritism. Boaventura Kloppenburg wrote most of the books himself.
15. "Questão de Honra para os Católicos a Reeleição do Deputado Eurípides Cardoso de Menezes," *A Cruz*, September 28, 1958, 1.
16. "Lançado o Livro Vermelho da Igreja Perseguida," *A Cruz*, November 30, 1958, 1.
17. "Questão de Honra," 1.
18. Dom Jerônimo de Sá Cavalcante, "A Presença da J.U.C.," *Diário de Pernambuco*, March 25, 1950.
19. Ibid.
20. Ibid.
21. Dom Jerônimo de Sá Cavalcante, "Por uma democracia cristã," *Diário de Pernambuco*, September 28, 1955.
22. "Apreciação valiosa," *Âncora*, June 29, 1950.
23. "Labores, lutas, folguedos da Mocidade da 'ÂNCORA,'" *Âncora*, December 15, 1948.
24. "Esperantina contra o Protestantismo," *Âncora*, January 29, 1951, 1.
25. Ibid.
26. Ibid., 4.
27. Frei Otávio de Terrinca, "Prefácio," in Frei Damião de Bozzano, *Em Defesa da Fé* (Recife: Edições Paulinas, 1955 [1953]), np.

28. Ibid.

29. "Evangélicos perseguidos!" *Norte Evangélico* 7.7 (July 1958): 1, 5.

30. "Perseguição em Patos," *Norte Evangélico* 7.6 (June 1958); "Evangélicos persegui-dos!" ibid.; "Perseguições religiosas," *O Jornal Batista*, July 31, 1958; "Ainda a Perseguição em Patos, Paraíba," *O Jornal Batista*, August 14, 1958; "A liberdade de consciência," *O Jornal Batista*, October 23, 1958; "Harmonizar a situação em Patos," *Correio da Manhã*, July 24, 1958.

31. "Até onde irá a fúria do Padre Dutra?" *O Correio da Paraíba*, May 6, 1958.

32. "Harmonizar a situação em Patos," *Correio da Manhã*, July 24, 1958.

33. The themes of ecumenism and religious tolerance were woven through the entirety of the Second Vatican Council, but two documents addressed them directly: *Unitatis Redintegratio* (Decree on Ecumenism, 1964), which officially endorsed the ecumenical movement and encouraged all Catholics to participate; and *Dignitatis humanae* (Of the Dignity of the Human Person, 1965), which explicitly supported religious freedom and religious pluralism.

34. Quoted in Moura, *Frei Damião e os impasses da religião popular* 47.

35. Mendonça, "O protestantismo brasileiro e suas encruzilhadas," 60–61; Coppe, "Os encontros e desencontros do Protestantismo Brasileiro."

36. Livro de Atas do Presbiterio de Pernambuco, ff. 1–13, SPN. The controversy was also detailed in the June, July, August, September, October, and November 1956 editions of *O Norte Evangélico*.

37. Rosa and Filho, eds., *Cristo e o Processo Revolucionário Brasileiro*.

38. Alves, *Protestantism and Repression*, 173, 175.

39. Ibid., xxii.

40. "Frente única," *A Ordem*, January 26, 1951.

41. Agnelo Rossi, "Protestantismo e comunismo," *O Correio da Manhã*, September 29, 1953, 2.

42. Alves, *Protestantism and Repression*, 173, 175.

43. Antônio Pimental, "Jerônimo Gueiros—O Protestante," *Diario de Pernambuco*, May 10, 1953, 2, 13.

44. Munguba Sobrinho, *Jerônimo Gueiros—O Protestante* (Recife: Departamento de Radio-Difusão e Imprensa da Junta Evangelizadora, 1954), 5, Arquivo do Seminário Teológico Batista do Norte do Brasil (STBNB).

45. For an analysis of the waves of Pentecostalism in Brazil, see Freston, "Pentecostalism in Brazil," 119–33.

46. Ibid., 126–28.

47. Alencar, *Matriz Pentecostal Brasileira*, 173.

48. Luiz Chaves, "Rio Tinto—Parahyba do Norte," *Mensageiro da Paz* 3.18 (September 1933): 6.

49. Bortoleto, "Não viemos para fazer aliança."

50. Junior, "10ª Caminhada em Defesa da Liberdade Religiosa."

Archives

Brazil

AAP	Arquivo Administrativo de Paraíba, João Pessoa, PB
ACMB	Arquivo da Confederação Nacional de Congregações Marianas do Brasil, Aparecida, SP
ACMRJ	Arquivo da Cúria Metropolitana do Rio de Janeiro, Rio de Janeiro, RJ
AHP	Arquivo Histórico Presbiteriano, São Paulo, SP
AMCSP	Arquivo Metropolitano da Cúria de São Paulo, São Paulo, SP
AN	Arquivo Nacional, Rio de Janeiro, RJ
AAOR	Arquivo da Arquidiocese de Olinda e Recife, Recife, PE
ACNSR	Arquivo do Convento de Nossa Senhora do Rosário, João Pessoa, PB
ACNSP	Arquivo do Convento de Nossa Senhora da Penha, Recife, PE
ADC	Arquivo da Diocese de Cajazeiras, Cajazeiras, PB
ADP	Arquivo da Diocese de Pesqueira, Pesqueira, PE
ADM	Arquivo da Diocese de Mossoró, Mossoró, RN
AIECCR	Arquivo da Igreja Evangélica Congregacional de Catolé do Rocha, Catolé do Rocha, PB
AMSB	Arquivo do Mosteiro São Bento, Rio de Janeiro, RJ
APAB	Arquivo da Paróquia de Areia Branca, Areia Branca, RN
APCR	Arquivo da Paróquia de Catolé do Rocha, Catolé do Rocha, PB
APCG	Arquivo da Paróquia de Campina Grande, Campina Grande, PB
APE	Arquivo da Paróquia de Esperança, Esperança, PB
APF	Arquivo da Paróquia de Flores, Flores, PE
API	Arquivo da Paróquia de Ipojuca, Ipojuca, PE

APNSP   Arquivo da Paróquia de Nossa Senhora da Piedade, Cajazeiras, PB
APPes   Arquivo da Paróquia de Pesqueira, Pesqueira, PE
APPic   Arquivo da Paróquia de Picuí, Picuí, PB
AEP   Arquivo Eclesiástico da Paraíba, João Pessoa, PB
APEJE   Arquivo Público Estadual Jordão Emerenciano, Recife, PE
BMAM   Biblioteca Municipal Augusto Maciel, Catolé do Rocha, PB
BMP   Biblioteca Municipal de Picuí, Picuí, PB
CAALL   Centro Alceu Amoroso Lima para a Liberdade, Petrópolis, RJ
CEDIC   Centro de Documentação e Informação Científica, São Paulo, SP
CPDOC   Centro de Pesquisa e Documentação da História Contemporânea do
          Brasil, Fundação Getúlio Vargas, Rio de Janeiro, RJ
FJN   Fundação Joaquim Nabuco, Recife, PE
IHGP   Instituto Histórico e Geográfico Paraibano, João Pessoa, PB
IAHGP   Instituto Arqueológico, Histórico e Geográfico Pernambucano, Recife, PE
IPCO   Instituto Plínio Correa de Oliveira, São Paulo, SP
MHC   Museu do Homem do Curimataú, Cuité, PB
MHLE   Museu Histórico Lauro da Escóssia, Mossoró, RN
MP-REP   Museu Republicano "Convenção de Itu," Itu, SP
PACM   Personal Archive of Crisólito Marques, Cuité, PB
STBNB   Seminário Teológico Batista do Norte do Brasil, Recife, PE
SPN   Seminário Presbiteriano do Norte, Recife, PE

United States

BL   Burke Library at Union Theological Seminary, Special Collections (BL),
          New York
LC   Library of Congress, Washington, DC
SBHLA   Southern Baptist Historical Association (SBHLA), Nashville, TN

Secondary Sources

Albuquerque, Epitácio Pessoa Cavalcanti de. *Desmascarando um mistificador: erros e desmandos do atual governo da Paraíba, 1935–1940*. Rio de Janeiro, 1940.

Albuquerque Júnior, Durval Muniz de. *The Invention of the Brazilian Northeast*. Translated by Jerry Dennis Metz. Durham: Duke University Press, 2014.

Alencar, Gedeon Freire de. *Assembléias de Deus: origem, implantação e militância (1911–1946)*. São Paulo: Arte Editorial, 2010.

———. *Matriz Pentecostal Brasileira: Assembleias de Deus, 1911–2011*. São Paulo: Novos Diálogos, 2013.

Almeida, Elpídio de. *História de Campina Grande*. João Pessoa: Editora Universitária UFPB, 1979.

Almeida, Maria das Graças Andrade Ataíde de. *A construção da verdade autoritária*. São Paulo: Humanitas FFLCH/USP, 2001.

Alves, Rubem. *Protestantism and Repression: A Brazilian Case Study*. Translated by John Drury. Maryknoll: Orbis Books, 1979.

Annais do III Congresso Eucharistico Nacional. Recife: Jornal do Commercio, 1940.

Aquino, Rubim Santos Leão de, et al. *Pernambuco em Chamas: revoltas e revoluções em Pernambuco*. Recife: Fundação Joaquim Nabuco, 2009.

Arquivo da Congregação Mariana da Mocidade Académica: Terceiro Volume. [Pernambuco], 1940.

Azzi, Riolando. *A Neo-Cristandade: um projeto restaurador*. São Paulo: Paulus, 1994.

——. *O estado leigo e o projeto ultramontano*. São Paulo: Paulus, 1994.

——. *Os pioneiros do Centro Dom Vital*. Rio de Janeiro: Educam, 2003.

Azzi, Riolando, and José Oscar Beozzo. *Os religiosos no Brasil: enfoques históricos*. São Paulo: Edições Paulinas, 1986.

Azzi, Riolando, and Klaus van der Grijp. *História de Igreja no Brasil: ensaio de interpretação a partir do povo—terceira época (1930–1964)*. Petrópolis: Editora Vozes, 2008.

Bandeira, Marina. *A Igreja Católica na virada da questão social (1930–1964)*. Rio de Janeiro: Editora Vozes, 2000.

Bautista García, Cecilia Adriana. "Hacia la romanización de la Iglesia mexicana a fines del siglo XIX." *Historia mexicana* 55.1 (2005): 99–144.

Bear, James E. *Mission to Brazil*. n.p.: Board of World Missions of the Presbyterian Church of the United States, 1961.

Bellotti, Karina Kosicki. "Pluralismo protestante na América Latina." In *Religião e Sociedade na América Latina*, edited by Eliane Moura da Silva, Karina Kosicki Bellotti, and Leonildo Silveira Campos, 55–71. São Bernardo do Campo: UMESP, 2010.

Beozzo, José Oscar. *História da Igreja no Brasil*. Petrópolis: Editora Vozes, 2008.

Bireley, Robert. *The Refashioning of Catholicism, 1450–1700: A Reassessment of the Counter-Reformation*. New York: Macmillan Press, 1999.

Blackbourn, David. *Marpingen: Apparitions of the Virgin Mary in Bismarckian Germany*. Oxford: Oxford University Press, 1993.

Blake, Stanley E. *The Vigorous Core of Our Nationality: Race and Regional Identity in Northeastern Brazil*. Pittsburgh: University of Pittsburgh Press, 2011.

Bortoleto, Milton. "Não viemos para fazer aliança: Faces do conflito entre adeptos das religiões pentecostais e brasileiros." Master's thesis, University of São Paulo, 2015.

Bozzano, Frei Damião de. *Em Defesa da Fé*. Recife: Edições Paulinas, 1955 [1953].

Bruneau, Thomas C. *The Political Transformation of the Brazilian Catholic Church*. Cambridge: Cambridge University Press, 1974.

Burdick, John. *Looking for God in Brazil: The Progressive Catholic Church in Urban Brazil's Religious Arena*. Berkeley: University of California Press, 1996.

Butler, Matthew, ed. *Faith and Impiety in Revolutionary Mexico*. New York: Palgrave Macmillan, 2007.

——. *Popular Piety and Political Identity in Mexico's Cristero Rebellion.* New York: Oxford University Press, 2004.

Caldas, Joaquim Moreira. *Porque João Dantas assassinou João Pessoa.* Rio de Janeiro: Est. de Artes Graf. C. Mendes Júnior, 1935.

Camargo, Cândido Procópio Ferreira de, ed. *Católicos, Protestantes, Espíritas.* Petrópolis: Editora Vozes, 1973.

Campbell, Courtney J. "The Brazilian Northeast, Inside Out: Region, Nation, and Globalization (1926–1968)." PhD diss., Vanderbilt University, 2014.

Campos, Leonildo Silveira. "Del monopolio católico a la diversidad, el pluralismo y el cambio religioso en Brasil en el siglo XX." In *Pluralización religiosa de América Latina,* edited by Olga Odgers Ortiz. México, DF: CIESAS, 2011.

——. "El campo religioso brasileño: Pluralismo y cambios sociales—Protestantismo y pentecostalismo entre los años 1970 y 2000." *Sociedad y Religión* 20.30–31 (2008): 31–57.

——. "Pentecostalismo e Protestantismo 'Histórico' no Brasil: um século de conflitos, assimilação e mudança." *Horizonte* 9.22 (July–September 2011): 504–33.

——. "O protestantismo de missão no Brasil, cidadania e liberdade religiosa." *Educação e Linguagem* 17.1 (January–June 2014): 76–116.

Campos, Reynaldo Pompeu de. *Repressão judicial no Estado Novo: esquerda e direita no banco dos réus.* Rio de Janeiro: Achiamé, 1981.

Carneiro, Maria Luiza Tucci, and Boris Kossoy, eds. *A Imprensa confiscada pelo DEOPS, 1924–1954.* São Paulo: Ateliê Editorial/Imprensa Oficial/Arquivo do Estado, 2003.

Carpeaux, Otto Maria. *Alceu Amoroso Lima.* Rio de Janeiro: Edições Graal, 1978.

Carvalho, Martha M. Falcão de, and M. Santana. *Poder e intervenção estatal: Paraíba, 1930–1940.* João Pessoa: Editora Universitária, 2000.

Castro, Eduardo Góes de. *Os "quebra-santos": anti-clericalismo e repressão pelo DEOPS/SP.* São Paulo: Humanitas, 2007.

Chatellier, Louis. *Religion of the Poor: Rural Missions in Europe and the Creation of Modern Catholicism, c. 1500–c. 1800.* Translated by Brian Pearce. Cambridge: Cambridge University Press, 1997.

Chesnut, R. Andrew. *Born Again in Brazil: The Pentecostal Boom and the Pathogens of Poverty.* New Brunswick: Rutgers University Press, 1997.

——. *Competitive Spirits: Latin America's New Religious Economy.* New York: Oxford University Press, 2003.

Cintra, Sebastião Leme da Silveira. *A carta pastoral de S. Em. Sr. Cardeal D. Leme quando Arcebispo de Olinda, saudando os seus diocesanos.* Petrópolis: Editora Vozes, n.d. [1916].

Conde, Emílio. *História das Assembléias de Deus no Brasil.* Rio de Janeiro: CPAD, 1960.

Coppe, Moisés A. "Os encontros e desencontros do Protestantismo Brasileiro: Lacunas que favoreceram o desenvolvimento da UCEB." *Reflexus* 6.7 (2012).

Cordeiro, Domingos Sávios de Almeida. *Um Beato Líder: Narrativas memoráveis do Caldeirão.* Fortaleza: Imprensa Universitária Universidade Federal do Ceará, 2004.

Corten, André. *Pentecostalism in Brazil: Emotion of the Poor and Theological Romanticism*. Translated by Arianne Dorval. London: Macmillan Press, 1999.

Costa, Gutenberg. *A presença de Frei Damião na literatura de cordel: uma antologia*. Brasília: Thesaurus, 1998.

Costa, Marcelo Timotheo da. *Um itinerário no século: mudança, disciplina e ação em Alceu Amoroso Lima*. Rio de Janeiro: Editora PUC, 2006.

———. "Los tres mosqueteros: una reflexión sobre la militancia católica lega en el Brasil contemporáneo." *Prismas* 11 (2007): 57–75.

Crabtree, Asa Routh. *Baptists in Brazil: A History of Southern Baptists' Greatest Mission Field*. Rio de Janeiro: Baptist Publication House of Brazil, 1953.

Crivelli, Camillo. *Directorio Protestante de la America Latina*. Liri: Tipografia Macioce e Pisani, 1933.

Cunha, Euclides da. *Os Sertões*. São Paulo: Ediouro, 2009.

Dale, Romeu. *A ação católica brasileira: documentos*. São Paulo: Edições Loyola, 1985.

Dawsey, Cyrus B., and James M. Dawsey, eds. *The Confederados: Old South Immigrants in Brazil*. Tuscaloosa: University of Alabama Press, 1995.

De Groot, C. G. *Brazilian Catholicism and the Ultramontane Reform, 1850–1930*. Amsterdam: CEDLA, 1996.

Della Cava, Ralph. "Catholicism and Society in Twentieth-Century Brazil." *Latin American Research Review* 11.2 (1976): 7–50.

———. *Miracle at Joaseiro*. New York: Columbia University Press, 1970.

Diacon, Todd A. *Millenarian Vision, Capitalist Reality: Brazil's Contestado Rebellion, 1912–1916*. Durham: Duke University Press, 1991.

Dias, Romualdo. *Imagens da ordem: a doutrina católica sobre autoridade no Brasil (1922–1933)*. São Paulo: UNESP, 1996.

Dias, Zwinglio Mota, Rodrigo Portella, and Eliza Rodrigues, eds. *Protestantes, evangélicos, e (neo)pentecostais*. São Paulo: Fonte Editorial, 2014.

Duarte, Raymundo. "Um movimento messiânico no interior da Bahia." *Revista de Antropologia* 11.1–2 (June–December 1963): 41–51.

Dulles, John W. F. *Sobral Pinto, the Conscience of Brazil*. Austin: University of Texas Press, 2002.

Dutra, Natércia Suassuna. *Antônio Mendes Ribeiro—O Benemérito*. Paraíba: n.a., 2009.

Edwards, Lisa M. *Roman Virtues: The Education of the Latin American Clergy in Rome, 1858–1962*. New York: Peter Lang, 2011.

Eire, Carlos. "The Concept of Popular Religion." In *Local Religion in Colonial Mexico*. Ed. Martin Nesvig, 1–36. Albuquerque: University of New Mexico Press, 2006.

Episcopado do Brasil. "Estatutos da Ação Católica Brasileira." In *A Ação Católica: documentos fundamentais*. Ed. Romeu Dale, O.P., 27–31. São Paulo: Edições Loyola, 1985 [1935].

Espinosa, Gastón. *William J. Seymour and the Origins of Global Pentecostalism*. Durham: Duke University Press, 2014.

"Estatutos da Liga Eleitoral Católica." In *A Igreja e a política no Brasil: documentação do partido católico à LEC (1874–1945)*. Edited by Oscar de Figueiredo Lustosa, O.P. São Paulo: Edições Loyola, 1983.

Estrela, Raimundo. *Pau-de-colher: um pequeno Canudos*. Salvador: Assembleia Legislativa do Estado da Bahia, 1998.

Fallaw, Ben. *Religion and State Formation in Postrevolutionary Mexico*. Durham: Duke University Press, 2012.

Faria, Francisco Leite de. *Os barbidinhos franceses e a restauração pernambucana*. Coimbra: Coimbra Editora, 1954.

Faustino, Lindomarcos. *Memorial dos Sacerdotes de Mossoró*. Mossoró: Fundação Vingt-Un Rosado, 2012.

Fenwick, John R. K., and Bryan Spinks. *Worship in Transition: The Liturgical Movement in the Twentieth Century*. New York: Continuum, 1995.

Ferreira, Julio Pires. *Almanach de Pernambuco para o ano 1909*. Recife: Imprensa Industrial, 1908.

Ferreira, Lúcia de Fátima Guerra. *Igreja e Romanização: a implantação da Diocese da Paraíba (1894/1910)*. João Pessoa: Editora UFPB, 2016.

Fitzpatrick-Behrens, Susan. *The Maryknoll Catholic Mission in Peru, 1943–1989: Transnational Faith and Transformation*. Notre Dame: University of Notre Dame Press, 2012.

Fragoso, Hugo. "O apaziguamento do povo rebelado mediante as missões populares, Nordeste do II Império." In *A Igreja e o controle social nos sertões nordestinos*, edited by Severino Vicente da Silva, 10–53. São Paulo: Edições Paulinas, 1988.

Franca, Leonel. *Catolicismo e protestantismo*. Rio de Janeiro: Agir Editora, 1954 [1933].

——. *A Igreja, a reforma, e a civilização*. Rio de Janeiro: Agir Editora, 1958 [1923].

——. *O protestantismo no Brasil*. Rio de Janeiro: Agir Editora, 1952 [1937].

French, John D. *Drowning in Laws: Labor Law and Brazilian Political Culture*. Chapel Hill: University of North Carolina Press, 2004.

Freston, Paul. "History, Current Reality, and Prospects of Pentecostalism in Latin America." In *The Cambridge History of Religions in Latin America*, edited by Virigina Garrard-Burnett, Paul Freston, and Stephen C. Dove. New York: Cambridge University Press, 2016.

——. "Pentecostalism in Brazil: A Brief History." *Religion* 25 (1995): 119–33.

——. "Protestantes e política no Brasil: da constituinte ao impeachment." PhD diss., Universidade Estadual de Campinas, 1993.

Freyre, Gilberto. *The Masters and the Slaves*. Translated by Samuel Putnam. Berkeley: University of California Press, 1986.

Gabaglia, Laurita Pessoa Raja. *O Cardeal Leme (1882–1942)*. Rio de Janeiro: Livraria José Olympio Editora, 1962.

Gabrielli, Cassiana Maria Mingotti. "Capuchinhos bretões no estado do Brasil: estratégias políticas e missionárias (1642–1702)." Master's thesis, Universidade de São Paulo, 2009.

Garcia, Simone. *Canudos: história e literatura*. Curitiba: HD Livros Editora, 2002.

Gardelin, Mario, and Alberto Victor Stawinski. *Capuchinhos italianos e franceses no Brasil*. Porto Alegre: EST/EDUCS, 1986.

Garrard-Burnett, Virigina, Paul Freston, and Stephen C. Dove, eds. *The Cambridge History of Religions in Latin America*. New York: Cambridge University Press, 2016.

Giombi, Samuele. "Predicazione e missioni popolari." In *I cappuccini in Emilia-Romagna: storia de una presenza*, edited by Paolo Prodi and Giovanni Pozzi, 472–515. Bologna: Grafiche Deboniane, 2002.

Gomes, Antônio Máspoli de Araújo. "A destruição da terra sem males: o conflito religioso do Caldeirão de Santa Cruz do Deserto." *Revista USP* (June–August 2009): 54–67.

Gomes, Frei Jociel. *Frei Damião: apóstolo do Nordeste, traços biográficos*. Recife: Causa de Beatificação e Canonização de Frei Damião, 2013.

Guerra, Flávio. A *Questão Religiosa do Segundo Império Brasileiro; Fundamentos Históricos*. Rio de Janeiro: Irmãos Pongetti, 1952.

Guilhon, Norma. *Confederados em Santarém: saga americana na Amazônia*. Rio de Janeiro: Presença, 1987.

Gurjão, Eliete de Queiróz. *Morte e vida das oligarquias: Paraíba (1889–1945)*. João Pessoa: Editora Universitária UFPB, 1994.

Hahn, Carl Joseph. *História do culto protestante no Brasil*. Trans. Antonio Gouvêa Mendonça. São Paulo: ASTE, 1989.

Hauck, João Fagundes, et al., eds. *História da Igreja no Brasil: ensaio de interpretação ao partir do povo. Segunda época — século XIX*. Petrópolis: Editora Vozes, 1980.

Hentschke, Jens R. *Reconstructing the Brazilian Nation: Public Schooling in the Vargas Era*. Baden-Baden: Nomos, 2007.

Holanda, Sérgio Buarque de. *Roots of Brazil*. Notre Dame: University of Notre Dame Press, 2012.

Hoornaert, Eduardo. *O cristianismo moreno no Brasil*. Petrópolis: Editora Vozes, 1990.

———. "Perspectivas históricas da obra educacional do padre-mestre Rolim." In A *Igreja e o controle social nos sertões nordestinos*, edited by Severino Vicente da Silva, 107–17. São Paulo: Edições Paulinas, 1988.

Inojosa, Joaquim. *República de Princesa (José Pereira x João Pessoa — 1930)*. Brasília: Civilização Brasileira, 1980.

Isnard, Clemente Gouveia. *Dom Martinho: vida e obra do grande abade do Mosteiro de São Bento do Rio de Janeiro e iniciador do movimento litúrgico no Brasil*. Rio de Janeiro: Edições Lumen Christi, 1999.

Ivereigh, Austen, ed. *The Politics of Religion in an Age of Revival: Studies in Nineteenth-Century Europe and Latin America*. London: Institute of Latin American Studies, 2000.

Junior, Walmyr. "10 Caminhada em Defesa da Liberdade Religiosa." *Jornal do Brasil*, September 15, 2017. http://www.jb.com.br/comunidade-em-pauta/noticias/2017/09/15/10a-caminhada-em-defesa-da-liberdade-religiosa/. Accessed September 19, 2017.

Klaiber, Jeffrey. *The Catholic Church in Peru, 1825–1985: A Social History*. Washington, DC: Catholic University of America Press, 1992.

Kselman, Thomas. *Miracles and Prophecies in Nineteenth-Century France*. New Brunswick: Rutgers University Press, 1983.

Lehmann, João Baptista. *O Brasil Católico: Synopse da hierarchia ecclesiastica brasileira, inclusive Ordens e Congregações religiosas*. Juiz de Fora: Typographia Lar Catholico, 1936 (1938, 1942—III and IV editions).

Leitão, Deusdedit. "Padre Rolim: aproximações biográficas." In *A Igreja e o controle social nos sertões nordestinos*, edited by Severino Vicente da Silva, 82–95. São Paulo: Edições Paulinas, 1988.

Leite, Lisânias de Cerqueira. *Protestantismo e romanismo*. Vol. 1. Rio de Janeiro: n/a, 1936.

———. *Protestantismo e romanismo*. Vol. 2. Rio de Janeiro: n/a, 1938.

Léonard, Émille-G. *O protestantismo brasileiro: estudo de eclesiologia e história social*. Translated by Linneu de Camargo Schützer. São Paulo: Aste, 1963.

Levine, Robert. *Pernambuco in the Brazilian Federation, 1889–1937*. Stanford: Stanford University Press, 1978.

———. *Vale of Tears: Revisiting the Canudos Massacre in Northeastern Brazil, 1893–1897*. Berkeley: University of California Press, 1995.

Lewin, Linda. *Politics and Parentela in Paraíba: A Case Study of Family-Based Oligarchy in Brazil*. Princeton: Princeton University Press, 1987.

Lima, Alceu Amoroso (Tristão de Athayde). *A contra-revolução espiritual*. Cataguases: Spinola e Fusco Editores, 1932.

———. *Memórias improvisadas: diálogos com Medeiros Lima*. Petrópolis: Editora Vozes, 1973.

———. "Notas para a história do Centro Dom Vital (VIII)." *A Ordem* 59.6 (June 1958): 39–45.

———. *Pela Cristianização da Idade Nova*. Vol. 1. Rio de Janeiro: Livraria Agir Editora, 1946.

———, and Jackson de Figueiredo. *Correspondência: Harmonia dos Contrastes*. 2 vols. Edited by João Etienne Filho. Rio de Janeiro: Academia Brasileira das Letras, 1991–92.

Lustosa, Oscar de Figueiredo, ed. *A Igreja e a política no Brasil: documentação do partido católico à LEC (1874–1945)*. São Paulo: Edições Loyola, 1983.

Luzzatto, Sergio. *Padre Pio: Miracles and Politics in a Secular Age*. New York: Metropolitan Books, 2007.

Mafra, Clara. "Casa de Homens, Casa de Deus." *Análise Social* 42.182 (2007): 145–61.

———. *Os evangélicos*.

———. *Na Posse da Palavra: Religião, conversão, e liberdade pessoal em dois contextos nacionais*. Lisbon: Imprensa de Ciências Sociais, 2002.

Mainwaring, Scott. *The Catholic Church and Politics in Brazil, 1916–1985.* Stanford: Stanford University Press, 1986.

Maior, Mário Souto. *Frei Damião: um santo?* Recife: Fundação Joaquim Nabuco, Editora Massangana, 1998.

Maritain, Jacques. *Freedom in the Modern World.* Translated by Richard O'Sullivan. New York: Charles Scribner's Sons, 1936.

Mariz, Cecília Loreto. *Coping with Poverty: Pentecostals and Christian Base Communities in Brazil.* Philadelphia: Temple University Press, 1994.

Mariz, Cecília L., and Roberta B. C. Campos. "Pentecostalism and 'National Culture': A Dialogue between Brazilian Social Sciences and the Anthropology of Christianity." *Religion and Society: Advances in Research* 2 (2011): 106–21.

Mariz, Celso. *Cidades e homens.* João Pessoa: Comissão do IV Centenário da Paraíba, 1985.

———. *Evolução Econômica da Paraíba.* João Pessoa: A União Editora, 1939.

Marques, Crisólito da Silva. "Fé e Poder Andando Juntos: Estudo sobre a vida sacerdotal, política, e social do Padre Luiz Santiago na cidade de Cuité-PB." Undergraduate thesis, Universidade Estadual da Paraíba, 2010.

Martins, Mário Ribeiro. "O radicalismo batista brasileiro." Master's thesis, Seminário Teológico Batista do Norte do Brasil, Recife, 1972.

Mendonça, Antonio Gouvêa. *O celeste porvir: a inserção do protestantismo no Brasil.* São Paulo: Edusp, 1995.

———. "O protestantismo brasileiro e suas encruzilhadas." *Revista USP* 67 (September–November 2005): 48–67.

Mendonça, Antonio Gouvêa, and Prócoro Velasques Filho. *Introdução ao protestantismo no Brasil.* São Paulo, Edições Loyola, 1990.

Mesquita, Antônio. *História dos Batistas no Brasil: de 1907 até 1935.* Rio de Janeiro: Casa Publicadora Batista, 1962 [1940].

Miceli, Sergio. *A elite eclesiástica brasileira.* Rio de Janeiro: Editora Bertrand Brasil, 1988.

Monteiro, Felipe Pinto. "Peregrinação, violência e demonofobia: novas interpretações sobre o movimento messiânico-milenarista de Pau de Colher." *PLURA* 4.1 (2013): 62–92.

Monteiro, Yara Nogueira. "Congregação Cristã no Brasil: da fundação ao centenário—a trajetória de uma Igreja brasileira." *Estudos de Religião* 24.39 (July–December 2010): 122–63.

Montenegro, Abelardo F. *Historia do fanaticismo religioso no Ceará.* Fortaleza: Editôra A. Batista Fontenele, 1959.

Moura, Abdalaziz de. *Frei Damião e os impasses da religião popular.* Petrópolis: Editora Vozes, 1978.

Myscofski, Carole. *When Men Walk Dry: Portuguese Messianism in Brazil.* Atlanta: Scholars Press, 1988.

Nascimento, George Silva do. "Patrio-Biografia: Horácio de Almeida e sua história da Paraíba." Master's thesis, Universidade Federal da Paraíba, 2010.

Nembro, Metodo da. *Storia dell'attività missionaria dei minori cappuccini nel Brasile.* Rome: Institutum Historicum Ord. Fr. Min. Cap., 1958.

Neri, Marcelo Côrtes. *Novo Mapa das Religiões.* Rio de Janeiro: Fundação Getúlio Vargas, 2011.

Nesvig, Martin Austin. Ed. *Religious Culture in Modern Mexico.* Lanham: Rowman and Littlefield, 2007.

Neto, Frei Francisco Lopes de Sousa. *Frei Damião: o missionário.* Fortaleza: Armazén da Cultura, 2011.

Nogueira, Hamilton. *Jackson de Figueiredo.* São Paulo: Edições Loyola, 1976.

Octávio, José, ed. *A Paraíba: das origens à urbanização.* João Pessoa: Fundação Casa de José Américo, 1983.

Oliveira, Ernesto Luiz de. *Roma, a Egreja, e o Anticristo.* São Paulo: Empresa Editora Brasileira, 1931.

Oliveira, Gledson Ribeiro de. "Bodes, hereges, irmãos: Igrejas presbiterianas e batistas no Ceará do primeiro novecentos." PhD diss., Universidade Federal do Ceará, 2012.

Oliveira, Lucia Lippi. "Vargas, os intelectuais, e as raízes da ordem." In *As instituições brasileiras da era Vargas,* edited by Maria Celina D'Araujo, 83–96. Rio de Janeiro: EdUERJ/Fundação Getúlio Vargas, 1999.

Oliveira, Pedro Ribeiro de. *Religião e dominação de classe.* Petrópolis: Vozes, 1985.

Oliveira, Pedro Ribeiro de, and João Everton da Cruz. "Frei Damião: a metamorfose do missionário." *História Agora* 10 (2011): 287–317.

Oliveira, Plínio Corrêa de. *Em Defesa da Ação Católica.* São Paulo: Editora Ave Maria, 1943.

Oliveira, Zaqueu Moreira de. *Perseguidos, mas não desamparados: 90 anos de perseguição religiosa contra os batistas brasileiros (1880–1970).* Rio de Janeiro: JUERP, 1999.

Overmyer-Velásquez, Mark. *Visions of the Emerald City: Modernity, Tradition, and the Formation of Porfirian Oaxaca, Mexico.* Durham: Duke University Press, 2006.

Palacios, Guillermo. "Política externa, tensões agrárias e práxis missionária: os capuchinhos italianos e as relações entre o Brasil e o Vaticano no início do segundo reinado." *Revista de História* 167 (July–December 2012): 193–222.

Pang, Eul-Soo. "The Changing Roles of Priests in the Politics of Northeast Brazil, 1889–1964." *The Americas* 30.3 (January 1974): 341–72.

Pecklers, Keith F. *The Unread Vision: The Liturgical Movement in the United States of America: 1926–1955.* Collegeville, MN: Liturgical Press, 1998.

Pedavoli, Celestino de. *Combate ao protestantismo: virgindade perpetua, maternidade divina, e conceição imaculada de Maria.* Recife: Empreza d'A Provincia, 1904.

———. *Mais um triumpho do Catholicismo sobre o Protestantismo.* Recife: Empreza d'A Provincia, 1898.

Pereira, Eduardo Carlos. *O problema religioso na América Latina: estudo dogmático histórico.* São Paulo: Empresa Editôra Brasileira, 1920.

Pereira, Nilo. *Dom Vital e a Questão Religiosa no Brasil.* Recife: UFPE Imprensa Universitária, 1966.

Pessar, Patricia. *From Fanatics to Folk: Brazilian Millenarianism and Popular Culture.* Durham: Duke University Press, 2004.

Pew Research Center. "Brazil's Changing Religious Landscape." Washington, DC: Pew Research Center, 2013.

Pierson, Paul Everett. *A Younger Church in Search of Maturity: Presbyterianism in Brazil from 1910 to 1959.* Philadelphia: Temple University Press, 1974.

Piletti, Nelson, and Walter Praxedes. *Dom Hélder Câmara: profeta da paz.* São Paulo: Contexto, 2010.

Pimenta, Pedro Simões. *O diário de Vovô Pedro: autobiográfico.* Cuité: n.p., 1986.

Pinheiro, Jorge, and Marcelo Santos, eds. *Os batistas: controvérsias e vocação para a intolerância.* São Paulo: Fonte Editorial, 2012.

Pinto, Luis. *Fundamentos da história e do desenvolvimento da Paraíba.* Rio de Janeiro: Editora Leitura, 1973.

Pompa, Maria Cristina. "Leituras do 'fanatismo religioso' no sertão brasileiro." *Novos Estudos* 69 (July 2004): 71–88.

———. "Memórias do fim do mundo: o movimento de Pau de Colher." *Revista USP* 82 (June–August 2009): 68–87.

Pozzi, Giovanni, and Paolo Prodi. *I Cappuccini in Emilia-Romagna: storia di una presenza.* Bologna: Grafiche Dehoniane, 2002.

Premack, Laura. "'The Holy Rollers Are Invading Our Territory': Southern Baptist Missionaries and the Early Years of Pentecostalism in Brazil." *Journal of Religious History* 35.1 (March 2011): 1–23.

Procópio, Severino Gomes. *Meu Depoimento: Revolta de Princesa, Revolução de 1930.* João Pessoa: Grafica A Imprensa, 1962.

Prodi, Paolo. "I nuovi Ordini religiosi e l'identità cappuccina nella Chiesa dell'età moderna." In *I cappuccini in Emilia-Romagna: storia di una presenza,* edited by Paolo Prodi and Giovanni Pozzi, 8–19. Bologna: Grafiche Dehoniane, 2002.

"O programa de 1933 da LEC." In *A Igreja e a política no Brasil: documentação do partido católico à LEC (1874–1945),* edited by Oscar de Figueiredo Lustosa, O.P., 104–26. São Paulo: Edições Loyola, 1983.

Queiroz, Maria Isaura Pereira de. *O messianismo no Brasil e no mundo.* São Paulo: Dominus, 1965.

A Questão Protestante no Brasil: Semana de Estudos sobre "O Protestantismo no Brasil," realizado no Seminário Central de Ipiranga, de 19 a 23–8–1940. São Paulo: Tipografia Orfanato Cristovão Colombo, 1940.

Ramírez, Daniel. *Migrating Faith: Pentecostalism in the United States and Mexico in the Twentieth Century.* Chapel Hill: University of North Carolina Press, 2015.

Ramos, Severino. *Agripino: o mago de Catolé.* João Pessoa: Editora A União, 2014.

Regni, Pietro Vittorino. *Os capuchinhos na Bahia.* 2 vols. Translated by Fr. Agatângelo de Crato. Salvador: Convento da Piedade, 1988.

Rego, José Lins do. *Pedra Bonita.* Rio de Janeiro: Editora José Olympio, 2011.

Reid, Alcuin. *The Organic Development of the Liturgy: The Principles of Liturgical Reform and Their Relation to the Twentieth-Century Liturgical Movement Prior to the Second Vatican Council*. San Francisco: Ignatius Press, 2005.

Ribeiro, Boanerges. *Protestantismo e cultura brasileira: aspectos culturais da implantação do Protestantismo no Brasil*. São Paulo: Casa Editora Presbiteriana, 1981.

Rodrigues, Ines Caminha Lopes. *A revolta de Princesa: poder privado-poder instituido*. São Paulo: Brasiliense, 1981.

———. *A revolta de Princesa: uma contribuição ao mandonismo local (Paraíba, 1930.)* João Pessoa: Secretaria de Educação e Cultura, 1978.

Rolim, Francisco Cartaxo. "Padre-mestre Inácio de Souza Rolim, um retrato esquecido." In *A Igreja e o controle social nos sertões nordestinos*, edited by Severino Vicente da Silva, 96–106. São Paulo: Edições Paulinas, 1988.

———. *Pentecostais no Brasil: uma interpretação sócio-religiosa*. Petrópolis: Editora Vozes, 1985.

Rosa, Wanderley Pereira da, and José Adriano Filho, eds. *Cristo e o Processo Revolucionário Brasileiro: A Conferência do Nordeste 50 anos depois (1962–2012)*. Rio de Janeiro: MAUAD Editora, 2012.

Rosas, Suzana Cavani, and Tanya Maria Pires Brandão, eds. *Os sertões: espaços, tempos, movimentos*. Recife: Editora Universitária UFPE, 2010.

Rossi, Agnelo. *O Diretório Protestante no Brasil*. Campinas: Tipografia Paulista, 1939.

———. *Flores em meus 50 anos de sacerdócio*. Campinas: PUCCAMP, 1987.

Sanchis, Pierre. *Catolicismo: cotidiano e movimentos*. São Paulo: Editora Loyola, 1992.

———. *Catolicismo: modernidade e tradição*. São Paulo: Editora Loyola, 1992.

———. *Catolicismo: unidade religiosa e pluralsimo cultural*. São Paulo: Editora Loyola, 1992.

Santana, Martha M. Falcão de Carvalho e M. *Poder e intervenção estatal: Paraíba, 1930–1940*. João Pessoa: Editora Universitária, 2000.

Santiago, Luiz. *Serra do Cuité: sua história, seus progressos, suas possibilidades*. João Pessoa: A Imprensa, 1936.

Santos, Ednaldo Araújo dos, and Ricardo Grisi Velôso. *O Ano Sacerdotal e o Clero da Arquidiocese da Paraíba*. João Pessoa: A União Editora, 2010.

Santos, Fernando Pio dos. *Apontamentos biográficos do clero pernambucano*. 2 vols. Recife: Arquivo Público Estadual Jordão Emerenciano, 1994.

Santos, João Marcos de Leitão. "A ordem social em crise: A inserção do Protestantismo em Pernambuco: 1860–1891." PhD diss., Universidade de São Paulo, 2008.

Santos, Lyndon de Araújo. *As outras faces do sagrado: protestantismo e cultura na Primeira República Brasileira*. São Luís de Maranhão: Edufma, 2006.

Sarzynski, Sarah R. "History, Identity, and the Struggle for Land in Northeastern Brazil." PhD diss., University of Maryland, College Park, 2008.

Serbin, Kenneth. *Needs of the Heart: A Social and Cultural History of Brazil's Clergy and Seminaries*. Notre Dame: University of Notre Dame Press, 2006.

Silva, Cândido da Costa e. *Roteiro da vida e da morte: um estudo do catolicismo no sertão da Bahia*. São Paulo: Ática, 1982.

Silva, José Ariovaldo da. *O movimento litúrgico no Brasil*. Petrópolis: Vozes, 1983.

Silva, José Bonifácio de Sousa e. *O pendão real: esboço histórico da "Egreja Evangelica de Monte Alegre.*" Recife: Ed. of Author, 2012.

Silva, José Luiz. *Frei Damião: edição comemorativa da visita do Santo Padre ao Brasil*. João Pessoa: MARKET, 1991.

Silva, Lêda Cristina Correia da. "Práticas e representações hagiológicas: a devoção a Frei Damião de Bozzano (1931–2008)." Master's thesis, Universidade Federal de Pernambuco, 2009.

——, and Sylvana Maria Brandão de Aguiar. "Frei Damião: Trajetórias de vida, missões, carisma e poderes." *Paralellus* 6.13 (July–December 2015): 445–66.

Silva, Rogério Souza. "A política como espetáculo: a reinvenção da história brasileira e a consolidação dos discursos e das imagens integralistas na revista *Anauê!*" *Revista Brasileira de História* 25.50 (July–December 2005): 61–95.

Silva, Severino Vicente da. *A Igreja e o controle social nos sertões nordestinos*. São Paulo: Edições Paulinas, 1988.

Simões, Daniel Soares. "O Rebanho de Pedro e os Filhos de Lutero: O Pe. Júlio Maria de Lombaerde e a Polêmica Antiprotestante no Brasil (1928–1944)." Master's thesis, Universidade Federal da Paraíba, 2008.

Slater, Candace. *Stories on a String: The Brazilian Literatura de Cordel*. Berkeley: University of California Press, 1982.

Sobrinho, Reinaldo de Oliveira. *Anotações para a história da Paraíba* Vol. 2. João Pessoa: Idéia, 2002.

Souza, Edilson Soares de. "Cristãos em confronto: discórdias entre intelectuais religiosos num estado não-confesional (Brasil, 1890–1960)." PhD diss., Universidade Federal do Paraná, 2012.

Souza, Jessie Jane Vieira de. *Os círculos operários: a Igreja e o mundo do trabalho no Brasil*. Rio de Janeiro: UFRJ, 2002.

Souza, Luiz Alberto Gómez de. *A JUC, os estudantes e a política*. Petrópolis: Vozes, 1984.

Souza, Robério Américo do Carmo de. "Vaqueiros de Deus: a expansão do protestantismo pelo sertão cearense, nas primeiras décadas do século XX." PhD diss., Universidade Federal Fluminense, 2008.

Steigenga, Timothy J., and Edward L. Cleary. "Understanding Conversion in the Americas." In *Conversion of a Continent: Contemporary Religious Change in Latin America*. Ed. Timothy Steigenga and Edward Cleary. New Brunswick: Rutgers University Press, 2007.

Suassuna, Ariano. *Romance d'A Pedra do Reino e o príncipe do sangue do vai-e-volta*. Rio de Janeiro: Editora José Olympio, 1971.

Sylvestre, Josué. *Da revolução de 30 à queda do Estado Novo: fatos e personagens da história de Campina Grande e da Paraíba, 1930–1945*. Brasília: Centro Gráfico, 1993.

Tarsier, Pedro. *História das perseguições religiosas no Brasil.* 2 vols. São Paulo: Cultura Moderna, 1936.

Todaro, Margaret. "Integralism and the Brazilian Catholic Church." *Hispanic American Historical Review* 54.3 (August 1974): 431–52.

——. "Pastors, Prophets, and Politicians: A Study of the Brazilian Catholic Church, 1916–1945." PhD diss., Columbia University, 1971.

——. "The Politicization of the Brazilian Catholic Church: The Catholic Electoral League." *Journal of Interamerican Studies and World Affairs* 16.3 (August 1974): 301–25.

Trindade, Hélgio. *Integralismo: o fascismo brasileiro na década de 30.* São Paulo: Difusão Européia do Livro, 1974.

Unknown. *Lembrança das Santas Missões que os missionarios capuchinhos pregam nos Estados da União do Brasil—Pernambuco, Parahyba, Rio Grande do Norte e Alagôas—distribuido por elles gratuitamente.* Recife: Typ. J. Agostinho Bezerra, 1909.

Vale, Terezina. *Profeta da Paz: Frei Damião.* Recife: Avellar, 1991.

Vásquez, Manuel A. *The Brazilian Popular Church and the Crisis of Modernity.* Cambridge: Cambridge University Press, 1998.

Vieira, David Gueiros. "A Historical Study of the Missionary Work of Dr. George W. Butler and an Analysis of His Influence on Brazil." Master's thesis, University of Richmond, 1960.

——. *O protestantismo, a maçonaria, e a Questão Religiosa no Brasil.* Brasília: Editora Universidade de Brasília, 1980.

Vieira, Dilermando Ramos. *O processo de reforma e reorganização da Igreja no Brasil (1844–1926).* Aparecida: Editora Santuário, 2007.

Villaça, Antonio Carlos. *História da Questão Religiosa.* Rio de Janeiro: Livraria F. Alves Editora, 1974.

Voekel, Pamela. *Alone Before God: The Religious Origins of Modernity in Mexico.* Durham: Duke University Press, 2002.

Weinstein, Barbara. *The Amazon Rubber Boom, 1850–1920.* Stanford: Stanford University Press, 1983.

——. *The Color of Modernity: São Paulo and the Making of Race and Nation in Brazil.* Durham: Duke University Press, 2015.

Wright-Rios, Edward. *Revolutions in Mexican Catholicism: Reform and Revelation in Oaxaca, 1887–1934.* Durham: Duke University Press, 2009.

Zagonel, Carlos Albino, ed. *Capuchinhos no Brasil.* Porto Alegre: Edições EST, 2001.

Zemon Davis, Natalie. "The Rites of Violence: Religious Riot in Sixteenth-Century France." *Past and Present* 59 (May 1973): 51–91.

Zovatto, Pietro. "Dalla spiritualità del settecento ai nostri giorni." In *Storia della spiritualità italiana*, edited by Pietro Zovatto, 445–708. Rome: Città Nova, 2002.

INDEX

abjurations of faith. *See* conversion cere-
monies
Abreu, Capistrano de, 218
Ação Social Católica, 91
Ação Universitária Católica, 249 (n.27)
Afogados de Ingazeira, 258 n.4
Afro-Brazilian religion, 50, 78, 128, 144, 231,
232, 245
Agua Preta, 111, 268 (n.65)
Alagoa Grande, 76
Alagoa Nova, 179
Alagoinha, 116
Albuquerque, Epitácio Pessoa Cavalcanti
de, 138
Almeida, Horácio de, 144
Almeida, José Américo de, 138–39, 144
Almeida, Lindonio de, 125; Catholic perse-
cution of, 130–32; and effort to obtain
justice for Catholic attacks, 143–45,
151–52
Almeida, Manoel Francisco de, 83
Almeida, Nemesio de, 143
Almeida, Rômulo de, 144–45
Alves, Ana, 83–84, 85
Alves, Josué, 125; and Catholic persecution
of, 130–32
Alves, Rubem, 239
Amaral, Dom João da Mata, 218, 220, 223
Amaro, Severino, 121, 136, 146, 147, 156, 157
Amazônia, 7, 60, 69, 77; and Confedera-
dos, 6–7; and origins of the Assembléia
de Deus, 75–76
Anauê! (journal), 50
Âncora, 234–35
Anglican church, 6, 20, 52

anticlericalism, 10–11, 31, 33, 41, 44, 278
(n.11)
antisemitism, 45, 166, 212, 240
Araújo, Helon Dinoá, 71
Arcoverde (town), 62, 137, 187, 258 (n.4);
and Integralism, 102–3; and Frei
Damião, 187, 199–200
Arcoverde, Antonio Napoleão, 102–3
Arcoverde, Joaquim Cardinal, 218
Arehart, Raynard, 73, 82
Areia Branca, 95, 114, 116, 137
Assembléia de Deus, 7, 61, 75–77, 244–45,
262–63 (n.76), 263 (n.85); and drought/
migration, 81, 83–84; and conversion
journeys, 85–87; in Mossoró, 95; in
Areia Branca, 95, 116; in Arcoverde, 102;
in Campina Grande, 112; in Catolé do
Rocha, 126, 134; and growth in Cuité,
126–27; and persecution in Cuité, 80,
107, 121, 135–37, 146–148, 150–151, 156–
157; in Cajazeiras, 219–20; in Rio Tinto,
244–45; and "traditionalization" in the
1950s, 241–42. *See also* Pentecostalism

Bandeira, Hildon, 274 (n.89)
Baptist church, 20, 21, 52, 61–63, 67, 69, 74,
84–87, 144, 169, 209; in Pesqueira, 43–
44, 92–94; and relationship with Pentecostals, 7, 21, 75, 79; and growth of
Brazilian leaders, 61–62, 71; and the
Radical controversy, 64–66, 69, 71–72;
in Sousa, 67; in Cajazeiras, 67, 194–96,
219–22; expansion into rural sertão, 69,
71–72; and drought, 81–82; and violence
in Nísia Floresta, 89; in Flores, 101, 107;

Baptist church (*cont.*)
in Arcoverde, 102, 187; in Ipojuca, 106; in Campina Grande, 112, 193; in Jaguaquara, 115; and fanaticism, 149, 176–77; in Itambé, 190–91; in Bezerros, 192, 194; in Gravatá, 192; in Itabaiana, 192–93; and santas missões/Frei Damião, 190–96, 199, 210, 219–22; in Patos, 236; and ecumenism, 240
Barreto, Dom Francisco de Campos, 52–53
Barros, Artur de, 163, 189
Baturité, 71
Bear, James, 69
Berg, Daniel, 75, 262 (n.76)
Bezerros, 192, 194
Borges, José Francisco, 206
Brasil, Antonio Correa, 147
Brasil para Cristo, 241
Brazilian Empire. *See* Imperial Brazil
Brejo dos Cavalos, 120, 132–33, 144, 151–52, 155–56, 262 (n.67)
Briault, Harry George, 73, 75, 124–25, 129, 132, 143–44, 151, 262 (n.67)
Brito, Dom Luiz Raimundo da Silva, 168, 178
Britto, Cândido, 92
Butler, George, 69

Cabral, João Passos, 59–60
Cajazeiras, 67, 98–101, 107, 111, 113, 116, 118, 137, 159, 244; and Frei Damião, 194–96, 221–23, 236; religious history of, 218–19, 287 (n.70); and anti-Protestant preaching tour, 220–21
Cajazeirinhas, 132, 271 (n.31)
Caldeirão de Santa Cruz do Deserto, 153–54, 214
Callou, José de Anchieta, 92–93
Câmara, Alfredo de Arruda, 94
Câmara, Dom Jaime de Barros, 99–100, 229–30, 232; and time in Mossoró, 94–96; and Frei Damião, 210–12
Câmara, Hélder, 16, 230, 249–50 (n.39)
Campello, Francisco Barretto, 183
Campina Grande, 81, 125; and construction of chapels, 112–13; and preaching tours,

114; and Protestant-Catholic debate, 73, 193–94, 216
Campinas, 51–53
Campos, Francisco de, 43–44
Canudos, 3, 5, 78, 149, 154, 209, 215, 280 (n.43)
Capuchin Order, 21–23, 104, 223, 234–35; and santas missões, 107–8, 162, 164–65, 169–75; history of, 165–69, 277 (n.5–6); and accusations of fanaticism, 176–78; and the Catholic Restoration, 178–83; and Padre Pio, 206–8; and reaction to Frei Damião, 212–14; and promotion of Frei Damião's sainthood cause, 224; and pacification of popular rebellions, 280 (n.43); and Holy Week missions, 288 (n.85). *See also* Damião, Frei; santas missões populares
Carlson, Joel, 77
Carneiro, Rui, 137–40, 147
Caruaru, 110–11
Carvalho, João, 49
Carvalho, José Borges de, 99
Carvalho, Marcionilo, 67
catechism, 12, 92, 95, 100, 114, 117, 170, 172, 177, 179, 212, 220–21
Catholic Action, 12–14, 38, 91, 94, 100–101, 219, 229–30, 233–34, 238, 240, 248–49 (n.27); and Marian Congregations, 46–47; and Agnelo Rossi, 51, 56; and santas missões/Third Order Franciscians, 180–81
Catholic Confederation of the Archdiocese of Rio de Janeiro, 232
Catholic Decalogue, 42
Catholic Restoration, 2–3, 9–19, 29–32, 129–30, 158, 226–33, 242–44; and LEC, 42–46; and Marian Congregations, 46–50; and Agnelo Rossi, 50–58; and Pentecostalism, 78–80; and Restorationist priests, 96–100, 124–28, 140–42; and santas missões, 178–83; and Frei Damião, 183–89, 191, 196–97, 213–23
Catholic Workers' Circles, 94, 127, 219
Catolé do Rocha, 55, 97, 219, 244; persecution of Protestants in, 120–21, 128–34;

Cuité, 80, 107, 114; persecution of Protestants in, 121, 134–37; growth of Pentecostalism in, 126–27; and Catholic Restorationism, 127–28; and local politics, 140–43; and prosecution of Catholics, 145–48, 155–58, 161; and religious fanaticism, 150–51, 155–57
Cunha, Euclides da, 3
Cunha, Liomio, 85, 149

Dainese, Cesar, 47, 50
Damião, Frei, 107–8, 118, 164–65, 179–80, 235–37, 243, 277 (n.2); and the Catholic Restoration, 183–89, 217; early life of, 184; and creation of anti-Protestant rites, 186–88; and accusations of violence against Protestants, 189–90, 194–95, 222–23, 236; and debates with Protestants, 190–94, 216–17; relationship with civil authorities, 195–96; and accusations of religious fanaticism, 199–200, 208–13; and identity as a popular saint, 202–8; and relationship with religious authorities, 213–18, 223–24, 236–37; and controversy in Cajazeiras, 218–23; and sainthood cause, 224–25; and *Em defesa da fé*, 235
Dantas, José Adelino, 98
Daughters of Mary, 127
debates, religious, 73, 129, 190–94, 216–17
Delgado, José de Medeiros, 112–14
Departamento Estadual de Ordem e Social (DEOPS), 144–45, 151, 250 (n.40)
Departamento Nacional de Defesa da Fé e da Moral (DNDFM), 54, 230
dictatorship of 1964, 237
divorce, 42, 44, 216
Dozio, João, 146
drought, 3, 20, 59–61, 80–84, 108–9, 114 170
Dutch occupation of Brazil, 30–31, 59, 165–66, 182–83
Dutra, Manoel, 236–37

ecumenism, 8, 16, 18, 143, 165, 197, 226, 228, 230–31, 237–42
Edinburgh World Missionary Conference, 8

elections of 1933 and 1934, 41–46
Epitacinho. *See* Albuquerque, Epitácio Pessoa Cavalcanti de
Era Nova, 92
Escada, 71
Escola Normal Dona Francisca Henriques Mendes, 127–28
Esperança, 107–8, 137, 187–88, 190, 193, 221
Esperantina, 235
Estado Novo, 49, 100, 138, 144–45, 161, 209–10, 227
Estrela do Mar, 47–48
Eucharistic adoration, 92, 47
Eucharistic Congress, 29–31, 128, 179, 183
Eucharistic Crusades, 127
Eucharistic procession/march, 114, 179
Evangelical Union of South America (EUSA), 73–74, 125

Fábrica Peixe, 91
Falcão, Apolonio Marinho, 190–92
Falcão, Orlando, 191
Falcão, Silas, 199–200, 210
fanaticism, religious, 3–5, 23–24, 26, 41, 78–79, 122–24, 148–62, 163–64, 176–78, 190–91, 193–94, 199–202, 208–17, 222, 232, 237, 243
Faustino, Antonio, 103
Federação de Escolas Evangélicas do Brasil, 8
Federação de Igrejas Evangélicas do Brasil, 8
Feitosa, José Alves, 62, 71
Ferreira, Joaquim de Assis, 99, 123; and the Catholic Restoration, 127–28; and persecution of Protestants, 130–31, 133, 159; promotion of, 134; and relationship with local authorities in Catolé do Rocha, 139–40, 142; and relationship with Tribunal de Segurança Nacional, 145; and religious fanaticism, 152; and relationship with Catholic leaders, 159
Ferreira, José Martins, 67, 73
Ferreira, Manoel, 68, 71
Ferreira, Silvestre, 106